Laura Esquivel's Mexican Fictions

This book is dedicated to the women
who direct Mexico's domestic life
and occupy its "kitchenspaces" and to
Mexico's women writers and creative
artists and, naturally, to our loved ones.

Laura Esquivel's
Me**X**ican
Fictions

Like Water for Chocolate
Como agua para chocolate

The Law of Love
La ley del amor

Swift as Desire
Tan veloz como el deseo

Malinche: A Novel
Malinche: novela

Elizabeth Moore Willingham
EDITOR

sussex
ACADEMIC
PRESS
Brighton • Portland • Toronto

2 4 6 8 10 9 7 5 3 1

First published in 2010 by
SUSSEX ACADEMIC PRESS
PO Box 139
Eastbourne BN24 9BP

and in the United States of America by
SUSSEX ACADEMIC PRESS
920 NE 58th Ave   Suite 300
Portland, Oregon 97213-3786

and in Canada by
SUSSEX ACADEMIC PRESS (CANADA)
90 Arnold Avenue, Thornhill, Ontario L4J 1B5

British Library Cataloguing in Publication Data
A CIP catalogue record for this book is available from the British Library.

Library of Congress Cataloging-in-Publication Data
Laura Esquivel's Mexican fictions : Like water for chocolate, The law of
  love, Swift as desire, Malinche: a novel / edited by Elizabeth Moore
  Willingham.
    p. cm.
Includes bibliographical references and index.
ISBN 978-1-84519-410-9 (h/c : alk. paper)
    1. Esquivel, Laura, 1950– —Criticism and interpretation.
2. Mexico—In literature. I. Willingham, Elizabeth M. (Elizabeth Moore)
PQ7298.15.S638Z76 2010
863′.64—dc22
                                                                              2009053097

Mixed Sources
Product group from well-managed
forests and other controlled sources
www.fsc.org Cert no. SGS-COC-2482
FSC © 1996 Forest Stewardship Council

Typeset and designed by Sussex Academic Press, Brighton & Eastbourne.
Printed by TJ International, Padstow, Cornwall.
This book is printed on acid-free paper.

Contents

Contents

Acknowledgements

Many colleagues and friends have been instrumental in shaping and directing this collection. I owe a debt of gratitude for support of various kinds to Yolanda Bache Cortés of UNAM (Universidad Nacional Autónoma de México), to Marian Y. Ortuño and Manuel Ortuño of Baylor University, and to Sifrejido Loa of the Baptist University of the Américas. Linda McManness provided invaluable suggestions for the book, Guillermo García Corales offered a series of important and formative criticisms, and Baudelio Garza provided editorial guidance on the subject of Mexico's cuisine. Julie Kisacky generously aided me with an accurate correction and translation of an evidently misprinted Italian source. Oswaldo Estrada of the University of North Carolina at Chapel Hill kindly provided a copy of his article on *Malinche: A Novel* from a new volume of work dedicated to Professor Luis Leal.

Jackie Maloy McClendon, former Office Manager for the Department of Modern Foreign Languages, and Sherry Alejandro, former departmental associate, provided technical and material support for the formative years of the project, and Ann Westbrook contributed her expertise and reassurance to meeting the final manuscript submission requirements. Linda J. Capps and Linda Conlon provided other kinds of essential technical support. Without their grace and know-how, the project would have been severely hampered.

Janet Jasek and Laura Summerall and other librarians in Baylor University's Interlibrary Loan Department were remarkable for their resourcefulness in searching for materials. Only their experience in the work and their indomitable grace and efficiency have allowed this work to proceed and to include the range of printed materials that is necessary to this kind of study.

Special thanks go to Joan E. Supplee, former Director of Latin American Studies at Baylor University, who provided expert advice on matters of Latin American political and economic history, made possible Elena Poniatowska Amor's visit to Baylor University, and facilitated other opportunities related to Mexican geography and culture. We are all grateful to Ms. Poniatowska for her generosity toward this project.

Joseph F. Vélez, Professor *Emeritus* at Baylor University, generously

Acknowledgements

refereed two of the essays and improved several sections of this volume, offering corrective and formative suggestions, and saving the volume from a number of infelicities.

Miguel González Gerth, Professor *Emeritus* at the University of Texas at Austin, was the earliest source of encouragement and advice on this project and remained so throughout, kind and generous with his ideas and critical perceptions. His contacts with scholars in Latin American fiction and culture proved invaluable to the formation of the volume.

The Nettie Lee Benson Latin American Collection at the University of Texas at Austin was essential to the research for the volume, and I appreciate having had generous access to its collections, both rare and circulating. Its librarians were supportive and accommodating in every sense.

The periodical and book collections of the Sterling Memorial Library at Yale University and its generous extension of research privileges to visiting scholars served this volume over several summers.

Thomas Colchie and Random House assisted the project with advance copies of two of the novels. We appreciate the kind assistance of actor-director Alfonso Arau and actress-writer Yareli Arizmendi in clarifying biographical data. Anne E. Merchant copy-edited drafts of the essays and offered many helpful suggestions. Austin College (Sherman, Texas) provided support for translation of one of the essays. For these acts of support and generosity, we are grateful.

Jeffrey Oxford, María Elisa Christie, and Lydia Rodríguez offered essential corrections, suggestions, and additions to the Glossary.

Finally, I remain deeply indebted, personally and professionally, to the scholars who contributed to this volume. Each has graciously honored the highest standards of collegiality and professionalism through the years of its development. Their insightful and informed readings of Esquivel's work, their thoroughness and care as researchers and writers, their good advice to the editor, and their ever-patient reception of editing requests give this collection the value and truth it possesses. I hold their scholarship and professionalism, as well as their friendship, in the highest regard.

The shortcomings and errors in this volume are mine.

ELIZABETH MOORE WILLINGHAM
Baylor University

Works by Laura Esquivel in English and Spanish

Between Two Fires: Intimate Writings on Life, Love, Food & Flavor. Trans. Stephen Lytle. New York: Crown, 2000.

Como agua para chocolate: Novela de entregas mensuales con recetas, amores y remedios caseros. México: Planeta, 1989.

Estrellita marinera: una fábula de nuestro tiempo. Mexico: Planeta, 1999.

"Foreword." *An Appetite for Passion.* Ed. Lisa Fine, Ivana Lowell, and John Willoughby. New York: Miramax, 1995.

"Foreword." *The Secrets of Jesuit Breadmaking: Recipes and Traditions from Jesuit Bakers Around the World.* Rick Curry. New York: Morrow, 1995.

Íntimas suculencias: tratado filosófico de cocina. Madrid: Ollero & Ramos, 1998.

The Law of Love. Trans. Margaret Sayers Peden. New York: Crown-Random, 1996.

La ley del amor. Mexico: Grijalbo, 1995.

El libro de las emociones: son de la razón sin corazón. Barcelona: Plaza & Janés, 2002.

Like Water for Chocolate: A Novel in Monthly Installments with Recipes, Romances and Home Remedies. Trans. Carol Christensen and Thomas Christensen. New York: Doubleday, 1992.

Malinche: A Novel. Trans. Ernesto Mestre-Reed. New York: Atria, 2006.

Malinche: novela. New York: Atria, 2006.

"Prólogo." *La cocina del chile.* Patricia Van Rhijn. Mexico: Planeta, 2003.

Swift as Desire. Trans. Stephen A. Lytle. New York: Crown-Random, 2001.

Tan veloz como el deseo. Barcelona: Plaza & Janés; New York: Anchor-Doubleday, 2001.

A listing of English and Spanish editions of Esquivel's novels appears in the Works Cited.

Editor's Preface

This book presents a critically insightful and timely collection of essays on Laura Esquivel's four novels to date and the film version of *Like Water for Chocolate*. Ancillary materials and an introduction to twenty years of Esquivel criticism offer additional support for informed readings of the chapter essays and of Esquivel's novels and for a more insightful viewing of the film. The volume is intended for scholars, researchers, teachers, non-specialists, and students having various levels of experience with Mexican and Spanish American women's fiction, film, and criticism. Those new to these areas of study and non-academic readers will find sections of the book and certain aspects of the apparatus designed especially to facilitate their readings. We hope that more experienced readers will be able to skim over tutorial elements of the volume without undue distraction.

The Essays

The chapter essays are grouped according to the novel each addresses, and the novels are treated in order of publication. Linda Ledford-Miller's biography of Esquivel opens the work and is followed by "An Introduction to Esquivel Criticism" (Willingham). This critical introduction provides an overview of the popular and academic reception of Esquivel's novels and the film and suggests future critical directions. Like the volume, it considers the novels in order of publication, with the extensive body of material on *Like Water for Chocolate* consuming a significant portion of the chapter. The seven chapters that follow the critical introduction treat *Like Water for Chocolate*, beginning with Elena Poniatowska Amor's response to the novel.

Elena Poniatowska Amor, whose award-winning books in testimonial literature have represented Mexican women's voices and lives with nuance and realism, provides an eclectic and electric context for Esquivel's fiction. Poniatowska's consideration of Esquivel's literary roots ranges from the Colonial Period to contemporary feminist theater and from lyric poetry to the testimonial narrative. In addition, her conversation with Esquivel elicits a telling view of men and food as parallels in the universe of the kitchen where the female acts of grinding, kneading, smoothing, stirring, timing, measuring – and so on – are organizing and sensual principles in the shared lives of men and women. The English translation of Poniatowska's essay precedes its Spanish original, the inclusion of which provides the reader the only means of access to a literary document written by one of Mexico's foremost authors. The editor's notes to the English translation support Poniatowska's wide-ranging literary allusions in the interest of the reader who is new to Mexican Letters. The notes summarize material by paragraph in order to intrude as little as possible on the literary and creative nature of the text.

Patrick Duffey examines the phenomenon of the film version in conjunction with the novel in "Crossing Gender Borders: Subversion of Cinematic Melodrama in *Like Water for Chocolate*." Esquivel's exploitation of character, space, and plot conventions, according to Duffey, emerges from models promulgated in Latin American and Hollywood melodrama of the 1940s and 1950s, an influence he traced at length in a volume on Mexican narrative in the twentieth century (1996). Duffey shows how Esquivel makes mimetic use of certain cinematic features and parodies others, and he notes Esquivel's "revolutionary" shift of violence and power into women's spaces in and around the home and her gender blending and bending operations on Mexican archetypes. Duffey's reading / viewing affirms that Esquivel has adapted types and conventions to stage a comic "melodrama" of subtle construction with its roots in Mexican cinema.

Jeffrey Oxford illuminates another subtle aspect of perspective in a statistically detailed and enlightening analysis of the male characters in *Like Water for Chocolate*. Oxford notes that feminist critical treatment of gendered roles in Hispanic fiction has often focused on the work of Spain's male writers, and his essay both reverses and expands that inquiry by applying its principles to a work of Latin American women's fiction that is widely thought of as having few male characters. In "Unmasked Men: Sex Roles in *Like Water for Chocolate*," Oxford enumerates a surprising number of male characters and observes how Esquivel's reversals of gender in roles and traits of character structure her fictional society and appropriate power within it. Oxford's work is foundational to further study of Esquivel, and it forms a connection here with the essays of Patrick Duffey and Debra D. Andrist, who explore questions of gender and mimesis in *Like Water for Chocolate* from other perspectives.

In "The Absence of God and the Presence of Ancestors," Stephen Butler Murray considers another category of subversion and reversals and examines the tension between Mexico's Catholic tradition and the role of indigenous spirituality in the novel. Murray grounds his reading by quantifying the Church's role and the quality of its interventions against the spirituality of *indigenismo* as presented in *Like Water for Chocolate*. The issue of how religious practice and spirituality work in the Latin American novel is one of understudied and understated importance. It is noteworthy in this context that what reviewer J. M. Labanyi finds "perhaps the most interesting" of Donald L. Shaw's conclusions in his 1981 work on the *nueva narrativa* (of the Boom and post-Boom) is that those narratives were obligatorily set against "the background of a loss of religious belief" (216).

Rural Mexican women's experience in "kitchenspace" is a subject of María Elisa Christie's more than two decades of research in cultural geography and development and is the focus of her essay in this volume. Christie places her field work in cultural geography in Mexico into the fictional context of Esquivel's *Like Water for Chocolate* in "Gendered Spaces, Gendered Knowledge: A Cultural Geography of Kitchenspace in central Mexico." Christie's term "kitchenspace" designates gendered space within and surrounding the home and the kinds of knowledge that support, foster, and perpetuate family and community cultures. Kitchenspace also implies its own internal culture, including language, rules, and rituals, a culture whose elements and experience are shared and extended – and sometimes contested – by its fictional representation in Esquivel's novel. Christie's beautiful and detailed photographic images (after page 106) of women in their kitchenspaces in central Mexico enrich the reader's perspective on the novel.

As Christie's study affirms that *Like Water for Chocolate* resonates with Mexico's real-world experience, Debra D. Andrist finds that modern science validates certain mythical and "magical" elements of the novel. Having had many years of directing and teaching specialized courses in Medical Spanish, Andrist uses her knowledge of that field and of Mexican culture and literature to examine the novel's supernatural and fantastic elements within the contexts of medical and scientific literature. Andrist's "Transformation, Code, and Mimesis: Healing the Family in *Like Water for Chocolate*" reveals how Esquivel codes narratives of illness, injury, madness, and recovery to create paradox and mimesis that shape the larger narrative. Although most readers find the novel more comic than serious, Andrist suggests a darker reading of *Like Water for Chocolate* in which the characters and their relationships develop through pathological or wounded narrative environments by signs of paradox and mimesis toward healing and resolution.

Elizabeth Coonrod Martínez formulates a critical bridge between *Like Water for Chocolate*, set in the early twentieth century, and Esquivel's futuristic second novel, *The Law of Love*, in her essay, "Cultural Identity and the Cosmos: Laura Esquivel's Predictions for a New Millennium."

Coonrod Martínez finds that Esquivel projects the familiar quest for Mexican identity into a twenty-third century Mexican society, where gender and nationality are fluid, but where, despite the science-fiction technologies that move the plot along, the culture is anchored in the urban chaos of Mexico City. It is telling, as Coonrod Martínez points out, that Esquivel's twenty-third century society makes claims to honor its past, but paradoxically prohibits access to it, setting the stage for Esquivel's problematic and innovative heroine, Azucena, to break social and political rules in her no-holds-barred search for love. Although Azucena is ostensibly engaged in a quest for her soul-mate, she soon finds that what Coonrod Martínez characterizes as an indigenized Mexican *karma* leads her toward a larger purpose and moves her away from the petty concerns of contemporary, inter-galactic strife towards a more transcendent set of issues.

In proposing an alternative reading of *The Law of Love*, Lydia H. Rodríguez considers the novel as an effective piece of science fiction in "Laura Esquivel's Quantum Leap in *The Law of Love*." Basing her examination on the work of Jean Baudrillard and Robert Scholes, Rodríguez affirms that *The Law of Love* mingles the "strange" and the "known" in order to produce an authentic examination of life, identity, and humanity. Rodríguez's reading adds theoretical depth to the study of the novel and contributes new perspectives to the field of Hispanic science fiction.

Esquivel's *Swift as Desire* narrates another quest: on one level, it is that of Mexico's search for an embraceable identity, and, on the other, the individual search for place and purpose. "The Two Mexicos of *Swift as Desire*" (Willingham) considers the resolutions and impasses in broken relationships and the politics of individual and communal freedom and power in Mexico. Esquivel's next novel, *Malinche: A Novel*, returns to the site of Mexico City in the time of the Conquest, and, like *Swift as Desire*, narrates a quest for true love and a series of homecomings.

Malinche: A Novel revives two of the most potent and enduring symbols of Mexico and *mexicanidad*, La Malinche and the Virgin of Guadalupe, whose precedent deity in Nahua culture provides the title character the reconciliation she seeks. As Jeanne L. Gillespie points out in her essay on *Malinche: A Novel*, images of La Malinche are ubiquitous in the contexts of Mexican popular drama, parades, and *fiestas*; in public art, on posters and postcards; and in philosophical texts and popular speech. Gillespie's reading of the novel emphasizes the Mesoamerican models of discourse, religious practice, and material culture that anchor Esquivel's presentation of Malinalli, the title character's reconstructed indigenous name, and links the novel to Doris Sommer's theory of "domestic tranquility." Esquivel appropriates historical documents to

inform some aspects of her narrative, but written history does not determine her narrative. Gillespie emphasizes the connections between the
historical record and Mesoamerican culture and Esquivel's rendering of
Malinalli and the events of her life. The narrative confirms Cortés's rape
of Malinalli and emphasizes Malinalli's passions, dreams, and ideas in the
context of her personal and cultural history. By the time of Malinalli's
death, the responsive reader has given credibility to her human side and
female voice and has participated in Esquivel's historically grounded, but
imaginative resuscitation of Malinalli.

Ryan F. Long, in his study of *Malinche: A Novel*, examines the
contested constructions surrounding the title character's name,
chronology, and nature in previous treatments. Long reads Esquivel's
self-reflective text as implying a dual consideration: first, that of Malinalli,
Esquivel's organically motivated and self-determining protagonist; and
second, that of the iconic "La Malinche," whose culturally charged image
has evolved over the past several hundred years. As La Malinche had no
word in shaping the changing perceptions of her role in history,
Esquivel's Malinalli is similarly propelled through the events of her life
by powerful forces. Like Tita in *Like Water for Chocolate*, however,
Malinalli eventually mediates her own space and realizes her desires. Long
characterizes Esquivel's text as a work of "translating the translator," in
which Esquivel acknowledges the irony that her construction of Malinalli
stands only to be revised and reshaped by dynamic cultural and artistic
forces that are constantly at work on La Malinche.

Argentine critic Alberto Julián Pérez closes the collection with an essay
that re-examines Esquivel's work in the context of what Pérez terms *la
nueva novela de mujeres* [the new women's novel]. Beyond the "new
historical novel" that has been theorized and examined frequently over
the last twenty years, Pérez emphasizes the formidable production of
Latin American women's fiction in recent decades, and the distinctive
quality of the feminist perspective in fiction concerned with historical
periods. Pérez, who published his initial exposition on these ideas in
1995, affirms Donald L. Shaw's observation (2002) that what may
become known as the most significant marker of Spanish American
fiction since the mid-1970s is "the emergence of a large body of women
writers of notable talent" (6–7). Of interest to the present study, Shaw
identifies "[a] significant group of newer writers," including Isabel
Allende and Esquivel, as aiming toward "relevance to Spanish American
conditions" and turning away from some of the perceived qualities of the
Boom writers (6–7).

While Pérez's literary historiography encompasses an extensive
international list of thinkers and artists, he proposes that Latin America's
creative movements, in particular, have prodded readers and viewers to

see art, history, politics, and society in a new way by challenging imposed boundaries. Indeed, the movement in women's writing that Pérez describes has challenged traditional ideas about Latin American fiction, defied categories of genre, and created modes that are more responsive to women's experience and concerns than traditional forms have been.

Apparatus

For those who prefer to read in English, this collection provides a fully accessible text, and for those new to the study of Latin American literature and culture, it provides a glossary of terms. We hope that those who read in Spanish and those who are experienced in Hispanic literature and culture will not be distracted by these features. The essays provide systematic access to chronology in literature and criticism, especially in the opening and closing chapters, which are particularly dedicated to examining critical perspectives. In the following paragraphs, we note features of the volume's apparatus and explain the rationale behind our choices in questions of translation and citation.

Translations into English

The chapter essays provide direct translations of passages from literary work, including, of course, Esquivel's novels. Unless otherwise stated, quotations of Spanish narrative material shown in English are the translations of the editor or the essayist working from the Spanish original. The reader should consult the notes to each chapter for verification of the source of the text. Where the original text cited by the essayist provides <<and>> (double angle brackets) for quotation marks, this volume uses English text symbols ("and") and U.S. style, enclosing punctuation of other kinds within the quotation marks.

Reviews and criticism in this volume include work in several languages, most often Spanish or English. Where a quotation from a critical work originally in a language other than English is shown here in English, the translation belongs to the editor or chapter author, or is their combined work. In one instance, at the recommendation of the essayist, an extended critical passage in Spanish is given in the notes to the essay in order to give the reader easy access to the original.

Words and phrases that are judged to be descriptively unique in the original language and that fit fluidly into the syntax appear in the original language with a bracketed English translation at the first instance. Certain Spanish and Nahuatl words continue to appear in the text following the initial translation and are shown in italics at each occurrence. Our usual practice is to show the English translation within brackets following the Spanish, but in a few instances, where syntax and need are amenable, the English rendering comes first and the Spanish word or short phrase appears parenthetically afterward so that the reader may consider a translation that might otherwise be in doubt. Naturally, some Spanish or Nahuatl words and expressions do not lend themselves to word-for-word equivalency in academic work, and others merit a fuller explanation than will fit smoothly into the primary context. These words and phrases are printed in italics within the essays and will be found in the "Glossary" (Glossary) in this volume.

In the matter of translating non-English titles of literary works, again, there are several matters to consider. All Esquivel's books have been translated into English, and we refer to them throughout the volume by their English titles. To avoid confusion with the material in the opening sections, the first mention of each of Esquivel's novels in Ledford-Miller's Biography and in the critical Introduction gives the English title followed parenthetically by the year of first publication and the Spanish title and year of first publication (if the two years are different). For example, *Like Water for Chocolate* (1992. *Como agua para chocolate* 1989) and *Swift as Desire* (2001. *Tan veloz como el deseo*). Because *Like Water for Chocolate* has been published in several editions and formats in both languages, each chapter essay specifies which edition the essayist has used. A listing of Esquivel's published work appears immediately preceding this Preface, and information for each of Esquivel's novels is given in the Works Cited, where some entries incorporate bracketed bibliographic notes to assist in distinguishing editions.

Citations of non-English titles of literary works other than Esquivel's follow two formats, depending upon whether or not the work is published in an English translation. For the first mention of a work of literature that has been translated into English, the English title is given, followed parenthetically by the year of its publication, with the title of the original and its year of publication following. For example, *Here's to you, Jesusa* (2001. *Hasta no verte Jesús mío* 1969) and *Massacre in Mexico* (1975. *La noche de Tlatelolco* 1971). The chronology given is meant to be that of first publication in the language, but the reader should be aware that other editions may exist, and also that in some instances, there is conflicting information about the first year of publication. Multiple editions of older works in history and literature may have been published in English and Spanish many times over decades or centuries, and we cite readily available editions of those works. Translated works are given in their English titles following their first mention in the book.

For non-English titles that have not been translated into English, the editor's English translation of the title is shown within brackets following the year of publication for the original edition of the work; for example: *El tren pasa primero* (2005 [*The Train Passes First*]). Subsequent mentions of non-translated works keep the original book title. Film titles are translated at the first mention and given chronology parenthetically in the notes or main text.

References to critical work by the author's name are accompanied by the parenthetical year of publication; for example: Ángel Flores (1955). The parenthetical citation (Anderson 1996 3) is read as the surname of the author, the year of publication of the book or article, and the page number where the reference may be found.[1] Where authors have several entries, or a given work has several editions, the year of publication is an aid to finding the correct entry in the Works Cited. Where critics have the same surname, first names or initials disambiguate the reference. Where an author has published multiple items listed in the Works Cited in the same year, the text directs the reader to the correct work with a phrase or key word from the title given parenthetically with the page number. Where we cite two or more essays from the same collection, we use the MLA method of cross-referencing the volume by including the editor's name, under which the volume is cited, and year of publication. Where the translation of a title is not transparently the title of the Spanish work, we place the original title in brackets for clarification, as in Rosario Ferré's *The Youngest Doll* [*Papeles de Pandora*]. Print media, film, and literary reviews and criticism (academic and popular) use like formats.

Style, notes, and chronology

When syntax and sense allow, we incorporate biographical and publishing chronology into the flow of discourse or place the information parenthetically into the main text, as we have shown above in citing literary works. Where the syntax does not lend itself to a smooth inclusion of data, those details appear in the essay's endnotes, and full information, in the Works Cited. At the first mention of literary authors' publications in the critical introduction and in Pérez's concluding essay, we provide parenthetical chronology in the main text where syntax allows. We adhere closely to the "main text" rule for chronology in these chapters because of their focus on critical background. We have sought to include chronology throughout the volume in passages or notes where a listing of authors or critics' work provides a chronologically anchored background on some point of critical interest. For the reader's convenience, notes to all essays and ancillaries are endnotes attached to each text.

Biographical chronology for writers and artists is given in the notes to Poniatowska's English essay and in the main texts of the critical introduction and Pérez's essay, and in other instances where chronology is considered foundational to the discussion. Biographical data comes from several sources. It is often that supplied by the Library of Congress. We also consulted standard reference works in the field such as Diane E. Marting's *Spanish American Women Writers: A Bio-bibliographical Source Book*; María Claudia André and Eva Paulina Bueno's *Latin American Women Writers*; Carlos Solé's *Latin American Writers*; Robert Aldrich and Garry Wotherspoon's *Who's Who in Contemporary Gay and Lesbian History, from WWII to Present Day*; and information provided in editions of the writers' works. Years of birth and death are given parenthetically; a year followed by an en dash signifies a living writer at the time of this writing. Persons who are principally critics and not writers of literature are not usually identified with a parenthetical chronology.

While we have linked the chapter essays for a "read through" volume and hope that the volume will serve a good number of readers in that way, specific research topics and usual scholarly practice will lead readers directly into one essay or another. Cross-references and the repetition of certain information aims to serve the reader who opens the collection somewhere other than the beginning.

In the matter of ellipses, we follow a conservative path. In quotations where the essayist has omitted words from an original text, we signal the omission by ellipsis within brackets. All other ellipses appear in the original. Since Esquivel's texts show ellipses, this method serves to distinguish the two possibilities. The English translations of Spanish quotations that contain imposed ellipses suppress the brackets, since the nature of the omission has been already indicated in the Spanish quotation.

Using the Works Cited

The principle of the Works Cited is to provide the reader with enough information to locate material referenced in the text of the chapter essays and ancillaries. Primary and secondary materials, including book reviews, and criticism on Esquivel's novels and film appear in the extensive first section of the Works Cited. Smaller divisions of the Works Cited are meant to serve readers with specialized disciplinary interests in accessing a body of references by a direct path: Films; Television Programming; Film Reviews and Box Office Reports; and Medical Humanities resources related to readings of *Like Water for Chocolate*. Information is compressed in keeping with the principles of MLA style, using abbreviations and shortened forms where those strategies do not detract from clarity.

Book reviews, found in the first section, show the wording "[Review of]" followed by the title of the book under review. Review articles and reviews of a group of books are usually assigned titles (as if the material were critical essays); the reader will know the nature of these items by the indications [Review] or [Review Article]. Print reviews of novels and films that comprise a single page are cited with the page number following the first reference if clarity permits; the Works Cited entry will confirm that the review consists of only one page. Because confusion arises when dates indicating periodical publication date and dates referring to last-access to internet sites are presented in the same format, we differentiate purpose by format. The periodical publication date appears in the usual U.S. dating format as month/day/year (July 4, 1776), followed by a colon and pagination, as with academic periodical articles. Where the article is available on the internet, the date of access is shown as day/month/year (4 July 2009) without punctuation. Where the name of the print publication serves as the reference within the essay text, the review is staff-written and is listed in the Works Cited as [Anonymous/Staff] and alphabetized accordingly.[2] Online reviews are listed by the author's name or sponsoring entity. To assist the novice or non-academic reader in locating source information, the chapter or ancillary text provides direction to headwords.

Entries for internet sites throughout the Works Cited seek to honor the spirit of the *MLA Handbook* 7th edition's observations on the flexible and changing nature of internet sites (5.6–5.7.1).[3] We list websites in one of two ways: by author name(s) or by a title. Personal names are given as with print material (last name first); otherwise, sites are listed by the name of the site (shown in italics), or by the title of the essay or text contained there (within quotations). In two instances, we impose a simple rubric (Piedras Negras, Coahuila) for clearer reference, and the site title follows. Sub-heads appear within quotations, following the model of chapter and essay titles in printed material. In every case, the citation within the main text of the book directs the reader to the correct online entry.

Depending on the availability of information, the Works Cited entry for an online resource includes the following, in order: (1) the name of the site or the name of the author(s), followed by a main title and any pertinent sub-head(s), with the elements separated by periods; (2) the date of the text material and (if different and provided) the site's last update or copyright date as (month/day/year), with the two dates separated by a period. In the case of a periodical article posted online, the name of the periodical, date of publication, and page and column designations (as applicable) follow; (3) site sponsorship information, followed by a period; (4) finally, the date of our most recent access of the site in day/month/year order and the URL within angle brackets, followed by the final period.

A list of abbreviations used in the volume, including those of the

Works Cited, is presented in the end matter particularly in the interest of readers new to academic reading and research or to some of the fields addressed in this collection. We employ abbreviations where they pose no challenge to sense, most often in notes and ancillaries.

We hope that these apparatus decisions and their results will serve the reader, making the experience with this volume accessible, productive, and enriching.

ELIZABETH MOORE WILLINGHAM
Baylor University

Notes

1 In referring to page numbers, we fully represent numbers 10–99 to comport with reading practice and to make the reference clear: 92–97, not 92–7; 232–39, not 232–9.

2 For example, in the case of reviews in *Publishers Weekly*, where Sybil S. Steinberg was the book review editor over the period in question, unsigned reviews, presumably written by editorial staff members, are found under "Anonymous/Staff" in the Works Cited.

3 The *MLA Handbook* lists material by section and subdivides its sections as necessary. Section 5.6 begins on page 181 of the 7th edition, for example. Readers will be able to discern between print and electronic sources in the Works Cited, so we do not use the prescribed MLA 7th edition notation at the end of each citation.

The Cover Image
Frida Kahlo, 1932

The original photograph is a 25 × 19 cm. silver gelatin portrait of Mexican artist Frida Kahlo taken by Carl Van Vechten (1880–1964) on March 19, 1932.[1] Kahlo is perhaps best known for her self-portraits, and this image may be considered in significant ways a part of that genre.

Rather than the Diego Rivera-scripted Tehuana dress that is typically associated with Kahlo, her costume and ornaments in this image suggest the Nahua-Mixtec culture that informed her early life and whose signs often appear in her work. The heavy, polished-stone necklace, shimmering earrings, and embroidered white *huipil* draw the eye, but Kahlo's oblique glance – fierce, resentful, defiant? – and the shining tray balanced on her head ask the viewer to linger, to contemplate the portrait's mystery and indeterminacy.[2]

That a portrait somehow captures the identity of its sitter is a given, and most viewers would agree that Mexican womanhood and *mestizo* national identity are also in play in this portrait. I suggest that Kahlo's merging of identities here may allude to "Frida [as] La Malinche." This interpretation is consistent with the aims of expressing layered views of identity in the portrait and with our knowledge of Kahlo's life and work. Her artistic representations of Nahua monuments, deities, and cultural symbols are frequent, and in her life and art, Kahlo connected herself to La Malinche in various ways. Kate Burton of the Tate Modern writes that in the "conflicted character" of La Malinche, "Kahlo found a mirror for her own anxieties, sometimes signing her letters 'Frida, La Malinche,'" and that in her self-portrait *The Mask* (1945), Kahlo paints a carnivalesque face of La Malinche over her own face.[3] Kahlo's 1937 painting of her native wet-nurse in *My Nurse and I* (*Mi nana y yo*) suggests Kahlo's vital connections to the indigenous maternal figure.[4]

In the Van Vechten image, we see the young Kahlo, a contested icon of Mexican womanhood in our day, perhaps giving Mexico's most vexed representation of national identity a compellingly human interpretation in which the twenty-four-year-old Kahlo's potential for creativity and suffering speaks through the mask of costume and prop.

Notes

1   The image is owned by the Beinecke Rare Book and Manuscript Library and is a part of the Yale Collection of American Literature. It is used by permission of the Beinecke and the Carl Van Vechten Trust, Dr. Bruce Kellner, Trustee.

2   Kahlo's maternal grandfather, Antonio Calderón, came from Morelia in Michoacán (where she and Rivera lived in 1938), and Kahlo grew up in Coyoacán in Mexico City. I am indebted to Elena Poniatowska and Jeanne Gillespie for their study of the photograph and their comments regarding the objects in this image. The opinions expressed in this essay are mine alone, however, except where noted. Poniatowska corrects certain possible misconceptions (20 November 2009): "Frida Kahlo carries on her head a *batea* (tray) that the women from Juchitán [a Zapotec community in Oaxaca] carry [. . . .] She also has a [pre-Hispanic] necklace of very heavy stones given to her by Diego Rivera. [. . .] She had great courage because it was difficult to wear such a heavy necklace and not bend her neck [and it is difficult to hold a *batea* on your head]. The necklace is not jade [. . . but] just polished stones." Juchitán is northeast of Tehuantepec, the region of the Tehuana *huipiles* that Kahlo often wore at Rivera's urging.

3   The weeping mask may be read as conflating Malinche and *La Llorona*, the weeping woman, as Jeanne Gillespie points out is a frequent result in Mexico's popular culture. See Gillespie's chapter in this collection.

4   Margaret Lindauer comments at length on Kahlo's "missing mother" in the context of *My Nurse and I*, and on the role women play in constructing Post-Revolutionary identity for the nation and the individual, a construction to which Kahlo contributes in the Van Vechten photograph. The Malinche figure in José Clemente Orozco's mural *Cortés and Malinche* (1926) seems to anticipate Kahlo's "Nana." See Gillespie, in this volume, n. 8.

A Biography of
Laura Esquivel

LINDA LEDFORD-MILLER

Laura Alicia Palomares Esquivel was born in Mexico City on September 30, 1950 to Josefina, a homemaker, and Julio Caesar Esquivel, a telegraph operator who suffered from Parkinson's disease. The family home was located in a "nice" neighborhood, and Laura was the third of four children, a son and three daughters.[1] The couple eventually divorced, and Julio Esquivel's final illness and death in 1999 became the inspiration for Esquivel's third novel, *Swift as Desire* (2001. *Tan veloz como el deseo*).

Esquivel completed her teacher training at Mexico City's Escuela Normal para Maestros, the national college for teacher preparation. She taught elementary-age children for eight years, and, with the collaboration of friends, founded a children's theater workshop, Taller de Teatro y Literatura [Workshop for Theater and Literature]. Esquivel also produced dramatic pieces for children's theater and wrote for children's public television in the late 1970s and early 1980s. She married Alfonso Arau, an actor, director, and producer. The couple has one daughter, Sandra, born in 1976. In 1985 Esquivel and Arau collaborated on the film production of her screenplay for *El chido guan: Tacos de oro* [*The Cool One: Gold Tacos*], also known as *Tacos de oro* and *Chido One*.[2] Esquivel's screenplay was nominated for best screenplay by the Mexican Academy of Motion Pictures.

In 1989 Esquivel published what would quickly become a mega-best seller in Mexico and abroad: *Like Water for Chocolate: A Novel in Monthly Installments, with Recipes, Romances, and Home Remedies* (1992. *Como agua para chocolate: novela de entregas mensuales con recetas, amores, y remedios caseros* 1989). Esquivel originally conceived of the project as a screenplay, but the cost of financing a film with a period setting led her to tell the story as a novel. For the 1993 film, Esquivel and Arau collaborated on the adap-

1

tation and production of the novel as a film, with Esquivel as screenwriter and Arau as director. The film garnered enormous popularity, supporting sales of the book in several languages and winning ten Ariel awards (the Mexican equivalent of the Oscar), including Best Direction and Best Screenplay, and was nominated for the Golden Globe for best foreign film. The novel has enjoyed enduring popularity and is frequently used in high school and college literature classes in Spanish or in translation. Esquivel received the ABBY (the American Booksellers' Book of the Year) award in 1994 for the novel.

Esquivel's second novel, *The Law of Love* (1996: *La ley del amor* 1995), combined romance with Mexican and Mesoamerican culture and science fiction. Esquivel styled it the first "multi-media novel." The setting is simultaneously the sixteenth-century Mexico of Hernán Cortés's conquest of the Aztecs and the twenty-third-century future in the same location. The media include color comic-book panels to illustrate the text and a compact disc of musical recordings meant to be used at specific narrative junctures.

In Esquivel's third novel, *Swift as Desire*, a telegraph operator of Mayan heritage has an uncanny ability to understand the unexpressed feelings of those around him. The fourth of her novels, *Malinche: A Novel* (2006), was begun at the suggestion of Mexico's Santillana publishing house. Esquivel reports that the novel is based on two years of research on the historical record of Malinche's life and Mesoamerican culture. Despite the range of her fictional mode, her productivity, and serious approach to her craft, and the critical treatment of her work by scholars since the early 1990s, Esquivel is considered a "popular" rather than a "literary" writer by some critics.

Esquivel has often commented on the influence of her family on her writing, particularly that of her grandmother, in whose kitchen she learned much of the culinary lore that shapes *Like Water for Chocolate*. Esquivel's interest in food and cooking is evident as well in *Between Two Fires: Intimate Writings on Life, Love, Food & Flavor* (2000. *Íntimas suculencias: tratado filosófico de cocina* 1998). She has also written the "Prologue" to *La cocina del chile* (2003 [*Cooking with Chiles*]) and the forewords for *An Appetite for Passion* (1995) and *The Secrets of Jesuit Breadmaking: Recipes and Traditions from Jesuit Bakers Around the World* (1995). Continuing her interest in writing for children, Esquivel published *Estrellita marinera: una fábula de nuestro tiempo* (1999 [Little Sea Star: A Fable of Our Time]). Esquivel is also the author of a self-help book, *El libro de las emociones: son de la razón sin corazón* (2000 [*The Book of Emotions*]), which is meant to be a guide to recognizing and expressing emotions authentically.

Divorced from Arau following the release of the film version of *Like Water for Chocolate*, Esquivel is now married to Dr. Javier Valdez, a dentist, and they make their home in Mexico City. Esquivel is listed as a member of the faculty of the College of Political and Social Sciences and the faculty of Post-graduate Studies on Latin America at UNAM (Facultad de Ciencias Políticas y Sociales).

Additional reading on Laura Esquivel's biography includes interviews conducted with the author by Molly O'Neill and Claudia Loewenstein. See reference works on Latin American women writers published or re-edited since 2000, such as the revised edition of the *Encyclopedia of Latin American History and Culture* (Tulchin) and *Latin American Women Writers: An Encyclopedia* (André and Bueno).

Notes

1　See Esquivel's interviews with Molly O'Neill and Claudia Loewenstein for her comments on her early life.
2　The Library of Congress gives the title as *Tacos de Oro – el Chido Guan* (1986). 1985 is the Award year and is provided at IMDb.

An Introduction to Esquivel Criticism[1]

Elizabeth Moore Willingham

Like Water for Chocolate

Esquivel's *Like Water for Chocolate* (1992. *Como agua para chocolate* 1989) precipitated a stunning literary and film event in the last decade of the twentieth century: the film and book created a single-author economic boom, unprecedented in Mexican literature or film of any period by any author; moreover, this author was a woman with a first novel. In Mexico, the novel went into second and third printings in the first year of its release and reached the second place in sales in 1989.[2] *Like Water for Chocolate* was Mexico's "bestseller" in 1990.[3] Gastón Lillo (1994) explains that the commercial success of the novel was an outstanding example of postmodern modes of production:

> Vale recordar que la novela [. . .] fue inicialmente publicada por la multi-nacional Editorial Planeta; en 1992 pasaba ya de las 16 reimpresiones, cada una con una tirada mínima de 25,000 ejemplares y había sido traducida a veinte idiomas. Su feliz adaptación a la pantalla y la distribu-ción en video de la película no han hecho más que incrementar su éxito inicial. (488 n. 6)

> [It is worth remembering that the novel . . . was first published by the multi-national (concern) Planeta Publishing; in 1992 it had already gone beyond 16 reprints, each one with a printing of 25,000 books and had been translated into twenty languages. Its fortunate adaptation to the screen and the distribution of the film on video has done nothing except add to its initial success.]

As Lillo indicates, the film version had great appeal, and it dominated the annual Mexican film awards, the *Arieles*, and garnered "nearly two dozen" international awards (Karlin 34).[4]

4

Like Water for Chocolate resonated with readers and viewers around the world, making it clear that book buyers and film audiences outside Mexico did not need to understand the culinary and figurative meaning of the main title, serialized women's novels, the Mexican Revolution, or Mexico's culture in order to embrace the narrative. In all languages, the number of copies of *Like Water for Chocolate* in print is given variously as between thirty and forty-five million, and the book and the film have both been translated into an impressive number of languages.[5] These numbers, even in conservative versions, speak to a level of reader response that prompted editorial confidence. That confidence is evident in the number of reprints and multiple editions of *Like Water for Chocolate* and in the release of translations of Esquivel's subsequent novels to coincide with the release of the Spanish version. Esquivel's skill with narrative, mode, voice, and character is deft storytelling, and the narrative mirror that she holds up to Mexican woman-hood, family dynamics, gender roles, religion, society, history, and politics has given readers a truth-telling fiction that speaks across political boundaries.

Like Water for Chocolate: The Novel's Early Critical Reception

In the first years after the novel's publication, a good number of reviewers and literary critics on both sides of the border dismissed Esquivel's debut novel as an entertaining romance, an unremarkable melodrama, or a weak attempt to imitate the pantheon of male Boom writers, and some derided it with excoriating phrases. Salvador A. Oropesa (1995) details the ironies inherent in the "críticas negativas" [negative reviews], citing literary criticism published in the Mexican periodicals *Plural* and *Unomasuno* (*MR* 252–53). Debra A. Castillo (2007) comments on the broad disdain that greeted *Like Water for Chocolate*: "Esquivel's book was universally panned by the male-dominated literary establishment as 'lite lit'" ("Anna" 98). Castillo's assessment references book reviews like Antonio Marquet's 1991 essay in the Mexican literary magazine *Plural*, which provided a range of the kinds of complaints that male (and female) critics would lodge against the novel, but at least one Mexican women's magazine, *Fem*, took another position.

Carmen Ramos Escandón's *Fem* review (1991) emphasizes the coherence of Esquivel's integration of narrative and recipes in a feminist narrative with an infrastructure adapted from nineteenth-century women's magazines and the women's sections of large daily papers, which were seeking to increase circulation by attracting new female readers (45). About mid-century, as Ramos Escandón records, publications for women were being called *calendarios para señoritas* [calendars for young ladies]; these *calendarios* included moralizing narratives, instructions for embroidery, recipes, home remedies, and serialized novels (45). This content, then, provided a specific literature for women, and it was accessible only to those who were "initiated" in the case of certain types of needlework and cooking instructions, just as certain elements of *Like Water for Chocolate* are fully accessible only by the initiated (45). Ramos Escandón views the recipe motif in relation to the women's daily-life patterns on the ranch and in Tita's prescribed destiny as caretaker for her mother (47a). The recipe is also a mode of transition to the narrative, and through the recipe, the narrator speaks intimately to her implied audience (a cooking class), and, by extension, to the reader (47c). *Like Water for Chocolate* unfolds as a narrative of a Mexican "Everywoman" in which the protagonist "defies the traditional recipe imposed upon her by her life, family, and epoch" – and fittingly, the novel's creative form also defies traditional recipes of novel writing (48c). Ramos Escandón's reading of the novel emphasizes its unity in form and content; the appropriate, layered functions assumed by the recipes in the narrative; and the effectiveness of the work as fiction.

Antonio Marquet's *Plural* essay, referenced above, emerged in 1991 and quickly took its place as the model negative review of *Like Water for Chocolate*. The substantive oppositions between Marquet's essay and Ramos Escandón's illustrate the potential for a gendered divide in reading and assessing the novel. In another example of that divide, Marquet parodies the novel's elements in an effort to trivialize the work, but Kathleen M. Glenn (1994) notes Marquet's ironic failure "to have realized that *Como agua* is a parodic text" (41). Kristine Ibsen (1995) characterizes Marquet's attack on the novel as a "virulent denigration" and writes that examples of his mistaken reading are "too numerous to mention" (133). Cecelia Lawless (1997) points out that the "popular response" to *Like Water for Chocolate* that Marquet decries "demonstrates that there exists a female community of readers that could potentially be rather powerful [. . .], and this community inspires fear in [. . .] Mexican society" (226).

Marquet asserts that the novel is the calculated result of a predetermined formula for creating a "best seller" in women's novels, and that the cost of the book predicts the socio-economic level of its Mexican readership, thereby explaining its commercial success, in spite of its having no literary claims.[6] Marquet complains that *Like Water for Chocolate* shows little style or imagination, is generously endowed with *infantilismo* [childishness], and carries "a false air of popular literature," fit only for a narrow audience (58, 67). Playing on his "recipe for a best seller" motif, Marquet parodies the parody, claiming that "a pinch of imagination" may be added to the formula, but that it's not really necessary, *i.e.*, for the book's success, because writing in that genre requires no imagination (67). Marquet asserts that the book was designed only to be a novelty on the literary scene (58), a complaint echoed by U.S. critics following the release of the translation. Marquet's misstatements concerning the novel and his trivializing its affective and concrete elements are staples of subsequent negative Esquivel scholarship. Later critics adopt one of Marquet's erroneous readings – that Mamá Elena's labor with Tita is brought on by the death of her husband – and U.S. critics and reviewers have echoed Marquet's view of the novel as light reading.[7]

One of those who classifies the novel in the "light" category is Suzanne Ruta (1993), who reviews the English translation. Ruta suggests a number of useful critical directions in her review, but concludes that Esquivel "has bitten off more than she can chew" by treating lightly the deaths of Rosaura and Mamá Elena, who, according to Ruta, both die as bulimics, a mistaken notion. Ruta complains of too many events engineered by "magic realism" and concludes that *Like Water for Chocolate* is best read "for dessert" (7).[8] She implies that Poniatowska's *Here's to you, Jesusa* (2001. *Hasta no verte Jesús mío* 1969) would have been (in 1993) a more worthy subject of translation than *Like Water for Chocolate* because the former is a more serious kind of book, while Esquivel's novel is too superficial and comic to merit the investment and attention that translation requires.

Like Marquet, Ruta places *Like Water for Chocolate* into the Latin American *literatura lite* or *literatura fácil* [light or easy literature, reading for pleasure] category, a phenomenon that Debra A. Castillo (1998) characterizes as critical misogyny, which "implicitly recalls anxieties associated with the submerged metaphors of the transgressive woman" – in this case, the woman writer.[9] Castillo's characterization is ironic in the context of Ruta's review because the reviewer is a woman writing for a women's literary magazine, a point that at least one reader, Judith Richards, noted. Two months after the appearance of Ruta's review, Richards, in a letter seeking to mediate Ruta's conclusions, aptly refers to "a 'rich' Mexican women's literary tradition" out of which Esquivel writes. Richards describes other cooking narratives, those of Rosario Castellanos (1925–1974) and Sor Juana Inés de la Cruz (1651–1695), as points of departure in that history and takes issue with Ruta's implication that gritty testimonial literature is somehow truer or more valuable as reading material than writing that presents "survival through humor and irony" (4). Richards also notes the novel's "ironic use of a familiar mode" to construct a woman's individual history, its probing of "concepts like nostalgia and traditional family life," and the novel's "metaphoric inscription of Tita's spiritual female community" (4).

Like Water for Chocolate: The Novel and the Critics

Richards suggests critical directions that continue to be of interest to Esquivel scholars and to others who study and teach women's writing, as have the cultural, psychological, linguistic, and feminist critical explorations that Ruta suggests. In spite of Marquet's derisive comments and inaccurate reading of the novel, he, too, indicates critical approaches that scholars have since pursued. Ruta mapped some of these directions with greater clarity than Marquet by sketching bare theoretical and historical references around them. Ruta sets the role of Mamá Elena into the context of Rosario Castellanos's assertion that Mexican mothers are apt, not only to be self-sacrificing, but to sacrifice their daughters as well (7). Ruta also notes the novel's mythic connections to food and to the archetype of the "mother–daughter–food nexus" and its "gentl[e]" contradiction of philosopher and poet Octavio Paz's assertion of the paucity of Mexican contributions to global culture (7).[10]

Since Ruta's review, academic criticism has extended the possibilities suggested by references to Castellanos, Paz, and mother–daughter–food relationships, and has focused on Esquivel's construction of a space of rebellion in Mexican cultural and domestic life. Most early academic treatments of the novel focused productively on a cluster of essential elements: the novel's diverse mix of forms and genres; its parody of forms and traditions; the kitchen constructed as a locus of female power; aspects of food in the narrative; fairy tale elements in plot and character; the manipulation of gender and the anti-maternal mother figure; Tita's struggle for agency and identity against a patriarchal matriarchy; and the nature of the so-called "magical" events in the novel. In the mid-1990s, students in Hispanic literature wrote about the similarities between Mamá Elena's De la Garza ranch and the domestic milieu in Federico García Lorca's *The House of Bernarda Alba* (*La casa de Bernarda Alba* 1936), and they noted the "evil stepmother," the subjugated Cinderella, the thwarted love story, and other fairy tale elements present in the novel and film. These topics have also merited professional critical attention.[11]

Reviewers' comments and scholarly treatments based on food preparation and consumption have the weight of numbers in the body of work on the novel and film. Kathleen M. Glenn provides a telling summary, as of 1994, on the attention being given in the Academy to "culinary criticism" – even in the staid *PMLA* – and she affirms that such a critical approach to *Like Water for Chocolate* addresses narrative fundamentals. Tamar Heller, in a review of *Through the Kitchen Window* – provokingly titled "Asking for More" – suggests a rationale for the level of attention to the food elements:

In my own work on women and orality, I have been struck by how food is the most durably rooted of all metaphors in lived experience: the multiple meanings of hunger remind us of the link between body, mind and soul – realms that, for women, have often been the site of cruel opposition rather than of creative balance. (8)

In *Like Water for Chocolate*, character, metaphor, and plot are tellingly connected with food, hunger, and appetite.

Magdalena Maíz-Peña and Luis H. Peña (1991) followed the search for metaphor and meaning in the novel's food-based elements early in the life of *Like Water for Chocolate* in a presentation that asked how cooking and consumption determine character in the novel. The following year saw additional attention to this focal point of the text. Beatriz González Stephan's reading of the novel (1992) notes the marginalization of "imaginative literature" and suggests that reader involvement in the novel attaches to the cooking content, which "destabilizes" what is widely regarded as "good literature." She reads the novel as resisting traditional paradigms of power and repression through the appropriation of a catalog of genres.[12]

Lawless, whose comments on the negative reception of the novel were mentioned above, addresses the meaning and uses of cooking and the home-hearth environment in *Like Water for Chocolate* in two insightful essays. In 1992, she acknowledges that the novel's genre is "unclassifiable," but documents Esquivel's replication of the "almost formulaic" structure of a Gothic novel to produce a parody based on the language and spaces of food preparation (262–63).[13] Lawless's 1997 essay avails itself of the previous one in many instances, but emphasizes that the novel's material and its locus in the kitchen create a broad communal discourse based on recipes into which Tita's narrative is embedded and located appropriately in the kitchen.

For Lawless, the kitchen is a "productive site" for female and marginalized discourses (227), a "zone of transformation" (228), a space for women's voices and communal activity (228), a space where Tita stakes out a private realm and a source of power and voice (228), and a site of women's community (233). Lawless points out that reading the novel in the classroom extends the internal culinary community of the novel to create classroom conversation about individual culinary heritage – and even the production of cookbooks – and gives students a center around which to build solidarity and community in a context of diversity (221). She notes that while the ranch and family in the novel are transient, the cooks and their legacy endure.

A good number of commentators have treated the cooking-kitchen elements of *Like Water for Chocolate* as focal points. Glenn works through culinary elements as they are applied to Esquivel's parodic intentions and results, and she cogently emphasizes, in an exposition on parodic discourse and reader response, that the reader should be prepared to read in an ironic mode (39–41). Donna M. McMahon (1995) shows how, in the novel as well as in the screenplay, Esquivel constructs a feminine version of revolutionary history in which she allows the reader to witness multiple-perspective testimony, challenges to authority, and exaggeration within the narrative, inviting the reader or viewer to become involved in the indeterminacy of history and the feminine view of it. McMahon remarks the representation of meta-linguistic communication through cooking in the novel and the film in her article on the feminine voice (especially 25–27). Jeffrey M. Pilcher (1997) introduces his historical account of Mexico's cookbook production with a paragraph on *Like Water for Chocolate* (200) and concludes that the novel provides an apt metaphor for the transformation of Mexican cuisine and society when Tita rejects marriage with Dr. Brown and continues her illicit affair with Pedro, the Mexican boy-next-door (215).[14]

Also focusing on the recipe as text, Norwegian Hispanist Kari S. Salkjelsvik (1999) shows that in spite of its apparently fixed form, the recipe as a text is ripe for variations and departures. She notes that the form of the novel requires the reader who wishes to follow the "melodramatic love story" to read it by means of the recipes (171), whose representation as a fixed set of instructions is emphasized by the prescriptive text of Carreño's *Manual*, and even by John Brown's recipe for matches (177–78). Salkjelsvik considers oral and apprentice culinary traditions, individual gifts for cooking, and the pragmatics of the kitchen that result in the recipe as a "mutable" text, suggesting that putting kitchen recipes "into practice" requires creativity, relative adjustments to absolute textual terms, and even a rejection of the text (180).

The novel's recipe motif as a creative sign, including the potential for re-writing an apparently fixed text and for conveying wisdom for survival and healing, is an approach that Janice A. Jaffe (2003) also finds telling. She cites Chicana writer Helena María Viramontes (1954–) in Viramontes's description of her creative process in the context of cooking and the kitchen in "'Nopalitos': The Making of Fiction." Viramontes writes that she has "never been able to match her [mother's] *nopales*," but that she has inherited her mother's "capacity for invention" and has thus found her own "space on the kitchen table" for her writing (Jaffe 201).[15] Jaffe explores the workings of the cooking metaphor in the context of recipes, and she reads the kitchen as transformed into a site of rebellion, a position that Meacham (1998) earlier proposed in the context of the fairy tale structure.

Jaffe's reading of the title as representing "Tita's anger at her confinement to the kitchen" raises objections in light of Tita's productive behavior in the kitchen and because of the kinds of forces that really do "imprison" her (203, 209). On the other hand, Jaffe's emphasis on a community of women who defy norms and emphasize creativity as a means of agency and her many external references to that idea are especially fruitful (209). She also notes that in the narrator's final references to the narrative source as Tita's cookbook, the narrator is inviting the reader to turn back to the first chapter to read the story anew (208). In fact, this invitation is to reconsider the narrative as the narrator does, knowing in advance the staples of the tale and looking forward each time to "hearing" the story unfold again.

In a wide-ranging essay that shifts the conversation to the topic of genre and movement, Susan Lucas Dobrian (1996) characterizes the novel's form as "a pastiche of genres" and an "all-in-one" gathering of various kinds of narratives, including "magic realist" (56). Clearly, Esquivel parodies or subverts nearly every staple of the romance novel, from the cliché of "flaming passion" to the standard of the thoroughly masculine, masterful, male object of the heroine's longings. Dobrian views the novel's mother–daughter relationship, rather than the relationship between Tita and Pedro, as the vehicle through which Tita seeks to establish identity and autonomy (61–62). Dobrian's extended treatment of Gertrudis, the middle sister and Revolutionary *generala* (62–65), proposes that Gertrudis represents the "complete breaking away" from traditional female strictures and prohibitions and a weaving together of the "sexual and the political" in a character who "intercedes in the war waged around the family" (65).

Dobrian asserts that the novel works as a parody of romance myths that, if played straight, have a leveling effect on women's identities and desires, and that Esquivel's rather subtle way of "recod[ing]" and subverting romance staples is connected to the recipe format, which, in its unfolding, makes clear that neither women nor cooking "can be successfully created" according to "a predetermined set of ingredients" (58). In contrast to the assertions of subsequent critics, Dobrian reads the kitchen and cooking as "redefin[ed]" and the space and its activity, as liberating and powerful in the historical context of the Revolution (62–63). This critical position is subsequently contested by a number of Marxist viewpoints, but Esquivel's use of domestic space, culture, and activity continues to occupy critics who view them as telling elements of Latin American fiction and film.

Esquivel's handling of parody has played a part in critical efforts to define the novel as "postmodern" or to set it into Latin America's "post-Boom," for its use of romance conventions, kitchen discourse, and other traditional discourses that together form a pastiche. Some of the novel's so-called postmodern elements do not require much parsing. Gastón Lillo and Monique Sarfati-Arnaud (1994), for example, point to the "recycling" of mass-culture genres in the narrative, its various "pastiches," and the forms of mass production that have made possible the success of the novel and the film. Lillo and Sarfati-Arnaud also validate the "magic realism aesthetic" in *Like Water for Chocolate*, particularly in the use of hyperbole (485) and in the reduction of the Revolution from national meta-narrative into scenes of adventure or melodrama that lack historical and critical content (486).

Their work characterizes the novel and film's "exploitation" of "subgenres" that are linked to mainstream mass-marketing potential, interestingly, as "un especie de coqueteo" [a kind of flirtation] (481), and they remark the ambiguous "oscila[ción]" [swinging back and forth] between "el ethos burlón de la parodia y un registro neutro" [the mocking ethos of parody and a neutral register] that serves the love story (483–84). Images of "flirtation" and "swinging back and forth" also describe women's bodies engaged in sexual and erotic behaviors – perhaps a subtle parody of the target text and its marketing devices? Lillo and Sarfati-Arnaud regard the film and the novel as representations of the most "acritical" and "celebratory" currents of Latin American postmodernism (488).

John H. Sinnigen (1995) also references postmodern critical terms as being useful in reading *Like Water for Chocolate* from a political perspective based on Mexican programs of development in the 1980s and on a reading of the novel as a "feminocentric national allegory," in the sense of Doris Sommer's "foundational fictions." He recognizes "the recipes and the descriptions of the preparation and consumption of food" working as "textual supports of the plot" as they are central to the "mother–daughter conflict" (117). The allegory in *Like Water for Chocolate*, according to Sinnigen, is rooted in "a central female figure through whom meaning is channelled [*sic*]"; in psychosexual conflict; in the presumed binary oppositions based on gender, race, and family and social position; and in other cultural factors, represented by the female characters and presented equivocally in the novel (117–19). In his reading of the characters, Sinnigen notes that because Mamá Elena's lover and the father of Gertrudis is José Treviño, the result of Gertrudis's giving orders to Sergeant Treviño subjects "the paternal surname [. . .] to the disobedient daughter's commands" (121), and that it is Gertrudis alone who "seem[s] to be successful" in the Revolutionary context. In the end, however, her appearance at the wedding as wife and mother shows that she has given up those aspirations in exchange for the trappings of conventional modern life (122; see also 126).

Sinnigen nuances Jean Franco's "generalized conclusion" in her 1989 critical work *Plotting Women* – namely, that "it is simply not possible to retain verisimilitude and make women into national protagonists" because they are never in the plot, but "definitely somewhere else" (Franco 146) – by pointing out that Esquivel moves the kitchen to the center of the allegory and "evokes" not only the Revolutionary period, but also the 1930s and the 1980s of the novel's publication (119).[16] He notes that the apartment building and parking lot that replace the ranch are something of a sell-out, a "reconciliation with a bourgeois, U.S.-style patriarchy," and that the U.S. "achieves ascendancy" in the marriage of Esperanza to Alex, "restor[ing] and reform[ing the] patriarchy" (126).[17]

Glenn (1994), whose work is referenced above, reads the novel as a postmodern parody that uses hyperbole, "abuse of coincidence" (44), reversal of narrative modes, and language play such as ironic assignments of language among the characters, cliché, and double meanings (42–44) to produce parody. Ibsen (1995), likewise mentioned above for her comments on the novel's early negative criticism, also treats the novel's parodic elements, but she presents the novel as a post-Boom parody in which the narrative stages follow the structure of the romantic novel-in-installments as featured in women's magazines of the mid-twentieth century (and earlier) with which *Like Water For Chocolate* explicitly identifies itself in the title. Esquivel appropriates this popular form to structure and define her narrative.[18] Ibsen also regards Esquivel's use of magic realism as an appropriation and parody of a masculine form (134–35). Claudine Potvin (1995) disagrees that the parodic elements are successful, and she regards the possibility of parody as having been lost to a one-dimensional view of women's culture and "una montaña de clichés imposibles de tragar" [a mountain of clichés that are impossible to swallow] (65).

Also pointing to postmodern parody, María Elena de Valdés, in her study of the portrayal of women by male as well as female authors in Mexican literature (1998), characterizes *Like Water for Chocolate* as "a postmodern celebration of being a woman" and emphasizes that it works as a parody of literary and popular genres, in the same way that *Don Quixote* parodies the chivalric novels of Cervantes's day.[19] Unlike Ibsen, González Stephan, Glenn, and others who write that the novel resists classification and merges traditional genre borders, De Valdés views Esquivel's parody as centered on nineteenth-century women's magazines, the *calendarios para señoritas*, described by Ramos Escandón. De Valdés emphasizes that these publications reflected and sustained a particular kind of "Mexican female culture," partly through their serialized romantic novels (183), whose heroines were able to "transcend the conditions of life and express [themselves] in love and creativity" (184).

Oropesa (1992), whose mediation of the early negative reviews is cited above, focuses his critical eye on Esquivel's use of Spanish America's arbiter of deportment, *El manual de urbanidades y buenas maneras* (1853) by Manuel Antonio Carreño (Venezuela 1812–1874).[20] In an insightful critical reading of *Like Water for Chocolate*, Oropesa shows how Esquivel creates "a new cultural space" in the genre of fiction in which the body forms an integral part of the narrative, challenging the patriarchal circumscriptions of the *Manual* with feminine desire, voluptuousness, and maternity. Referencing Roselyn Costantino's dissertation on Mexican women writers, Oropesa cites Mexican lesbian novelist Rosa María Roffiel (1945–) as finding Esquivel's challenge to the patriarchy incomplete and, thus, failed.

Though Roffiel is speaking about *Like Water for Chocolate*, her comments about the novel's "protagonists" could apply to Esquivel's more recent protagonists as well: "[L]as protagonistas de Esquivel [presumably Tita, Gertrudis, and Esperanza, and perhaps the unnamed narrator] salen del huacal pero sólo llegan hasta los nuevos límites que la nueva sociedad patriarcal les ha marcado" [Esquivel's protagonists liberate themselves, but they only get as far as the new boundaries set by the new patriarchal society] (Costantino 29).[21] Oropesa observes the "correctness" of Roffiel's search for utopias "outside society's norms" (*fuera del juacal*), but makes the important observation that Esquivel's mediated "feminism" is validated by the state of transition in which Mexico and other Latin American societies find themselves.

Where women read, it is virtually a given that cruel stepmothers, enchantments, and heroic tasks that achieve deliverance – fairy tales, in other words – form part of the reader's worldview, and such elements in a narrative will get immediate notice – even Marquet perceived Tita as a Cinderella figure. Many critics of *Like Water for Chocolate* mention or make much of the fairy tale presence. Glenn cites the reversals of fairy tale elements in the novel (44), and Cherie Meacham (1998) presents a convincing exposition showing how Esquivel creates an updated version of the ancient form with reversals and mediations of certain standard elements, with mythical oppositions to enrich the tale, and an appropriately "revolutionary" cultural setting. Esquivel's ostensible prince-hero, Pedro, is not the ideal figure of fairy tale, myth, or legend, and Meacham's compact commentary on Pedro is insightful (126). The narrative closure, rather than the standard happy ending of a love story, is ambiguous, and Meacham suggests several possible perspectives from which to regard its signs (16–27). Like many fairy tales, *Like Water for Chocolate* centers on a mother–daughter conflict in a domestic situation where the father is absent. Meacham finds Cinderella-Tita's hearth to be a "place of great power and prestige" (127) and the narrative outcome, a "victory" (125).[22] Sarah Appleton Aguiar's *The Bitch is Back* (2001) suggests an updated

14

approach to the paradox and mimesis suggested by Mamá Elena and her pallid clone Rosaura in the context of a feminist-Jungian reading.

Parallels between *La casa de Bernarda Alba* and *Like Water for Chocolate* are especially suggestive to readers with a background in twentieth-century Peninsular literature. Eva L. Santos-Phillips (1997) has written an insightful study on the maternal discourse of domination as a "régime of truth" operating in the film versions of the two works. She bases her study on Michel Foucault's theory of domination, and she notes that even as the mothers monitor their daughters' behavior and sexuality and threaten and punish them, the powerful maternal figures also demonstrate signs of repression. Other occupants of both households adopt the example of exerting power subversively, and the mothers take progressively more extreme action to retain hegemony as the daughters rebel. While Adela and Tita are both dead at the conclusion of their narratives, the former is a dark victory and the latter wins something, if only for subsequent generations.

Reading *Like Water for Chocolate* through its fairy tale structure or through a comparative or mythic approach using *The House of Bernarda Alba* or other pieces of literature is likely to lead to work in Jungian theory on archetype and myth. Spanish critic Ana Ibáñez Moreno (2006) explores the Jungian archetype of the *madre terrible* (the bad mother, castrating and unfeeling, who consumes her young) in *The House of Bernarda Alba* and *Like Water for Chocolate*. Ibáñez Moreno describes the maternal dysfunction present in both works and demonstrates other parallels between them in the contexts of women's discourse and ritual and in the protagonists' responses to their fates.

Tina Escaja presents a study of archetypes in which she finds that Mamá Elena embodies *malinchismo* violence in her treatment of Tita (582), and that Esquivel evokes La Malinche in Gertrudis, the bastard child, both as "hijo de la chingada" [child of the "violated" woman] and as La Malinche herself (583).[23] She casts Tita as a type of Penelope because Tita crochets a blanket that is a substitute for love and lover, a blanket whose many colors offer her an escape from the severity of her mother (584). Escaja's ideas are suggestive for future work on the issues of identity in Esquivel based on Mexican and Classical archetypes.

For a few critics of the novel, *Like Water for Chocolate* has also provided a fruitful ground for studying literary *costumbrismo*, which, in a Mexican novel, implies narrative representations of indigenous people and cultural elements, including language, culinary arts, home remedies, *refranes*, dress, and worldview that structure and determine the narrative. These elements may be romanticized or presented as realistic or parodied.[24] One of the earliest academic presentations on *Like Water for Chocolate*, for example, was María de Jesús Páez de Ruiz's cultural and linguistic approach to the text. She pointed out that a significant number of words and expressions in the novel are given unique meaning in Mexican Spanish and that these expressions contribute to the novel's cultural character.[25]

Some of these themes have been re-examined and developed with fresh perspectives in more recent critical work. On the question of Mexican identity, and more specifically, women's identity, Kathleen Johnson (2002) emphasizes a historical retrofitting of feminine identity and self-determination in the Revolutionary-period character of Tita. According to Johnson, Tita rejects the suffering silence of *la abnegada* when she establishes a "room of her own in the kitchen" and its environs. From this domestic space, Tita energetically resists the tyranny of maternal and cultural expectations with ritual, experimentation, and imagination. Tita "maximizes" her power to determine her destiny as she masters the kitchen (37) and communicates by means of the dishes she prepares, eventually making her great-niece, the book's narrator, her present-day legatee, both in Mexico's traditional culinary arts and as a Mexican woman with the freedom to shape her own identity (42).

Several studies centered on women and feminism also take a cultural approach to the novel. María Elisa Christie (2002) relates elements of identity and cultural practices of women living in Mexican communities having Nahua cultural roots to *Like Water for Chocolate*. Maite Zubiaurre (2006) discriminates between "kitchen narratives" and "table narratives" and rejects *Like Water for Chocolate* as a feminist narrative. She classifies it as a "kitchen narrative" and shows how the novel validates traditional boundaries and women's identity. She establishes only "table narratives" as genuinely feminist in that they liberate women from the kitchen and food preparation and make women consumers, locating women in the public sphere and expanding their roles beyond traditional boundaries.

Many commentaries on *Like Water for Chocolate* include mention of one or more aspects of its symbolic and allegorical content apart from political and historical references. Yael Halevi-Wise (1999) develops the symbolism of the novel's birds, including domestic fowl used for meat and eggs, and its use of fire, absent a focus on myth. Contrary to the usual symbolic meaning of the bird in art and narrative as representing liberty, or a yearning for liberty if the bird is caged, Halevi-Wise projects a slightly different meaning, that of Tita's "distorsionado destino" [distorted destiny], as Mamá Elena imposes it upon her (513). Tita's life is to be dedicated to the service, pleasure, and comfort of her mother, who consumes her life as birds are consumed at dinner. Like the fattened capons served up at the wedding feast, Tita is "castrated" by her destiny to be "served up" to her mother's convenience.

Halevi-Wise views the novel's instances of castration – Pedro's sexual separation from Tita, and Pedro and Tita's "castrated" love affair, along with Tita's sterile destiny – as represented by birds (514). Tita has an especially close relationship with birds and eggs: she hallucinates the peeping of a chick within a fresh egg; she carries eggs fresh from the hens in her blouse to take advantage of their warmth; as a child, she gags on a soft-cooked egg, force fed to her by her mother; she associates the eggs that she handles in cooking with testicles; when the first band of Revolutionaries pillages the ranch, she notices the absence of the doves' cooing from the raided dovecote, adopts the only survivor, a hatchling, and then remains in the dovecote to escape Mamá Elena's wrath; at John Brown's ranch, she envisions her idle hands as birds, the first time, Halevi-Wise notes, that the novel makes the more traditional association between a longing for freedom and the image of birds – though some readers might see the previous images as compatible with that idea as well.[26]

Halevi-Wise further comments that images of fire and heat are associated transparently and directly with sexual desire and erotic activity, and that fire and heat connect indirectly to desire and eroticism through the association of heat and fire with food preparation and digestion (516–18). The "fire" of Mamá Elena's outrage burns Pedro when her spirit upsets an oil lantern, and the smell of burned feathers hangs in the air, recalling the earlier associations with the birds and identifying Pedro, according to Halevi-Wise, as the "'gallina' cobarde que es a lo largo de la obra" [the cowardly hen that he is throughout the novel] (519). The "marriage" bed at the end of the novel is lighted by thousands of candles, and Tita and Pedro's union on earth ends with an even longer and more vigorous display of fireworks than their first sexual encounter produced.

Halevi-Wise invokes classical references in his commentary on the novel's closing love scene: the staging of the bedroom recalls the reunion of Penelope and Odysseus, and Tita's decision to follow Pedro into the tunnel mirrors Juliet's decision to reject life without Romeo. The regeneration of the land from the ashes is reminiscent of the fiery renewal of the Phoenix, dying in its nest to rise anew from the ashes (519–20). Also remarking on the conclusion of the novel, Miguel A. Segovia (2003) views the final conflagration as creating "death and rebirth," and as "repressed, circumscribed, and coded desire that in this story can be funneled only through the body and through ritual cooking" (168).[27]

Segovia's reading enlarges the novel's allegorical possibilities, proposing that Mamá Elena, having killed Tita's father with her secret, becomes Tita's father, and a "love-hate relationship" develops between Tita and Mamá Elena (167), a woman with a "colonizing gaze" (173) and the "nation's queer mother" (170). In Segovia's perception, the novel "stages" Tita's "ambivalent" relationship with "her seductively masculine mother and Pedro, her effeminate lover" (168). The "signs of hatred" that Tita evinces toward her mother "[bleed] into the purview of love," and Tita "subconsciously desires her mother" for Mamá Elena's qualities of strength and "resolve" – qualities lacking in Pedro (172).

Segovia further asserts that Mamá Elena "protect[s Tita] from herself" and "silence[s]" her, not only "because of 'family tradition,'" but also "because of a mother's queer love for her unsuspecting daughter," a "'dark' secret" that "resembles her [Mamá Elena's] affair with a mulatto" (167). Segovia writes that when Tita counsels Paquita Lobo that the secret ingredient in a special dish is "love," that Tita "is saying more about her mother than about the recipe" (168). Segovia's work presents novel ideas, but the basic premise of a secret sexual attraction between Mamá Elena and Tita, upon which the rest turns, does not withstand the weight of textual evidence that points in other directions.

In another study that rests on allegory, Catherine Fox-Anderson (2000–2001) recalls the lead from Janet Maslin's 1993 *New York Times* film review (discussed below): "Food and passion create a sublime alchemy in *Like Water for Chocolate*." Fox-Anderson makes a great deal of medieval alchemic discourse and suggests that the novel's magic and mystery pose an alchemical allegory set into a hermetic environment, an argument whose connections to the narrative are thin.

Elyette Benjamin-Labarthe (2003), writing about the film, and Georgina J. Whittingham and Lourdes Silva (1998), comparing *Like Water for Chocolate* to Gabriel García Márquez's *Of Love and Other Demons* (1995. *Del amor y otros demonios* 1994), consider at greater depth the simple equation of food signifying passion and find that food represents love, as well as erotic experience.[28] Benjamin-Labarthe recalls the soothing, aphrodisiac, and magical properties assigned to native foods and the ritualistic preparation of chocolate by Mesoamerican societies (35–36) and suggests Tita as a shaman or priestess through her connection to rituals of food preparation. Whittingham and Silva emphasize lovemaking and the erotic as "aesthetic acts" and representations of the repression of female desire and the cultural prohibitions connected to that repression in *Like Water for Chocolate* and *Of Love and Other Demons*.

Like Water for Chocolate: The Film and the Critics

Following a phenomenally successful run on home turf, the film opened in select U.S. markets, including New York, on February 17, 1993. Its international release served to awaken global interest in the novel, popularized Mexican film worldwide, inspired investment in film in Mexico, and coaxed open the doors of Hollywood to Mexican filmmakers.[29] While Deborah A. Shaw (2003) agrees that *Like Water for Chocolate* "has come to symbolize the development of Mexican film in the 1990s," she cautions reserve in estimating the level of Mexican government support to film in the period and in overstating the quality of Mexican domestic-market film; she also cites the limited extent of Mexican film releases.[30]

In 2003, Joseph Contreras and Scott Johnson, writing for *Newsweek*, recalled the effect of *Like Water for Chocolate* on Mexico-U.S. film relations and warned that federal spending cuts in Mexico would send even more Mexican movie makers north:

> If approved, the government spending cuts will surely accelerate the exodus of Mexican talent to El Norte. The directorial diaspora was set in motion in 1993 by Alfonso Arau's romantic fantasy, *Like Water for Chocolate*, which set a U.S. box-office record for a foreign movie. After that, Mexican filmmakers became all the rage in studio boardrooms across Hollywood. Now they are just as likely to venture out on their own; Guillermo del Toro, the director of comic-book-inspired films like *Cronos*, moved to Austin in the late 1990s and cofounded the Tequila Gang production company with Alfonso Cuaron and *Like Water for Chocolate* screenwriter Laura Esquivel.[31]

Success of the film release in the U.S. correlated with the generally positive reviews of the film in U.S. magazines and newspapers, which emphasized the film's hearth–heart relationship, romantic and erotic aspects of the love affair, and its magical events and transformations. Janet Maslin, reviewing the film at the time of its North American release for *The New York Times*, found the film "lively" and "enchanting" (B4), "presenting a torrid, slow-burning love affair and never losing its own bright, original flame" (C13). Not all viewers, however, found the film "original" or "enchanting."

Dissenting U.S. views on the film soon emerged in the elite U.S. weeklies *The New Yorker* and *The New Republic* and trickled in from elsewhere, mostly – but not entirely – coming from male critics. *New Yorker* film critic Anthony Lane's review lived up to the magazine's monocled logo and disdainfully pronounced the film "sticky, lusty, and rather ludicrous" and dismissed the food-and-kitchen metaphors with "the kitchen stands for the bedroom, and that's that." Lane declared that the movie felt "like second-hand Magic Realism," taking "a shortcut to weirdness without hooking into anything substantial."[32] Stanley Kauffmann in *The New Republic* responded to the film with words like "pummeled," "barrage," and "assault," and found that the film was a "rag-bag" of "components," and that Arau had directed "without distinction of any kind" (26). British film critic Jonathan Romney in *The New Statesman and Society* (1993) found Arau's film overdone, simplistic, and "schmaltzy" (33).

The academic audience apparently found its own way through the film, which gained access to university classrooms and film series, encouraging broader study of the novel, and the novel and film continue to be used together in academic settings.[33] De Valdés (1995) makes an early point-by-point comparison between the novel and film, singling out two problematic aspects of the translation from print to film: first, that Tita is an abused "Cinderella" in the film, but not in the novel (with which some viewers and readers would disagree); and, second, that Mamá Elena immediately dies from the marauders' attack in the film, as opposed to her lingering in a paralyzed state before dying in the novel (which may be inferred from the film's handling by the viewer familiar with the novel). It is interesting that Claudine Potvin, at about the same time (1995), declares, "Es casi imposible separar la adaptación al cine [. . .] de la novela" [It's almost impossible to separate the film adaptation from the novel] (56).

In addition to De Valdés's distinctive perception of substance and style between novel and film, her observations about the potential problems encountered by male readers and viewers of *Like Water for Chocolate* are also ground for further investigation. Her keenest insights, however, lie in the summary assessments of the novel that frame her essay, assessments that speak at once to the basic "what it's about" and to reader (and viewer) response, as well as to Esquivel's work as a writer. De Valdés's primary assertion about what kind of film this is ("a postmodern celebration of being a woman") has been cited above, and she adds that the novel is a "feminist recuperation of artistic creativity within the confinement of the house" that is presented not as an "ideological argument," but as "an intertextual palimpsest" (190). These phrases suggest critical points of departure from which to approach and move through the novel and the film reflectively.

As we have seen, following the release of the film, critical work began to combine – or conflate – the novel and the film as objects of criticism, while in only a few cases, such as in Miriam López-Rodríguez's essay on Mexican identity, the film alone is considered. Because later critical treatments so often refer both to the print and film versions, and because many converge in their critical approaches to one or both, the following discussion will deal with criticism on the film and print versions of *Like Water for Chocolate*.

Victor Zamudio-Taylor and Inma Guiu (1995) ponder the process of the written text becoming film and ask what is lost, gained, and mediated when words are made into speech, action, and (film) set, eliminating the "'adjectival' depth" of the literary text (47–48). Zamudio-Taylor and Guiu point out that the film and novel of *Like Water for Chocolate* share certain concepts: the "literary *topos* of the found book"; the reading of the book; its authorship by a character within the narrative; and the circularity of the opening and closing scenes (50). In response to reviews that emphasized the film's "magic" and culinary adventures, Zamudio-Taylor and Guiu observe that "there is more" to the film and novel than "magical realism and food," but they remark that the most important historical events of the period – the armed conflicts of the Revolution and the Mexican War with the U.S. – "radiate in their absence," and that neither film nor novel engages the Revolution's aims of social change (51).[34] Subsequent views have examined the film's omissions of historical, economic, and social content more critically and have put a fine point on claims of "magical realism."

Julianne Burton-Carvajal, in an essay on "Mexican Melodramas of Patriarchy" (1997), calls the film a "postmodern hypermelodrama" and affirms that Sommer's theory of "foundational fictions" finds resonance in *Like Water for Chocolate* for its effort "to narrativize the nation" and its use of the couple as "an analogue to the process of nation formation" (229).[35] She notes that the film "elevate[s]" its female characters while "stereotyping" the male characters, and that it exploits popular film genres for a hyperbolic representation of sexuality and the body. For Burton-Carvajal, Mamá Elena is an example of perverse *matria potestas* [maternal power] in countering her daughters' "emotive fertility."[36] Peering "[b]eneath this film's captivating charm," Burton-Carvajal detects a misogynistic, racist subtext in Gertrudis's "rhythm," in what is perceived as the novel's superficial treatment of Chencha's rape, and in its facile resolution of Alex's claiming Esperanza in marriage.

Similar complaints form the substance of later criticism. In the new century, a pattern of criticism flowered in which critics took Esquivel – and Arau – to task for being acritical – for failing to engage authentically with issues of race, class, economics, history, and gender that fragment the nation and fragment identity. Along these lines of thought, critics found the comedy less funny and the parody, less ironic and more clichéd, and some critics, it turned out, loved to hate *Like Water for Chocolate*. In her discussion of the representation of women in the film version of *Like Water for Chocolate*, for example, Harmony H. Wu (2000) revises the view of the film as providing a positive model of Mexican womanhood and female identity. She concludes that the film enjoyed "immense success" in the "usually hermetic U.S. film market" because it "commodifies" an image of Mexico (and Latin America) that satisfies the need of U.S. filmgoers to see Mexico as "magic, folkloric, exotic, provincial," and, concurrently, as separate from their own, privileged culture.[37]

Wu's point of departure is Sommer's affirmation (in *Foundational Fictions*) that Latin American fiction sought to create nation and national identity through novels that allegorize nation building and create new identity in romances that put the European or Creole into amorous contact with an "other." In a union thus characterized and determined by race, class, or national origin, the newly formed couple then founds the new nation and forms its identity. Wu extends Sommer's theory to Mexico's "revolutionary melodrama" film, where internal conflict is added to the basic social clash of the "mixed" romance that also breaks with the past and presages the future (174–75). Wu finds *Like Water for Chocolate* not to be a "liberal, feminist treatise" but a "conservative text" that "doubles back" on its "feminist pretensions" and replaces the "class conflict" of Sommer's national novel with "feminine [. . .] desire" opposing the established order (178–79). Wu's concern with the film's failure to engage social reality is subsequently echoed by other critics.

Deborah [A.] Shaw (2003) explores identity in the film and approaches *Like Water for Chocolate* by comparing the kind of Mexican "national image" it promulgates with that presented by *Amores perros* (2000. *Love's a Bitch*). Shaw points to director Arau's missed opportunities to tackle Mexico's social and economic issues using parody and the film's historical focus, and she makes much of Esquivel's failure to create nuanced women characters within a critically imagined milieu. Shaw asserts that the film is so conservative in these respects that it was sure to please both the Ministry for Tourism and the government of Coahuila (39). National Tourism was gratified, according to a statement on the subject by Arau, with the film's representation of "a conservative, romantic image of rural Mexico" (39). For Shaw, that image primarily reflected a "nostalgia for a mythical past," and its representation "belied the reality of mass poverty and ever increasing urbanization, seen in Mexico City's vast shanty-towns" (39).

Like Wu, Shaw views the film as "ignor[ing]" such issues as "modernization, the increase of social inequality, and the growth of feminism," and as "reinvent[ing] the past in such a way as to negate social history" (39). Shaw describes the film's representations of gender as "clearly delineated," and the realities of "class and ethnic tensions," as "ignored" (39). Shaw cites Claudia Loewenstein's 1994 *Southwest Review* interview with Esquivel as articulating what Shaw calls Esquivel's "essentialist image" of women who are divided between "natural" and "unnatural" women (Shaw 40, 48–49) and containing Esquivel's "attack" on how women are located within "materialism and modernity" (40). In such a simplistically predetermined cinematic environment, Shaw asserts, the viewer lacks "freedom of interpretation" (43). A pervasive part of this environment is what Shaw describes as the film's seductive veneer of "folkloric romanticism," a mask for an antagonistic posture toward social change, particularly feminism (67).

Concurring with Shaw and Wu's "conservative text" assessment, Victoria Martínez (2004) tests that critical judgment against a reading of Mexico's economic and political history. Martínez's political criticism is initially bolstered by John H. Sinnigen's discussion (1995) of *Like Water for Chocolate*'s "oblique" references to the "ongoing burning political and cultural questions" of the 1980s and Carlos Salinas Gotari's "modernizing project" that sought to straddle Mexican heritage and the "first world" aspirations of its leadership (114). Like Deborah A. Shaw and Wu, Martínez finds the novel's supposed feminism insincere and intentionally so, "a false feminist message" (35, 38, 40) that is subject to critical deconstruction (28). She elaborates the novel's "neo-liberal" politics as "falsely" representing the historical Revolution as a moment of "liberation of the economically and gender oppressed [*sic*]" (28–29).[38] Her work on Pedro, who usually gets cursory critical attention, is insightful and perceptive, but she is mistaken in writing that the "other Mexican men in this text are revolutionaries" (32), as Oxford explains in his essay in this volume.

Martínez makes dark assumptions regarding Tita and Chencha's mistress–servant relationship late in the novel (34), finds John Brown's affection for his grandmother patronizing in some respects (35), and points to the disappointing bourgeois image of the post-Revolutionary Gertrudis (37–38) and the unchallenged economic well-being of the De la Garza family. Martínez concludes that the novel must reflect the government's neo-liberal policies, a nostalgia for the economics of the *Porfiriato*, and a longing for U.S. cultural influence – referencing John Brown's medical science and the "successful union" of Esperanza and Alex in producing a child who survives (38–39). No "real revolution" appears in the novel (36), and there is simply "nothing subversive" in it (41), she concludes.

Dianna C. Niebylski ("Passion" 2004) likewise laments Esquivel's failure to grapple critically with Mexico's historical violence and present-day injustices in the novel and screenplay. She affirms that the novel disappoints, and that the film falls into the genre of *comedia ranchera*, an unfortunate result in her estimation, given the nature of the material (263).[39] The comic and "potentially parodic" elements in the novel, according to Niebylski, work only in the short term – "temporarily" or "at least initially" (253–55). She blames the novel's "insufficiently revisionist tactics" for helping to make it a short-term publishing wonder and distancing it from any claim to literary merit. Niebylski emphasizes the author's "intent[ion]" toward parody, which "is compromised by the inconsistent tone of the narrative" (255), later characterized as "tonal instability" (270 n. 11). Niebylski observes that Esquivel's tone "shifts from comic carnivalesque to comic sentimental and [to] sometimes openly maudlin and nostalgic, often within a single sentence" (255). Niebylski notes that these instances are not systematic enough to construct a parody of the "careless semantic and stylistic abuses" that one finds in poor examples of serialized romance fiction or television soap operas (255).

Niebylski also comments on Esquivel's representation of the grotesque in Rosaura and on Esquivel's ambiguous, essentially failed characterization of Tita, both of which link representations of the body in *Like Water for Chocolate* to violence as a theme. Rosaura is rendered as an object "of social denigration and cultural rejection," which unjustly "reproduces the pernicious cultural prejudices that turn pregnant, unloved, and overweight women into women who 'explode,'" according to Niebylski. Esquivel implies, then, that Rosaura, the "most repressed" of the sisters, "deserve[s] her miserable fate" (257). Tita, Niebylski observes, is doubly trapped by the author, first, in an "idealized femininity" and, second, in an "anti-carnivalesque containment" based on "the author's refusal to let the novel's heroine enter the sphere of the properly carnivalesque" (257). Niebylski writes that Esquivel's Tita attains "the properly carnivalesque" only at her death when she eats the matches and spontaneously combusts, allowing her body to control her and "defil[ing] her body simultaneously" (258). Niebylski asserts that Esquivel's discourse of the body as "bawdy, grotesque, and steamy" links to culinary discourse, and culinary discourse, to violent death by "self-poisoning," which links to "the theme of violence" (260–61).

Niebylski notes Esquivel's broad "indifferen[ce]" to historical events, which represent no more than "local flavor" in the novel, and she takes Esquivel to task specifically for the family's perceived indifference toward Chencha's having been raped by raiders (261). Niebylski charges Esquivel for her failure to "explore the links" to violence outside the ranch (*e.g.*, the hangings in the town, battles in the distance, and the wet-nurse killed by a stray bullet) as connections to social conflicts involving gender, class, and race (261). Niebylski concurs with film reviewer Romney, mentioned above, that the film fails to capitalize on comic and carnivalesque elements present in the novel that could have been transformed into edgier material, more focused on the historical period (263).

To take nothing away from her insightful unpacking of the ostensible parody and comedy of the novel and the author's missed opportunities, some few of Niebylski's statements about plot and character merit clarifying. She locates the "love story and the cooking lesson" in "the rural and border town of Coahuila" (252), which is inaccurate since Coahuila is a state, and most of the narrative takes place on a ranch in a rural area near the town of Piedras Negras, a town in the state of Coahuila.[40] By the close of the novel, in the present of the 1980s, an apartment building and parking lot sit on the formerly rural site, and the old ranch property has become urban or suburban. Niebylski cogently asserts that the melodramatic figure of Gertrudis as a general in the Revolutionary army is based on María Félix's idealized portrayal of such figures, but her stipulation that Gertrudis as a female general makes "an improbable historical figure" because Villa's army "had none" is worth clarifying with historical data.[41] She also writes that Pedro "suffers a stroke" during sex and dies, but within the context of novel, at the moment of sexual climax, Pedro's spirit accesses the tunnel from which he came into life, and he returns there – dead of too much joy.[42]

Helene Price (2005) also considers both the film and the novel and parodies the novel's focus on food to introduce its "Unsavoury Representations." Price asserts that the contradictions between Esquivel's "tablespoon of magic" and true "magical realism" are apparent "with little more than a second glance" at the novel or film. While she develops an argument that is close in aim and certain points to Wu's treatment and repeats conclusions enjoined by Wu (using William Spindler's bimodal geographic perspective) and Martínez, the difference is that Price's "magic realism" dichotomy is framed in an internally authentic critique.[43] Price demonstrates that the "magic" in *Like Water for Chocolate* has no authentic roots in the "Boom" tradition of magic realism, not because Esquivel's "magic real" comes from the wrong part of the world, but because it fails to meet the true aims and to satisfy the political rationale that Price attaches to true magic realism. Price finds that *Like Water for Chocolate* fails to use its magic to distance Mexican identity from its historical patriarchy and class divisions and to reshape national identity as a liberating and leveling discourse, the distinctive function of magic realism, according to Price.

Price echoes Marquet in finding that *Like Water for Chocolate* has "all the right 'ingredients'" for commercial success, but asserts that those who have attributed "magic realism" to certain events in the narrative and film (as many have) are falling for style – the appearance of "fantastic occurrences" being equivalent to magic realism – and missing the essential substance of magic realism. Price asserts, instead, that *Like Water for Chocolate* "go[es] entirely against the grain of the revolutionary ethos" (181) and that its "magic" elements serve only to bolster and support the patriarchy's traditionally oppressive gender and class divisions. She charges that *Like Water for Chocolate* fails to challenge discrimination and traditional gender roles, and that its "magic" elements work to make Mexico a palatable dish for those who like to think of the nation as harmoniously quaint, charming, and backward, and as separate and marginal when compared to U.S. culture. Whether French, German,

British, Irish, Indian, and Italian readers' and viewers' responses would be similar if gauged from this perspective is ground for further investigation.

In her distinctive treatment of the film, López-Rodríguez (2004) considers the "Mexicanness" of the film version and focuses on the relationship between the women in the film and food as revealing Mexican identity. López-Rodríguez relates the historical roots of two of Tita's special dishes, *mole de guajolote con almendra y ajonjolí* [turkey *mole* with almonds and sesame seeds] and *chiles en nogada* [chiles in walnut sauce]. The former, according to López-Rodríguez, was "forbidden to women during the colonial period" for its alleged aphrodisiac powers, and the latter was created in Puebla to honor Mexican independence (64). López-Rodríguez also provides a useful outline on Mexican cuisine (65–66), suggesting that Tita's menus, as the products of her self-liberation and her transformations of the kitchen and cooking, are "post-revolutionary" and "multicultural" in the context of Mexican identity (67–68. 70–71). According to López-Rodríguez, Tita's cookbook, with its mix of women's genres, contains a version of Mexican history that creatively breaks down borders and difference and gives the written word to women – whose access to other forms of literacy is limited or barred (70).

Stephen M. Hart, in his "Prologue" to *A Companion to Latin American Film* (2004), calls the film "playful" and "lighthearted" (vii) and addresses the matter of "magical realism" in the film. He emphasizes that "magical realism" is a means "for depicting Latin American reality" and constructing "cultural identity" and includes *Like Water for Chocolate* and Isabel Allende's *The House of the Spirits* (1985. *La casa de los espíritus* 1982) among those works where "magical realism" is found (*Film* 176). Hart also mentions the fairy tale elements of "Cinderella" as they apply to *Like Water for Chocolate* (176).[44] Hart (177), with Claudine Potvin (55) earlier, affirms that the film is very like the novel. Hart pays particular attention to how cinematic techniques are used to portray and differentiate the ghostly from the living appearances of Mamá Elena and Nacha, and he finds the fire scenes (the burning shower and the final scene), by comparison, "less visually convincing" (177).

The Law of Love

Two years after the release of the English translation of *Like Water for Chocolate* and the global release of Arau's film (1993), Esquivel's second novel, *The Law of Love* (1996. *La ley del amor* 1995) was published in Spanish.[45] Global sales for *Like Water for Chocolate* and the economic success of the film apparently prompted the simultaneous release of the

Spanish novel in the U.S. and motivated arrangements for timely releases of the novel in translation. This procedure has operated for each of Esquivel's subsequent novels, but only *The Law of Love*, so far as can be determined at this writing, has been slated for filming. Esquivel's later novels have not had *Like Water for Chocolate*'s transformative effects on fiction writing or filmmaking, yet each has deepened Esquivel's fictional exploration of Mexican identity and culture and individual and communal realization. She has contested Mexico's views of gender, history, time, tradition, class, race, and identity, and she has appropriated and combined established genres of the novel in ways that are distinctive – for a result that is perennially styled as "new" in the parlance of Latin American literary criticism.

With *The Law of Love*, Esquivel risked her popular – and literary – reputation with an experiment in science fiction and further endangered the experiment in genre by including images, authorial instructions, and music – including lyrics by Liliana Felipe – to accompany the narrative.[46] Esquivel, however, like Ray Bradbury, writes science fiction with a soul, which is to say that in the midst of gadgetry, space and time travel, and futuristic technology, the reader discovers the human heart, roused to the old struggle for agency, identity, and belonging.

Elizabeth Coonrod Martínez (1998) reviewed *The Law of Love* for *Hispania*, drawing comparisons between Esquivel's modes and concerns in her first novel and the second. She noted that the two share a comic presentation and "political undertones" – like "class hierarchies" and "political abuse" – but that *The Law of Love* strives for the ambitious aim of achieving "a *fin de siécle* assessment of human nature and Mexican society" within the context of Mexico's urban popular culture and social stratification (891). Robert Houston in *The New York Times Book Review* found the CD that accompanies the book "a delight." *Publisher's Review* found the novel "propelled by the same jolly, reckless storytelling energy" of *Like Water for Chocolate*, but noted that "skimpy character development" and a "[B]yzantine plot" work against the novel's success (225). Lillian Pizzichini (1996) harkened acritically toward magic realism and science fiction, but for her, the multi-media reading became tedious (23).

Concepción Bados-Ciria (1996), like Houston, found much to like in the CD, and she parses Esquivel's choices and placement of the music in enlightening ways. She writes that "the novel presents itself as an interactive body between the reader and the protagonists" (38), and she ably unpacks the musical (opera and *danzón*) elements and reveals their narrative connections in a smooth tutorial, rendering the "complex plot" richer and more connected to the narrative and images. Briefly, opera accompanies narrative events involving tragedy and emotional suffering

27

(39–40), and popular music reinforces the stance of a protagonist with sympathetic energy, pleasure, and resistance (41).

Lisbeth Gant-Britton (2000) assesses *The Law of Love* as a work of futuristic fiction in which technology is used in a productive sense to "introduce a trope in which the 'soul' is the repository of the mind-spirit connection" as a "motif of an inner self that continues to exist" (268). This rendering contests the position taken by other Latina and Latin American women writers who implicate technology in the destruction of indigenous culture and people and, instead, "signals the development of a Latin American futurism" that honors a "mind/body/spirit connection" that specifically avails itself of global technology (268). Carla Fernandes (2001) writes that although the novel advertises its innovations in terms of media and its futuristic topic, its narrative is firmly grounded in the past, and Esquivel emphasizes traditional literary themes, even in her choices of "multi-media" ancillaries (670). In spite of its references to technology and mechanization, Fernandes writes, the plot rests on a parable of universal harmony (671) – a perception that readers and listeners like Bados-Ciria might observe is rendered audible in the musical accompaniment to the narrative.

The Law of Love has found a more receptive audience to debate its modes and readings in comparative and theoretical academic treatments, but, as was the case with *Like Water for Chocolate*, some critical pronouncements shed more heat than light on *The Law of Love*.[47] For example, Ilan Stavans adopted a Marquet-like hostility in his inventive, drive-by attack on *The Law of Love*, describing Esquivel as "a shadowy screenwriter" who had "gone amok" with her second novel, using "mere gags" to "discuss" futuristic devices (112). He characterizes the progress of the plot as "unravel[ing]" and summarizes the action of the novel in a way that conflates temporally separate events (110). In her review of *The Law of Love*, Barbara Mujica emphasizes Esquivel's "gimmickry" but, perhaps surprisingly, Mujica singles out the music and the CD (rather than the science fiction) as the "gimmick" (61). Mujica finds the story "so confusing and convoluted" that "nothing – not even Puccini – can save it." Following this statement, however, Mujica perseveres through six more paragraphs on the novel, finding it "impossibly silly and complicated," but making a great deal of sense about the plot.

Ryan Prout suggests that in *The Law of Love*, Esquivel combines romance with "an adventurous patriotic futurology," including reminders of "the national rape" (51), a narrative combination that, he notes, did not play well in Mexico. Prout, reporting the novel's "hostile" reception at home, explains the reaction "as symptoms of its negotiation of opposing models of Mexican national identity" (43).[48] Claire L. Taylor (2002) also notes the poor reception among reviewers in the U.S. and

U.K. (324 n. 2) and modifies Prout's designation of "romance" to "New Age romance" (329). Taylor points out that the novel's science fiction elements ironically threaten the romantic storyline because the protagonists' "constantly changing bodies" (329) work as a "distorting force" on their "subjectivity" (330) and "serve to undermine a straight reading" of either of the genres (328).

Swift as Desire

Genre mix and pastiche are absent in Esquivel's straightforward third novel, *Swift as Desire* (2001. *Tan veloz como el deseo*). In *Swift as Desire,* Esquivel makes transparent a hidden tale of love, rancor, and longing emerging from the warring worldviews of post-Revolutionary Mexico. In reviewing the novel for *Hispania* in 2002, I pointed to its representation of opposed national forces and its insistence on reconciliation, also noting the apparent incoherence in the narrative voice. Sylvia Santiago, reviewing the novel for *Herizons,* called upon the food metaphor and parodically described *Swift as Desire* as "artificially sweetened" in comparison to *Like Water for Chocolate* (35). She remarks that the novel frequently "resembles the *telenovelas*" and warns potential readers "with little patience for melodrama [. . .] to steer clear" (35).

Editorial confidence remained sufficiently high, however, that in 2001, Random House audio released the English translation of *Swift as Desire* read by Elizabeth Peña to positive reviews (O'Gorman, Kellerman). Rachel Cooke in the *New Statesman* (U.K.) recalls Esquivel's "sexy little [first] novel" and finds this "fable" disappointing – "glib" and "hackneyed" – by comparison. She expresses the problem in culinary terms as one of "far too much sugar and not nearly enough spice" (39). *Publishers Weekly* (U.S.) opted for a "sweeter" critical view, noting that the "fourth" – in reality the third – novel by the "princess of modern Latin American literature" is "another quirky and sensual story with a moralistic twist" that "succeeds in conveying a touching message of the power of familial and romantic love" (165). Criticism in this volume intends to provide a more careful reading and insightful critical view of *Swift as Desire.*

Malinche: A Novel

Esquivel's fourth novel again placed the author's interest in Mexican history and her willingness to integrate other media into the text at the service of a woman's historical narrative. *Malinche: A Novel* debuted in a promising way, first in the U.S. and then in Mexico. A few months after the initial release, *Malinche* (as I will refer to the novel henceforward) was reported to be in its second printing. Fonolibro soon released an audio version recorded by Lucía Méndez with a tantalizing promotion for the "controversial" history of the "enigmatic" title character.[49] Two of the major-outlet reviews in the U.S. are representative of the popular media's response to the novel: *Publishers Weekly* found Esquivel's novel to be "disjointed storytelling," lacking in "narrative immediacy," and giving "short shrift" to its title character (31). The *Philadelphia Enquirer's* long-time reviewer and Latina novelist Tanya Barrientos was likewise disappointed in the book's failure to realize its potential and distanced by its fabulist "New Age babble." Victor Cruz-Lugo's book-tour interview with Esquivel offered no critical view or new information about Esquivel's process in writing the novel.

In the U.K., Alice O'Keeffe's consideration of Allende's *Inés of My Soul* (2006. *Inés del alma mía*) and Esquivel's *Malinche* for *The New Statesman* records several interesting responses to Esquivel's novel. O'Keeffe reflects upon the kinship that Latin American women – even those from the higher socio-economic classes who appear to be European in their heritage – demonstrate with the "conquered" rather than with the conquering Europeans. O'Keeffe attributes this "white" sympathy with the oppressed indigenous people to the U.S. presence in Latin America, which, she notes, makes "even relatively well-off Latin Americans [. . .] keenly aware of how it feels to be at the mercy of an imperialist power" (52).[50] She views the two novels, both treating women who had intimate relationships with Spanish conquerors, as "contribut[ing] to the process of reconciliation." Unfortunately, O'Keeffe finds Esquivel's novel otherwise tedious, "undermined by Esquivel's meandering, shapeless narrative, which lapses into clichéd mysticism." O'Keeffe wonders at the "confusing" matter of Esquivel's referring to Cortés as "Malinche" and writes that the "codex" Esquivel commissioned to double the narrative looks "like second-rate cartoons" that "if anything, detract from the novel's credibility." The reviewer is apparently unaware that Cortés *was* "Malinche," and that Nahua codices, images of which are readily available online and in print reproductions, are quite similar to the result that Jordi Castells achieves for the reverse of the novel's book jacket.[51]

Oswaldo Estrada (2007) considers *Malinche* in the context of Latin America's new historic novel, "self-conscious rewritings of history" that pose questions of identity that began with the Conquest and continue to be debated (617–18). *Malinche* is exceptional within the genre in that the protagonist is an indigenous woman whose image and narratives extend outside Mexico and appear in other national literatures. Estrada compares

Malinche's currency as a cultural icon with Don Quixote's and Don Juan's. In addition, he finds that although *Malinche* responds to the "new historical novel" in a few basic respects, Esquivel uses forms that are "radically different" from those employed by the genre's "most outstanding and successful practitioners" (620). Esquivel's aim, according to Estrada, is to take an entirely different tack from those who have used Malinche for their own ends. Instead, Esquivel attempts "to deconstruct the conquest from within" and recreate it from the perspective of an indigenous female character (624–25). Estrada observes that when Malinalli is born with the umbilical cord between her teeth, the "anachronistic" image intimately connects her to the mythic founding of the Aztec empire (626).[52]

Though he finds ample evidence of Esquivel's use of contemporary chronicler Bernal Díaz de Castillo's *The History of the Conquest of New Spain* (2008. *La historia verdadera de la conquista de la Nueva-España*), Estrada affirms that Esquivel inscribes her Malinalli with emotions and behaviors that counter Díaz de Castillo's representation of Doña Marina's compliant character (624–25; 630–32). Estrada characterizes the dialogue that put off some reviewers as Esquivel's erring in giving her protagonist a voice that sounds like W. H. Prescott's idea of "the language of love" in his *Conquest of Mexico* (625).[53] In the same vein, Estrada remarks that discourse attributed to Malinalli's mother when they are reunited long after the mother has sold her into slavery, "debilit[a] la representación del sujeto indígena en la novela" [weakens the representation of the indigenous subject in the novel], harkening back to nineteenth-century characterizations of indigenous people "en que los indios son descritos con tonos románticos, como si fueran parte del paisaje" [in which Indians are described in romantic terms, as if they were part of the landscape] (632).

This kind of discourse, however cloying, outdated (629), and hackneyed (632), Estrada observes, serves to emphasize Esquivel's "intención política" [political aim] (632). Esquivel's enslaved Malinalli, in Estrada's reading, is not the "open, raped" mother that Octavio Paz philosophizes (in "Los hijos de La Malinche"), but a woman conscious of the power of language and of her power as a translator who controls her situation by managing both sides of the translation to her advantage (633–34).[54] Estrada notes that Esquivel's Malinalli, in spite of her agency as translator, shows an uneasiness about her identity; she senses that she is losing her culture and becoming identified with the Spanish, an aspect of character that one does not detect in the Doña Marina of the *Historia verdadera* (634).

For Estrada, the only redeeming feature of the novel's ending is that Esquivel constructs a fresh myth that fuses the raped woman with the

Virgin, in a scene that stands "en total contradicción con la historia escrita" [in total contradiction to written history], as Malinalli communes with the Aztec goddess Tonantzin, who takes on the guise of the Virgin of Guadalupe (636). This scene serves to throw older versions of history into doubt and constructs new myths using old ones, or, put another way, recycles all kinds of cultural knowledge and opens up possibilities about the identity of La Malinche (636–37).[55] In these ways, Esquivel responds to questions of female and *mestizo* identity and poses the problem anew for the global generation (637).

The essays on *Malinche* in this volume also take up questions of identity and contested cultural representations related to the character of Malinche.

Future Directions in Esquivel Criticism

Beatriz González Stephan's 1991 observations on *Like Water for Chocolate* are valuable as a productive philosophy upon which to contemplate future critical work on Esquivel's fiction and on fiction by other women who write in non-traditional and experimental modes. González Stephan reminds her reader that "Las formas literarias alternativas presentan una infinita riqueza, y que siempre cualquier intento taxonómico corre el riesgo de simplificarlas" [Alternative literary forms present infinite richness, such that in any effort to categorize them, we always run the risk of simplifying them] (214). A re-examination of reductionist efforts practiced on Esquivel's fiction would be productive critical effort. In this regard, María Elena Soliño's detailed work on Spain's women writers' use of fairy tales (2002) makes several points that suggest critical perspectives on *Like Water for Chocolate*. She writes about the influence of fairy tales on the *novela rosa*, with which Esquivel's first novel has been identified in a pejorative sense by some critics and in an intentionally parodic sense by others. Soliño's positing the fairy tale as a purveyor of social and political norms and thus apt for subversion and parody in women's fiction suggests a fresh avenue into fairy tale theory for Esquivel critics.

Florinda Riquer Fernández (1992), addressing matters of feminist outlook and practice in Mexico, suggests that created spaces such as Tita's kitchen and its environs, usually sites and signs of patriarchal domination and female life-sentences, have the potential to become spaces defined and dominated by women, who take their identity from affirming their own qualities and activities rather than defining themselves via negative comparisons to patriarchal attributes and values. In real life, she asserts, women can successfully challenge the patriarchy. She writes that if a woman's identity is based on her "qualities" and "activities" rather than on a negative perspective of her "position," one based on her interactions "in certain contexts [social, religious, cultural, familial] through her life," that women's identity moves beyond the gender-based and oppositional ideas of "feminine" (60). Moreover, she suggests that women identifying themselves in ways that reject binary oppositions based on a rubric of masculine attributes and activity "also recover the active roles that they play," perhaps "transcending" their subordinate roles, and, at the very least, contesting them (60). It is possible, according to Riquer Fernández, that individual women, living in a time and place particular to them, can redefine the way they see themselves. In the same way, it is critically valid to read Tita and some of Esquivel's other female characters as rejecting the oppressed role of the *madre* – or *mujer* – *abnegada* [the self-effacing, self-denying martyr-mother or -wife] within a time and place without rejecting their personal attributes or the nature of their activity.[56] Riquer Fernández's essay finds much support also in the cultural geography studies conducted and presented in the context of *Like Water for Chocolate* in this volume by María Elisa Christie.

On the other hand, Wu, (Deborah A.) Shaw, Niebylski, and Price present counter arguments, characterizing such points of view as validating patriarchal discourse and further subjugating the disadvantaged. From a feminist perspective, the motivations of Esquivel's heroines are interesting for what they are and are not. Tita longs for love, marriage, and children; Azucena rushes headlong through the universe, searching for her "soul mate"; Lluvia wants to help her dying father "talk" and longs for a reconciliation between her parents; and Malinalli insists on her right to freedom and a life with her children and Jaramillo. These are not the stuff of any standard feminist agenda, seen through the gendered, binary lens of supposedly masculine values, but they convey the kinds of concerns, qualities, and activities that other Mexican and Latin American women writers have also treated with power and affection and that social scientists have validated and documented in their work.[57]

Rosario Castellanos's frequently cited description of the woman's congenital lot in Mexico suggests that what Esquivel has done in each of her novels is not as acritical as some critics have charged. In *Mujer que sabe latín* (1973 [*A Woman Who Knows Latin*]), Castellanos writes,

> Por eso desde que nace una mujer la educación trabaja sobre el material dado para adaptarlo a su destino y cultivarlo en un ente moralmente aceptable, es decir, socialmente útil. Así se le despoja de la espontaneidad para actuar; se le prohíbe la iniciativa de decidir; se le enseña a obedecer los mandamientos de una ética que le es absolutamente ajena y que no tiene más justificación ni fundamentación que la de servir a los intereses, a los propósitos y a los fines de los demás. (14)

[For that reason, from the moment that a woman is born, the system works through the curriculum to adapt the "material" to her destiny and to cultivate it to yield a morally acceptable being, that is to say, one useful to society. Thus she is deprived of her spontaneity in taking action; she is prohibited from taking the initiative in making decisions; she is schooled to obey the charges of an ethic that is completely outside herself and that has no more justification or foundation than that of serving the interests, aims, and ends of others.][58]

Castellanos's focus on Mexican education for girls anticipates Esquivel's treating the theme in *Like Water for Chocolate* and its implicit lesson in each of her novels. Tita laments the lapses in her formal education, and Esquivel's women characters – Tita, Gertrudis, Mamá Elena, Nacha, Luz del amanecer, Lluvia, and Malinalli – are, in some way, expected to bend to an external ethic that makes them serviceable to others.

Following Rosario Castellanos's unexpected death in August 1974, Mexican poet José Emilio Pacheco (1939–) wrote about her focus on Mexican women's identity in his Sunday newspaper feature "Inventario." Pacheco cited precisely the kinds of obstacles that work against a validating view of the Mexican woman's identity and acknowledged the grasp that Castellanos had attempted:

Cuando pase la conmoción de su muerte y se relean sus libros, se verá que nadie entre nosotros tuvo en su momento una conciencia tan clara de lo que significa la doble condición de mujer y de mexicana al hizo de esta conciencia la materia misma de su obra[,] la línea central de su trabajo. Naturalmente no supimos leerla. El peso de la inercia nos embotaba, la oscuridad de las nociones adquiridas nos cegaba, la defensa instintiva de nuestros privilegios nos ponía en guardia. (16)[59]

[When the shock over her death has passed, and we re-read her books, we'll see that none of us in our time was as completely conscious as she was of what it means to have the twin conditions of being female and Mexican, as she made that understanding the very substance of her work, the true thread that runs through it. Of course, we never knew how to read her work. The weight of inertia made us dull, the darkness of our traditional notions blinded us, the instinctive defense of our privileged situation put us on guard.]

Clearly the consciousness of what it means to be a woman in Mexico continues to develop, while elements of culture, family, religion, and society that sustain the patriarchy prosper in critical and real-world applications, perhaps, as Pacheco writes, precisely because there is so much to lose in rejecting their comfort. Some of the "ways" in which Esquivel's women characters "serve themselves" are subversive, and others are openly rebellious. Like the personal testimonies of Mexican writers and artists, the work of social scientists who study gendered roles in Mexican culture suggests connections to Esquivel's fictional worlds, as we see in this volume in Christie's essay.[60] Critical assessments that find *Like Water for Chocolate* insufficiently politicized or socially unconscious suggest closer examination of the work; moreover, an extension of this line of investigation making use of Esquivel's later novels, along with *Like Water for Chocolate*, would provide a more insightful set of observations.

Much remains to be done on reading the integration of modes and material in *The Law of Love*. The multiple ways of looking at the novel in the contexts of Mexican identity and nation have barely begun to be explored, and even the novel's place in the science-fiction genre, glob-ally or across Latin America, is not established, judging by the indices of work on the broad field of recent science fiction. Lydia H. Rodríguez, in her chapter of this volume, cites the *Revista monográfica* issue entitled *Hispanic Science-Fiction and Fantasy* (1987), which predates *The Law of Love* and includes several essays on detective and "sleuth" fiction. Because these elements form a part of the layered-genre structure of *The Law of Love*, further work on the novel as a part of those science fiction sub-genres in Latin America is in order. It is interesting that Carlos Fuentes's *The Eagle's Throne* (2006. *Silla del águila* 2003), like Esquivel's *Law of Love*, adapts science fiction to the writer's purpose (politics and sex) and mode (epistolary) and may appropriately be described as a futuristic political farce.[61] A comparative consideration of these two novels and compara-tive work between *The Law of Love* and other Latin American science fiction that directs its attention to nation, identity, and agency would be projects of interest to the field. A film version of *The Law of Love* would create still other possibilities.

Swift as Desire has been critically ignored, possibly assumed to be unworthy of academic attention because of its openly experiential and biographical ties, its woman's voice, and its material: parental caretaking, laying out the dead, and mourning, which are perceived as woman's work. José Joaquín Brunner's provocative essay on Latin American iden-tity (translated in Volek by Moseley) would make a productive starting point for a consideration of Esquivel's search-for-identity narratives, including *Swift as Desire*. Brunner writes:

> The epic and original features of our identity remain trapped in that place of origin where Nature is larger than man and where the Word is mar-ried with [*i.e.*, to] Nature [. . .]. [T]his paradise, without a doubt, excludes Modernity. [¶] The utopian identity as historical evolution [. . .] sup-

poses [. . .] a reconciliation with the part that is found to be torn [. . .]."
(115)

Esquivel's emphasis on finding the "torn" part and seeking reconciliation of the two halves is realized in Lluvia's activity in *Swift as Desire* on a mundane, contemporary level, and more fancifully and romantically in her other novels. The idea of "repairing" what is "torn," or refashioning a whole out of "what is left" and the underlying implication of work associated with women's hands, such as quilting, darning, crocheting, (re)weaving, embroidery, needlepoint, ironing, blocking, and stitching, are modes present in women's writing about history and identity that remain under-explored in literary criticism.

Swift as Desire is Esquivel's only novel to date that focuses on life within the present-day capitol, and future criticism on *Swift as Desire* would be well served to consider "the city." Mexico City might productively be considered, in the words of Elisabeth Guerrero and Anne Lambright (2007), as "a product and a generator of modern culture," as a cultural entity that gives the novel and its characters their context (xi). Urban cultural geography and constructions of the individual and society within that space suggest germane critical directions for *Swift as Desire*, in the same way that parallel considerations have served in the rural context for thinking critically about *Like Water for Chocolate*.

Franco's *Plotting Women*, Sommer's theorizing the national novel, and Debra A. Castillo's *Easy Women* (1998), with its warning of fear of a "literal and figurative feminization of literature" (218), suggest interesting – and untapped – critical intersections with Esquivel's fiction. For example, Castillo's consideration of readers' and characters' agency, of fictional prostitutes and sexual attitudes, and of the public fascination with the prostitute character finds intersections with Esquivel's Gertrudis, with Lucha and her alleged sin, and with Lolita, whose rape is kept silent. The most obvious connections between Castillo's work and Esquivel's lie, of course, in *Malinche: A Novel*.[62]

Also suggestive is Franco's writing that Elena Garro, in *Recollections of Things to Come* (1969. *Recuerdos del porvenir* 1963), "escapes from verisimilitude through fairy tale but thereby cannot insert her heroines into history," and that Castellanos's effort in *The Book of Lamentations* (1998. *Oficio de tinieblas* 1962) to be "true to history means that she dooms her protagonist" (146). Esquivel also avails herself of the fairy tale realm and "dooms her protagonist," but might one argue cogently that *Like Water for Chocolate* is somehow successful in producing a national allegory with women characters composing the center and advancing a heroine? That is an argument yet to be made.

There is also the matter of women who write about the past and leave the great events and actors of history on the edge of the plate as inedible garnish. As Alberto Julián Pérez suggests in the final chapter of this volume, this fiction merits serious continuing critical consideration, not for what it does *not* do, but for what it accomplishes – or seeks to accomplish. One productive critical direction in this regard is to examine the curative and reconciliatory power of Esquivel's historically grounded film and fiction in terms of reader response. Historian and poet Aurora Levins Morales writes of the historian as a *curandera/o* [folk healer], a telling characterization for the novelist who writes in a historical context in order to tell the stories of history's marginal actors and spectators.

Women writers' versions of history bring to mind Spanish expatriate José Moreno Villa's often-quoted observation about Mexico's way of regarding its history as if its heroes lived on, and its great events continued to unfold:

> La historia de México está en pie. Aquí no ha muerto nadie, a pesar de los asesinatos y los fusilamientos. Están vivos Cuauhtémoc, Cortés, Maximiliano, don Porfirio y todos los conquistadores y todos los conquistados. Esto es lo original de México. Todo el pasado suyo es actualidad palpitante. No ha muerto el pasado. No ha pasado lo pasado, se ha parado. (105)

> [Mexico's history is on its feet. Here, no one has died, in spite of the murders and deaths by firing squad. Cuauhtémoc, Cortés, Maximiliano, don Porfirio, and all the conquerors and all the conquered live on. This is what is original about Mexico. All of her past is throbbing reality. The past has not died. The past has not passed, but has halted.][63]

In the texts of women writers like Esquivel, the past becomes present in the microcosm of the fiction. In the work of women writers who recreate history as it is lived along the margins, history is centered in the private lives of individuals and families, and its presence is a spiritual and physical legacy where objects and memory tell a tale that has never been told before in quite the way these women writers tell it.[64]

Esquivel's small-lens view of history in *Like Water for Chocolate* and in episodes of *The Law of Love* and *Swift as Desire* works from a marginalized perspective, and in *Malinche*, she gives a conspicuous one-dimensional icon of Mexican popular culture a family history and human fears and aspirations.[65] Understanding how Esquivel's fiction fits into ways of theorizing and reading historical fiction in Latin America takes in work by Seymour Menton (1955, 1993), Linda Hutcheon (1988), Elzbieta Sklodowska (1991), Alberto Julián Pérez (1995), Peter Elmore (1997), Fernando Aínsa (1991, 1997), and Elisabeth Guerrero

(2002).[66] Aínsa (1997) points to the "explicit aim" of the new historical novel as "configuring identity" in "emergent" nations (113), which Menton had proposed in 1955. Fresh critical views that examine this "new novel" on its own terms will continue to expand ways of reading this fiction.

Finally, in the context of Mexican film history, the film based on *Like Water for Chocolate* suggests additional critical directions. One of these is the question of mother figures in Mexican film, and additional films based on Esquivel's fiction would add to the discussion. Diana Bracho, a Mexican actress and member of a distinguished film family, writes perceptively about women in Mexican film in an essay in 1985. She quotes Emilio García Riera's comment to her that "el cine estatal no tiene madre" [Mexican film has no mother] (421).[67] Bracho observes that when Mexican film has a "mother," she is not an object of reverence because Mexico, "llena de valores machistas y sexistas, no puede producir un cine que empatice con la mujer" [filled with sexist and machista values cannot produce a (national) cinema that empathizes with women] (421). Esquivel's contribution to reshaping this aspect of Mexican film – and fiction – merits further critical consideration.

Notes

1   In choosing which and how many works to reference in this essay, I have omitted some worthy contributions to the critical conversation for reasons of space, but have sought to represent the main currents of critical thinking on each of the novels and the film. Reviews treating Esquivel's novels, their recorded versions and translations, and the film of *Like Water for Chocolate*, along with news releases and stories related to the business side of the novels and film, are available in print and microfilm through research libraries; in online archives maintained by the media outlets in question; through online services available by private subscription; through electronic databases that serve university libraries (like MLA, InfoTrac-all, Book Review Digest, *etc.*); and in random postings of material at online sites. See the Apparatus section of the Editor's Preface of this volume for other details on citing reviews.

2   See Marquet, 89, col. c, and n. 3 concerning the novel's buyers. Debra A. Castillo ("Reading" 1999) provides an answer to the question of who reads novels today in Latin America, recalling a personal conversation with writer and critic Sara Sefchovich in 1994. Castillo reports that Sefchovich affirmed that "women, especially leisured middle-class women, read, and they overwhelmingly read works by other middle-class women in which women have positive protagonistic roles" (165). According to Castillo, Sefchovich was reflecting on the success of women writers like herself, Ángeles Mastretta (1949–), and Laura Esquivel (165).

3   Suzanne Ruta reports this record number of sales in *The Women's Review of Literature* (1993).

4   Susan Karlin reported in *Variety* (1993) that a longer version of the film, at 144 minutes, allegedly got a "lukewarm response" from "international critics" the previous year, but at her writing, the film, having had three cuts and several post-production fine tunings for better sound and visual quality, was "on the verge of becoming the highest-grossing foreign-language film in U.S. history." She reports that director Arau said that he favored the longer version (1, 34). The film was the largest grossing foreign film in history at $21,665,468 until *Crouching Tiger Hidden Dragon* (2000) surpassed it. The latter continues to hold the record at $128,078,872. *Pan's Labyrinth* (2006), at $37,634,615, also surpassed *Like Water for Chocolate*. These figures are reported at Box Office Mojo.

5   The film translation includes subtitled and dubbed versions. Heather Johnson, in an online report, documents translations into thirteen languages. I have found versions of the film with subtitles or dubbing in Bulgarian, Portuguese, Brazilian Portuguese, Italian, German, and English. The English subtitled version appears to be available widely in Western Europe. IMDb records fourteen translations of the film title, including Spanish and English.

6   The cost of books in Mexico has had much public attention, and this aspect of the novel's history, to whom it communicated and how, and what those effects have been socially and culturally would be useful to explore now with twenty years of hindsight. See María Elena de Valdés's brief discussion of the female reading public and reading material in Mexico (*Mirror* 5–8). Michael Schlig's work on the mirror as a metaphor mediating art and reality and as a metaphor and motif in Hispanic literature and art is useful for its commentary, as well as for its bibliography and notes on this vast subject.

7   Sánchez-Flavian repeats Marquet's error that Tita's birth is "premature" due to Mamá Elena's shock "at the tragedy" of her husband's death (no pagination).

In subsequent text references to *Like Water for Chocolate* in these notes, I use English (Doubleday hardcover 1992) and Spanish (Doubleday hardcover 1993) editions to guide the reader through whichever text is more accessible to him or her.

The novel's narrator makes clear that Tita's birth is early and that it is rapidly brought to a conclusion because of the infant's violent sobbing *in utero* because her mother is chopping onions (13 Spanish; 5–6 English). Juan de la Garza goes to celebrate Tita's birth in the local *cantina* and suffers a coronary there when a fellow patron tells him the "terrible" truth (131 Spanish; 138 English). He dies when Tita is two days old, presumably as the result of the coronary (14 Spanish; 6 English). Barbara A. Tenenbaum gets the death wrong, too (162), and her interesting article contains other misdirection. She makes assumptions that because Gertrudis is the daughter of Elena's mixed-race lover, Gertrudis must be the eldest daughter and that Elena must have been pregnant with Gertrudis when Elena married the unsuspecting Juan. However, Juan de la Garza fathers Rosaura; Elena and

José start their affair during the marriage, and Elena becomes pregnant. Tita, the youngest, must take care of their mother, rather than Rosaura, the eldest, who must marry first (18 Spanish; 13 English) à la Angustias in *The House of Bernarda Alba* (see n. 11, below). Tenenbaum observes that the film and book disagree on this point (162–63), but both make it clear enough that Rosaura is the eldest, and so marries first, and that Elena *begins* her affair with José Treviño, the first love from whom her parents sought to separate her by marrying her to Juan de la Garza. After her marriage, she corresponds with José and begins an affair, conceiving Gertrudis, her second daughter, with José while she is married to Juan, who later fathers Tita (130 Spanish; 137–38 English). Gertrudis is the mediating middle child, a role which we see her fulfill in the chapters "March" and "July." See "January" for Tita's birth, and "July," for the hidden events of Gertrudis's parentage and Tita's birth.

8   Readers should use caution in embracing the notion that Esquivel is dealing in "magic[al] realism." For a historical perspective, see the essays of Franz Roh (1925), Alejo Carpentier (1949), Ángel Flores (1955), Luis Leal (1967), Menton (1983, 1998), and Stephen M. Hart (2004). Zamora and Faris (1995) make the first four essays (and others) available in their magic realism reader. Stephen Hart's opening essay in his co-edited *Companion to Magical Realism* (2005) provides an excellent tutorial on these essays, a global view of the subject, and suggestions of problematic critical and practical aspects in "magical realism" (1–13). See Seymour Menton's article (1983) on Borges as a magic realist, Menton's historical overview of the subject, and his subsequent "true history" of the phenomenon (1998). See Irene Guenther's article in Zamora and Faris for the "magical" *versus* "mystical" discussion (especially 65–66 n. 24).

9   See Castillo's continuing discussion of this question and the connections she makes to Jonathan Culler's characterization of the functions of the prostitute in nineteenth-century French literature (*Easy Women* 215 *ff.*). Also see Beatriz González Stephan's catalog of the pejorative designations assigned to "marginal literatures" and the nature of critical treatment on them (1992, 201–2).

10 Presumably this conclusion is derived from a reading of *The Labyrinth of Solitude* (1961. *El laberinto de la soledad* 1950) written by Paz (1914–1988) during a sojourn in Europe.

11 The parallel between Mamá Elena and Mexico's Porfirio Díaz is based in her iron-fisted insistence on authority, tradition, and European- and North American-based social pretensions. García Lorca (1898–1936) wrote *Bernarda Alba* shortly before his death, making it the third drama of his "rural trilogy." The trilogy exposes the effects of Spain's oppressive cultural traditions on women. *Bernarda Alba* was not staged until 1945 in Argentina.

12 See especially 201, 206, 210–11.

13 Lawless (1997) cites Eve Sedgwick's description of the Gothic "recipe" (Lawless 219 quoting Sedgwick 9). See Sedgwick 9–11.

14 Pilcher's excellent article offers a number of insights on the *Calendarios para*

señoritas, whose form Esquivel adopts for *Like Water for Chocolate*, and on the prohibitions and warnings connected with food and cooking.

15 See Viramontes in the Works Cited.

16 Franco is discussing the frustrated quest in which Elena Garro and Rosario Castellanos find themselves in the early 1960s as they attempt to write fiction in a historical context *and* to make a female character central. Their effort is, in Franco's words, "to appropriate the then hegemonic genre – the novel as national allegory," and what is ultimately true is that women cannot be "national protagonists" (146).

17 Sinnigen perhaps misses the narrator's continuing presence through the book (and film) and that her narration at the opening of the book connects fluidly to the closing narration (125–26). He also writes that she "lacks Nacha and Gertrudis"; however, this is not necessarily the case, considering the novel's emphasis on spiritual links to ancestors in the novel and film (described in Stephen Butler Murray's chapter in this volume) and the fact that Gertrudis does not die in the late 1930s when Tita does, but could have lived into the lifetime of the novel's narrator, her great niece. Tita, viewed in the context of Unamuno's sense of "intrahistory" (described in this volume in Pérez's closing essay) does "acquire a name for posterity," but, as in the case of Malinche, "interpreting" Tita is a job for those who remain behind and have access to the documents and the oral intra-historians. Also see Franco (145).

18 The women's magazine, with its recipes, household hints, articles on home management and marriage, and the serialized novel (*novela de entregas*) containing a love story (a *novela rosa*), was a package designed for women's consumption. It promulgated acceptable standards of behavior, activities, and interests for women and offered monthly affirmations of the roles of wife and mother. The serialized novel entered the women's magazine format in the mid-nineteenth century, according to De Valdés.

19 De Valdés's book chapter is based on an article published in 1995 ("Verbal and Visual").

20 Oropesa's article is in Spanish, and the translations are mine. The reader of *Like Water for Chocolate* may recall that in one of Tita's recollections of the *Manual*, she curses it for having given her no training to equip her for the medical emergency of Roberto's birth (72 Spanish; 71–72 English). Carreño's *Manual* has been through many printings and editions from the mid-nineteenth century through the last quarter of the twentieth century.

21 Roselyn Costantino interviewed Mexican women writers, such as Roffiel, for her dissertation, and the *huacal* comments come from one of those meetings. Oropesa quotes Roffiel's comment from Costantino (29). Oropesa (259) cites Costantino as 30–31, but 29 is accurate according to the bound copy of the dissertation.

22 A paper presented at the 1998 "Hijas del quinto sol" conference (Willingham 1998) showed how the novel incorporates elements found in fairy tales, folk tales, and local legends, and how the nature of those events, characters, and modes of narration favorably affect reader involvement with *Like Water for Chocolate*.

41

23 See Jeanne L. Gillespie and Ryan F. Long's chapters in this volume for further discussion of these ideas.

24 In Latin American fiction, indigenous, *mestizo*, African, and *mulato* characters (as in the case of Gertrudis and her father) are juxtaposed with those who are "white" or "whiter." The latter possess superior economic and social access and advantages, and the former are unsullied by the greed and avarice of the hegemonic upper class. This dichotomy, founded on race, ethnicity, and color, creates a culture within the nation of the narrative.

25 Like the literary language of José Joaquín Fernández de Lizardi (1776–1827), considered Mexico's first novelist, the language of Esquivel's novels offers material for linguistic studies. Interestingly, Jack Emory Davis (1961), who studied Fernández de Lizardi's "picturesque 'americanismos,'" points to two examples of "estar como agua [or *agüita*] para chocolate" [being like water for chocolate] in Lizardi's work (74).

26 Halevi-Wise's citations involving Tita with eggs come from the Spanish edition. In English (Doubleday hardcover 1992), they are as follows: eggs compared with testicles, 26; the castration process, 27; the peeping egg, 28; swallowing the soft-cooked egg, 30; the warmth of eggs, 69; missing the cooing of the doves, 92; taking refuge in the dovecote, 99–101; Tita's hands as birds, 109; Esperanza's diapers destroyed by the hens, 217–18.

27 See also Halevi-Wise's essay on storytelling in *Like Water for Chocolate* (1997).

28 García Márquez (Columbia 1928–) won the Nobel Prize for literature in 1982, and his masterwork is usually considered to be *One Hundred Years of Solitude* (1981. *Cien años de soledad* 1979). This "Boom" novel is known by many for its use of magic realism. In this context, see n. 8, above, and Fredric Jameson (1986).

29 Janet Maslin's review for *The New York Times* appeared on the film's opening day.

30 See Shaw's discussion of Mexican film at this period in her chapter "Seducing the Public: Images of Mexico in *Like Water for Chocolate* and *Amores Perros*" (esp. 36–54). Shaw also takes on the question of "Feminist or Feminine," examining the criticism, most of which is focused on the novel, and concluding that Tita's "inability to live independently from Pedro" and her decision not to live without him "should trouble feminists" (50).

31 Another perspective of President Vicente Fox's proposed cuts was that Mexico would be flooded by American films. Esquivel is quoted by Mark Stevenson of the Associated Press (AP): "We [Mexicans] will be left to the mercy and whims of distributors of Hollywood's worst productions." See Stevenson in the Works Cited. The article is obtainable via a search of AP's 2003 archives and its purchase. It may be available through various news media subscribers to AP. *Asuntoscapitales.com* conducted an online survey the week of November 8, 2009, asking readers whether they advocated government support of film.

32 Reviews of the film appeared in newsweeklies such as *Newsweek* (David Ansen), *Time* (Richard Corliss), and *The New Republic* (Stanley Kauffmann), and in specialized periodicals such as *Sight and Sound* (John Kraniauskas), *Variety* (Susan Karlin), and *Films in Review* (Kenneth Geist).

33 For example, *Like Water for Chocolate* continues to be a chapter in Mary Gill, Deana Smalley, and Maria Paz Haro's *Cinema for Spanish Conversation*'s second edition (2006). The DVD, released in a wide-screen edition on March 14, 2000, was a *New York Times* Critics' Pick (*NYT. Like Water for Chocolate*).

34 Niebylski's 1998 essay in *Performing Gender and Comedy* catalogs a selection of these kinds of phrases from *USA Today and Glamour* that were featured on the cover of the English translation and in promotional materials (179–80). See also her note to this section describing the jacket's promotional perspectives (194 n. 1). Zamudio-Taylor and Guiu refer to Janet Maslin's review, cited earlier in this introduction.

35 The essay that I am commenting on is a revision to a version published in 1994 following its presentation at a conference in 1993. Burton-Carvajal's comments on misogyny and racism as sub-texts in the film and novel and her relating the film and novel to Sommer's theory predate the publications of other commentators who do not necessarily cite her work.

36 *Matria potestas* (Latin) is a reversal of *patria potestas*, patriarchal power or the power of the father, which references the power of the Roman father, as male head of household, over the members of the household.

37 Wu presented an earlier study on the topic, "Eating the Nation: Selling *Like Water for Chocolate* in the USA," at the LASA Congress, April 17–19, 1997, in Guadalajara.

38 Martínez relies also on previous work by John H. Sinnigen (1995).

39 Niebylski has written a number of similarly focused essays on *Like Water for Chocolate*, and I have chosen to comment on her 2004 essay, included in a volume on literary adaptations to film ("Passion" 2004), as particularly appropriate to the present examination and representative of her views. See the Glossary for *comedia ranchera*.

40 Piedras Negras, Coahuila, was founded in the early nineteenth century; across the border, which Chencha navigates in the narrative, is Eagle Pass. At the opening of the novel, until the time of the Revolution, the name of the town was officially, ironically, "Ciudad Porfirio Díaz" [Porfirio Díaz City], a name it was given through some part of the dictator's reign. As place names are a part of popular culture, it is likely that local people persisted in calling the city by its older name, Piedras Negras, the name it reassumed when the dictatorship ended. This information is known to a lesser or greater degree by those living in the region. See "Piedras Negras" in the Works Cited for two official websites of the municipality, where its history, location, and certain historical documents are available. During 1913 and 1914, Villa and Carranza were at odds, but there was no "public" break. Carranza had been born to an upper-class family in Coahuila and had served as its governor, so his sympathies would have lodged with

landowners like Mamá Elena and her social circle. Also see John Mason Hart's *Revolutionary Mexico* (267–72).

41 What is true or not true in personal and military history about that chaotic time is often difficult to extrapolate and much more, to ascertain. Villa's army is recorded as having at least one "coronela," a woman whose husband fought in the troop, and whose bravery in leadership, however much truth or legend, is preserved in an American newspaper story. See Elizabeth Salas's book for this and related information, especially 41–43. Concerning Villa's attitude toward military women, Niebylski may have in mind Villa's dramatic execution of some large number of *soldaderas* when one failed in an attempt to assassinate him (Salas 39). *Soldaderas* were not primarily armed combatants, but women regarded as wives or partners of soliders; they provided food, medical care, camp sites, laundry, and other necessary amenities to keep the solider fighting. Some took up arms periodically. Women participated in the Revolution as female soldiers, and some were made officers. See Anna Macias's article (esp. 73–75) and Poniatowska's testimonial book *Las Soldaderas* (2006. [Spanish] 1999).

42 In supposing a physical reason for Pedro's death during sex at about the age of forty, one might intuitively suggest a coronary ahead of a stroke, based on "urban legends" of men dying in local motels with their mistresses and the caveat about taking a male enhancement drug in combination with nitrites (prescribed for angina). In fact, men are highly unlikely to die during sex, according to cardiologist Graham Jackson (2004). Sex between long-term partners, as Tita and Pedro were, according to Jackson, "is not particularly stressful to the heart" (1). Risk factors governing the small number of coitus-related deaths in men include a significant age disparity between the partners, adultery, and alcohol and food consumption prior to the act (Jackson 1. See 1–6). Only the last of these might apply to Tita and Pedro's final lovemaking. Ischemic stroke during or after intercourse in three patients was not reported as fatal in a 2004 study (Becker). A report on a single patient with recurrent capsular ischemia following post-coital middle cerebral artery dissection (Prabhakaran 2006) included the comment: "First, MCA [middle cerebral artery] dissection is rare and, to our knowledge, has not been previously reported in the setting of coitus." (The patient did not die.) Subsequent studies did not report fatalities either. See "Resources in Medical Humanities" in the Works Cited for these full citations.

43 See Spindler (1993). Also see n. 8, above.

44 Hart (*Film*) gives the "fairy godmother" role to "Chencha, the Indian maid" (a girl and later a woman of about Tita's age). From the fairy tale perspective, Tita's "fairy godmother" is Nacha. Potvin calls Nacha Tita's "guardian angel" (62). Meacham, writing on the fairy tale structure, locates "two indigenous 'fairy godmothers'" (127) – Luz del amanecer and Nacha, both of whom come to Tita in spirit. Esquivel's name is often mentioned with that of the prolific short-story writer and novelist Isabel Allende (Chile 1942–). See Pérez's essay in this volume in connection with Allende.

45 IMDb records the release date in Mexico as April 16, 1992; the film was shown, according to the same source, at the Toronto Film Festival in September 1992, and it was released world-wide beginning in February 1993 in the U.S. The last releases recorded by IMDb are Poland, Finland, and the Netherlands, all in 1994.

46 Liliana Felipe, Argentina-born singer and songwriter, comedienne, and performance artist, now lives in Mexico and is one of its leading social/arts activists and stage performers. Felipe is the domestic and artistic partner of Jesusa Rodríguez. See Poniatowska's introduction and Jean Franco's article on Rodríguez.

47 Saïd Sabia addresses the issue of reader response to Esquivel's innovative presentation in *The Law of Love*. For additional perspectives on the "multi-media" novel, see also Ludmila Kapschutschenko-Schmitt (2004) and Ana María Rodríguez-Vivaldi (2003). The collection of essays edited by Janet Pérez and Genaro Pérez (*MR: Experimental Fiction by Hispanic Women Writers*) is the most useful collection to date for background and theory on the topic. Lilia del Carmen Granillo Vázquez explains that she found no positive reviews in Spanish American outlets for *The Law of Love* (110–11).

48 Prout lucidly theorizes homosexuality in *The Law of Love*.

49 See *Malinche*, an audiobook promotional video, in the Works Cited.

50 O'Keeffe appears to be unaware of the irony inherent in this statement. While the U.S. is a powerful force in the region, Great Britain was a true imperial power, with an Empress and the intention to build an empire. British possessions and British power over trade in Central and South America and the Caribbean, along with its island claims in the South Atlantic off Argentina, had great "imperialist" weight in the nineteenth century, and the last "imperialist" conflict between Britain and Argentina (over the Falklands) took place in the 1980s. I must also express doubt about the South American upper classes being generally more focused on indigenous citizens than on European culture.

51 In the paperback editions, the codex illustrations appear inside the book rather than on the reverse of the book jacket. See Jeanne Gillespie's chapter in this volume for appropriate references to images of the codices. See the following note as well.

52 It is likely that readers would also connect the image to the founding of the modern Mexican nation whose flag shows the eagle, perched on a *nopal* cactus, holding a serpent in its beak, the sign that the Aztecs took as pointing to the place where Tenochtitlan should be built. The Mendoza codex shows on its first folio the founding of Tenochtitlan with the eagle, serpent, and *nopal*.

53 Estrada does not note specific pages of Prescott's well-known history (1859), but Prescott writes, in the context of explaining that Doña Marina learned "Castilian" very quickly, that "[s]he learned it all the more readily, as it was to her the language of love" (1922 vol. I 170). Also see Ryan Long's essay in this volume and his n. 3.

54 Estrada refers to Paz's essay "The Sons of La Malinche." See n. 10, above

and n. 65, below. For the pejorative perspective on "Malinche," see the chapter essays here by Gillespie and Long.

55 Estrada references the "anachronism" because anachronism is an element of the "new" Latin American historical novel as Menton (1993) differentiates it from the older, romanticized historical novel. Menton describes these modes (including anachronism) in the "new" historical novel (25), in addition to the six primary characteristics that distinguish it (22–25).

56 This sentence does not reflect the wording of Riquer Fernández, but the editor's enlargement of her idea of the woman character who does not live in a "depressed" state. See Patrick Duffey's essay in this volume for his ideas on the *madre abnegada* in Mexican film. Riquer Fernández's essay presents theoretical and sociological concepts of "the feminine" in Mexican society, both from her own thinking and in her treatment of the work of others, that suggest applications in literary and film criticism.

57 I am thinking here, especially, of the work of Rosario Castellanos in defining what it meant to her to be a Mexican woman and a writer, discussed in subsequent paragraphs, but also of the life and work of Gabriela Mistral (1889–1957) and that of Nellie Campobello (1900–1986). See Franco (*Plotting*) on Castellanos's expression of her longing for motherhood (142–43), and for another perspective on Castellanos's view of motherhood, Lisa Davies's treatment (2000) of *The Book of Lamentations* (*Oficio de tinieblas*, in her title). See Pérez's essay in this volume for its discussion of feminist criticism.

58 See "Woman and Her Image" in *A Rosario Castellanos Reader* (esp. 240, Ahern's translation). The editor's translation was made prior to locating Ahern's. See also Carlos Monsiváis (1975) on Mexican sexisms.

59 The passage is quoted in Sarabia (82 n. 10). The "Inventario" column in *Excelsior*'s Sunday "cultural" supplement (*Diorama* August 11, 1974) is entitled, "Rosario Castellanos o la literatura como ejercicio de la libertad" [Rosario Castellanos, or Literature as an Exercise in Liberty] (16). There is no by-line, but Pacheco (who won the Cervantes Prize in literature on November 30, 2009) has written the column for about fifty years, since 1960. See, for example, a feature by Pedro González Olvera on Pacheco's lifetime of writing about Mexican culture in Costa Rica's *Áncora* (August 16, 2009).

60 María del Carmen Elu de Leñero (1969) studied gender in Mexican society in the third quarter of the twentieth century through a national survey, "Estudio sociológico de la familia mexicana" [Sociological Study of the Mexican Family]. In Elu de Leñero, see especially "Estereotipos tradicionales en los medios rurales" [Traditional Stereotypes in Rural Environments] (23 *ff.*) and "Actividades de la mujer en la familia" [Women's Activities within the Family] (105 *ff.*). José Cantú Corro's 1938 work on gender is of interest for its historical point of view, and Lesley Feracho (2005) treats Latin American gender theory from a socio-cultural perspective.

61 Concerning Fuentes (1928–), see the English translation of Poniatowska's essay, 57, n. 12.

62 Castillo (*Easy Women*) refers to "la Malinche" frequently (esp. 20–22), but considers Esquivel's fiction *literatura fácil*, so Esquivel's "easy women" remain to be studied within the context Castillo develops.

63 Moreno Villa (1887–1955) arrived in Mexico in 1937 at the age of 50 (Lida 52), exiled from Spain because of the Spanish Civil War. Moreno Villa's observation is widely quoted. Oswaldo Estrada opens his essay (2007) on *Malinche: A Novel* with Moreno Villa's wording to contextualize the emphasis on historical fiction in Mexico. Fernando Amerlinck used Moreno Villa's observation in an opinion piece (*Asuntos Capitales* Mexico) on 6 February 2007 in a call for better education of a public that thrives on a romanticized patriotic history and fails to recognize its living enemies to liberty. Moreno Villa's observation makes an appropriate point of departure for considering aspects of Mexico's popular culture, fiction, and film. The original source, I believe, is Moreno Villa's *Cornucopia de México* (1940 105), cited above. The newer edition (1985, 1992) is more likely to be accessible, and the quotation appears at 223–24. In either edition, the pertinent essay is "Diálogo Conmigo Mismo Acerca de México" [capitalization *sic* from the 1940 edition].

64 Women writing about women who navigate historical periods suggests Soledad Puértolas's award-winning, best-selling *Queda la noche* [*The Night Remains*], published in 1989 (as was *Like Water for Chocolate*). Puértolas (1947–) affirms that this first-person narrative *Queda la noche* is non-traditional in form, combining elements of various genres and presenting a protagonist who both lives under and contests the patriarchy. See Estelle Irizarry's discussion (1995) in which she compares *Queda la noche* to Carmen Laforet's *Nada* (1945. *Nada: A Novel* 2008) as "a novel of beginnings" and affirms that *Queda la noche* meets a critical description of *Don Quixote* as "a novel set in reality but anchored in history" (57), characterizations that suggest *Like Water for Chocolate* as well.

65 "La Malinche" has received much critical attention since the mid-1980s, much of it harkening back to Octavio Paz's essay "The Sons of La Malinche" (1961. "Los hijos de la Malinche." 1950). In this volume, see the chapter essays of Gillespie and Long. Re-assessments of Paz's work include Beth Miller's edited volume with essays by Luis Leal ("Female Archetypes") and Rachel Phillips (1983); Sandra Messinger Cypess's book (1991); and Margo Glantz's edited volume (1994), which holds Jean Franco's essay on Malinche. See the following also: Glantz's essay in Kohut (1991); Ricardo Herren's *Doña Marina* (1993); McCafferty and McCafferty on "Female Discourse" (online); Mary Louise Pratt's article on Chicana writers (1993); Frances Karttunen's "Rethinking" the cultural icon (1997); Norma Alarcón's work on the Chicana feminist view of self and literature (1989, 2001); Marta E. Sánchez's essay locating La Malinche's cultural function in Chicano fiction (1998); and Maarten Van Delden's article on recent treatments of La Malinche (2004).

66 William W. Moseley (1960) references the critical hesitation and lack of "enthusiasm" for the "historical novel" at the time of his writing on the

genre in Chile, a "nation of historians" influenced by Sir Walter Scott and Alexandre Dumas, where historical fiction was serialized early in the nineteenth century (338–39). Moseley asserts that this was not literature for women, but for men and patriots seeking to re-examine the Conquest and the Colonial Period. Mosely treats novels by women such as Inés Echeverría de Larraín (1868–1949) and Magdalena Petit (1903–1968), as well as those by better-known male authors like Alberto Blest Gana (1830–1920). See Aínsa's morphology of the genre (1991) and Menton's "empirical" approach (1993) to tracing the literary history of the genre through specific examples that justify its significance in Latin American Letters. See Menton's earlier examination (1955) of the Latin American historical novel where he defines the aim of the genre as "the search for nation" and national "unity." Menton emphasizes the particular tripartite unity "of land, people, and time." By "people," Menton refers to the novelists' treatment of racial unity.

67 Diana Bracho (1944–) is a Mexican film and television actress who has played many "Mexican mother" roles. In what was probably Mexico's most popular-ever *telenovela* [soap opera], *Cuna de lobos* (Carlos Téllez, dir. 1986 [*Cradle of Wolves*]), Bracho played the role of Leonora Navarra de Larios, who was duped, drugged, and forcibly estranged from her child. Bracho has a long institutional and familial memory of Mexican film. Her father, Julio Bracho (1909–1978), was one of the most highly regarded directors of Mexico's "golden age" in film, and other family members have also figured in the history of Mexican film. See Jesús Ibarra's *Los Bracho: Tres generaciones de cine mexicano* (2006).

Laura Esquivel's Mexican Chocolate[1]

ELENA PONIATOWSKA AMOR

"I, who do not eat, ate up the novel. Had Frida Kahlo read it, she would have run out to the market in Coyoacán to buy food, and wherever Marguerite Yourcenar may be, she would taste it." So says Jesusa Rodríguez, whose relationship with food was changed by *Like Water for Chocolate*.[2]

Apart from *Like Water for Chocolate*, very few novels are edible. Jorge Amado in *Dona Flor and Her Two Husbands* brings to life the extraordinary battle between the soul and matter when he tells us the adventures of doña Flor, director of the Taste and Art cooking school, who knows what to serve at a wake to support the morale and appetites of those who come to give their condolences, and also of those to whom sympathy is being offered: coffee or a *jicara* of chocolate at midnight with little balls of *mandinga*; corn tortilla, Mexican-style eggs on the following morning, ham and *mortadela*, biscuits, fried foods, croquettes of all types, varied sweets, and dried fruits to be eaten with beer or wine.[3]

In Puebla de los Ángeles, on Friday nights, the self-sacrificing wife used to prepare hot chocolate for her husband as a prelude to sex. The couple would then head toward the canopy bed – but before stepping on the immaculately white bed, they would kneel together in prayer:

> Neither for vice
> nor for lust
> but to make a child
> for Thy Holy Sacrifice.[4]

And wham! They dove in, falling right into the middle of the stream, in the very center of the place where the King's horses were watered. If the wife wore a long night gown with a strategically placed, embroidered opening, things might get a bit more complicated, but not so much. In any case, the virtuous woman and excellent housewife knew quite well that on a Friday night, when her husband ordered, "Make me a chocolate well blended with plenty of foam and very hot," that after consuming the contents of the clay cup – because chocolate tastes like it should only in a fat-bellied and echoing cup made of clay – they would ascend the stairs in a measured way and then hurry their steps toward the room of their love-affair. The next morning, the self-less, cherished Mexican mother, the dove of the nest, the house fairy, would have to change the sheets of the rumpled bed and remake the bed as an orderly port, converting it again into a silent vessel under the hands of her oarsmen, the Angels of Puebla.[5]

We women tend to write with sorrow. José Joaquin Blanco was partly right when he said that Rosario Castellanos was, in her poetry, like a hired mourner. Nostalgia tends to numb us, choking back memory, and the daily routine conquers us, covering all things with the grayness of its dust. It could never be affirmed that one of the characteristics of the literature of Angelina Muñiz, Elena Garro, Inés Arredondo, Julieta Campos, is gladness – they are not as happy as clams. In the past, only one woman writer, María Lombardo de Caso, has shown her readers a notable sense of humor. Indeed, the playful pages of *Una luz en la otra orilla* laugh among themselves.[6]

Guadalupe Dueñas, that profane nun who unwinds the rosary of her genius in her writing, is also funny, but a book like *Like Water for Chocolate: A Novel in Monthly Installments with Recipes, Romances and Home Remedies* has never been seen in the valley of tears of Mexican literature. It should be observed that men are also whiners, and with the exception of Jorge Ibargüengoitia, they all take themselves too seriously and sweat solemnity.[7]

I began to read *Like Water for Chocolate* in a bad mood, the thick manuscript of more than 200 pages weighing down on my knees, but as soon as I got to page fifteen time started to fly, and by the end I was sending blessings to Laura Esquivel. I had the urge to meet her, to marry her, to cry with joy over the finely chopped onions, to enjoy the smells rising from her stews, to know in the deepest sense all her life's recipes. I found out, as Tita did, what the gaze of love is:

> She was walking toward the table carrying a tray of egg-yolk candy, when she felt it, like fire, burning her skin. She turned her head and her eyes met Pedro's. In that moment she understood perfectly what the dough of a roll must feel when it comes into contact with the boiling oil. The sensation of heat was so real that it extended throughout her body, and she feared that, like a roll, she might begin to erupt in bubbles all over her body – her face, belly, heart, and breasts. Tita could not keep

her eyes on Pedro, and, lowering her eyes, she quickly crossed to the opposite end of the room where Gertrudis was playing the waltz Eyes of Youth on the pianola. (21–22)

In this milieu, amidst revolutionaries who come and go, government forces and rebels who gallop around the walls of the house at Piedras Negras – the house inhabited by northern women, beautiful and tough, plain-spoken and blunt, all of them flirtatious: from the terrifying and emasculating head of the family, Mamá Elena, to the servant Nacha who dies, to Chencha, her successor, to Tita as the heroine, to Rosaura, her older sister, and Gertrudis the second sister, to John's grandmother, Luz del amanecer (Morning Light), a Kikapú Indian and a marvelous character who functions as a folk-healer, Laura Esquivel interweaves the life of her women characters and gives us – in *salsa de molcajete* – their flesh and blood. Mamá Elena, who makes *chiles en nogada* [stuffed peppers in cream], not only can crack bag after bag of pecans and peel more than a thousand of them in a couple of days, but she relishes such tasks. She excels at crushing, splitting, and skinning – which are her favorite activities.

"When I serve food," says Laura Esquivel, "I feel that the gender roles are inverted: the male becomes the receptor. Through serving food, I become the one who penetrates. Furthermore, you are what you eat and with whom and how you eat it. In my family, food was always very important, and for my mother it was a medium of communication and a ritual in every sense. For those reasons, we enjoy each dish. It is an act that reaffirms the union of a couple, living with the offspring, and fellowship with friends. A family's history is its recipes, and it is imperative to keep them alive."

The family traditions and events are thus connected with food. "Food always brings back the past to me," says Laura. "This knowledge gave me the idea of writing a novel in which recipes were the foundation. As a young girl I was shocked to learn that my grandmother's sister was prohibited to marry so that she could take care of her mother in old age, and so I created Tita, my protagonist. Sacrificed by her mother, Tita is able to bring to fruition her love and do away with that terrible tradition of the youngest taking charge of the mother."[8]

But Tita obeys Mamá Elena: "You know very well that because you are the youngest of the girls, it is your duty to take care of me until the day I die" (17). Mamá Elena prevents Tita's marriage with Pedro and creates another imperative: If Pedro wants to marry one of Mamá Elena's daughters, he must marry Rosaura, the oldest daughter. Pedro accepts in the hope of being able to remain close to Tita. The only thing that escapes Mamá Elena's control is the food, and Tita prepares the wedding cake.

Tita communicates to the eggs and the flour, to the butter and the sugar, her anger and frustration, and the wedding guests fill themselves up, not with succulent delicacies, but with immense and bitter sorrow. During the wedding banquet, Rosaura becomes gravely ill, Pedro waits six months in doing a husband's duty, and the house is stained in melancholy. That is Tita's revenge as queen of the kitchen. In this role, during this period of sterility on the ranch, an image of Tita at work in the kitchen becomes sensual:

> Tita, on her knees, leaned over the *metate* and was moving rhythmically and in a cadence as she crushed the almonds and the sesame seeds.
>
> Under her blouse her breasts moved freely, for she never used a brassiere. Drops of perspiration ran along her neck downward, sliding along the furrow of flesh between her firm, round breasts.
>
> Pedro, unable to resist smells that were coming from the kitchen, went toward it and stood stock-still in the doorway, confronted with the sensual position in which he found Tita.
>
> [. . .] Pedro lowered his gaze and fixed it on Tita's breasts. She stopped grinding, straightened up, and proudly raised her chest so that Pedro could observe it fully. This study of which her breasts were the object changed their relationship forever. After that scrutinizing gaze that penetrated clothing, nothing could be as it was. Tita knew, personally, why contact with fire alters elements, why a piece of dough becomes a tortilla, why a breast without having been through the flames of love is lifeless, a ball of useless dough. In only a few moments, Pedro had transformed Tita's breasts from chaste to voluptuous without ever touching them. (68)

Before Laura Esquivel, the image of a woman in the kitchen had never been treated in this way, but in *Like Water for Chocolate* the kitchen is the house, the hearth of the home, the center of the earth, and the conscience of the fatherland. Through faith and the kitchen, our men have escaped death. Woman is the giver of remedies, the one who boils teas, the one who combines the herbs, the one who cures, and the one who cleans and separates the seeds, the one who spreads the *tortillas* on the *comal*. The kitchen works as a center of information, a new agency, and comforting place for sinners. All the family members are attracted to the kitchen because they know that, along with the sacred food, good advice will be served.

To the rhythm of the milling, to the toasting of coffee beans, in the bucket full of water that is used to make dough, women gradually arrange and smooth masculine insecurities, finding the right place for everything, and putting each thing in its proper place; annoyances go on a shelf and troubles, into a drawer. Women mill a man's anguish in a *metate* and filter his ideas through a colander in such a manner that a bit of "Royal" yeast lifts the feeling of self-worth when it is brought out of the oven and sprinkled with sugar. Woman kneads man, she slaps him, and extends him so that his being is flexible, she stuffs him, makes him *pan de muerto*, sweet bread, *rosca de Reyes,* croissants, and *pambazos*, and she serves him up again, like a soup of his own chocolate at lunch, stuffing him with raisins, and truffles, placing an apple into his little snout – a suckling piglet baked to a golden brown, crunchy and recently born, a roasted kid-goat of himself, accompanied by refried beans and *guacamole*.

"First, I chose the recipes I liked the most," says Laura. "The ones that had a special meaning because I ate them at Christmas or on my birthday or to celebrate an anniversary, and I pictured what sort of meaning these recipes would have in the lives of my characters. In accord with the recipes, I created a dramatic structure, the same one I used when I wrote movie and television scripts. (I wrote the script for Arau's *Chido One, Colombino*, and *Mujer Divina* with music by Agustín Lara.[9]) I chose the order in which the recipes would enter, the Christmas Cakes, when Pedro asks for Tita's hand in marriage and ends engaged with Rosaura, her sister. The wedding cake 'Chabela,' and the 'Quails in rose petals' when Tita and Pedro begin to communicate their love through food. The '*mole* with almonds and sesame seeds' celebrates the birth of Pedro and Rosaura's first born. The *chorizo norteño* appears on the day that Tita goes mad with grief and strips in the dovecote, and the mixture for matches when John, the doctor, saves her life."

The most bellicose of the recipes is the mixture for matches:

Ingredients:
1 oz. of salt peter
½ oz. of red lead
½ oz. of powdered gum Arabic
1 drachma of phosphorus
saffron
cardboard

Intimate suppers are almost always the beginning of an amorous act. "I am going to devour you like a mango," says the great poet Claudel.[10] At the end of the novel, Tita has to collect enough phosphorus to light the tunnel that will take her to rendezvous with Pedro, who is finally a widower because Rosaura has done them the favor of dying:

[Tita] began to eat the matches that were in the box one by one. While she chewed, she closed her eyes tightly and tried to reproduce the most exciting memories between Pedro and her: the first glance, the first brushing of their hands, the first bouquet of roses, the first kiss, the first caress, the first intimate encounter. And she accomplished her goal. When the matches made contact with the luminous images she evoked, they lit up. (221)

Cook, alchemist, long- and bejeweled-haired witch, lover of man and life, lopezvelardian, and erotic,[11] Laura Esquivel offers us a book that did not exist in Mexican Literature – on a silver platter. It is a book of love well-simmered, without boasting or high-sounding words, without resignation or vengeance, prepared like a *turrón* that melts in your mouth and fills your stomach, esophagus, lungs, and torso with joy. We chop the cilantro very fine, we chop our hearts like they were onions, and we begin to hand out the pieces, to throw them out the window, giving them to the first person who crosses our paths, throwing pieces of it from the entry of the house; we mix it in soft oil, and wash the other ingredients, soft feelings, in lemon water, we cut into slices the days to come, we salt and pepper the bed, we boil the virtues to remove the mold, and afterward we toss our political ideas (if we have any) into the casserole one by one, and we put our tongue and lips into *adobo* sauce for two hours to season them.

Like Water for Chocolate feeds the reader and makes the blood boil, grateful for its many true and nurturing words. "Feed your head" orders the Jefferson Airplane, and Laura Esquivel's *Like Water for Chocolate* fattens us up and leaves us like Christmas turkeys, even though in Mexico turkeys are called *guajolotes*. It is no wonder that this novel was on *The New York Times* "Best Seller" list for so many years, nor any wonder that Carlos Fuentes offered words of praise to the most loving of Mexico's women authors.[12]

Notes

1   Ms. Poniatowska's original essay in Spanish is given immediately following this translation. The English version is translated from the Spanish by Manuel Muñoz and the editor, with refereeing by Mexican literary scholar and Puebla native Joseph F. Vélez. Because a good number of Poniatowska's literary references have no translation into English, in these notes only, the editor places the Spanish, French, or Portuguese title first with the title of the English translation following in parentheses. If the work is not translated, the title's translation is the editor's and it appears within brackets. The Works Cited provides full bibliographic citations. Citations in this essay from *Como agua para chocolate* (1989; *Like Water for Chocolate*) come from the Doubleday Spanish edition (New York 1993).

Translations are the editor's.

2 Jesusa Rodríguez (1955–) is a Mexican iconoclast and social activist, writer, performance artist, award-winning actress, and director, whose satirical stage work is characterized by Jean Franco as "usually touch[ing] the raw nerves of nationalism and religious morality" (48). For further reading, see Jean Franco's "A Touch of Evil."

Frida Kahlo (1907–1954), Mexican artist and intellectual, was born in Coyoacan, near Mexico City, and lived in Mexico and the U.S.

Marguerite Yourcenar (1903–1987), a prolific and prize-winning Belgian-born novelist, poet, essayist, and translator, was educated in the classical languages and French literature by her Northern French father and was the first woman admitted to the 300-year-old French Academy (1980). Her first book was *Le jardin des chimères* (1921. [*Garden of Illusions*]). She continued to publish throughout her life, and the third volume of her memoirs, *Quoi? L'Éternité*, [*What? Eternity*] was released in 1988.

3 See the 1969 English version (3) and the 1981 Spanish version (17) for the reference, which is found on the first page of the first chapter ("De la muerte de Vadinho" [About the death of Vadinho]). Poniatowska expands on the original text with Mexican dishes, and she replaces "bollitos de bacalao" in the Spanish translation of the Portuguese with "bollitos de mandinga." See *mandinga* in the Glossary. Jorge Amado (1912–2001) is the Brazilian author of over twenty novels. *Dona Flor e seus dois maridos: história moral e de amor* (1966) was filmed in 1976 by Brazilian director Bruno Barreto and published in Spanish in the U.S. in 2008.

4 Puebla de los Ángeles is the capital city of the state of Puebla, lying to the south of Mexico City. In *Like Water for Chocolate*, Pedro recites a variation on this prayer the night he consummates his marriage with Rosaura (43). Moctezuma is said to have believed in the "male enhancement" powers of *chocolate* and to have consumed it before visiting his wives. See *chocolate* in the Glossary.

5 The idea of the housewives of Puebla as "angels" plays on the name of the city, Puebla de los Ángeles.

Rosario Castellanos (Mexico 1925–1974) adopted the idea of the "angel in the house" in "Woman and Her Image," citing Virginia Woolf (Ahern 236–44, esp. 239, n. 1). Virginia Woolf played on the idea of the idealized and magical housewife as the "angel of the house" in "Professions for Women" (1942), alluding to a popular Victorian poem of idealized domestic life, *The Angel in the House* by Coventry Patmore (1891). "Woman and Her Image" appeared in Castellanos's *Mujer que sabe latín* (1973. [*A Woman Who Knows Latin*]). See the note below for additional information on Castellanos. See also Pérez's essay in this volume for references to Woolf and Castellanos in the context of feminism.

6 José Joaquín Blanco (1951–) is a Mexican historian, activist, essayist, screenwriter, and poet. He is the author of *Se llamaba Vasconcelos* [*His Name was Vasconcelos*] and of the screenplay for *Frida, naturaleza viva* [*Frida, Living Nature*].

Rosario Castellanos was a newspaper columnist, literary critic, novelist, and poet. She was serving as Mexican ambassador to Israel at the time of her death. Her novels are *Balún Canán* (1957. *Nine Guardians* 1992), which reflects Castellanos's early life in Chiapas, and *Oficio de tinieblas* (1962. *The Book of Lamentations* 1998), which treats an indigenous rebellion in Chiapas. Also see the essay of Julián Pérez in this volume.

Angelina Muñiz-Huberman (France 1936–), an award-winning Spanish-Mexican-Jewish writer, came to Mexico at the age of ten. She is known for fiction in which she explores the lives and memories of *converso* Jews (Jewish converts to Christianity) living in Mexico. She is the author of *Huerto cerrado, huerto sellado* (1985. *Enclosed Garden* 1988), a collection of short fiction.

Elena Garro (1916–1998) was born in Puebla to a Mexican mother and Spanish father. Garro was a novelist, short-story writer, and playwright, best known for her novel of the Mexican Revolution *Los recuerdos del porvenir* (1964. *Recollections of Things to Come* 1969).

Inés Arredondo (Mexico 1928–1989), scholar, publisher, essayist, and fiction writer, won many honors for her writing, scholarship, and public service, among them the Xavier Villaurrutia Prize for *Río subterráneo* (1979. *Underground River* 1996). A collection of her complete works, *Obras Completas*, has seen two editions.

Julieta Campos (1932–), Cuban-born literary critic, political activist, novelist, and playwright, has lived for years in Mexico. Her published work includes *Tiene los cabellos rojizos y se llama Sabina* (1974. *She Has Reddish Hair and Her Name is Sabina* 1993) and *Reunión de familia* (1997. [*Family Reunion*]). Campos's collected works were published in 2005.

María Lombardo de Caso (1905–1964), a native of Puebla, has published a collection of short fiction, *Muñecas de niebla* (1955. [*Dolls of Fog*]), and two novels: *Una luz en la otra orilla* (1959. [*A Light on the Opposite Shore*]) and *La culebra tapó el río* (1962. [*The Snake Covered the River*]). Lombardo de Caso's complete works were published in 1999.

7   The novels of Guadalupe Dueñas (Mexico 1920–2002) include *Tiene la noche un árbol* (1958. [*The Night Has a Tree*]); *Imaginaciones* (1977. [*Imaginations*]); and *Antes el silencio* (1991. [*In the Presence of Silence*]).

Newspaper columnist, novelist, short-story writer, teacher, and play-wright Jorge Ibargüengoitia (Mexico 1928–1983) is the author of *Los relámpagos de agosto* (1965. *The Lightning of August* 1986); *Las muertas* (1977. *Dead Girls* 1983); and *Las ruinas que ves* (1975. [*The Ruins You See*]), novel of academic life in Ibargüengoitia's native Guanajuato.

8   Also see Poniatowska's foreword to Verónica Ortiz's collection of inter-views with Mexican women writers (2005), most of whom are indebted to Poniatowska for some aid in their writing careers, and Ortiz's interview with Esquivel, both of which address these matters.

9   Alfonso Arau Incháustegui (Mexico 1932–), an actor and director in Mexico and the U.S. and Esquivel's first husband, directed *Como agua para chocolate* (1992) as well as *El chido guan:Tacos de oro* (1985). According to

Arau, *Colombino* and *Mujer Divina* were screenplays written by Laura Esquivel for Arau's direction, but they were never produced (personal correspondence with Alfonso Arau, July 2007). See Ledford-Miller's biography in this volume.

Agustín Lara (Mexico 1897–1970) was a musician and prolific composer, popular world-wide, whose song "Mujer" features the phrase "Mujer, mujer divina" [Woman, divine woman], in its first line. Placido Domingo covers the song on the album *Por Amor* (Atlantic 1998).

10 Paul Claudel (France 1868–1955), poet and playwright, was called the "Patriarch of French drama" by Henri Peyre (1954). In Claudel's play *Partage de Midi* (1905. *Break of Noon* 1960), the character Ysé speaks: "[. . .] Ah viens donc et mange-moi comme une mangue! Tout, tout, et moi!" [Oh, come here and eat me up like a mango. All of it, all, and me, too!] (Act II 1026).

11 Ramón López Velarde (Mexico 1881–1921) was a lyric poet known for his surprisingly vivid expressions of passion and sensuality. He is celebrated for his inventive imagery, often religious or erotic or both, and his use of colloquial expression.

12 Carlos Fuentes (Mexico 1928–) is a novelist and essayist known for *La región más transparente* (1963. *Where the Air is Clear* 1960); *El gringo viejo* (1985. *The Old Gringo* 1986); and *La muerte de Artemio Cruz* (1967. *The Death of Artemio Cruz* 1964). Fuentes has been criticized for his portrayals of women characters in Mexican settings, but Maya Jaggi (2001) notes that in response to the pricking of his conscience after writing *La muerte de Artemio Cruz*, he wrote *Los años con Laura Díaz* (1991. *The Years with Laura Díaz* 2000) as an homage to his grandmothers, whom he describes as "brave young widows" to whom he was very close. Jaggi describes Fuentes as having "praised a constellation of women writers." His comment on Laura Esquivel comes from essayist Poniatowska's personal experience.

El chocolate mexicano de Laura Esquivel

Elena Poniatowska Amor

"Yo que no como, me comí la novela. De haberla leído Frida Kahlo, hubiera ido corriendo al mercado de Coyoacán a abastecerse y, donde quiera que se encuentre Marguerite Yourcenar la estaría saboreando" dice Jesusa Rodríguez a quien "Como agua para chocolate" le cambió la relación con la comida.

Pocas novelas son comestibles. Jorge Amado en su "Doña Flor y sus dos maridos" nos brinda la extraordinaria batalla librada entre el espíritu y la materia al contarnos la aventura vivida por doña Flor, la de Jorge Amado, directora de la escuela de cocina "Sabor y Arte", quién sabe qué servir en un velorio, cuidando de la moral y del apetito de los que se presentan a dar el pésame y a los que hay que ofrecer café o una jícara de chocolate a media noche con bollitos de mandinga, tortas de maíz, huevos estrellados a la mexicana a la mañana siguiente, jamón y mortadela, bizcochos, frituras, croquetas de toda clase, dulces variados y frutas secas acompañados de cerveza o vino.

En Puebla de los Ángeles, los viernes en la noche, la abnegada esposa solía prepararle a su marido un chocolatito caliente para fornicar. Luego se dirigían a la cama de baldaquín pero antes de abrir la cama de inmaculada blancura, rezaban arrodillados el uno junto al otro:

No es por vicio
ni es por fornicio,
es por hacer un hijo
en tu Santo Sacrificio.

Y ¡zás! se echaban un clavado y caían a la mitad del río, en el centro mismo del abrevadero de los caballos del rey. Si la esposa usaba un largo camisón con agujero, las cosas se complicaban un poco. Bueno, no tanto. En todo caso, la virtuosa señora y ama de casa sabía muy bien que cuando su esposo le ordenaba el viernes en la noche: "Prepárame un chocolate bien batido con mucha espuma y muy caliente", después de sorber el contenido del pocillo (porque el chocolate sabe como debe saber sólo en un pocillo de barro panzoncito y rumoroso) subirían comedidos y apresurarían el paso a la alcoba de los devaneos. A la mañana siguiente, ella, la abnegada madrecita mexicana, la paloma para el nido, el hada del hogar, tendría que cambiar las sábanas del lecho revuelto y regresar la cama a buen puerto, convertirla de nuevo en una embarcación silenciosa en manos de sus timoneles, los ángeles del Puebla.

Las mujeres solemos escribir triste. En parte tuvo razón José Joaquin Blanco cuando dijo que Rosario Castellanos era, en su poesía, una plañidera. Nos entume la nostalgia, nos engarrota el recuerdo, nos vence la cotidianeidad que todo lo cubre con la grisura de su polvo. Jamás podría afirmarse que una de las características de la literatura de Angelina Muñiz, Elena Garro, Inés Arredondo, Julieta Campos, es la alegría. No son precisamente castañuelas. En el pasado, sólo una escritora tuvo un notable sentido del humor, María Lombardo de Caso. Lúdica, las páginas de "Una luz en la otra orilla" se van riendo las unas con las otras.

También graciosa, Guadalupe Dueñas, esa monja profana que ha ido devanando el rosario de su ingenio. Pero un libro como "Como agua para chocolate", novela de entregas mensuales con recetas, amores y remedios caseros nunca se había visto en el valle de lágrimas de la literatura mexicana. Porque también los hombres son unos chilletas y, salvo Jorge Ibargüengoitia, todos se toman terriblemente en serio y sudan solemnidad a gotas.

Empecé a leerla de mal talante, el grueso manuscrito de más de doscientas páginas pesándome sobre las rodillas, a partir de la pagina 15 el tiempo se me fue volando y al terminarlo bendecía yo a Laura Esquivel, tenía ganas de conocerla, casarme con ella, llorar de felicidad sobre las cebollas finamente picadas, gozar del olor que despiden sus guisos, conocer a fondo todas sus recetas de vida. Supe como Tita lo que es una mirada de amor: " . . . caminaba hacia la mesa llevando una charola con dulces de yemas de huevo, cuando la sintió, ardiente, quemándole la piel. Giró la cabeza y sus ojos se encontraron con los de Pedro. En ese momento comprendió perfectamente lo que debe sentir la masa de un buñuelo al entrar en contacto con el aceite hirviendo. Era tan real la sensación de calor que invadía todo su cuerpo que ante el temor de que, como a un buñuelo, le empezaran a brotar burbujas por todo el cuerpo, la cara, el vientre, el corazón, los senos, Tita no pudo sostenerle esa mirada y bajando la vista, cruzó rápidamente el salón hasta el extremo opuesto, donde Gertrudis pedaleaba en la pianola el vals "Ojos de Juventud."

Así entre revolucionarios que van y vienen, federales y rebeldes que galopan en torno a los muros de la casa en Piedras Negras, habitada por mujeres norteñas, hermosas y bragadas, claridosas y despatoladas, todas ellas entronas, desde la espantosa y castradora mandamás Mamá Elena hasta la sirvienta Nacha que muere, Chencha su sucesora, Tita la heroína, Rosaura su hermana, Paquita Lobo, Gertrudis la segunda hermana, la abuela de John, "Luz del amanecer", (una india Kikapú que es un personaje maravilloso a la vez de curandera), Laura Esquivel va entretejiendo la vida de sus mujeres y dándonos en salsa de molcajete los rasgos de su carácter. Mamá Elena por ejemplo, es la de los chiles en nogada. No sólo puede partir costales y costales de nueces y pelar más de mil nueces en pocos días, sino que goza enormemente haciéndolo. Prensar, destrozar y despellejar son algunas de sus actividades favoritas.

"Cuando yo doy de comer, dice Laura Esquivel, siento que se invierte el papel sexual de la pareja y el hombre se convierte en el receptor. A través de los alimentos soy yo la que penetro. Además, tú eres lo que comes y con quién y cómo te lo comes. En mi familia fue siempre muy importante la comida y para mi mamá era un medio de comunicación y todo un rito. Por lo mismo disfrutamos mucho cada comida. Es un acto que reafirma la unión de la pareja, la convivencia con los hijos, el encuentro con los amigos.. La historia de una familia son sus recetas y es importantísimo mantenerlas vivas."

"Siempre la comida me remite al pasado", dice Laura "y de allá me surgió la idea de hacer una novela en la que las recetas fueran lo medular. De niña, me impresionó que a una hermana de mi abuela le impidieron casarse para que cuidara a su mamá en su vejez y así construí a Tita, mi personaje principal, que, sacrificada por su madre, logra realizar su amor y hacer morir esa tradición tan terrible."

"Tienes que hacerte cargo de tu madre." Tita obedece a Mamá Elena: "Sabes muy bien que por ser la más chica de las mujeres a ti te corresponde cuidarme hasta mi muerte" (17). Mamá Elena impide que se case con Pedro. Si Pedro se quiere casar tendrá que ser con su segunda hija: Rosaura. Pedro acepta con tal de permanecer cerca de Tita. Lo único que escapa al control de Mamá Elena es la comida y Tita confecciona el pastel de novios. Comunica a los huevos y a la harina, a la mantequilla y al azúcar toda su rabia y su frustración y los invitados se van llenando no de suculencias sino de una inmensa tristeza. Durante el banquete de bodas, la novia Rosaura enferma de gravedad, Pedro tarda seis meses en hacer obra de varón y la casa se tiñe de melancolía. Ésa es la venganza de Tita, la reina de la cocina. En este papel, en esta época de esterilidad en el rancho, Tita, trabajando en la cocina, llega a ser una imagen sensual:

Tita, de rodillas, inclinada sobre el metate, se movía rítmica y cadenciosamente mientras molía las almendras y el ajonjolí.

Bajo su blusa sus senos se meneaban libremente pues ella nunca usó sostén alguno. De su cuello escurrían gotas de sudor que rodaban hacia abajo siguiendo el surco de piel entre sus pechos redondos y duros.

Pedro, no pudiendo resistir los olores que emanaban de la cocina, se dirigió hacia ella, quedando petrificado en la puerta ante la sensual postura en que encontró a Tita.

[. . .] Pedro bajó la vista y la clavó en los senos de Tita. Ésta dejó de moler, se enderezó y orgullosamente irguió su pecho, para que Pedro lo observara plenamente. El examen de que fue objeto cambió para siempre la relación entre ellos. Después de esa escrutadora mirada que penetraba la ropa ya nada volvería a ser igual. Tita supo en carne propia por qué el contacto con el fuego altera los elementos, por qué un pedazo de masa se convierte en tortilla, por qué un pecho sin haber pasado por el fuego del amor es un pecho inerte, una bola de masa sin ninguna utilidad. En sólo unos instantes Pedro había transformado los senos de Tita de castos a voluptuosos sin necesidad de tocarlos. (68)

Antes de Laura Esquivel, la imagen de la mujer en la cocina no había sido tratada en esa forma. En *Como agua para chocolate* la cocina es la casa, el rescoldo del hogar, el centro de la tierra, la conciencia de la patria. A través de la fe y la cocina, nuestros hombres se han salvado de la muerte. Es la mujer la dadora de los remedios, la que hierve los tes, la que combina las hierbas, la que cura, la que separa y limpia las semillas, la que extiende las tortillas sobre el comal. La cocina es centro de información, agencia noticiosa, consuelo de pecadores. Todos los miembros de la familia van a la cocina porque saben que allá junto a los sagrados alimentos le servirán buenos consejos. Al ritmo de la molienda, del café que se tuesta, del agua en la cubeta para hacer la mezcla de la masa, la mujer va acomodándole al hombre en el armario sus inseguridades, encontrándole un lugar a cada cosa y poniendo cada cosa en su lugar, las desazones en una repisa y la inquietud en un cajón. Muele su angustia en un metate y filtra sus ideas a través de la coladera de tal manera que con un poco de Royal levanta el sentimiento del valor propio cuando lo saquen del horno y lo espolvoreen de azúcar.

La mujer amasa al hombre, lo tortea, lo extiende para que su pasta sea flexible, lo rellena, lo hace pan de muerto, pan de dulce, rosca de Reyes, cuernos y pambazos y lo vuelve a servir como una sopa de su propio chocolate, a la hora de la merienda, encajándole pasas, trufándolo, una manzana en su hociquito, lechón dorado al horno, crujiente y recién nacido, cabrito de sí mismo, con sus frijoles refritos y su guacamole de acompañamiento.

"Primero elegía las recetas que más me gustaban", dice Laura, "las que tenían un significado especial porque las comía en Navidad o en mi cumpleaños o para festejar algún aniversario e imaginé qué significado podrían tener esas recetas en la vida de mis personajes. En función de las recetas hice una estructura dramática, la misma que utilizaba cuando hacía guiones de cine y de televisión. (Escribí el guión de *Chido One* de Arau, *Colombino* y *Mujer Divina* con música de Agustín Lara.) Escogí el orden en el que entrarían las recetas, las tortas de Navidad, cuando Pedro va a pedir a Tita y sale comprometido con Rosaura, su hermana, el pastel de Boda 'Chabela', y las 'Codornices en pétalos de rosa' cuando Tita y Pedro empiezan a relacionarse amorosamente a través de la comida. El 'Mole con almendras y ajonjolí' celebra el nacimiento del primer hijo de Pedro y Rosaura, el chorizo norteño hace su aparición cuando Tita enloquece y sube a desnudarse al palomar y la "masa para hacer fósforos" que da John el médico que le salva la vida."

La más belicosa de las recetas es la de la masa para hacer fósforos.

Ingredientes:
1 onza de nitro en polvo
1/2 onza de minio
1/2 onza de goma arábiga en polvo
1 dracma de fósforo
azafrán
cartón.

Los "soupers intimes" son casi siempre el inicio del acto amoroso. "Te voy a devorar como a un mango" dice el gran poeta Claudel. Al final de la novela, Tita tiene que reunir el suficiente fósforo para encender el túnel que la llevará al encuentro de Pedro por fin viudo porque Rosaura les ha hecho el favor de morirse:

> [Tita s]e empezó a comer uno a uno los cerillos que contenía la caja. Al masticar cada fósforo cerraba los ojos fuertemente e intentaba reproducir los recuerdos más emocionantes entre Pedro y ella. La primera mirada que recibió de él, el primer roce de sus manos, el primer ramo de rosas, el primer beso, la primera caricia, la primera relación íntima. Y logró lo que se proponía. Cuando el fósforo que masticaba hacía contacto con la luminosa imagen que evocaba, el cerillo se encendía. (221)

Cocinera, alquimista, bruja de cabellos largos y ensortijados, amante del hombre y de la vida, lopezvelardiana y lujuriosa, Laura Esquivel nos ofrece en charola de plata, un libro que no existía en la literatura mexicana, el del amor bien guisado, sin desgarramientos ni palabras altisonantes, sin resignaciones ni venganzas, a punto de turrón, que se hace agua en la boca y llena de felicidad el estómago, el esófago, los pulmones, la caja del pecho. Picamos el cilantro bien picadito, picamos nuestro corazón como una cebolla y empezamos a repartirlo, a echarlo por la ventana, a regalárselo al primero que pase, a aventarlo fuera del zaguán, lo mezclamos en aceite suave, lavamos en agua de limón los otros ingredientes, los sentimientos tiernos, cortamos en rodajas los días por venir, salpimentamos el lecho, hervimos las virtudes para quitarles el moho, después en la cacerola echamos una a una nuestras ideas políticas (si es que las tenemos) y ponemos en adobo durante dos horas nuestra lengua y nuestros labios para que se sazonen.

Como agua para chocolate lo alimenta a uno y hace burbujear la sangre agradecida por tantas atinadas y nutritivas palabras. "Alimenta tu cerebro" (ordena) Jefferson Airplane y Laura Esquivel con su *Como agua para chocolate* nos ceba y nos deja como pavitos de navidad, aunque en México a los pavos se les llame "guajolotes." Con razón esta novela se mantuvo tantos años en la lista de los libros más vendidos del *New York Times*, y con razón Carlos Fuentes felicitó a la más amorosa de las escritoras mexicanas.

Crossing Gender Borders: Subversion of Cinematic Melodrama in *Like Water for Chocolate*

PATRICK DUFFEY

As the introductory essay to this collection has demonstrated, early critical reaction to Laura Esquivel's popular novel *Like Water for Chocolate* was often quite negative. Antonio Marquet's dismissive assessment is well known: "[E]s simplista, maniquea [. . .] infantil [. . .] plagada de convencionalismos banales, despojada de una intención estilística definida y no tiene otra aspiración que ser novedosa" [It is simplistic, manichean . . . childish . . . plagued with banal commonplaces, stripped of any defined stylistic aims, and having no other purpose than being a novelty] (58). Within a few years of publication, however, scholars began to take notice of the novel's rich complexity. Carmen Ramos Escandón studied the "female language" of its culinary discourse, and Beatriz González Stephan examined how the novel makes parodic use of the *novela rosa* [romance novel], Mexican cookbooks, and Carreño's nineteenth-century book of etiquette.[1]

In one of the most important of these reevaluations of the novel, Kristine Ibsen contended that *Like Water for Chocolate* questions the boundaries between "serious art" and popular literature, since it is a "playfully parodic appropriation" of canonical magical realism (à la Gabriel García Márquez).[2] Extending Ibsen's analysis of the novel's parodic undercurrents, my study focuses on how the novel also appropriates and subverts many of the structures and themes of the cinematic melodramas produced both in Hollywood and Mexico during the 40s and 50s. It was natural for Esquivel to parody both magical realism and cinematic melodrama. At the time of the novel's publication, her involvement in the film industry was as important as her literary career.

In 1985, her screenplay for the film *El Chido Guan* was nominated for the Ariel prize in Mexico.[3] Her then-husband, Alfonso Arau, directed both *El Chido Guan* and the film version of *Like Water for Chocolate*. It is not surprising that her close relationship with cinema had an impact on her first novel. To provide a basis for my study of this impact, of how Esquivel subverts cinematic melodrama, I will begin by outlining a few pertinent ideas from recent film studies on Hollywood and Mexican melodrama.

Cinematic Melodrama in Hollywood and Mexico

Film scholars have considered the Hollywood melodrama of the 40s and 50s a subject worthy of study only since the early 70s. Since then, Christine Gledhill, Laura Mulvey, Mary Ann Doane, Jackie Byars, Tania Modleski and E. Ann Kaplan have revealed the structural, stylistic and ideological richness of the genre.[4] It was not until the early 90s, however, that film studies began to pay serious attention to the Mexican melodrama of the same period. Prior to this, film scholars such as Enrique Colina, Daniel Díaz Torres, Michael Chanan, and Carlos Monsiváis had written off the Mexican melodrama as escapist sentimentality.[5] Ana M. López, John King, and Laura Podalsky have initiated pioneering work in this area.[6] Film critics' late-twentieth-century studies of both Hollywood and Mexican melodramas offer several ideas that are quite pertinent to my reading of *Like Water for Chocolate*.

Laura Mulvey's 1986 essay "Melodrama Inside and Outside the Home" provides a useful definition of melodrama:

> The aesthetics of the popular melodrama depend on grand gesture, tableaux, broad moral themes, with narratives of coincidence, reverses and sudden happy endings organised around a rigid opposition between good and evil. Characters represent forces rather than people, and fail to control or understand their circumstances so that fate, rather than heroic transcendence, offers a resolution to the drama. (73)

In my opinion, Esquivel's novel offers a postmodern version of melodrama, a version of it that simultaneously takes advantage of and pokes fun at melodrama's excesses, the coincidences, the sometimes cartoon-like characters, the sudden happy ending. In Umberto Eco's terms, Esquivel "revisits" the melodrama, "but with irony, not innocently" (Eco *Postscript* 67). In the same essay, Mulvey points out how Douglas Sirk's 1955 melodrama *All That Heaven Allows* provides a window into the repressive attitudes of 1950s America in the way that the film represents space in terms of gender. The film links interior space inside the home with repression, motherhood and middle-class values. Jane Wyman plays a middle-aged woman whose husband has died and whose narrow-minded children want their mother to stay at home, watch television, and lead the quiet life of an asexual widow. They condemn her romantic relationship with a young gardener, played by Rock Hudson. According to Mulvey, Hollywood melodrama often identified interior space as female space, as a space in which mothers lived in middle-class material comfort, in an atmosphere of repressed sexuality (64). *Like Water for Chocolate*, like Hollywood melodramas, identifies interior spaces with women, but it subverts the traditional melodramatic order of things. For Tita and other characters in the novel, the interior space of the kitchen is a locus of power, a place of rebellion and independence.[7]

According to Ana M. López, Mexican family melodramas of the 40s and 50s focus on three conflicts: the clash between old feudal Porfirian values and modern, urban life; the resultant male identity crisis; and the resultant female identity crisis (see "Mediating" 153). Regarding the role of women in these films, she describes several categories of female characters: the *ángel del hogar* or saintly mother (*e.g.*, Sara García in *Cuando los hijos se van* [*When the Children Leave*]); the *mala mujer*, or the thoroughly evil woman (*e.g.*, María Felix in *Doña Bárbara*); the *mujer sufrida*, or the innocent, fallen woman/suffering mother (*e.g.*, Libertad Lamarque in *Soledad* [*Soltitude*]); or the seductive *cabaretera* (*e.g.*, Ninón Sevilla in *Señora Tentación* [*Madame Temptation*]). *Like Water for Chocolate* includes aspects of these melodramatic women in its cast of characters, but often the novel subverts the traditional limitations of women's roles and redefines them according to its postmodern version of melodrama.

The Revolution from the Inside; or, the Power of the Kitchen

Like many of the heroines of Hollywood family melodramas, Tita de la Garza is a woman who does not get out much. Throughout the novel, her life is at home, within the confines of the family ranch. Like the homes depicted in many Hollywood melodramas, Tita's home is a place of emotional and sexual repression. She may never marry since it falls to her to take care of her mother, Mamá Elena. No tears are allowed. The severe limitations of Tita's life are rigidly defined by her mother:

> Al lado de su madre, lo que sus manos tenían que hacer estaba fríamente determinado, no había dudas. Tenía que levantarse, vestirse, prender el fuego en la estufa, preparar el desayuno, alimentar a los animales, lavar

los trastes, hacer las camas, preparar la comida, lavar los trastes, planchar la ropa, preparar la cena, lavar los trastes, día tras día, año tras año. (104)[8]

[At her mother's side, the things her hands had to do were coldly prescribed – there was no variation. She had to get up, dress herself, light the fire in the stove, make the breakfast, feed the animals, wash the dishes, make the beds, make lunch, wash the dishes, iron the clothes. make dinner, wash the dishes, day after day, year after year.]

Despite the drudgery of Tita's everyday life at the family ranch, and despite the opportunity to leave it for good offered to her by Dr. Brown's marriage proposal, Tita never abandons the ranch for very long.

Although *Like Water for Chocolate*, like the Hollywood melodrama *All That Heaven Allows*, is a story of a woman who fights against social convention and finds freedom in the end, Esquivel's novel does not provide Tita with her freedom in the manner of traditional melodrama. While Jane Wyman leaves her repressive home behind and finds love and liberation in the arms of her young gardener, Rock Hudson, Tita lives out her life at the family ranch. Instead of fleeing from her repressive interior space, Tita transforms it into a locus of power. Through her kitchen and the magical food that it produces, Tita is able to find love and, eventually, some measure of independence.

The kitchen was always a place of freedom for Tita. Nursed on teas and atoles by the indigenous servant Nacha since her birth, Tita feels at home only in the kitchen , and she perceives the world in culinary terms:

No era fácil para una persona que conoció la vida a través de la cocina entender el mundo exterior. Ese gigantesco mundo que empezaba de la puerta de la cocina hacia el interior de la casa, porque el que colindaba con la puerta trasera de la cocina y que daba al patio, a la huerta, a la hortaliza, sí le pertenecía por completo, lo dominaba. (14–15)

[It wasn't easy for a person who knew the world only through the kitchen to understand the world outside. That gigantic world that began with the door of the kitchen toward the interior of the house, because the world that began with the back door of the kitchen and that opened onto the patio, to the orchard, to the kitchen garden, that belonged to her completely – she had mastered it.]

In the kitchen, Tita is in charge. Esquivel ingeniously inverts the usual structure of melodrama here, since Tita's interior space actually becomes similar to the male exterior space of traditional Mexican melodrama. In other words, her kitchen (female space) becomes the main setting for the action scenes of the novel, which in traditional melodrama usually happen outside the home (male space).

When film scholar Gustavo García describes the spaces of Mexican melodrama, they are predominantly male, exterior spaces: the *hacienda* [estate], the village, the countryside, and the *vecindad* [the neighborhood, vicinity] (156–57). One of Esquivel's extraordinary accomplishments in her first novel is that she inverts so skillfully the structures of several traditional genres, including the typical Revolutionary melodramas, such as Fernando de Fuentes's *El compadre Mendoza* (1933. [*Godfather Mendoza*]) or his ¡*Vámonos con Pancho Villa!* (1935. [*Let's Go with Pancho Villa!*]). Simply put, Esquivel moves the typically male violence of the Revolutionary melodrama from the countryside into the kitchen. In the Revolutionary melodramas, violence is often perpetrated for a just cause, the freedom of a downtrodden people. In the case of *Like Water for Chocolate*, the perpetrator of the violence in the kitchen is often Tita, and her cause is also just: the freedom of a downtrodden woman.

There are three striking examples of Tita's "revolutionary" violence in the kitchen. When Tita is preparing the 170-egg wedding cake for Rosaura's impending wedding with Tita's true love, Pedro, Tita associates the eggs she is cracking with the testicles of the male chickens that she castrated a month before, when she was preparing capons for the wedding dinner. She recalls that as she attempted to castrate the first one, her hands trembled and sweated, and she hesitated because she could identify with the chick. Mamá Elena, by denying Tita the right to marry, had effectively castrated Tita (I will discuss the gender-bending female castration going on here in the next section). Tita wants to scream at her mother that she should be castrating herself, because then there would be a reason for her inability to get married: "[S]e había elegido mal al sujeto apropiado para capar, la adecuada era ella, de esta manera habría al menos una justificación para que le estuviera negado el matrimonio [. . .]" [The right subject for castration had been poorly chosen – she was the right one, because that way, there would be at least some justification for denying her marriage] (32–33).

Later in the novel, when Tita is getting ready to cook quail in rose petals, she must wring the necks of six of birds. Once again, Tita associates the violence she commits in the kitchen with her own personal struggle. To give herself the courage to twist their heads off, Tita imagines that the birds have a soft-boiled egg stuck in their throats. By wringing their necks, she is liberating them from this problem. Tita comes up with this strange association, because when she was a girl her mother forced her to eat boiled eggs, which got stuck in her throat. By wringing the quails' necks she is freeing them from their imaginary boiled eggs, and she is symbolically freeing herself from the domination of her mother: "Sólo trataba de imaginar que cada una de las codornices tenía atorado un huevo tibio en el buche y que ella piadosamente las liberaba de ese martirio dándoles un buen torzón" [She tried to imagine that each of the quail had a soft-cooked egg plugging up its crop and that she was mercifully liberating them from that martyrdom by giving the neck a good twist] (51).

Another example of culinary violence occurs when Tita is understandably upset about the death of her infant nephew, a death brought on by Mamá Elena's sending the child and his parents to San Antonio to avoid contact between Pedro and Tita. When her mother forbids her tears, Tita cannot take it anymore, and she commits the most violent act of which she is capable. She destroys the food she is preparing:

> Tita sintió que una violenta agitación se posesionaba de su ser: enfrentó firmemente la mirada de su madre mientras acariciaba el chorizo y después, en lugar de obedecerla, tomó todos los chorizos que encontró y los partió, gritando enloquecida. (94)

> [Tita felt that a violent anxiety was taking possession of her: she firmly met the gaze of her mother as she stroked the sausage, and then, instead of obeying her [mother], she took all the sausages that she could get hold of and tore them apart, screaming as if she had gone mad.]

It should be noted that Tita's acts of culinary violence are not only acts of rebellion, but also often involve some amount of violence toward herself, as a reaction to her desperate circumstances (self-castration, wringing the necks of birds she identifies with, destroying her own cooking).

Tita's dual effect on the object of her violence and on herself is consistent with what Thomas Elsaesser has to say about the cinematic domestic melodrama:

> [T]he social pressures are such, the frame of respectability so sharply defined that the range of 'strong' actions is limited. The tellingly important gesture, the social gaffe, the hysterical outburst replaces any more directly liberating or self-annihilating action, and the cathartic violence of a shoot-out or a chase becomes an inner violence, often one which the characters turn against themselves. (qtd. in Gledhill 56)

In *Like Water for Chocolate*, the typically male violence of the outside world takes the form of an inwardly directed, female violence of the kitchen. But violence is not the only kind of power in Tita's kitchen. Her kitchen can also be a source of sensuality.

Tita's cooking expresses her repressed emotions. When she is devastated and bitter about Pedro and Rosaura's wedding, the wedding cake that Tita prepares makes everyone vomit with bitterness and remorse over their lost loves. At the end of the novel, when Tita and Pedro are celebrating the marriage of Esperanza with Dr. Brown's son, Alex (a particularly joyous event, since it breaks the tradition of the youngest De la Garza daughter not marrying), Tita's *chiles en nogada* causes everyone to be sexually excited. But perhaps the most powerful concoction of Tita's kitchen is her quail in rose petal sauce, since it causes two revolutionary events to take place in Mamá Elena's house: it precipitates Gertrudis's escape from the repression of the ranch, and it allows indirect sexual communication between Pedro and Tita. In fact, the effect of the quail is so strong that the action of the scene, which originates in the kitchen and dining room, spills out into the surrounding countryside, converting the traditional domain of male Revolution into a space of female liberation.

After eating the quail and serving as a willing medium for Pedro and Tita's sexual passion, Gertrudis must take a cold shower to calm her lust. The rosy aroma that she gives off invades the countryside and wafts so far that a *villista* passing by on horseback picks up the enticing scent, rides to find its source, and picks up a naked Gertrudis at full gallop, and they make love as they ride off together. One of the most action-filled scenes in the novel has its origins in the interior space of Tita's kitchen and the repressed desires within Tita herself. Remarkably, the narrator explicitly notes the cinematic quality of the scene that Tita and Pedro witness:

[C]omo mudos espectadores de una película, Pedro y Tita se emocionaron hasta las lágrimas al ver a sus héroes realizar el amor que para ellos estaba prohibido. (56)

[Like mute members of the audience at a film, Pedro and Tita were moved to tears when they saw their heroes achieve the love that was denied them.]

Tita and Pedro stand there and watch their cinematic "heroes," Gertrudis and her *villista*, ride off, as if she and Pedro were watching one of Fernando de Fuentes's Revolutionary melodramas.[9]

Here Esquivel explicitly pokes fun at the clichés of such melodramas, especially their chance occurrences and their depiction of macho soldiers carrying off young women whenever they pleased. In this case, it is the woman whose desire is overwhelming and whose scent carries the man away. Far from being a simplistic imitation of melodrama (as Marquet would have it), *Like Water for Chocolate* is an ingenious parody of it, often inverting the traditional gender roles with a thoroughly postmodern sense of irony.

Before examining Esquivel's inversion of gender roles in greater depth, I will conclude this section by pointing out that Tita is not the only woman in the novel who gains her freedom by means of the kitchen. Nacha, whose lover was turned away many years before by Mamá Elena's mother, finds fulfillment in teaching Tita all she knows about the wonders of cooking. Although Nacha regrets not being able to have her own family, Tita considers Nacha her real mother. Tita's niece, Esperanza, is raised in the kitchen just as Tita was, and she eventually is able to marry her true love.

Perhaps the most interesting example of the power of the kitchen concerns the life of Dr. Brown's Kikapú grandmother, Luz del amanecer (Chapter VI, "June"). When Tita has a nervous breakdown after her infant nephew's death, Dr. Brown takes her across the border to stay with him in his house. Tita's favorite room in the house is the doctor's small laboratory, which used to be his grandmother's room, the place where she researched the medicinal properties of plants. Although Luz del amanecer was shunned by the Brown family, she was a gifted healer, and she used the little room as a refuge in which to prepare her herbal remedies: "este cuarto le servía de refugio en contra de las agresiones de su familia" [this room served her as a refuge against the interference of (her husband's) family] (106). Like Tita's magical dishes, Luz del amanecer's herbal medicines are potent: when her father-in-law becomes gravely ill, only her concoction of herbs is able to save him, and she becomes a nationally recognized healer. Tita recognizes in Luz del amanecer another woman who utilizes the power of the kitchen to achieve some measure of freedom from familial repression.

Inversions, Castration Anxiety, and Melodramatic Gender-Bending

Like Water for Chocolate works effectively as a parodic inversion of family melodramas such as Juan Bustillo Oro's *Cuando los hijos se van* (1941). It also incorporates two other important female archetypes of the Mexican melodrama, as defined by Ana M. López: the *cabaretera*, the sexual siren portrayed by Ninón Sevilla, María Antonieta Pons, and others; and the innocent fallen woman/suffering mother portrayed so often by Libertad Lamarque. Esquivel's novel blends these melodramatic elements and puts them at an ironic, postmodern distance in two ways: first, it revels in gender-bending, having women play all of the major roles, even the traditionally male ones; and second, it attaches no shame to the roles of *cabaretera*/prostitute or innocent fallen woman/suffering mother.

One could compare *Like Water for Chocolate* to several other domestic melodramas of the "golden age" of Mexican cinema, but *Cuando los hijos se van* shares certain structural elements with the novel that make for an interesting comparison. The film deals with a provincial family broken apart when the rigid, insensitive father (Fernando Soler), influenced by the "bad" son, disowns the "good" son (sending him to the city), despite the protests of the sensitive, saintly mother (Sara García). In *Like Water for Chocolate*, Nacha is the only saintly mother figure, an indigenous sage who acts as Tita's surrogate mother. When she dies, Tita feels as if her "verdadera madre" [real mother] has died (49). Mamá Elena plays a part similar to the father's role in *Cuando los hijos se van*. She is the one who breaks up the family because of her rigidity and insensitivity.

In fact, the family sees Mamá Elena as an expert in breaking up things. She is the only one in the family who knows how to break apart a watermelon perfectly, and she utilizes her powers of disintegration with equal skill in her handling of familial relationships: "Indudablemente, tratándose de partir, desmantelar, desmembrar, desolar, desjarretar, desbaratar o desmadrar algo, Mamá Elena era una maestra" [Undoubtedly, in matters of splitting, dismantling, cutting up, destroying, hobbling, disrupting, or breaking anything, Mamá Elena was a master] (92–93). Like the father in *Cuando los hijos se van*, Mamá Elena banishes a "good" child – in fact, she banishes two "good" children, Gertrudis and Tita, at different points in the story. Mamá Elena plays the part of the patriarchal "heavy," and Gertrudis and Tita, as her "good sons," participate in a similar gender-bending that is apparent throughout the novel.

Mamá Elena demonstrates a traditionally male strength, as when she stares down the Revolutionary soldiers who enter the ranch in search of provisions. Her eyes make the *villista* captain feel like a guilty little boy:

> Realmente era difícil sostener la mirada de Mamá Elena, hasta para un capitán. Tenía algo que atemorizaba. El efecto que provocaba en quienes la recibían era de un temor indescriptible: se sentían enjuiciados y sentenciados por faltas cometidas. Caía uno preso de un miedo pueril a la autoridad materna. (87)

> [It was really hard to stand Mamá Elena's gaze, even for a captain. There was something about it that struck fear into people. The effect that it had on its victims was an indescribable fear: they would feel tried and convicted for crimes committed. One became prisoner to a childish terror of maternal authority.]

Another way to read this scene is in Freudian terms, with Mamá Elena's eyes giving the captain a Medusa-like stare that he fears because of castration anxiety. This is not so improbable, since Tita explicitly refers to her mother in Freudian terms, as "la mujer castrante que la había reprimido toda la vida" [the castrating woman who had repressed her all her life] (131). As we have seen, when Tita describes her unsuccessful attempt to castrate the chickens, she identifies with the male birds, stating that if she were castrated, at least there would be a reason for her not to marry. Of course, according to Freud, it is the son who develops castration anxiety, fearing that his father will castrate him because of the son's sexual desire for his mother. According to the Freudian model, both Tita and Mamá Elena are women who are playing roles usually associated with males.[10]

Gertrudis also takes over a traditionally male role in the novel. Like the banished "good" son in *Cuando los hijos se van*, she returns home as a great success. In Gertrudis's case, she has become nothing less than a *generala* in the Revolutionary army, earning her high rank, fighting harder than anyone else in battle: "Este nombramiento se lo había ganado a pulso, luchando como nadie en el campo de batalla" [She had earned her rank by fighting like nobody else on the battlefield] (165).

We see that Gertrudis and Tita are subversive characters, but not only because of their gender-bending. Each of them represents a postmodern version of a female archetype of the Mexican melodrama. Gertrudis runs off to live in a brothel. Her lust is as potent and unrepressed as that of any *cabaretera* in the movies, and yet the shame is missing for the most part. Her mother and the neighbors condemn her (Mamá Elena burns her birth certificate), but Gertrudis herself sees the experience as liberating. In a letter to Tita, she writes that "ahora después de que infinidad de hombres han pasado por mí, siento un gran alivio" [now after an infinite number of men have been with me, I feel a great relief] (121). Her experience in the brothel has calmed her lust and given her confidence. In contrast, the sexual sirens of Mexican *cabaretera* films use sex to express anger and exact vengeance. As López puts it, the *cabareteras* "project a virulent form of desire on to the screen," and they are always "cloaked with the shameful aura" of the original raped, "treacherous" Mexican woman, *la Malinche* (158–59).[11]

Gertrudis is an updated *cabaretera*, one for whom sex is a healthy means of self-expression. In a similar way, Tita represents a kind of updated fallen woman/suffering mother. Like many of the characters played by Argentine actress Libertad Lamarque in Mexican melodramas of the 40s and 50s, Tita, through no fault of her own, has become entangled in an affair that causes her to play, to some extent, the role of the fallen woman. Also like Lamarque's characters, Tita is a suffering mother, or at least a suffering surrogate mother for Roberto and Esperanza. Unlike

Lamarque's characters, however, Tita never allows herself to feel ashamed of her illicit relationship. Instead, she fights for the freedom to love the man whom she desires.

According to López, the ostensible message of *Cuando los hijos se van*, like that of many of the family melodramas of the period, is one which attempts to uphold the patriarchal family structure: "The film attempts to idealize the family as a unit whose preservation is worth all sacrifices, even death [. . .]" (154). What does Esquivel's novel attempt? It certainly does not idealize the patriarchal family structure. On the contrary, it supports two ideas that are antithetical to the traditional patriarchal order. First, it suggests that family traditions can be pernicious, repressive, and destructive to the family unit. Second, it loudly affirms that women are quite capable of handling the major roles of the family – and of the family melodrama – by themselves, if necessary. All of the male characters in the novel are weak to one extent or another. Esquivel's strong women take over traditionally male roles, sometimes bending gender in order to do so, inverting the usual order of the family melodrama.

Perhaps Mamá Elena sums it up best. When Father Ignacio worries about her sending Pedro and his family to San Antonio, he tells her that she, Tita and Chencha need a man around the house in order to protect them from the Revolution. Mamá Elena replies that she has never really needed a man:

> "[S]ola he podido con el rancho y con mis hijas. Los hombres no son tan importantes para vivir padre," –recalcó – . "Ni la revolución es tan peligrosa como la pintan, ¡peor es el chile y el agua lejos!" (79)

> ["I've handled the ranch and my daughters by myself. Men aren't so important for survival, Father," she emphasized. "Neither is the Revolution as dangerous as they paint it – it's worse to have the hot peppers and the water too far apart!"]

Esquivel's women are strong enough to take over many of the male roles of traditional melodrama. Tita and Gertrudis are confident enough to remake the melodramatic roles of the *cabaretera* and the innocent fallen woman into something less shameful, more liberating. Nacha, Tita, Luz del amanecer, and Esperanza are able to turn the kitchen – an interior space of repression in the Hollywood melodrama – into a place of rebellion and self-expression. Tita's culinary violence supplants the male violence of Revolutionary melodramas. It is worth noting that Tita's favorite Christmas gift as a child was a primitive film projector that Nacha gave her:

[S]u verdadero nombre era el de "zootropo" [. . . .] Cuántas tardes gozaron ella y sus hermanas viendo las imágenes en secuencia que venían dibujadas en tiras de cristal, y que representaban diferentes situaciones de lo más divertidas. (156)

[Its real name was "zoetrope". . . . How many afternoons she and her sisters had enjoyed as they watched the sequence of images that came drawn on sheets of glass and that showed a variety of the funniest situations.]

Like Tita, Esquivel remembers the cinematic images of her childhood with a certain fondness. As a novelist with screen-writing credits, Esquivel redefines those images, creating a new place for women in a new kind of melodrama.

Notes

1 See Willingham's critical introduction in this volume for additional discussion of Ramos Escandón's (1991) and González Stephan's (1992) readings of the novel.
2 See n. 28 in the critical introduction.
3 See Ledford-Miller's biography of Esquivel, Elena Poniatowska's essay, and the Glossary in this volume for additional information on *Chido Guan*.
4 See Christine Gledhill (1987); Laura Mulvey (1989); Jackie Byars (1991); E. Ann Kaplan (1992); Jacky Bratton, et al. (1994).
5 See Enrique Colina and Daniel Díaz Torres (1971); Michael Chanan (1985); Carlos Monsiváis (1985).
6 See Ana M. López (1991); John King (1990); John King, Ana M. López, and Manuel Alvarado (1993); Laura Podalsky (1993). See also Andrea Noble's *Mexican National Cinema*, especially chapter 4, "Melodrama, Masculinity and the Poltics of Space" (2005).
7 Esquivel validates her choice of melodrama as worthy of literary fiction in an *Excelsior* interview reported by Alejandro Semo and Juan José Giovannini (1990).
8 Quotations from *Como agua para chocolate* (Spanish edition) are from the Doubleday Spanish edition (1993). Translations into English are the editor's.
9 This is, of course, a humorous anachronism, since during the Mexican Revolution the film industry was in its infancy. Documentary films of the Revolution existed from the beginning of the conflict, but Revolutionary melodramas were years away. Esquivel's narrator does not hesitate to tell her tale with anachronistic flair, as when she compares Tita's pain to the black holes found in space (21).
10 See Sigmund Freud, "Some Psychical Consequences of the Anatomical Distinction Between the Sexes" (1925).

Unmasked Men: Sex Roles in *Like Water for Chocolate*

JEFFREY OXFORD

Feminism, inspired by "a desire for justice in the real–world apportion-
ment between men and women of power" (Lindstrom 1989 50), plays
an important role in *Like Water for Chocolate*. There are twenty-three
female characters in the work and a quantitatively significant number of
forty-five male characters.[1] However, of all these men, there are only two
which are qualitatively and fundamentally essential to the plot – Pedro
and Dr. Brown – while the elimination of any one of six of the women
– Mamá Elena, Tita, Nacha, Rosaura, Gertrudis, or Chencha – would
substantially change the plot. Male characters, in contrast to female characters, are much more frequently referred to in the plural, 20% versus
13% for groups of female characters. While one might argue that this
group gendering is due to the grammatical structure of Spanish, in which
a single masculine element causes the collective noun and adjective referring to the entire group to be masculine, a closer examination of the
masculine plurals within the novel reveals that, in fact, the individual
elements of each group are most probably masculine in gender.

On Mamá Elena's *rancho*, the man never succeeds in becoming equal
to the woman: Mamá Elena controls the property and all who come
there, including the revolutionary soldiers (89); after her death, Rosaura
takes over and forces Tita and Pedro to hide their affair (238), and Dr.
Brown never attempts to marry another after Tita's refusal to marry him
– so far as we know (243). Thus, the woman in *Like Water for Chocolate*
is not the stereotypically perceived weaker sex; she is, at her weakest, an
equal participant and, more frequently, higher up in the level of
command, dominating all the various aspects of society.[2]

We see this domination in Gertrudis's flight from the ranch:
"Gertrudis dejó de correr en cuanto lo vio [a Juan] venir hacia ella"
[Gertrudis stopped running as soon as she saw Juan coming toward her]
(54), waiting for him to catch her so that "le apagara el fuego abrasador

76

que nacía en sus entrañas" [he might put out the scorching fire that was growing in her belly] (54). Gertrudis has as much desire for the encounter as Juan has, and urgency drives her toward him: she must put out the fire within her. Even before Pedro forces Tita into sex, she has indicated a willingness for a sexual encounter: "se enderezó y orgullosamente irguió su pecho, para que Pedro lo observara plenamente" [she straightened up and proudly raised her bosom so that Pedro might have a full view of it] (67), an observation that "cambió para siempre la relación entre ellos" [changed forever the relationship between them] (67), a willingness more explicitly detailed later as "los senos que Tita le ofrecía" [the breasts that Tita offered him] (68).

In spite of the traditional stereotype of the dominant, even abusive, Mexican male, Laura Esquivel does not present "the *pelado* bolster[ing] his fragile self-confidence with boastful displays of his virility" (Ramírez Berg 68); as argued in the preceding paragraph, Pedro's "rape" of the willing Tita can hardly be qualified as a boastful display, as neither can his and Tita's twenty-year pact with Rosaura to "ser de lo más discretos en sus encuentros y a mantener oculto su amor" [be extremely discreet in their meetings and to keep their love a secret] (238). Esquivel, in effect, uses as principal characters men that are subject to the desires and mandates of women, thereby displaying an inversion of the traditional gender roles even in the most traditionally physical aspects of male–female relations: "De esta manera *penetraba* [Tita] en el cuerpo de Pedro, voluptuosa, aromática, calurosa, completamente sensual" [In this way, Tita penetrated Pedro's body, voluptuous, aromatic, warm, totally sensual] (51, emphasis added). Esquivel's narrative organization makes the female – in particular Mamá Elena and Tita – the focus of the narrative, controlling the ranch and imposing her will.[3] The female in charge becomes, through her actions and words, the "masculinized woman" (Franco 1989 147), and the male in the narrative is the marginalized entity. Dr. Brown understands that his marriage to Tita is not to be, and realizing that he is superfluous – "que estaba haciendo mal tercio" [that he was becoming a fifth wheel] – he takes his leave and withdraws (243). Even Pedro, who eventually is able to consummate his love with Tita, must hide the affair because of Rosaura's insistence that they "seguir aparentando que su matrimonio funcionaba de maravilla" [go on pretending that their marriage was working beautifully] (237) and because of Tita's desire to protect and nurture Esperanza.

This reversal of traditional gender roles is an important aspect of semiotics that has been studied frequently by feminist critics. However, as Beth Miller notes in an analysis of feminist peninsular criticism (1983), the "majority of such [feminist] studies to date have been devoted to female characterization in narrative and dramatic works by peninsular

Spanish male authors" (8). Without carrying out a scientifically statistical analysis, I believe that it can be said that a substantial percentage of Latin American feminist criticism also has focused on literature written by male authors. This arises, if for no other reason, from the discrepancy between the number of male and female members of the so-called accepted literary canon. The present study, encompassing much more than simply a quantitative approximation of the literature written by women, posits an analysis of a single work by a female writer and her textual representation of the male. Taking advantage of the findings of a more detailed examination, then, I theorize that Esquivel establishes a relationship between the sexes in which the impotence of the male reveals verisimilar cultural attributes not often examined by more traditional critics; that is, I would argue, the Hispanic male in actuality has a "fragile self-confidence" (Ramírez Berg 68), and the Mexican society of *Like Water for Chocolate* is much closer to the true nature of the matriarchy that really exists in the Hispanic world than male novelists care to present or male critics generally care to recognize.

Alan Riding, in his book *Vecinos distantes: Un retrato de los mexicanos* (1987), describes what he believes to be the "typical" Mexican man and writes that the non-Hispanic cannot truly understand the complicated nature of the family relationships in a Hispanic family.[4] In Mexican society, "tanto la Biblia como la Iglesia fomentan la relación tradicional entre hombres y mujeres, respaldando el dominio de los hombres, al tiempo que esperan que la mujer emule la abnegación, modestia y ternura de la virgen María" [the Bible, as much as the Church, engenders the traditional relationship between men and women, supporting male domination, while that women are expected to model the self-denial, modesty, and tenderness of the Virgin Mary] (290). Typically, Riding notes,

> la cadena de mando pasa por las manos de los hombres de la familia [. . .]. Empero, en muchos sentidos, todo esto es una máscara también. La verdadera fuerza y estabilidad de la familia la proporcionan las mujeres [. . .]. Incluso en los hogares que no se han roto, las mujeres resuelven la mayor parte de los problemas: son responsables y confiables, proporcionan continuidad y controlan el entorno emocional. (291)

> [the chain of command passes through the hands of the men in the family. . . . Nevertheless, in many ways, this is a mask as well. The women provide the true force and stability for the family. . . . Including in unbroken homes, women resolve most of the problems: they are responsible and reliable, they provide continuity and control the emotional environment.]

The "mask" that Riding notes here is also validated in a more recently published study showing how immigrant Mexican women holding traditional rural Mexican Catholic values have overtly assumed male roles in an effort to achieve economic well-being for their families in Mexico by working in the U.S., a "seemingly paradoxical relationship between ideology and behavior" (Baker 397).[5]

Riding's commentary about the true role of the women in the family is also supported philosophically by Octavio Paz's commentary concerning the duality of women's roles and nature in Mexican society. Paz commented on woman-based social "stability" in *The Labyrinth of Solitude* (1961. *El laberinto de la soledad* 1950): "La mujer mexicana, como todas las otras, es un símbolo que representa la estabilidad y continuidad de la raza. A su significación cósmica se alía la social: en la vida diaria su función consiste en hacer imperar la ley y el orden, la piedad y la dulzura" [The Mexican woman, like all others, is a symbol that represents the stability and continuity of the race. Her cosmic meaning is aligned with her social significance: in daily life her function consists of ensuring that law and order and piety and sweetness reign] (59).[6] Although Paz's sociological view is perhaps different from commonly accepted ones, the attitudes and actions Paz describes are embraced in the film version of *Like Water for Chocolate*, as director Alfonso Arau has affirmed.

Arau comments that "the heroine, Tita, and the maid Nacha represent intuition, passion, sentiment associated with the female mentality" and that the film is "about the superiority of intuition over reason" (Elias) – or, in other words, the superiority of female truth over male truth. Arau, then, intended to portray in the visual medium Esquivel's particular interpretation of the Mexican psyche using Esquivel's own screenplay of her novel. On the side of "reason" (Elias) as interpreted by authority and tradition, Mamá Elena brutally dominates the de la Garza ranch, permitting no dissent, and going to the extreme of destroying Gertrudis's childhood photographs and her birth certificate when she learns that the supposedly abducted Gertrudis is working in a brothel (58). Mamá Elena demands that the youngest daughter, Tita, submit herself to caring for her mother even when that precludes her marrying the man she loves. Mamá Elena justifies her decision categorically on her continuation of a family tradition of unknown origin; the reader and Tita only know that Mamá Elena continues to enforce it.

The men in the novel, too, fall under the control of Mamá Elena's "reason," and their presence or absence reveals additional insights into men's roles in Elena's matriarchal society. Only three men are ever supposedly in charge of the ranch, but the three either do not fulfill their duties or are replaced by another person, or both, because of direct actions by women. Juan, the husband of Mamá Elena, is responsible for

the ranch, but he dies shortly after Tita is born, two days after being
informed that Gertrudis is the product of an illicit affair between Mamá
Elena and José Treviño (138–39). Nicolás, the second man in charge of
the ranch, theoretically is "ranch manager" or foreman (*el capataz*) and is
responsible for carrying out business affairs such as buying and selling
stock (88), but this is not the role of Nicolás that is most often portrayed.
Of the six times that Nicolás appears in the novel, he is referred to as *el
capataz* only once, and in this instance, he leaves "su hijo Felipe al cuidado
del rancho" [his son Felipe in charge of the ranch], presumably because
he is away carrying out some errand of his mistress's (88), and Felipe
becomes the third man in charge of the ranch. Mamá Elena, however,
relieves him of the position and orders him to go to find out what has
happened to Pedro and his family (Rosaura and Roberto) in San Antonio
(88). Nicolás, in fact, even as "ranch foreman," is most often portrayed
as an emissary or servant on an errand. At Tita's request, he delivers a
suitcase of clothes that Tita has packed for Gertrudis (70); during Tita's
absence from the ranch, Nicolás brings news of Gertrudis and a letter for
Tita: "había regresado hacía poco con noticias de [Gertrudis]" [he had
returned a little earlier with news of Gertrudis] (125); after the rape, Tita
sends Chencha "con Nicolás a su pueblo" [with Nicolás to her town]
(135); and in the last chapter, Nicolás and Rosalío, dressed up in *charro*
costumes, collect the guests' invitations at the gate to the ranch at
Esperanza and Alex's wedding (235).

Clearly, Mamá Elena "wears the boots" in her family and in local
society. She emphasizes her position in this regard at Rosaura's wedding,
when she informs Padre Ignacio, the local priest, that she needs no man
on the ranch, a point given more discussion below. Elena is neither the
Mater dolorosa who suffers the injustices of men, nor the *Venus dolorosa*
that seduces men[7]; she "plays out [the] role as phallic mother" (Saltz 34).
Mamá Elena crosses over traditional female roles and takes on those of
the male attempting to become, in this cross–gendered manner, the
controlling power: "the will of woman is the subjugating type: she
enslaves herself and tries to enslave others" (Boschetto 127). Female
domination limits what the men can do, rendering the men impotent
when the traditional male characteristics of strength and power are most
needed, such as when Mamá Elena casts herself as the commander and
keeps the revolutionary troops from ransacking the house while the two
men (Rosalío and Guadalupe) stand mute at her side. To emphasize her
dominant role, the troop captain responds to her order, "Entendido, mi
general" [Understood, General] (89–91).

When Padre Ignacio tells Mamá Elena that she needs a man on the
ranch (a scene to which I referred above), she responds: "Nunca lo he
necesitado para nada, sola he podido con el rancho y con mis hijas. Los

hombres no son tan importantes para vivir, padre" [I have never needed a man for anything. On my own, I have dealt with the ranch and my daughters. Men aren't so important for survival, Padre] (82). In the same scene, she minimizes the hardships and dangers of the armed conflict to ranches like hers in Northern Mexico, asserting with bravado that the Revolution is less dangerous than having "el chile y el agua lejos" [the hot peppers and the water too far apart] (81).

Validating this attitude is a study carried out by Henry Selby between 1978 and 1990, which states that in Mexico "estar casado [era] positivo para los hombres y negativo para las mujeres en cuanto a la renta: los trabajadores reciben un premio de 25% por estar casados mientras que las mujeres de la población activa sufren una reducción de 6%" [being married is a positive for men's income and a negative for women's income: male workers get an extra 25% for being married while women in the workforce suffer a 6% reduction] due solely to their civil state (17). While *Like Water for Chocolate* is not set in the time frame of Selby's study, the legal and social mindset that men have superior rights to economic control and assets certainly existed at the time.

In *Like Water for Chocolate*, however, Mamá Elena asserts that she needs no man for economic, physical, or psychological gain since her cross-gendered role includes exercising authority over all levels of ranch society: the upper, middle, and lower classes. Esquivel, in fact, notes that she herself views "the mother as being equal to the masculine world" (Loewenstein 594). In the case of Elena, neither the doctor nor the priest nor the soldiers can oppose her. Bandits give her a blow that paralyzes her, but she continues her tyranny over the ranch and its visitors until her death (130 *ff.*). Even in death, Elena's spirit torments Tita (173, 199) and punishes Pedro (201). Tita, a woman and blood relative, is the only one who can break Mamá Elena's grip on the ranch. When Tita tells her mother's apparition, "¡la odio, siempre la odié!" [I hate you, I've always hated you!] (200), Mamá Elena's angry spirit burns Pedro in a final act of rage and disappears "para siempre" [forever] (200).

The violation or transgression of traditional gender roles is practiced by a number of characters. Mamá Elena, after the death of her husband, rejects social wisdom that she should remarry and voluntarily remains a single mother. Taking on all the responsibilities of the ranch, Mamá Elena assumes the roles stereotypically played by the man and never demonstrates the traditional maternal characteristics of love and nurturing that aid the stability of the home. Mamá Elena's comments to Padre Ignacio are directed not toward an inferior person but to someone who, through cross-gendered roles, is on the same social plane as herself. Ecclesiastically, as "the Bride of Christ,"[8] the priest metaphorically becomes a single mother (or parent) for the parishioners, supposedly comforting, helping and raising the local "children of God" in the physical absence of the Father. What most limits Padre Ignacio's power in his relationship with Mamá Elena is his crossed-gender roles.

The priest has placed himself as the only guardian of his "family," but he has never felt, much less experienced, the power of worldly love – though one wonders just how he finds out that Gertrudis is housed in a brothel. Instead of those realizations of active sexuality, he has, figuratively, become a eunuch by taking vows that prohibit his marrying and fathering children. Thus, the priest composes an amalgam of all possible sexualities (except perhaps homosexuality): physically he is masculine, spiritually he is feminine, and figuratively he is neutered. It is, then, Padre Ignacio's blurred cross-gendering, not his position of clerical authority, that permits Mamá Elena to speak to him as an equal, and he is not able to offer valuable, acceptable advice to Mamá Elena to bring peace (and gendered order) to the ranch. As Elena rebuffs the *Padre*, Nacha, Tita's true "mother," dies alone in her room dreaming of the lover that Mamá Elena's mamá had run off generations before.

Besides Padre Ignacio, Dr. John Brown, another visitor to the ranch, attempts to intercede on Tita's behalf with Mamá Elena on several occasions, but to no avail, and he cares for Tita during her period of "lunacy" (Chapter VI "Junio") rather than commit her to an insane asylum. Tita meets John's kind and nurturing grandmother, Luz del amanecer, when she is at John's home, and this relationship *away from the ranch* begins her healing process. The doctor, however, is unsuccessful or ineffectual in some respects, and Tita's healing is not a direct response to his intervention. Though he is not Mexican, John Brown becomes the personification of what Birgitta Vance describes as an "aspect of the character of the Latin male: "his acute [*sic*] susceptibility to women" (111). This possibility works because John Brown, with his indigenous grandmother and constant contact with Mexico, is culturally influenced to the point of reflecting that susceptibility. When Pedro goes in search of John at the time of Rosaura's giving birth to Roberto, the two fail to arrive promptly, and Tita serves as midwife for Rosaura, who suffers from pre-eclampsia during the delivery (72–74).[9] Since Rosaura has suffered complications, and Mamá Elena believes that Rosaura needs constant attention, the doctor agrees to the suggestion of the matriarch that he return every day. Dr. Brown's true desire – which Mamá Elena fails to realize – is to see Tita, "la niña dientona que él recordaba [que] se había transformado en una bellísima mujer sin que él lo hubiera notado" [the toothy little girl that he remembered who had been transformed into a very beautiful woman without his having noticed it] (75).

Dr. Brown's challenges to Mamá Elena's decision about Tita's future are weak and sporadic. He attends the baptism of the child "sólo para ver si podía conversar con [Tita] a solas" [only to see whether he would be able to talk with Tita alone] (79). While he is there, he is told that Mamá Elena has prohibited Tita from getting married. He responds that such a prohibition is "una tontería" [a piece of foolishness] (80), but he does not pursue the challenge vigorously and marry Tita. He quietly contravenes Mamá Elena's insistent order that he institutionalize Tita, but does not oppose Mamá Elena openly (108). Though there are other factors at work (Tita's love for Pedro as chief among them), John's disinclination to oppose Mamá Elena makes him incapable of taking the necessary measures to obtain independence for Tita and himself. It is only much later that John Brown broaches the subject of marriage with Tita (108). His proposal comes after Tita's period of "lunacy" and her gradual restoration to health in Dr. Brown's house, away from Mamá Elena's demands and influence, and he is only successful in winning her hand after her mother's death, which he attends as her physician ("Noviembre").[10]

Besides Dr. Brown, Gertrudis, another visitor to the ranch, also consoles and advises Tita, and arrives at an important time, when Tita thinks she is pregnant (188–91). Thus, we see that the stability of the family, the modeling of male and female roles, the nurturing that traditionally proceeds from the maternal figure, is supported only by Nacha, the "mothering" figure on the ranch before her death, and, later, by Tita, when she is able to "mother" Roberto in secret. When Esperanza arrives, Tita's mothering is sufficiently guarded to avoid upsetting Rosaura, and Tita refuses to nurse Esperanza. With these exceptions, mothering *arrives* on the ranch as an external agency, which is to say that it comes from those with no permanence – and little or no influence – on the ranch: the Priest, Dr. Brown, and the spirits of Nacha and Luz del amanecer, and the runaway daughter, Gertrudis. Significant conflicts are amplified and extended because of the collisions between role-reversed characters, because of the confusion resulting from role-reversals, and because Mamá Elena cannot fulfill the role of mother by offering nurturing and unconditional love to her family. Only Tita and Nacha carry out that role as residents on the ranch, and they do so from positions of weakness.

Tita and Nacha are the chief victims of Mamá Elena's tradition of absolute power: Nacha was prevented from marrying her true love by Mamá Elena's mamá, and Tita is so prevented by Mamá Elena. Thus the principal struggle in the novel deals with the theme of independence from the mandates of Mamá Elena. Joan Cammarata notes, "En esta novela fémino-céntrica donde la mujer no es sólo un pretexto sino el texto mismo, la mujer tiene la opción de desarrollar su potencial completo y sus propias habilidades" [In this female-centered novel where the woman is not only a pretext, but the text itself, the woman has the choice of developing her full potential and her own abilities] (96). I would argue, however, that as long as Mamá Elena controls their lives, no woman – or man – has any option of developing potential or abilities, as my observations here confirm. In the central conflict, Mamá Elena forbids Tita's engagement to Pedro, and Mamá Elena instead proposes the arranged marriage between Pedro and Rosaura (12–13).[11]

While Tita and Gertrudis may fight for their autonomy from Mamá Elena, the men do not fight. Rather, they accept almost with resignation what Mamá Elena and other women say and want. The only occurrence of a man's fighting physically or psychologically on the ranch is when a gang of roving bandits – "un grupo de bandoleros" – comes to pillage the farm: "A Chencha la violaron y Mamá Elena, al tratar de defender su honor, recibió un fuerte golpe en la espalda y éste le provocó una paraplegia que la paralizó de la cintura para abajo" [They raped Chencha and Mamá Elena got a fierce blow to the back in trying to defend Chencha's honor, which caused her to be paralyzed from the waist down] (130). This typically brutal male violence against women during a period of legal and moral chaos is realistically drawn from the pages of the disordered Revolution. Even paralyzed, however, Mamá Elena continues to terrorize Tita, Chencha, and John Brown until she dies.

The male characters suffer enormously from this feminist cross-gendering, but some manage to take advantage of it as well. In spite of the fact that Dr. Brown does not follow Mamá Elena's orders to carry the disobedient and insane Tita to the sanatorium, it is not his masculine defense of Tita or Dr. Brown's knowledge of medical science that draws Tita from her stupor. It is, instead, Dr. Brown's feminine heritage in the forms of knowledge passed down from his grandmother and his maternal qualities that presage Tita's recovery; moreover, her full recovery occurs only when she tastes Chencha's ox-tail soup, and its flavor and aroma place Tita again in the nurturing presence of Nacha.

A part of John's knowledge comes from one of the indigenous characters in the novel, his grandmother, Luz del amanecer: he honors "los conocimientos que su abuela le había dado en sus inicios" [the knowledge that his grandmother had given him in his early life] (114). John's daily transfiguration inside the lab into what Tita recognizes as the "difunta abuela" [dead grandmother] (111)[12] eventually brings John to the point of playing a game with Tita that he and his grandmother used to play – writing invisible words on the wall with phosphorous and reading what is written at night when the phosphorous glows in the dark. Tita's writing on the wall marks her "primer paso hacia la libertad" [first step toward freedom] (119). John's grandmother's affectionate teaching and nurturing provide him a true understanding of medicine and continue to inspire him even after his studies at medical school: "Desde que mi abuela murió he tratado de demostrar científicamente esta teoría [de la abuela]. Tal vez algún día lo logre" [Since my grandmother died, I have tried to prove her theory scientifically. Maybe some day I will be able to do it] (118).[13]

Although Tita is engaged to marry Dr. Brown for some time, she is never strongly passionate in her desire for him. In fact, "esperaba que su alma por tanto tiempo enmohecida lograra poco a poco encenderse con la cercanía de este hombre" [she hoped that her soul, which had been damp for so long, would little by little be able to rekindle its fire because of her closeness to this man] (129). Dr. Brown, on the other hand, and in spite of being "plenamente convencido de que él se casaría con Tita con o sin la autorización" [fully convinced that he would marry Tita with or without the consent] (133) of Mamá Elena, never presses the matter, but allows Tita to control the destiny of them both. As an answer to the confession of Tita of her sexual relations with Pedro and feelings for him, Dr. Brown simply responds that she will have to decide whether he is the man she wants to marry or not: "[Q]uiero que pienses muy bien si ese hombre soy yo o no. Si tu respuesta es afirmativa, celebraremos la boda dentro de unos días. Si no, yo seré el primero en felicitar a Pedro y pedirle que te dé el lugar" [I want you to think very carefully about whether I am that man or not. If your answer is "yes," we will celebrate the wedding within a few days. If it's "no," I will be the first to congratulate Pedro and ask that he give you your place] (224). Tita decides to call the marriage off, and she and Pedro carry on an illicit affair for some twenty-plus years (237).

While Pedro, on the other hand, is able to express his "manliness" in his sexual desire for Tita (159, *etc.*) and in drinking and singing (200–201) in a celebratory way with Gertrudis's troops, even he is very much subject to the whims and dictates of the females. Upon Pedro's agreeing to Mamá Elena's proposal to marry Rosaura when he has already sworn his love to Tita, his father is confused: "Quedamos en ridículo aceptando la boda con Rosaura" [We'll look ridiculous accepting this proposal to marry Rosaura] (14). Pedro's answer, as the reader hears through the feminine voice of Nacha, is that he has taken the only way open to him to be close to Tita if he cannot marry her (14).[14]

This logic proves faulty as Pedro is incapable initially of taking advantage of Tita's willingness to give herself to him. When he could have run away with Tita, following Gertrudis's example, he chooses instead to flee by himself from Mamá Elena's scream: "Si Pedro le hubiera pedido a Tita huir con él, ella no lo hubiera pensado ni tantito, pero no lo hizo" [If Pedro had asked Tita to run away with him, she would not have hesitated for a moment, but he didn't ask] (55). On another occasion, he rushes out of the kitchen when Chencha enters instead of caressing "los senos que Tita le ofrecía" [the breasts that Tita offered him] (68). Their eventual union only comes about because Pedro observes Tita taking a shower (154) and pursues her and virtually rapes her, taking her virginity. Pedro and Tita submit to a pact with Rosaura, in which he and Tita agree to "mantener oculto su amor" [keep their love hidden] (238).

This pact further demonstrates the general state of impotence on the part of Pedro, who cannot make a decision that runs contrary to the desires of a woman.[15] Pedro has a youthful passion for Tita and wants to marry her, but he quickly agrees to marry Rosaura when Mamá Elena denies him his wish and offers him Rosaura as an alternative. Having married Rosaura, he postpones consummating the marriage until she refuses to let him "rehusarse a realizar su labor de semental por más tiempo" [refuse to do his husbandly duty any longer] (39). Pedro is subject to Rosaura, incapacitated to carry out his own desires, and must perform according to her will, which is validated by religious and social demands. When Rosaura prepares their first dinner, Pedro comments, "No, para ser la primera vez no está tan mal" [No, for the first time, it's not so bad] (49); however, when Tita cooks, he declares, "¡Éste es un placer de los dioses!" [This is a treat of the gods!] (50). Mamá Elena immediately silences him.

Only a short time later, at the moment when Gertrudis flees, "[h]ubo un momento, un solo instante en que Pedro pudo haber cambiado el curso de la historia" [there was a moment, just an instant in which Pedro could have changed the course of history] (55) by running away from the ranch with the willing Tita. Instead, he loses his courage when Mamá Elena shouts at them, demanding to know what is happening: "[Pedro] montando rápidamente en la bicicleta se fue pedaleando su rabia" [Pedro quickly jumps on his bike and pedals away his anger] (58). Later he gives in when Tita demands that Pedro not "honor" her by naming his daughter for his true love: "Pedro había insistido en que la niña [su hija] llevara el mismo nombre de Tita, Josefita," [Pedro had insisted that the child would have the same name as Tita, Josefita] (146). He changes his mind and names her Esperanza, the name that Tita chooses.

In *Like Water for Chocolate*, Esquivel makes weakness a typical masculine trait, and strength is more typically associated with women characters. The aforementioned theories proposed by Alan Riding, Octavio Paz, and others regarding the role of women in Mexican society support that claim and validate the authentic impotence of men in the matriarchal society represented in the novel. As the men abandon their "traditional" roles of power and authority (by death, profession, or some compromising situation), the women assume those roles, cross-gendering and taking greater control over people and events. In the face-to-face encounters between men and women, the masculine character generally submits himself to the desires or demands of the woman.

The woman in *Like Water for Chocolate* is indeed the one who commands, and she assumes roles traditionally considered masculine. The reversal of performances and roles in *Like Water for Chocolate* exposes relationships between the sexes in a telling and compelling way. While this factor has been often ignored or dismissed by writers, critics, and social scientists, it has been convincingly argued by Paz, Riding, Berg, and others as a dynamic presence in Mexico's familial and social reality, and Laura Esquivel validates it in her fiction.

Notes

1   Quotes and citations from *Like Water for Chocolate* come from the Anchor-Doubleday edition (paper 1992), in which the narration opens on page three. Translations from the Spanish belong to the editor. See Naomi Lindstrom's essay on feminist criticism (1989).

This number of men may seem like an unbelievably high number to the casual reader of the novel; for that reason, I have taken the pains to name the various characters below. While some may argue with my placement of certain characters into the "minor," as opposed to "major" category, my intent here is not related as much to the character's importance to the novel as much as to the frequency of their appearance. Thus, among the female characters, in alphabetical order along with the page of their first appearance in the novel, are eight major characters: Chencha (8), Esperanza (3 as "Mamá"; 146), Gertrudis (6), Luz del amanecer (111), Mamá Elena (3), Nacha (3), Rosaura (6), and Tita (3); a dozen minor (singular) characters: the lover of the enemy spy (194), Caty, Dr. Brown's cook (108), Dr. Brown's dead wife (75), a beautiful black woman who is the mother of José Treviño, the son (138), the sister of Sergeant Treviño (195), Lupita (76), Sergeant Treviño's mother (195), Schoolmistress Jovita (71), Mary, Dr. Brown's great-grandmother (112), Mary, Dr. Brown's aunt (156), Paquita Lobo, the neighbor (15), and La Ronca, the prostitute (195); there are three collectively identified groups of minor female characters: generations of youngest daughters (10), the prostitutes (195), and the *soldaderas* (203). The male characters can be divided into groups of seven major characters: Dr. John Brown (71), Juan Alejandrez (50), Juan de la Garza, Tita's father (4), Nicolás (70), Father Ignacio (58), Pedro Muzquiz (8), and Roberto, the son of Pedro and Rosaura (65); twenty-nine minor (singular) characters: Dr. Brown's grandfather (111), Alex (108), Brandt (114), the wrangler (30), the driver who loses control of his wagon (36), the Chinese contraband merchant (31), an enemy spy (194), Miss Jovita's son (220), Gertrudis's son with Juan (181), the unknown murderer killed by Sergeant Treviño (139), Felipe (88), Guadalupe (88), Nacha's brother (11), Jesús Martínez (152), Jorge Lobos (241), José Treviño, Mamá Elena's lover (138), José Treviño,'s father (138), Mamá Elena's father, Manuel M. Ponce, song-writer (200), Nacha's sweetheart (34), Pancho Villa (69), don Pascual, Pedro Muzquiz's father (11), Peter, the great-grandfather of Dr. Brown (112), the mayor of Piedras Negras (89), Mamá Elena's cousin (52), ranch-hand Rosalío (88), an unnamed sargent (90), Sargento Treviño in Gertrudis's troop (194), the man who used to make animals out of elongated balloons (6), and a soldier who comes with his captain (90); and nine collectively identified groups of minor male characters: Juan de la Garza's companions in the cantina (139), two trustworthy workers (88), the Federal soldiers (53), the white men who paid Mamá Elena's cousin for his invention (53), townsmen (36), schoolmasters (72), boys of the town (35), boys who threw a rocket (36), and revolutionary soldiers (with various names) (53).

2   Citing the film in this regard, Helene Price (2005) takes issue with this perception of female equality or domination in transactions between the sexes in *Like Water for Chocolate* and asserts that Pedro controls Tita. She claims that "it is a man [John Brown] who has the final say in this female-dominated film" as he "recite[s] his grandmother's theory, with which the novel ends" (168). While these are ideas worth exploring, the novel, of course, ends with Tita's great-niece's narration of a prospective event – a birthday celebration – that is imbued with women's knowledge and genealogy. The theory of the matches is not mentioned explicitly in the final pages though Tita acts on its principles as she eats the matches.

3   Obviously, Tita is able to impose her will more openly only after the death of Mamá Elena, but still in a somewhat limited way under Rosaura. After their mother's death, Rosaura and Tita are at a stalemate: Rosaura owns the house, but Tita has Pedro, so they make a treaty. While it may not appear that Tita exerts her authority as forcefully as her mother had, Tita is able to impose her will on the education of Esperanza through "extracurricular" lessons during meal times. Tita's control of Pedro remains strong; Pedro decides to not remonstrate with Dr. Brown because "Tita no se lo perdonaría" [Tita would not forgive him] (233).

4   Riding, formerly Mexico City bureau chief for *The New York Times*, first published his book in English as *Distant Neighbors: A Portrait of the Mexicans* (1984). A 1989 paper edition by Vintage is more readily available.

5   Phyllis L. Baker's study of gender among Mexican immigrant women in Iowa cites several earlier social science studies published between 1996 and 2001 that speak to the continuing perception of the hierarchical structure of the Mexican family and adherence to gender roles (397–98). See Baker's conclusions on transgressing gender in real life at (405–406).

6   For the citation, see chapter two, "Máscaras mexicanas" ("Mexican Masks") in *El laberinto de la soledad* (Penguin ed. 1997).

7   I use the terms *Mater dolorosa* [suffering mother] and *Venus dolorosa* [Suffering Venus] as the Spanish novelist Vicente Blasco Ibáñez used them in his detailed study of the stereotypes of the Hispanic female in *Los enemigos de la mujer* (from *Obras completas* 1987). Since that writing, many critics have written on the topic, giving the "grieved mother" such names as the "ángel del hogar"[hearth angel, angel of the home] (Aldaraca); "la mujer virtuosa" [the virtuous woman] (Andreu); "the fruitful, lifegiving mother" (Boschetto); as "Venus," the character may be fruitfully

compared to the Spanish "La Celestina" and the historical-mythical version of "La Malinche," for which the reader may wish to refer to essays in this volume on Esquivel's *Malinche: A Novel.*

8 Perhaps it is also worth noting that while priests do take a vow of celibacy, they do so because of their "marriage" to Christ. Many, in fact, also wear wedding bands, thereby making a public show of the mystical union.

9 Indigenous and Mexican midwives are prepared to intervene in medical emergencies, as we see in Nacha's advice to Tita during the delivery, so Tita's female role remains arguably intact although she has done "the doctor's job" in saving Rosaura. See also the essay in this volume by Debra Andrist.

10 It should also be noted that by this time Mamá Elena has disinherited Tita; "Mamá Elena no le perdonaría jamás a Tita que, loca o no loca, la hubiera culpado de la muerte de su nieto. Y al igual que con Gertrudis tenía vetado inclusive el que se pronunciara su nombre" [Mamá Elena would never forgive Tita, who, crazy or not, had blamed her for the death of her grandson. And as she had done with Gertrudis, Elena erased Tita from the family, forbidding that Tita's name be mentioned] (125). Tita, of course, never marries John, though she is briefly engaged to him. At her death, Elena deeds the ranch to Rosaura (215).

11 Interestingly, Mamá Elena's mother, another strong woman, "se había encargado de ahuyentar" [had taken it upon herself to run off] Nacha's sweetheart (35).

12 Dr. Brown does not literally transfigure into his grandmother, Luz del amanecer, but Tita "sees" her, so she is Tita's reality; Tita does not see a male figure. Thus, I would argue that it is, indeed, the feminine influence – or Dr. Brown's (unconscious) cross-gendering – that is the catalyst for beginning Tita's recuperation.

13 Although John's Kikapú grandmother is given the role of *médico de la familia* [family doctor] after her cure of her father-in-law (John's great-grandfather, Peter; see 112 *ff.*), that her role thus becomes "male" in that capacity is not clear. Her mother-in-law had nursed Peter before Luz del amanecer takes over, and afterward, Luz del amanecer retains her low social status as well as her indigenous appearance. When Tita sees her, she is "una mujer callada" [a silent woman] seated before the fire, "con su gran trenza cruzada sobre la cabeza" [with her great braid crossed over her head] (119), which surely reflects John's image of his grandmother.

14 Thus, not only is Pedro subject to feminine control, but the reader's version is subjected to the feminine narrative filter several times over: the conversation between Pedro and his father is transmitted from Nacha to Tita and from Tita, perhaps, to Esperanza, and then to the narrator (Esperanza's daughter), who passes the story to the reader.

15 The one exception would be the continuation of the illicit relationship with Tita and their refusal to allow Rosaura to prohibit Esperanza's marriage. However, even then Pedro has the express agreement and cooperation of Tita, who controls the kitchen (food, remedies, *etc.*), to oppose Rosaura.

The Absence of God and the Presence of Ancestors in *Like Water for Chocolate*

STEPHEN BUTLER MURRAY

Laura Esquivel's *Like Water for Chocolate* has been a favorite novel for many, those who study literature and those who do not, and a frequent subject for cultural criticism. It is a tale that shatters standard types and genres, offering a seamless blend between the utterly commonplace events of life and those uproarious occurrences that one can only attribute to the influence of the supernatural.[1] With an appreciation for the sheer practicality of living, Esquivel's characters continue their daily tasks and dwell in their worldly concerns, at times affected by the unexpected entrances and influences of otherworldly sources, but the presence and activity of these spirits never succeeds in overwhelming them.

Given Esquivel's interweaving of the extraordinary and the banal, it is surprising that, aside from reviews in both academic and popular publications, this book has received little scholarly attention among theological circles or in religious studies.[2] I would hazard a guess for this lack of theological inquiry: the presence of religious institutions is obvious throughout the novel, but they are of little importance to the advancement of the story. The Church is, in effect, a mute presence throughout the book. Because Tita has been reared a Roman Catholic, she recalls or is involved in religious rituals such as weddings, baptisms, and funerals (34), and she reports the words of the family's priest about Gertrudis's disappearance (58), but the Church itself has no agency as it is represented within these pages. Although a number of characters pray to God in the course of the novel, God is never active in the narrative that unfolds. Perhaps only twice is there any expectation that the God to whom the characters pray will affect their lives in any immediate way. It is indeed difficult for theologians to discuss a book where God is absent; nevertheless, it is a matter of theological interest as well as a matter of literary criticism to understand how it is that the Church and God play a minor role in a work whose ostensible religious foundation is Catholic. It is also useful to understand what it is that replaces them and how these "replacement" elements work to develop the fictional milieu and to reflect an authentic cultural reality.

Vitally important to creating a narrative culture and forwarding the plot is the agency of the spirits who populate the pages of *Like Water for Chocolate*. The spirits are never random, nameless phantoms, but the very ancestors of those who live and breathe in the world of the novel: *Nacha, Mamá Elena, Luz del amanecer*. Each of them enters the narrative reality as a spirit and behaves according to her nature in life, intervening and interfering in the lives of the living, offering succor or harm. What's more, these ancestral spirits influence the physical world, as might a poltergeist, but they interact dialogically with the living characters of the book. Thus, the ancestors are truly present, not as mere shades, but as intercessors between the wisdom of the spirit world and the chaos of the physical world and are active agents for good and evil within the narrative.

I assert that this spiritual "presence" and "agency" is what Esquivel offers those who read her book with theological eyes: an examination of a religious family that lives through the absence of God and with the presence of ancestors. *Like Water for Chocolate* is a story worthy of examination by those with religious concerns, whether literary or real-world, for the reason that Esquivel provides an insight into the way that many people live in this world: as practicing Christians who are, nonetheless, influenced deeply by the religious themes that were alive for their ancestors.[3] These religious foundations informed native cultures and worldviews before the introduction of Christianity into their communities by missionaries. As such, these ancestral principles and practices color contemporary Christian faith and observance around the world, maintaining vitality and praxis while rooted syncretically in a location's dominant contemporary religion, which for *Like Water for Chocolate* is Mexico and Roman Catholicism.[4]

This essay first explores the novel's presentation of the absence of God despite the signs of Roman Catholic institutions and practices in the narrative. Second, it examines the presence of ancestors in the novel, and how this respect, love, and fear of one's ancestors is appropriate to the cultural legacy to which these characters organically belong. Finally, this essay demonstrates the means by which the integration of these two themes shapes and determines narrative and character in *Like Water for Chocolate*.

The Absence of God

Esquivel's novel provides a fascinating contrast between religious practice and native custom. On the one hand, the text contains a significant number of references to God and the Church. With the events of Rosaura's wedding (Chapter 2, "February"), Roberto's christening (Chapter 4, "April"), and Alex and Esperanza's wedding (Chapter 12, "December"), for example, the narrative asserts the devout, orthodox nature of religious practice in Tita's family and among their friends and neighbors. On two other occasions, prompted by delight and terror, respectively, Gertrudis and Chencha sincerely ask for Divine intervention, and once, Pedro repeats a standard prayer. (I describe these prayers in detail below.) The images and dialogues of these scenes – the weddings and baptism and the offerings of prayer – suggest that it is important that the reader see the characters as religiously observant women, conscious of the Christian teachings, rituals, and signs that ostensibly inform Mexican culture and their lives.

It is useful to note that Esquivel's narrative places greater weight on the Church as part of the *social* fabric of the community – as an excuse for a party and special food – than on its dogma and prescribed observances. Furthermore, the characters' thoughts and actions are seldom shown to be shaped or influenced by their faith, and characters do not find theological matters to impact their moral reflections or their ways of living in the world. As examples, consider these: Mamá Elena has an affair during her marriage and produces a child, but her concern over this is social; her husband dies when he learns of it, from shame and surprise, we are led to believe; the community accepts these circumstances and socializes with the family on every special occasion; Mamá Elena forbids Tita to marry and hands off Tita's sweetheart to her older sister, both apparently socially acceptable actions; Mamá Elena beats Tita cruelly after Rosaura's wedding and later breaks Tita's nose with a blow from a kitchen spoon; Gertrudis works in a brothel without experiencing doubt or remorse on moral grounds; Mamá Elena angrily disinherits Gertrudis for social reasons; Pedro marries a woman whom he does not love to be near his true love; Tita and Pedro live as a married couple on the ranch with his wife and child; and the local priest has some unspecified business around a brothel on the border. These characters live their lives according to measures and guides that exist apart from Catholic teaching, which plays not even a superficial or hypocritical role in their speech or thinking.

Early in *Like Water for Chocolate*, Tita supplies the first reference to the Church in a defining moment for her character and the novel. While baking a cake for the wedding of her beloved Pedro and her sister

Rosaura, Tita is stricken emotionally by the sugar intended for the frosting and constructs the most intensive and detailed image of the Church in the novel:

> The whiteness of the granulated sugar frightened her. She felt power-less against it, feeling that at any moment the white color might seize her mind, dragging along those snow-white images from her childhood, May-time images of being taken all in white, to offer white flowers to the Virgin. She entered the church in a row of girls all dressed in white and approached the altar, which was covered with white candles and flowers, illuminated by a heavenly white light streaming through the stained-glass window of the white church. Never had she entered that church, not once, without dreaming of the day she would enter it on the arm of a man. (54)

Tita's reflection on the Church, in which she connects its predilection for "purity" with the guise of "whiteness," indicates a fundamental lack of interest in its ecclesiastical role as a house of worship, whereby her progress through the rites of passage toward adulthood would be blessed and oriented by the Church. Instead, the Church's rituals have misled her with what she now views as false milestones and empty promises.

Tita's focus, as she stirs her sister's enormous wedding cake, is upon her dreams of her own marriage and the sensory images by which the physical structure of the church – the building itself – would have been instrumental to her future. Before the betrothal between Rosaura and Pedro, members of the congregation had observed Tita and Pedro pass a perfumed love letter between them during High Mass (37). For Tita, the Church has been the place where she was able to foster a romantic rela-tionship with her beloved Pedro. She had constructed the basis of the future she envisioned as her own wedding in the church. In her time of need, the Church's rules and teachings provide no support or consola-tion to Tita by which she can resist her mother's prohibitions or graciously accept her fate, or avoid Pedro's amorous advances, or relin-quish him to her sister. The white things of the Church merely haunt her vision and taunt her with her spoiled expectations, blinding her to color.

For the remainder of the book, comments about the Church relate only to ceremonies of rearing children in the Catholic faith. When Gertrudis is discovered to be working in a brothel, Mamá Elena effec-tively "excommunicates" Gertrudis from the family by burning her baptismal certificate (58–59). Contradicting her mother's edict, Tita selects clothing and mementos for her sister and places them into a travel bag, but more than clothing, Tita tries to pack Gertrudis's childhood memories (70). The first aspect of Gertrudis's past that Tita places into the valise is "the day the three of them made their First Communion." The physical religious items associated with the day, icons and symbols of the ritual, can be placed into the suitcase: the veil, the prayer book, and the photo taken outside the church; however, what unnerves Tita is that she cannot pack what is for her the more significant aspect of the day: the sensory delight of "the taste of the *tamales* and *atole* Nacha had made, which they had eaten afterward with their friends and families" (70 italics added). What is significant about the day of Tita's first celebration of the Eucharist is *not* that she has been moved spiritually by ingesting the body and blood of Christ in communion or by becoming a formal member of the Church, but the sensory pleasure she experienced in eating Nacha's food in community with family and friends.

Later, when Rosaura's first child, Roberto, is baptized, the narrative focus is upon Tita's attachment to Roberto and on her joy and pride in acting as his "mother" – more than as his aunt – since Rosaura, still ill from the pregnancy and birth, can take part in no more than the church service. The religious significance of the baptism has no role in the narrative, and associating the negative character of Rosaura solely with the Church ceremony casts a negative light on that aspect of the day.

With Rosaura having taken to her bed upon returning home from church, Tita acts as hostess at the post-baptism banquet and carries the baby among the guests, showing him off, as people do with their infants (78). For Tita, this is the first party that she has enjoyed in her sixteen or so years of life, and this is because she is holding Roberto. Her brief period of euphoria transfers to the guests in her food, and they are happy in the midst of the violence and deprivation of the Revolution. No religious importance accrues to the day other than the extra-textual observance that provides the impetus for the events of the banquet. The role of the parish priest, Father Ignacio, in this chapter of Roberto's baptism, is limited to Father Ignacio's offering timid – and superfluous – advice to Mamá Elena when Mamá Elena determines to separate Tita and Pedro by sending Pedro, Rosaura, and Roberto to San Antonio (80).

Father Ignacio, indeed, receives sparse and equivocal treatment in the narrative. The first time that he is mentioned (58), it is to report Gertrudis's fate after she has supposedly been carried off by one of Pancho Villa's men. Father Ignacio announces that Gertrudis is working in a brothel on the border, but his revelation reveals more than Gertrudis's sin. Esquivel makes a suggestive observation regarding the priest's discovery: "and who knew how he found out about it" (58). The narration suggests that perhaps Father Ignacio found out about Gertrudis during one of his own visits to the whorehouse. In this compressed glimpse of his nature and habits, Father Ignacio is presented as – possibly

– relaxing the observance of his vows and failing to uphold his role as a model to the religious community. As with Father Ignacio's implied desire, the erotic and sensual appetites of Esquivel's other characters are shown to win out over dictates of the Church.

In another kind of reversal of the sensual and the religious in *Like Water for Chocolate*, Esquivel creates household "rituals," which must be rigorously observed under Mamá Elena's vigilance. Most of these involve food preparation and preservation (discussed in detail in Andrist's essay in this volume), but Esquivel's narration of Tita's bathing of Mamá Elena, brushing her hair, and dressing her uses discourse that sets the homely procedure into a higher, quasi-religious context. The procedures must be carried out incrementally with careful timing; Tita must use approved procedures and ingredients; and the ritual takes place only in a specific space (93 *ff.*). Tita is the only member of the family permitted to see her mother's naked body or to perform these rituals of preparation and cleansing. Her role is described as a "mission," and Mamá Elena's *toilette*, as a "ceremony" and a "liturgy" (94).

In these sequences, Esquivel presents mundane, secular activity as being invested with ritualistic detail and as having almost religious significance within the household. When Tita "falls short" in her preparations or movements, Mamá Elena is quick to scold her into an improved performance (94–95). In the case of the highly circumscribed bathing ritual, it is as if Mamá Elena's "cleanliness," achieved with the sensual components of warmth, touching, and fragrance, really were "next to godliness" – or perhaps a substitute for it.

Further distancing the characters from orthodox religious experience, the narrative generally invests their prayers with inefficacy or irony. The suggested irony of the rote prayer Pedro recites before his first sexual encounter with Rosaura lies in its incongruousness in the context of the narrative (40). Its stilted, dispassionate piety is comic in an atmosphere where religious observance is secondary to sensual experience, and Pedro's nervous dread at the thought of making love to Rosaura undercuts his profession of aloofness to supposed pleasure in sex. When Pedro can delay his conjugal duties to Rosaura no longer, he kneels by the bed and prays, "Lord, this is not lust or lewdness but to make a child to serve you" (40).[5]

Roberto, the son conceived from this union, does not live to serve God, as the prayer hopes he will, but his brief life brings Tita her first joy since Rosaura and Pedro were married, and it brings Pedro and Tita closer together. At Roberto's christening, Mamá Elena's attention falls on Tita and Pedro's attraction to each other, and Roberto dies when Mamá Elena sends Rosaura and her family away, out of reach of the milk and care that has kept him alive. He falls into the inept hands and dry breasts of his mother, and he dies as a result. Mamá Elena effectively sacrifices the child in her effort to quell the rising passion between Tita and Pedro. The intent of Pedro's prayer, that a child be created to serve God, is undermined, in a sense, by Mamá Elena's efforts to control the sensuality in her household.

In another instance of prayer, Gertrudis makes a spontaneous and informal prayer of gratitude, asking that Tita be granted many more years in which to prepare the family recipes, as neither she nor Rosaura knows how to make them (179). Gertrudis fears that the recipes will one day die along with her sister. Her prayer is answered in a miraculous – or magical – event. Tita dies, but the recipes do indeed survive and are carried on in the family, having been passed along to the narrator of the story, Tita's great-niece, by the miraculous cookbook-journal and Esperanza, the narrator's mother. Tita's cookbook-journal is the only material item to survive the apocalyptic conflagration that closes the novel, and it is her legacy to the great-niece who narrates her story *and* her recipes (246). Despite Gertrudis's prayer for her sister's longevity, Tita lives to be only thirty-nine years old and dies by following a recipe and a principle that she has recorded in her cookbook-journal.

Perhaps the sincerest intentional prayer in the novel occurs when Chencha believes that she is seeing the spirit of Mamá Elena "walk" on the ranch. She falls to her knees and prays to the Virgin to take Mamá Elena's soul and stop it from wandering in "the shades in purgatory" (159). The irony is that otherworldly lights and fireworks that the servant Chencha takes for Mamá Elena's spirit are signs of Tita and Pedro's first sexual encounter in the room where Mamá Elena formerly had Tita serve her in the bath.

The weight assigned in the narrative in favor of the sensual over the sacred, the lack of sincerity and efficacy associated with prayers to God, and the irony these prayers imply within their narrative contexts tends to confirm that both God and the Church are distant and ineffectual entities in the narrative world of *Like Water for Chocolate*. Despite the ostensible Catholic beliefs of the characters, neither God, nor angels, nor even Mexico's patron saint, the Virgin of Guadalupe, possesses agency in the narrative. Aside from lifeless institutions and virtually meaningless Church rituals, God and the saints are absent.

The Presence of Ancestors

While the narrative sets God and the Church aside, ancestors are forces of vital importance to the very nature of the narrative. Three ancestral spirits have a high degree of involvement and agency in the story: Mamá

Elena, Nacha, and John Brown's grandmother, Luz del amanecer. These are not mere specters, but intercessory agents, enabling events among the living, and moving freely around their spaces in the narrative. Luz del amanecer appears in John Brown's laboratory, which had been her own room across the patio from the house (110–11). The spirits of Nacha and Mamá Elena roam the De la Garza ranch house, appearing in the kitchen, in the parlor, and in the larder, as well in as the bedrooms.[6] It is significant that these spiritual beings are more than featureless ciphers from the Beyond, and that each has a name and identity. The mortal-life tendencies assigned to these spirits may be exaggerated, but each behaves consistently with her character in mortal life. As such, each ancestor performs a vital intermediary role for Tita and helps to drive the action of the narrative to its climax.

After Tita's nervous breakdown, Dr. John Brown takes her into his home rather than commit her to an asylum, as Mamá Elena has cruelly demanded that he do. While Tita is with Dr. Brown, he has difficulty connecting with her since she refuses to talk. The turning point occurs one day when Tita investigates an interesting smell that suggests to her that someone is cooking, and Tita encounters Luz del amanecer:

> She strode across the patio and opened the door; there she met a pleasant woman around eighty years old. She looked a lot like Nacha. A thick braid was wound around her head, and she was wiping the sweat from her brow with her apron. Her features were plainly Indian. She was making tea in an earthenware pan.
>
> She looked up and smiled kindly, inviting Tita to sit down next to her. Tita did so. The woman immediately offered her a cup of the delicious tea.
>
> Tita sipped it slowly, drawing maximum pleasure from the aroma of the herbs, familiar and mysterious. How welcome its warmth and flavor! She stayed with the woman for a little while. The woman didn't speak either, but it wasn't necessary. From the first, they had established a communication that went far beyond words.
>
> From then on, Tita had visited her there every day. But gradually, Dr. Brown began to appear instead of the woman. The first time this happened it had surprised her – she wasn't expecting to see him there, nor the changes he had made in the room's furnishings. (110–11)

Luz del amanecer is the intermediary through whom Tita begins to reconnect with the world around her from her "insane" state, and she is the means by which Tita finds a true friend in John Brown.

Luz del amanecer meets Tita's wounded, confused silence with a welcoming, reassuring silence of her own, and she draws Tita back into relatedness with her surroundings and people. In time, Tita comes to understand that the woman who keeps her company is none other than Luz del amanecer, John's deceased Kikapú grandmother. In death as in life, Luz del amanecer is a healer. Her quiet presence provides Tita the first bridge to her recovery. Just as Luz del amanecer was the source for John's interest in the Native medicine that augments his traditional Western medical practice (117), she acts as an extension of his healing efforts with regard to Tita's condition. Luz del amanecer's healing presence gradually merges, in Tita's perception, with John's, and prepares Tita for her full recovery when Chencha arrives bearing ox-tail soup, transporting Tita back into the fullness that Nacha's presence had given her: "With the first sip, Nacha appeared there at her side, stroking her hair as she ate, [. . .] kissing her forehead over and over" (124). This epiphany provides Tita's restoration to sanity and her reconnection to tears, laughter, voice, and activity.

The spirit of Mamá Elena is likewise the very essence of who she was in life, a presence best described by her talent for cutting watermelons, a keen metaphor for her way of interacting with others: "Unquestionably, when it came to dividing, dismantling, dismembering, desolating, detaching, dispossessing, destroying, or dominating, Mamá Elena was a pro" (97). In her tireless quest to squelch the vivacity of all around her, the spirit of Mamá Elena, in afterlife as in life, sometimes miscalculates and helps to bring about the very events she most wants to prevent. The prime example of this misfiring is her first spiritual manifestation, which so amazes and distracts Rosaura and Chencha that Tita and Pedro are able to make love for the first time undisturbed and undetected (158–59). Mamá Elena's act of coming back into the world provides Tita and Pedro their unchecked opportunity to become lovers, the outcome that Mamá Elena has striven most fervently to thwart.

Having the opposite force and effect of the spirit of Luz del amanecer, Mamá Elena's spirit is aggressively intrusive and interferingly obvious, intentionally destructive in her intercourse with the living. Her first manifestation, her coming into being as a spirit in the world, induces fear in all those conscious of her unnatural presence. Her second appearance is violent:

> [A] strong gust of wind banged the kitchen door wide open, causing an icy blast to invade the room. The napkin flew into the air and an icy shiver ran down Tita's spine. She turned around and was stunned to find herself face to face with Mamá Elena, who was giving her a fierce look. (172–73)

During this second appearance, Mamá Elena indicts Tita for her affair with Pedro, cursing Tita and her supposed unborn child. In spite of her fearsome presence, Mamá Elena flees when Chencha enters the kitchen. Maybe the spirit flees because Chencha is not "family," and the ancestral spirit of Mamá Elena would have no power over her. In any case, in this instance it would seem as though Mamá Elena's spirit is only willing to confront Tita.

Mamá Elena's third appearance is less violent, but equally threatening in tone. As Tita and Pedro cross a hallway, Tita sees her mother beside the door to the dining room, "throwing her a furious look" (173). Tita is terrified, as is the dog Pulque, when Mamá Elena advances on Tita threateningly. Because of the presence of her mother's spirit, Tita is no longer able to live life comfortably. Instead, she lives as though at "any minute some awful punishment was going to descend on her from the great beyond, courtesy of Mamá Elena" (119). As Mamá Elena did in life, her spirit intimidates her daughter emotionally, robbing Tita of peace and autonomy and limiting Tita's ability to claim her own identity and agency in the world.

In her final manifestation, Mamá Elena finally oversteps the boundaries and exceeds Tita's patience. While Mamá Elena threatens that "blood [will] flow" in the house (199) if Tita does not stop her affair with Pedro, it becomes apparent that the limits of Mamá Elena's abuse toward Tita are merely emotional and that she cannot follow through with any physical manifestation of her curses and threats. Tita's real power comes to the fore when she confronts Mamá Elena with Elena's prior hypocrisy: an affair that produced her illegitimate daughter (Gertrudis). Abandoning any attachment to the mother who terrorized her in life and from beyond the grave, Tita literally "casts out" Mamá Elena's spirit when she shouts that she hates her mother and has always hated her (199). Departing the room in a ghostly rage, Mamá Elena's spirit finds sufficient momentum to overturn a suspended oil lamp onto a campfire near Pedro, engulfing him in flames (200). Although Mamá Elena's spirit is unable to confront Tita's honesty and strength, Pedro's weakness in his drunken stupor allows Mamá Elena one last strike. Again, Mamá Elena's intention to interfere results in an irony: Pedro, suffering the pain of his burns, publicly rejects Rosaura's comfort and begs Tita not to leave his side (201). Tita reassures him, in front of the household and visitors, that she will not. Mamá Elena's spirit never resurfaces.

The last and arguably the most important of the spirits whose presence affects the narrative is Nacha, the half-deaf cook who nurses Tita through her infancy and is her closest confidante and foster-mother. Nacha passes away early in the story, due in part to Tita's irresistible tears mixed into the *chabela* wedding cake for Rosaura and Pedro (41). Unlike Luz del amanecer or Mamá Elena, Nacha's presence takes no physically visible form that is observed by Tita, though the reader catches sight of her final appearance, which discussed below (243). Nacha effects changes and provides love and counsel in a more subtle way, in keeping with her character and following the manner of the servant she was in life.

The circumstances that lead to Nacha's first spiritual manifestation are also different from those of the other two spirits. When Tita is holding the bloody roses from Pedro, Nacha whispers a Nahua recipe into her ear, setting off the adventure of Gertrudis's flight from the ranch (49). When Rosaura has difficulty giving birth, Tita prays for a long time to Nacha to enlighten her, to provide help in the emergency (72–73). The only effective prayer in the novel, this one brings Nacha's help, which is so efficacious that the birth of Rosaura's son is instantaneous after the lengthy bout with pre-eclampsia. Following the birth, Nacha instructs Tita in cleaning and dressing the newborn. There is no flurry of other-worldly light or sound, simply the very real effect of Nacha's supernatural influence. Similarly, after Pedro has been seared by Mamá Elena's spirit, Tita is frantic to prevent scarring. Again, Nacha provides the remedy by helping Tita realize that the bark of the *tepezcohuite* tree will help heal Pedro's burnt flesh (202). Nacha, like the best of servants, offers succor quietly, without fanfare.

The pattern continues when Nacha's spirit appears for the final time following Alex and Esperanza's wedding. Tita and Pedro are alone on the ranch for the first time, and the two lovers enter the dark room where Mamá Elena used to bathe, only to find it "completely transformed":

> All the furniture had disappeared. There was just the brass bed standing royally in the middle of the room. The silk sheets and bedspread were white, like the floral rug that covered the floor and the 250 candles that lit up the now inappropriately named dark room. Tita was moved at the thought of the work that Pedro had done to prepare the room in this way, and so was Pedro, thinking how clever she had been to arrange it all in secret. (243)

In fact, neither Tita nor Pedro had labored to create the romantic atmos-phere for this first and only time that they make love unrestrained by the presence of others in the house; they are not concerned that they will be discovered, and Rosaura has died. This is, in effect, their own wedding night. Nacha creates this special moment for them and unceremoniously departs once her task is done. After lighting the last candle, Nacha "raised her finger to her lips as if asking for silence, and faded away" (243). This is the last appearance of the surrogate mother who has watched over Tita since her first day and who brings her gracefully into her last moments. It is difficult to surmise whether Nacha's thoughtful gift is the final act of the ancestral spirits in the book, or whether Esquivel implies that Nacha is the one who saves the cookbook from the inferno of Tita's passion – or whether Tita's spirit does that.

Finding Synthesis

Esquivel's characters are affected in three ways by the motif of God's absence, as it is interwoven concurrently with the presence and agency of ancestral spirits. Through these three elements, Esquivel affirms certain ideas about God and ancestors within her narrative. First, the question raised by the presence of prayer and its efficacy within the book is intriguing. Four characters offer prayers: Pedro, Gertrudis, Tita, and Chencha. Each prays but once. Pedro and Gertrudis offer their prayers to God with rather ineffectual results, and Chencha's prayer to the Virgin is based on a false premise. On the other hand, Tita's prayer to Nacha's spirit brings to pass an immediate response of assistance leading to the healthy birth of Roberto.

The intentional acts of praying are relatively sparse in this book, so its occurrences, as extremities of action under some level of emotional stress at important narrative junctures, are telling. The prayers to God are ineffectual in some sense, whereas the prayer to one of the ancestral spirits, Nacha, has immediate and potent results. God is viewed as remote, and the Church and the priest are mere shadows of the Catholic presence in social and private space. What is dynamic and essential in private life is the characters' deep engagement with their ancestors, an association so palpable that the characters speak to the spirits, and the spirits' actions have palpable consequences in the characters' lives.

Second, it is important to discern the nature of the actions taken by the ancestral spirits. They show up purposefully and have a critical role in moving the narrative and in developing character and situation by means of actions that are consistent with their personalities and character in life. Luz del amanecer's constant, serene presence is what enables Tita's emergence from the psychological morass that neither her own forces nor medicinal means are able to resolve. Mamá Elena's actions disturb and disrupt the narrative in a purposeful way, permitting and then condemning the infidelities, and reminding the reader of the powerful parallel to Tita's situation in Mamá Elena's past. Nacha sympathetically aids Tita in her quest for happiness, whispering the recipe for quail in rose petal sauce, helping to deliver Rosaura's baby, instructing Tita's care for the baby following the birth, providing the ingredients for the balm that heals Pedro's burns, and facilitating the final romantic moment that Tita and Pedro share.

In these scenes, ancestors as spiritual intermediaries have the function that the Virgin or saints might otherwise claim, but the supernatural powers of the narrative's ancestral spirits are less than supreme. Even though ancestral spirits serve as agents who act upon the mortal characters in the novel, usurping the intercessory role, the nature of these spirits shifts the relative agency of the living human beings because ancestral spirits are unlike God and the saints in important respects. Ancestral spirits are not, as God is, utterly mysterious and untouchable, but intimately familiar to the living, and they are not invincible like God or the Saints, but vulnerable. We see that weakness in an evil spirit when Tita overcomes Mamá Elena as if Tita were the medieval Virgin ordering a devil back to hell with a threat. The narrative ethic validates kindness and love, real-world and spiritual, and shows the defeat of evil, even when the evil is otherworldly. Esquivel advances a vision of the individual and the community as final arbiters of their own agency and self-sufficiency, an embrace of Humanist ideals made possible because of the spirits' limited supernatural abilities and the fore-knowledge that the living possess of them. An intercessory Christian deity, on the other hand, would likely not allow such human determinism.

Third, the pervasive activity of the ancestral spirits yields a distinctive result in the sort of moral reflection exhibited by Esquivel's characters. A plethora of interpersonal discussions and internal dialogues regarding ethical behavior takes place, yet these conversations make no consideration of God or religious dogma. None of the characters engages in moral reflection that is defined by religious commitment and training. No one consults the parish priest for pastoral care, and in the Spanish edition, Mamá Elena rejects the priest's counsel absolutely (79).[7] Retribution and consequences are based on human judgments and meted out by Rosaura and the living Mamá Elena and, after her death, by Mamá Elena's spirit. Prayers are offered for assistance in a task, performance of a ritual, or protection, not for moral guidance in the midst of ambiguity. Consequences of behavior that might be considered morally questionable in the Catholic worldview are not the result of Divine intervention, and we see that forgiveness and closure in the narrative do not come from God.

Even in death, the ancestors' most substantive impact on the living is not based in their intercessory activities, but arises from a sense of mutual ethical obligation and affection. Tita and John Brown have such "obligations" to Nacha and Luz del amanecer, respectively, and the spirits continue to guide and sustain them spiritually. The living characters reference the spirits of the dead in the course of moral reflection, in performing mundane tasks, and in desperate moments when they need counsel or ideas. Thus, if we ask what determines ethical considerations and informs religious or spiritual practice in *Like Water for Chocolate*, humanistic and practical impulses are the clear answer, but it is honest to add that it is the internal emotional lives of the characters and their external challenges that provide the impetus.

In seeking deeper truths such as philosophies or principles behind those moral perspectives, one finds neither God nor the Church, but the characters' ties to their ancestors. Even when Tita chooses a course of action, her affection for the ancestral spirit – or her fear, in the case of Mamá Elena's spirit – often provides an external impetus. Even for the novel's narrator, the spirits of Tita and Esperanza are guiding and informing forces worthy of affection and honor: "My mother! . . . How I miss her seasoning, the smells of her kitchen, her chatting as she would prepare our meal [. . . .] Tita, my great-aunt, [. . .] will live on as long as there is someone who cooks her recipes."[8] The ending affirms that the spiritual legacy endures, informing the cultural inheritance and the artifact of the cookbook that bears them witness.

Notes

1 Quotations from *Like Water for Chocolate* in this essay come from the Doubleday English-language translation (1993).

2 On a religious topic that has no relationship to my present approach, Elizabeth Willingham (1998) explored the narrative uses of the biblical Apocalypse in the novel.

3 For the native peoples of Mexico, the living and the dead maintain active lines of communication. See H. B. Nicholson's article in the *Handbook of Middle American Indians*. In a study devoted to death practices in a variety of present-day and historical cultures, Peter Metcalf and Richard Huntington describe interesting parallels to the conception of death and ancestors portrayed in *Like Water for Chocolate*. Metcalf and Huntington point out that rather than understanding death as the absolute termination of life, some cultures hope for continuing aid and influence from their deceased ancestors (see especially, 70, 74, 100–101). See also Robert Carlsen and Martin Prechtel (1991). Patricia A. McAnany (1995) has made a fascinating study of the web of relationships that exist among ancestors, lineage, and land among the Maya. See Esquivel's handling of ancestors' spirits in *Swift as Desire*, treated in an essay in this volume by Willingham, and in *Malinche: A Novel*, discussed in this volume by Jeanne L. Gillespie and Ryan F. Long. See Coonrod Martínez's essay, here, for Esquivel's statements about her observance of Mayan traditions in the *Southwest Review* interview with Claudia Loewenstein (*SR* 598).

4 I use syncretism in the sense that David Carrasco (1990) defines it: "The complex process by which rituals, beliefs, and symbols from different religions are combined to create new meanings. Syncretism is most clearly represented in ritual performances that enable people to locate themselves within the new world of meaning" (169). Carrasco more recently dedi-

cated a paragraph to the inadequacy of syncretism in theory and teaching in his essay in Jacob K. Olupona's *Beyond Primitivism* (2004), where Carrasco describes syncretism as a "ubiquitous and lazy category" (133). Nevertheless, his emphasis there falls on the creative interweaving of concealed narrative themes in Christian ritual, specifically at Holy Week, in "a drama where the differences of these gods are activated and worked out" (137), a focus that comports with my use of "syncretism" here. See Carrasco's essay and that of Alfredo López Austin for an overview of religious tradition and history in Mesoamerica and a comparative approach to the subject, both in Olupona's edited collection.

5   See Elena Poniatowska's slightly different version of the prayer in her essay in this volume.

6   Ruth Bunzel (1952) notes, "The house is the everlasting home of one's own ancestors, where they are invoked as private persons, as family men and women maintaining order in their homes" (270).

7   This pagination is from Doubleday's 1993 Spanish-language edition. See the English edition version of this exchange (80). It is somewhat less definitive than the Spanish.

8   This passage appears on page 245 of the translation. The English given here is the editor's translation of the Spanish edition (Doubleday 1993).

Gendered Spaces, Gendered Knowledge: A Cultural Geography of Kitchenspace in Central Mexico

MARÍA ELISA CHRISTIE

Laura Esquivel's *Like Water for Chocolate* affirms my research on food preparation in central Mexico and my years of living in Xochimilco: food is the thread that weaves community together and women are the undisputed authorities in the kitchen.[1] Life in Xochimilco is *siempre de fiesta* [always celebrating] because every day of the year, at least one of its seventeen traditional *barrios* [outlying villages] is celebrating with fireworks, flowers, food, and drink. The term *fiesta* refers to social gatherings in which culinary feasts play a key role in bringing people together to celebrate a particular event, often a traditional ritual. In each case, a group of women work together for hours, days, and sometimes weeks to prepare elaborate dishes for guests. The reputation of the host family and neighborhood is literally in the hands of the *cocineras* [cooks] that volunteer their services for the event.

In Esquivel's text, the *fiestas* – including two weddings, a baptism, a welcome-home party (for Gertrudis), two "engagement dinners" (for Dr. John Brown and Tita), and a Christmas party – also bring people together and showcase the skills of the cook. A perspective from the kitchen in *Like Water for Chocolate* provides a unique window into Mexican culture and identity. In Esquivel's fictional place – Mamá Elena's ranch near the Texas border – people's sense of home is locked into the aromas and flavors of the *torrejas de natas* [cream fritters] or *caldo de colita de res* [oxtail soup] from childhood. With regional variations on the theme, things are not that different in Mexico today. This essay considers parallels and contrasts within that context between today's central Mexico and Tita's

105

world of Northern Mexico in *Like Water for Chocolate*. The gendered nature of "kitchenspace" and the gendered knowledge transmitted to younger generations within its realm are essential elements in the fictional and real world of Mexican society. The intersection of the two – gendered space and gendered knowledge – helps explain the powerful place of food preparation in central Mexico and Esquivel's text.

Kitchenspace, a place where food is prepared, whether indoors or outdoors, is a term I invented that encompasses activity associated with everyday routines as well as with ritual celebrations. The ordinary definitions and connotations of "kitchen" fail to incorporate the complexity and nature of the spaces in which I found women preparing food in Xochimilco and other Mexican communities. For me, coming from a Western European tradition, the word *cocina* or "kitchen" brings to mind an indoor space with four walls and a roof. Yet the food preparation sites I explored in central Mexico often had no walls at all, and if they did, the "kitchen" seemed to spill over into the outdoors or house-lot garden (plate 1). Food preparation for *fiestas* usually took place in the *cocina de humo* or *cocina de fiesta* [smoke or *fiesta* kitchen]. This space was always separate from the main structure and often fully out of doors (plate 2).

When Esmeralda, an informant in Tetecala, made a comment about not wanting to spend her life *"dentro de estas cuatro paredes"* [within these four walls] as she felt her family wanted her to do, I chuckled because the space in which she prepared food all day long had three walls and not four. While she – like Tita – felt trapped by the social expectations that restricted her movement and options, the physical structure of her kitchen did not match her mental image of a closed space. Clearly, the boundaries of kitchenspace are defined by social activity and gendered relationships rather than by physical structures. Kitchenspace is created – sometimes on a periodic basis – by the food preparation activity carried out by gendered subjects. In this sense, kitchenspace provides a framework for the exploration of what Judith Butler calls "the performance of gender" (1990) and is a world with its own specialized knowledge and particular perspectives.

Few things link humans to the earth as concretely as food or reflect cultural traditions as clearly as food preparation, yet kitchenspace and other gendered spaces are often ignored in academic circles, in part because of their inaccessibility to male researchers. The resulting lack of research obscures an understanding of cultural and physical spaces of importance to society as a whole. My project takes cuisine as an expression of cultural identity and cooking practices and everyday living as spaces where ordinary people express desires and tastes, and resist the powerful forces that rework the social environment.[2] In many communities in central Mexico, kitchenspace is so critical to social dynamics that

Plate 1 Doña Eustoquia, in her outdoor kitchen in Tetecala, gives shape to *memelas*, thick corn cakes, that will be cooked on the *comal* (griddle) and served with cheese and salsa over them.

Plate 2 María Teresa's large *cazuelas moleras* (clay pots) are used for making *mole*, in her "smoke kitchen" in Ocotepec, a community in central Mexico.

Plate 3 Ornamental plants in retired kitchen pots are a constant throughout central Mexico, denoting women's aesthetics in the house-lot garden. A woman brought this "wild" cactus from the hills into her kitchen, where she nurtures it like a member of the extended family for whom she cooks on a daily basis.

Plate 4 A gendered perspective from kitchenspace: surrounded by her colorful kitchenware, a woman looks out into her garden. She uses the cups on the back wall for serving coffee to her many guests at the wakes she has for "sending off" her dead, a necessary ritual in which many friends and family participate.

Plate 5 Esmeralda and her sister make sweet corn *tamales de elote* with raisins to celebrate the corn harvest.

Plate 6 Señora Marcela makes traditional *tlapiques* (fish tamales). Once daily fare, they are now only served on special occasions because of degradation of Xochimilco's waterways.

Plate 7 Hot chili peppers often lead to "spicy" conversations and jokes about sex among women as they cook and work in "kitchenspace."

Plate 8 A child plays with corn while the women of the *barrio* (neighborhood) work to prepare food for the extensive Niñopa celebrations in Xochimilco.

to ignore it is to miss an essential component of the construction of identity and meaning of life.

Certainly the construction of identity, culture, and setting in *Like Water for Chocolate* depends upon that social dynamic, its role in the kitchen, and the cook. Despite the fantastic tendency towards exaggeration that characterizes the women in *Like Water for Chocolate,* the text is more successful than much non-fiction at providing us with a taste of reality in the extraordinary and gendered world of traditional food preparation in Mexico. Like that of most women in my research, Tita's kitchenspace extends beyond the parameters of the indoor kitchen and includes the outdoor space behind the house. The text describes Tita's domain as a "gigantic world" through which she comes to know life and which stands in contrast to the world outside:

> No era fácil para una persona que conoció la vida a través de la cocina entender el mundo exterior. Ese gigantesco mundo que empezaba de la puerta de la cocina hacia el interior de la casa, porque el que colindaba con la puerta trasera de la cocina y que daba al patio, a la huerta, a la hortaliza, sí le pertenecía por completo, lo dominaba. (14–15)[3]

> [It wasn't easy for a person who knew life through the kitchen to understand the outside world. That gigantic world that began at the kitchen door towards the interior of the house, because the one that adjoined the back door of the kitchen and that led to the patio, the orchard, and the vegetable garden, that one belonged to her completely, she dominated it.]

Here, Esquivel defines Tita's territory as distinctly separate from the "exterior" or public world, though it does include the space outside the walls of the indoor kitchen. As in my research sites, many food preparation activities are carried out in the uncovered patio behind or at the center of the house. Kitchenspace is a "gigantic world" as Esquivel writes, but not one necessarily distinctly separate from the world outside, according to my observations. It is often impossible to draw a line marking where the "kitchen" ends and the "yard" or larger world begins – in *Like Water for Chocolate* and in the communities under study. In addition, the dichotomy between private and public space to which Esquivel alludes contrasts with the situation I have documented. There, the collective work structures and solidarity networks that bring women and their *comadres* [co-godmothers] together to prepare food for different types of celebrations blur the distinction between private and public.

In the field sites of my research, kitchenspace is at once the center of the household, and – in times of traditional celebrations – the center of community life. It is semi-public space that has little to do with the social isolation associated today with the suburban housewife or with the rural setting in Esquivel's novel. Because of the essential role women's kitchenspace practices play in establishing alliances and maintaining reciprocity networks, kitchenspace becomes a privileged site of social reproduction. Besides transmitting social customs, values, and relationships, kitchenspace keeps alive ways of doing and being to new generations, thus facilitating cultural reproduction as well.

Observing and Writing "Kitchenspace"

My research explores gendered spaces in Xochimilco, Ocotepec, and Tetecala that are associated with food gathering and preparation where women have unquestionable authority and responsibility. I investigated women's knowledge about their environment, their interactions with nature, gendered spaces in the landscape, and women's adaptation to changes in these spaces during their lifetimes. Finally, I asked what women's narratives about food tell us about their culture and identity. I also considered social, aesthetic, and symbolic aspects of food gathering and preparation. In this essay, I consider testimonies from several women of different generations and communities – Esmeralda in Tetecala, María Soledad and María Teresa in Ocotepec, and Marcela and Margarita in Xochimilco. Their testimonies suggest real-life parallels with Tita's fictional world.

My work draws on literature from the social sciences concerning social reproduction and feminist critiques of Western science that argue for the validity of knowledge gained from the lived experience.[4] The mind/body, nature/culture, and other Cartesian dichotomies that serve as the basis for the dominant methodologies in the production of Western knowledge exclude the majority of women's contributions throughout history and those kinds of knowledge that do not fit into a positivist approach to reality.[5]

I incorporate the concept of embodiment as the existential ground of culture and self, and, as Thomas J. Csordas writes (1994), "to insert an added dimension of materiality to our notions of culture and history" (4). Paying attention to women's hands at work from the perspective of embodiment – rather than the body – allows me to approach people as subjects transforming their environment rather than as objects of investigation or victims of change. Incorporating embodiment also facilitates my experiential approach to individuals dwelling or being in particular environments, including their sensory perceptions and emotions. My approach is grounded philosophically in the writing of Martin Heidegger

(1889–1976) in *Poetry, Language, Thought* (1971), and it is set into the disciplinary context in David Seamon and Robert Mugerauer's collection of essays on phenomenology in geographical studies (1985) and by Miles Richardson's work on the meaning of "place" (1982, 1984).

With its emphasis on gendered spaces and women's knowledge in relationship to natural resources and the environment, geography's feminist political ecology (FPE) provides a useful framework from which to approach gender, nature, and cultural identity in food preparation.[6] Calling for the "inclusion of a gender-based analysis of how spaces and places are used, valued and struggled over in specific cultures" with the goal of protecting women's source of income and livelihood, Dianne Rocheleau points out that men and women can have dramatically different relationships to particular resources. Feminist political ecology is the point of departure for this inquiry. The focus, however, is more the transmission of culture than the physical survival of either humans or the environment, though the three are tightly linked in the realm of food preparation.

Gendered Spaces and Perspectives

Like Esquivel in *Like Water for Chocolate*, I present gendered perspectives from kitchenspace in my work. While feminist in approach, subject, and spaces, my research is on many levels traditional, field-based, cultural geography that aims to understand how people live in specific and different places.

How is kitchenspace constituted as feminine? Kitchenspaces in Xochimilco, Ocotepec, and Tetecala – as in many other Mexican communities – are primarily inhabited by the women who cook in them anywhere from three to ten hours a day. Men come, wait to be served, eat, and leave. They speak little, rarely interrupt the woman of the kitchen, and leave their dishes on the table. Women's words – as well as men's relative silence – fill kitchenspace with gendered narratives; together with women's physical occupancy, their words mark it as gendered territory. Women's ornamental plants, decorative use of wall space, and the many concave receptacles used for food preparation and storage create an overwhelmingly feminine landscape (plate 3). Kitchenspace is not only constituted as feminine but also serves to reinforce parameters of the "feminine." A refuge to some, a jail to others, kitchenspace is a vitally important and clearly gendered social space (plate 4).

How do women feel about their kitchenspace? Independently of the cultural and social importance of food preparation in central Mexico, many women are resentful of their role in kitchenspace. Young women in particular often feel trapped by the roles imposed on them in the kitchen and the lack of opportunities outside the home. They may be eager to escape from the kitchen – and not just for the daily run to the market or the *tortillería* [tortilla factory]. In Tetecala, Esmeralda fantasized about escaping the tedious work in the kitchen and chafed under the strict limits her family imposed on her life (plate 5). Like Esmeralda – and Tita – Maria Soledad, an unmarried woman with no children of her own, was also in charge of cooking for her extended family and resented the hours in the kitchen. On the other hand, older women like Señora Marcela (my neighbor in Xochimilco) who work outside the home are often eager to retire and regain control of their households from their positions in the kitchen (plate 6).

Women's Work

One of the reasons for women to flee from the kitchen whenever possible is that work in the kitchen can be backbreaking. "La cocina es muy laboriosa!" [Kitchen work is hard work!] women in central Mexico often say. Traditional dishes like *mole, tamales,* or *chiles rellenos* are particularly tedious. In *Like Water for Chocolate,* the preparation of *chiles en nogada* is described as "un trabajo muy laborioso" [very hard work] and "un trabajo tan intenso" [a really difficult job] (210). These and other labor-intensive favorites require hours of preparation and frequently involve cooperation among several women, as when the women in *Like Water for Chocolate* sit around the kitchen table to make chorizo, *tortas de Navidad,* or some other family specialty.

In times of celebration, food preparation requires more prolonged physical effort than everyday cooking. For Pedro and Rosaura's wedding cake, Tita beats 170 eggs (31–33). In the final chapter of Esquivel's novel, we find Tita and Chencha preparing the *chiles en nogada* (209), mentioned above, for Alex and Esperanza's wedding. Despite some help, after cracking and cleaning one-thousand walnuts, Tita is physically exhausted: "[. . .] a Tita aún no le llegaba la hora del reposo. Su cuerpo le pedía a gritos, pero le faltaba terminar con la nogada antes de poder hacerlo" (234). [Tita's time to rest had not yet arrived. Her body screamed at her for a break, but she had to finish the walnut sauce before she could do so.]

While these quantities of food – a thousand walnuts and 170 eggs – in *Like Water for Chocolate* may seem surrealistic, they correspond in magnitude to what takes place in the communities I have studied. For example, February 2, *Día de la Candelaria,* is celebrated with food and *fiesta* throughout central Mexico and is referenced in *Like Water for Chocolate* (162). In Xochimilco, it is the largest celebration of the year, coinciding with the day of the *Niñopa* ("child of the place" in Nahuatl). Nothing brings more people together in Xochimilco than this most venerated and "miraculous" of Baby Jesus figures. A small wooden statue treated like a live child, the *Niñopa* hearkens to pre-Hispanic religious beliefs – notwithstanding the devout Catholicism of His followers. Breakfast for the *Niñopa* and his visitors (February 2, 2001) included seven large pots of hot, chocolate *atole* [a drink made of ground maiz] made from fresh-ground blue corn from the nearby *chinampas* [islands of land created for farming].[7] For the mid-day meal, the women prepared a dozen gigantic pots of rice to accompany the barbecued beef and side dishes. When I arrived early that morning, the three women who had begun preparing the *atole* before dawn were complaining of sore backs. Despite complaints about the taxing nature of kitchen work, most of the women I met derived a sense of satisfaction from helping prepare the food in honor of the local patron saint, as well as from feeding the family, perhaps especially so in dire economic circumstances. As in Tita's case, they took pleasure in bringing happiness to people at their tables.

Despite strict social and cultural parameters regulating women's activity in kitchenspace, the sensual and erotic nature of food and food preparation give it a subversive quality. Indeed, the *cocinera* [woman cook] is a magician or an alchemist of sorts (as Tita is), capable of transforming raw ingredients into exquisite aromas and flavors and, through these, affecting the physical and emotional state of those around her. This transformation is vividly illustrated on a mythic level in Esquivel's novel, when Tita's emotions – her grief, passion, sexual energy, bitterness, or joy – are expressed through her culinary creations and the emotional reactions they release in those around her. Cooking provides a vehicle whereby Tita penetrates beyond the kitchen's boundaries into strictly forbidden territories.

Within the women's "territory" of the kitchen, Rosaura seeks Tita's advice to help get Pedro's attention (159–60) and later confronts Tita concerning Pedro and Esperanza (193–96), and Tita and Gertrudis speak of sexual matters and their relationships as Tita cooks ("September" and "October"). As might be expected in the sensual realm of food, talk in real kitchenspace is often "spicy," full of details relating to bodies and desire. Working with women to prepare food before a *fiesta*, I was often surprised at the facility with which talk turned to sex and personal details that were not heard in mixed company (plate 7). The collective, gendered, semi-public space of food preparation seemed to invite hearty laughter and intimate conversation, as in those instances already

111

mentioned in *Like Water for Chocolate* and when Gertrudis, taking leave of the ranch, advises Tita on avoiding a future pregnancy (185).

One informant told me that without women cooking, community celebrations would be nothing more than drunken gatherings of men. Instead, special events bring men, women, and children together to share meals and merriment in collective bonding rituals ranging from praying for the deceased to agreeing on commitments towards the next barrio celebration. According to María Teresa, "Sin cocinera, no hay nada," [Without a cook, there is nothing]. Women and men alike agreed that good food brings family and community together and is key to the success of any wedding party or community *fiesta*. María Teresa explains the role of the cook, elaborating on the importance of the love she puts into her efforts:

> The meal is a point of gathering and union. [. . .] The cook is very important in all of this. Without the cook, there would be no meals, and the food would not be so well prepared. [. . .] Above all else, *la cocina* requires time and calm. Because you cannot do things in a hurry. Preparing meals takes time . . . a lot of time. It is like people should be in the kitchen with pleasure, all of the people in the kitchen. Because eating is supposed to be a pleasure. So if there is somebody that is cooking all upset, then that is why the food feels that. It should be something that one savors. And not that we all become angry. Otherwise, maybe the family would become disunited.

In Esquivel's novel, too, Tita's cooking brings her and Pedro closer than Mamá Elena might have wished. Food is at the center of human relationships, community life, and Tita's relationships with the significant people in her life – her longing and passion for Pedro, her happiness for Roberto, and her bitterness toward Mamá Elena.

La cocinera has social status and is subject to approval or criticism by society depending on the quality of her cooking. In *Like Water for Chocolate*, the narrator suggests a hierarchy of *cocineras* in her references to a *caldo que se respete* [respectable broth] (119) and *un platillo* that is among those *más prestigiados en las buenas mesas* [a dish . . . among the most prestigious on the best tables] (32). In the communities where I have done research, women are much more likely to receive recognition in celebrations that showcase their skills, than in the more private setting of everyday meals where their work and skills are often taken for granted.

Older women with knowledge of culinary traditions play a particularly important role. In *Like Water for Chocolate,* Tita's status as *cocinera* is Nacha's legacy. In Xochimilco, a great-grandmother of eighty-one with few responsibilities at home was grateful for the opportunity to contribute – and for the recognition and respect – when her neighbors summoned her to help with the cooking for a special celebration: "Aquí me quieren mucho; me llaman por venir a hacer el arroz," she said as she stirred the mole and kept watch over the bean tamales. [They love me a lot here; they call me to come make the rice.]

Some women I met avoided cooking for the community in fear of the criticism they would receive if their dishes did not meet expectations. My neighbor, Señora Marcela, has terrible memories about arriving early to a *fiesta* and being asked to make rice for over a hundred guests. She stayed away from *fiestas* after that, allowing her sister to represent the family at important events. Nonetheless, Señora Marcela's kitchen is a privileged place from which to experience family and neighborhood relationships. Without leaving the stove where she spends much of each day cooking for her extended family and networks, Señora Marcela participates in many social events outside her home through the preparation and exchange of special foods. To my great pleasure and satisfaction, I could taste and observe important family and community events from Señora Marcela's kitchen through the flow of food gifts.

Like Tita, who nurtured her niece and nephew with her food and attention from the kitchen, though on a larger scale, Señora Marcela also fed nieces and nephews who lived with her on a daily basis. When members of her household attend a fiesta without her – as she prefers to stay in her own kitchen – they bring her back a plate or basket of food. When there is a death in the neighborhood, she invariably receives some of the special meatless tamales prepared for the nine-day mourning ritual. In turn, she prepares and sends out dishes on request. Now and then, she hosts a special meal for a birthday or a rosary prayer session, or prepares a meal to feed the men who bring the fireworks to the neighborhood fiesta. Like Tita, her contributions to her family and greater community are often products of her work in the kitchen.

Gendered Knowledge

Kitchenspace is at once a cultural archive and a laboratory. In *Like Water for Chocolate*, Tita's cookbook-journal is a physical archive for the gendered knowledge and culture of the kitchenspace. It is a place where women nurture and educate children, transmitting recipes, organizational forms, food preferences, and a particular vision of life from one generation to the next. It also requires certain technical expertise and a practical knowledge of basic chemistry to transform elements of the natural landscape into edible dishes. The importance of using fresh ingredients and the knowledge of their proper use and storage required on the part of the cook – particularly when working with large quantities – are highlighted in *Like Water for Chocolate*. For instance, the cook must know how to keep eggs fresh (31), and how to raise, catch, and kill quail (54). Food conservation techniques such as burying chickens in ash, making sausage correctly, or conserving eggs as Tita does – or salting beef, in the case of my informants – extends the life of fresh ingredients.

As an aspect of knowledge and its correct application, several of my informants mocked women who were selfish or stingy with their recipes. A recipe alone is not enough to reproduce a coveted dish, they remarked: it requires a special touch as well. In a place with elaborate culinary traditions such as those of Mexico, the *cocinera* must also know when it is culturally appropriate to offer certain dishes, and what she should or should not serve with them. This knowledge is handed down from one female cook to another, though each must use her intelligence and creativity to adapt to constantly changing circumstances. Indeed, the *cocinera* is a repository of cultural information – recipes, home remedies, and the accompanying philosophies about life – and her body is the vehicle of transmission. With her knowledge and practice informing her choices and actions, the *cocinera* uses her hands and body to beat, grind, chop, and stir ingredients. In a real sense, one sees her putting heart and soul into her work, making a conscious effort to produce culturally acceptable and delectable dishes.

Ecology and Natural Rhythm

Kitchenspace in the research communities is also a place of heightened awareness of nature's rhythms and cycles – where society's relationship with the natural environment is central to everyday routines and seasonal celebrations. Not every household in my research sites has a pig, vegetables, or a fruit tree in the garden, but enough do that a sense of immediate connection with living food is part of the collective experience. While nature and society in Tita's world differ from those in the subject of my research – the fish and vegetables that form part of Xochimilco's food traditions are a product of its unique raised-bed agriculture and canals, for instance – the reader finds that kitchenspace links fictional nature and society as well. Through her work in the kitchen, Tita comes into direct contact with nature as she gathers fruit, eggs, and beans, and when she collects ingredients from the orchard, the poultry houses, the grainery, and the market.

In the real world, Señora Marcela's menus reflect what is in season, as well as the social events in the neighborhood. Rarely does someone slaughter a pig without sending her a basket of warm, crunchy pork-rinds.

Eating at her table, I knew when local vegetables such as the *huauzontles* or *romeritos* (traditional vegetables that are part of Xochimilco culinary traditions) were growing nearby, or when plums were ripe in her house-lot garden. When she makes *tlapiques*, tamales traditionally made with fish from local canals, her narratives of nostalgia for old times and stories of environmental degradation are inevitably part of the menu. Though her now-deceased parents and grandparents ate *tlapiques* practically on a daily basis, today *tlapiques* are only on the menu for special occasions (plate 6). Due to extensive water pollution that is one of the collective tragedies in Xochimilco, Señora Marcela must now purchase the fish at the local market, an expense she rarely can afford. Alterations in the environment – and the marketplace – push women to find ways of adapting ingredients and preparations to achieve some balance between the natural landscape and the kitchen.

With such ecological alterations and the ordinary change of season, the *cocinera* must know how to obtain what she needs in the kitchen, adapt a recipe when the ingredients of choice are not available, and combine things in such a way as to achieve the desired product and flavor. Just as Tita substitutes pheasant with quail (50), women throughout Mexico today substitute the native *guajolote* [turkey] with chicken. In fact, many ingredients introduced to the Americas after the Conquest are now integrated into the Mexican diet – such as the fresh cream and cheese that usually top corn-based *antojitos* or snacks – improving the flavor and nutritional value of traditional foods. Despite the weight of tradition, represented in the novel by Tita's fear of punishment by Mamá Elena – or her ghost – if she fails to follow a recipe to the letter (199), a cook constantly adapts to circumstances, walking the fine line between tradition and innovation.

Esmeralda includes ingenuity as a key characteristic of a *cocinera* that, together with patience and curiosity, is something she says a cook must draw upon to substitute missing ingredients: "Si no tienes lo necesario, tienes que ingeniártelas para reemplazarlo con algo que le de el mismo sabor," she says. [If you do not have what you need, you have to "engineer" things to replace some of the ingredients with something that will give it the same flavor.] Women's adaptive strategies are essential in kitchenspace, where the cook is always adjusting her menus and recipes, based on the availability of ingredients, cookware, and fuel – not to mention accommodation for changes in her life cycle and response to the demands of people around her.

The knowledge transmitted from one generation to another in kitchenspace is shared only with certain members in a given household or community. Many times only one of several sisters inherits the culinary tradition. In *Like Water for Chocolate*, both Gertrudis and Rosaura

115

prove their inadequacy in the kitchen. It is Tita, the youngest sister, that keeps family culinary traditions alive.

> Tita era el último eslabón de una cadena de cocineras que desde la época prehispánica se habían transmitido los secretos de la cocina de generación en generación y estaba considerada como la mejor exponente de este maravilloso arte, el arte culinario. (49)

> [Tita was the last link in a chain of cooks that since pre-Hispanic times had been transmitting to each other the secrets of the kitchen from generation to generation and was considered the best exhibitor of this marvelous art, the culinary art].

Tita inherits traditions primarily from Nacha, through hours of being nurtured by the stove at her side and later as her apprentice. Though Tita dies before the end of narrative, she leaves behind a cookbook to her niece, Esperanza, who keeps the culinary heritage alive.

Maternal Space

The fact that kitchenspace is a place where children play and learn helps explain its importance in transmission of culture – not only recipes – to new generations (plate 8). Both Tita and Dr. Brown grew up at the side of elderly, indigenous women who taught them about life as they played beside the stove. "Entre juegos me transmitió todos sus conocimientos" (111) [She transmitted all her knowledge to me in between games], Dr. Brown tells Tita. Just as Nacha molded Tita's tastes, children throughout Mexico are raised in kitchenspace, their tastes trained by the woman at the family hearth. In *Like Water for Chocolate*, Nacha and Luz del amanecer represent the indigenous element in Mexican heritage and identity that – like many foods and food preparation customs – survived the painful and complex process of *mestizaje* thanks in part to the work of indigenous women in kitchenspace.

Nacha is the indigenous "mother" for Tita, and in the novel – as in the research communities – kitchenspace is maternal space. Full of nourishing liquids, it is womblike in many ways. Mothering and kitchenspace are linked through the capacity to nurture life. Beginning with Tita's birth among tears and onions on the kitchen table, Esquivel develops the imagery of the kitchen as a source of continuing life and tradition. The kitchen is a metaphoric womb, and the *cocinera*, a nurturing mother or breast. In Esquivel's novel, it is not her biological mother but the indigenous cook, Nacha, who nurtures Tita. Tita too serves as a surrogate mother, caring for her sister's son when Rosaura proves unable to breast-feed him. At one point, Tita tries to pacify the screaming baby with her own virgin breast. When she satisfies little Roberto's hunger by lactating unexpectedly, the text compares her with the food goddess, Ceres. "Tita era en ese momento la misma Ceres personificada, la diosa de la alimentación en pleno" (75–76). [Tita was at that moment Ceres herself personified, fully transformed into the goddess of food.] Later, Tita nurtures Rosaura's second child with love, *tés*, and warm corn gruels in the kitchen (138).

Love, Embodiment, and Living Food

The idea that cooks must be happy persists in my research communities. *La cocinera* is expected to express love for her family through her food, no matter how tired or upset she might be. Tita tells her envious neighbor that love is the secret ingredient in her delicious mole (78). Mexican women often say that the secret to making satisfying food is the love the cook puts into her efforts. The cook must show reverence and respect for the food as well, and this aspect of kitchen lore appears in *Like Water for Chocolate*. When the beans refuse to cook, Tita guesses it is because she and Rosaura have argued in the kitchen, making the beans angry. Following Nacha's counsel, she sings to the beans so that they will soften in the broth (198–99).

While the idea of cooking with love is not unique to Mexico, its present form in these sites is grounded in Mesoamerican pre-Hispanic culture, which the reader can guess is the source of Nacha's advice about arguments in the kitchen and the "remedy" that allows the "angry" food to cook. Particularly when cooking with corn and making tamales, the sacred food par excellence in the Nahua culture region of central Mexico, one must observe certain rituals that reflect traditional beliefs. Nacha tells Tita that tamales will remain raw no matter how long they are cooked if two or more people have argued during the preparation because the tamales are "enojados" [angry] and that the only thing to be done is to sing to them (198). "Ears" made of corn husks are tied onto the handles of the pot holding the tamales in order to keep the tamales from "hearing" arguments and becoming upset. In Ocotepec, women go the extent of dancing around the pot "if necessary" to make the tamales happy. Just as Tita recalls Nacha's warning, each of my informants had stories about tamales that did not cook well because the women making them had an argument or otherwise permitted discord to enter the kitchenspace during their preparation. When Tita concludes that her beans are still raw because they witnessed her fight with Rosaura, she attempts to alter her mood and sings to them with love: "[. . .] no le quedó de otra que tratar

de modificar su estado de ánimo y cantarles a los frijoles con amor . . . "
(198). [She had no other choice but to try to change her mood and sing
to the beans with love.]

The precise ritual surrounding particular dishes varies slightly from
one community in central Mexico to the next, but all unmistakably
communicate the delicacy and sacred nature of the task entrusted to the
cocineras. The same woman who begins to stack tamales in the pot must
complete the task, for example. The woman who begins to stir the mole
must continue until the end or it will spoil, staying near the pot until she
is finished serving. Often, this means she works all day and into the night.
The responsibility of caring for the mole at a *fiesta* is a commitment
women take on with seriousness, pride, and tremendous respect for the
sacredness of food and tradition – but as one of the informants noted
(above), "Kitchen work is hard work!"

Power and Gendered Territory

Kitchenspace is a source of power for many women in my region of
study. Never is this more evident than when a woman shares a house
with her mother-in-law. It should come as no surprise that in a matriarchal culture where women's power is rooted in their role as nurturers,
older women are reticent to give up their power in the kitchen – or their
sons for that matter – to a younger woman. Evidently, many women in
Mexico find in food preparation an effective mechanism for nurturing
and controlling members of the household. Women are often territorial
about their kitchens and recipes, even in relation to their own daughters
and granddaughters. Several young women I met expressed frustration at
being kept out of the secrets of the kitchen until the *abuelita* of the house
was ready to pass them on. One woman said her grandmother always
managed to send her away on an errand at a crucial moment in the mole-
making process so that she never learned exactly how many or which
ingredients her elder put into the pot.

When Rosaura makes a feeble attempt to displace Tita from the
kitchen and impress her husband with what turns out to be a dismal meal,
the text alludes to an incursion into Tita's territory: "[Q]uién sabe si por
querer impresionar a Pedro, su esposo, or por querer establecer una
competencia con Tita en sus terrenos, en una ocasión [Rosaura] intentó
cocinar. [. . .] Obviamente el arroz se la batió, la carne se le saló y el postre
se le quemó" (51–52). [. . . who knows if she wanted to impress Pedro,
her husband, or because she wanted to establish a competition with Tita
in her territories, on one occasion she tried to cook. [. . .] obviously the
rice was mushy, the meat was too salty, and she burned the dessert.]

Unlike Tita, Rosaura does not have the knowledge, skill, or embodied love necessary to be a successful cook, mother, or lover; her efforts to impress Pedro or claim Tita's domain are unsuccessful.

Like the kitchen at the Rancho De la Garza of *Like Water for Chocolate*, "kitchenspace" in my own research implies a center of powerful gendered space and a privileged site of social and cultural reproduction in central Mexico. There, society's relationship with nature is inscribed in the patterns of everyday life and ritual celebrations, and gendered subjects work within the parameters of cultural boundaries to accommodate changes in the natural and social landscapes. Territoriality and hierarchies within kitchenspace reflect its vital importance to the reproduction of social relations within and beyond the household and its value as a living cultural archive and laboratory. In addition to reflecting the economic status of a particular household and often the climate and vegetation of its geographic location – as Tita's kitchen in *Like Water for Chocolate* repeatedly does – real kitchenspace affirms factors such as ethnicity, religious practices, and generational differences. A sensitive observer of culture can find, in the persistence of food traditions, locally specific manifestations of attachment to place and women who are experts at adapting to change.

While feminist scholars protest the lack of women's power in public spaces in Latin American societies where men appear to make all the decisions, women generally "run the show" in their homes, where the seat of that power is the kitchenspace. Esquivel emphatically validates this perspective in *Like Water for Chocolate*. In many communities, *las cocineras* have considerable impact on social relations *outside* the home, though, like Señora Marcela and Tita, they may seldom venture from the kitchen and its immediate and related area. Perhaps, as Esquivel does in *Like Water for Chocolate,* such truths are best told through literary fiction.

Notes

1   This essay is based on a year of ethnographic research in the semi-urban communities of Xochimilco, Ocotepec, and Tetecala in central Mexico during the 2000–2001 academic year, a period of work which also informs Christie's 2008 book, *Kitchenspace: Women, Fiestas, and Everyday Life in Mexico*; photographs and material used in this chapter and previously published in this book are used by permission of The University of Texas Press. Text and photographs previously published in articles that appeared in *The Geographical Review* (The American Geographical Society) and the *Journal of Latin American Geography* and used in this chapter are used by permission of the Society and the two journals. Permission to use text and photos appearing in this chapter that previously appeared in the journal article, "Kitchenspace: Gendered territory in central Mexico," published in *Gender, Place & Culture: A Journal of Feminist Geography* (13.6 [2006]:

653–61) are used by permission of the Taylor and Francis Group, Ltd., Publishers. Translations from Spanish and photographic images are the author's.

2 For cultural perspectives on food, see Frederick Simoons (1994); Carole M. Counihan and Penny Van Esterik (1997); and Deane W. Curtin and Lisa M. Heldke (1992).

3 Page numbers from *Like Water for Chocolate* refer to the hardcover Spanish edition (Doubleday. April 1993).

4 See Carolyn Merchant (1990) and Sandra Harding (1991).

5 See Merchant (1980), Susan Bordo (1986), Butler (1993), and Gillian Rose (1996).

6 See the essay collection edited by Dianne Rocheleau, Barbara Thomas-Slayter, and Esther Wangari, (1996).

7 See Crossley in the Works Cited and the Glossary for *chinampas*.

Transformation, Code, and Mimesis: Healing the Family in *Like Water for Chocolate*

Debra D. Andrist

In the film and print versions of Laura Esquivel's *Like Water for Chocolate*,[1] space and time create reality that resonates for most readers and viewers, yet the details of cooking, eating, illness, and madness appear to transcend scientific and medical principles, squarely situating this work in the genre of magical realism. In Esquivel's fiction, food is infused with the emotion of the cook and translates that emotion to those who consume it; healthy and pathological responses to food, environment, and healing are indicative of character. Elements of paradox (joy and grief, heat and cold) and mimesis (in character and situation) heighten pathos and emphasize the coded messages in pathology and healing. These narrative effects provide information to the astute reader or viewer about plot, character development, and narrative tone. The novel's physical consequences, viewed through a medical and scientific (biological, chemical) representation of the body by means of illness, injury, treatment, and death focus especially on the negative physical pathology and on the psychological effects that self-manifest in destructive social behavior.[2] Using a semiotic approach, this essay explores examples of such situations in the novel and points to the central roles of the magical and the scientific and medical representations that develop plot and character.

The transitions and transformations that occur because of these magical and scientific aspects are clarified through the application of Alicia Suskin Ostriker's theories on women writers as revisionist mythmakers.[3] Ostriker theorizes that all women writers are foreigners to, or at least on the margins of, the traditional system of symbols. Women have to create everything anew; they create new myths because they have to

121

recreate everything from the feminine point-of-view rather than from the masculine. This revision of myths especially stands out in the works of women writers like Esquivel who choose genres of the fantastic such as magical realism. Although Ostriker was theorizing about women's writing and not about Latin American magical realism, she proposes three strategies that are telling in the context of *Like Water for Chocolate*: (1.) transformation, or a radical change in physical representation; (2.) writing in code, or concealment of the theme or message of the work by coding messages; and (3.) mirroring or mimesis, in the exhibition or development of shared characteristics or behaviors, as if one character or event could stand for the other.

Tita's great-niece narrates the novel through a reading of recipes from Tita's cookbook-journal. The journal and recipes represent a codification or concealment of the theme or message of the work, according to the Ostriker model. An ingredient of the first recipe, onion, and the tears shed due to the fumes released when cutting them,[4] not only establish the leitmotif of tears, but also mirror the affinity between protagonist and narrator, whose response to onions is associated with Tita's: "Mamá decía que [yo lloraba tanto al cortar la cebolla] porque yo soy igual de sensible a la cebolla que Tita, mi tía abuela" [Mama used to say that I would cry so much when onions were cut because I was just as sensitive to onions as Tita, my great-aunt] (3).

Salt, one of the chemical requirements of life and a staple in the kitchen, is emphasized as a component of tears, beginning with Tita's audible sobbing from the womb when Mamá Elena chops onion, and continuing with Tita's birth on the kitchen table amid a salty flood of tears (rather than amniotic fluid), which provides seasoning in the kitchen for a considerable period.[5] Thus, too, begin Tita's ties to the kitchen, to food itself, to cooking and its substitutions, and to paradoxes. Mamá Elena's husband dies of a heart attack two days after Tita's birth, and Mamá Elena has no milk for her. While the stated message is that Mamá Elena is overwhelmed with grief and responsibility, the coded inference is distinct: the narrative later reveals that Mamá Elena's consternation may have resulted from fear of social exposure of her earlier infidelity. Her inability or unwillingness to nurture Tita, either physically or emotionally, is emphasized repeatedly and is mirrored in Rosaura, the eldest and the daughter most like Elena.

Nacha, ranch cook and Tita's substitute mother, rescues Tita: "se ofreció a hacerse cargo de la alimentación de Tita [. . . quien] se mudó a la cocina y entre atoles y tés [en lugar del mamar] creció" [she offered to take charge of Tita's feeding and Tita moved to the kitchen and with the *atoles* and teas instead of mother's milk, she grew up] (4–5). As a result of living vicariously through kitchen activities and food, Tita sees an equation where most observers would see a paradox: "no diferenciaba bien las lágrimas de la risa de las del llanto. Para ella reír era una manera de llorar [hasta el punto de confundir] el gozo del vivir con el de comer" [she did not differentiate properly between tears of laughter and tears from weeping. For her, to laugh was a way of crying, to the point of mixing up the pleasure of living with that of eating] (5). Even Tita's childhood toys and games are paradoxical substitutions: she transforms the trademark sausage of the family ranch into imitations of balloon animals she has seen and makes a game of sprinkling water on the hot griddle to see it dance.

When Pedro announces his love to Tita one Christmas in the kitchen, Tita has already recognized his interest in the drawing room because of the heat she felt from his gaze, "quemándole la piél" [burning her skin] (15). When Pedro agrees to marry Rosaura to remain near Tita, Tita feels a cold so intense and dry invading her body that her cheeks paradoxically burn and redden as they did under Pedro's gaze at the Christmas party (13). John Brown will later explain her joy and suffering in terms of his grandmother's theory of the internal matches (16–17), but for now, Tita can only suffer from the literal and metaphorical cold without understanding it. For many years, Tita tries to relieve her physical and mental suffering with an activity that implies warmth and manual occupation, "tejir a gancho" – crocheting an afghan:

> Sacó de su costurero una colcha que había empezado a tejer el día en que Pedro le habló de matrimonio [. . . .] tejió y lloró, y lloró y tejió, hasta que en la madrugada terminó la colcha y se la echo encima. De nada sirvió. (18)

> [She took a blanket from her workbox, one that she had begun to crochet the day that Pedro had spoken to her about marriage. . . . she crocheted and wept, and wept and crocheted, until by dawn she had finished the blanket, and she threw it over her. It didn't keep her warm.]

Throughout her life, Tita's efforts to find warmth will be in vain, but she continues to add to her *colcha*.

During the wedding preparations, Mamá Elena forbids Tita to cry, but Tita sobs as she prepares Pedro and Rosaura's wedding cake and icing (*fondant*) and even the nougat (*turrón*) (34), her tears blending with the batter.[6] The wedding sweets induce a bitter-sweet response among the guests, who weep for their own lost loves to the point of nausea and vomiting. Seen another way, consumption of the cake and other sweets prepared by the psychological-but-not-physical bride cause vomiting as a metaphor for the social rejection of Pedro and Rosaura's inappropriate marriage.[7] Paradoxically, Pedro whispers his continuing devotion to Tita at the wedding reception, and only months later does he finally consummate his marriage to his substitute-wife (39).

Following the wedding, the story's paradoxical events and responses continue. Tita is severely beaten by Mamá Elena, partly because Nacha cannot corroborate her innocence in putting a vomitive in the wedding cake because, the reader is rather belatedly informed, Nacha is dead. Nacha dies the night before the wedding, yearning for her lost love, a yearning presumably inspired by her tasting Tita's *fondant* (34), which results in a headache and her death: Tita finds Nacha dead, with medicinal leaves on her temples and clutching a photo of her own lost love, a man chased away by Elena's Mamá (40), in another mirroring of circumstance. With Nacha gone, Tita, who has just been suspected of poisoning the guests, becomes the official ranch cook. Substitute-wife, Rosaura, is not able to substitute as cook, though she tries her hand, and the entire family suffers indigestion. When Tita has been ranch cook for one year, Pedro offers Tita a bouquet of roses. In the moment of Tita and Pedro's joy, Rosaura cries with jealousy, and Mamá angrily warns Pedro and orders Tita to throw out the roses. Tita clutches the roses to her bosom, and the thorns pierce her skin, staining the roses redder with her blood, in a metaphorical consummation of her love with Pedro.

Rather than dispose of the roses, Tita decides to prepare a meal of quail in rose petal sauce, a literal and figurative reinforcement of the "deflowering" metaphor already suggested. Now Tita's blood blends with the sauce recipe. A second metaphor is obvious when Tita only injures the first quail rather than dispatching it – to her horror (47–48). Tita relates the half-dead bird's physical pain to her own psychological suffering – the analogy of the broken bird to her broken heart – and she realizes that she must imitate her mother's forcefulness in killing, but out of mercy. Tita, determined not to cause them to suffer, is able to kill the birds decisively and finish the dish. Both the birds and Tita are implicated in the sacrifice of the innocent.

Consuming the dish awakens overwhelming sexual arousal (felt as heat) in all the dinner guests. Notably, Mamá Elena complains that the dish contains too much salt![8] The passion that should have been physically consummated between Tita and Pedro, but which was dispassionately consummated between Rosaura and Pedro, will now be psychologically displaced upon the second sister, Gertrudis. This danger was noted (unscientifically) in the recipe: "Se desprenden con mucho cuidado los pétalos de rosas, procurando no pincharse los dedos, pues [. . .] los pétalos pueden quedar impregnados de sangre y esto [. . .] puede provocar reacciones químicas [. . .]" [One detaches the rose petals with great care, trying not to stick one's fingers because

. . . the petals can become soaked in blood, and this can cause chemical reactions] (45). Gertrudis sweats pink, rose-scented drops that
evaporate into a cloud as she tries to chase away the all-consuming heat
with a cold shower. Crazed with passion, she is carried away, literally
and figuratively, by a Revolutionary soldier, to consummate her awakened, displaced passion. Their psychological pathology – the idea of
being "crazy with passion" – and the social pathology – aberrant
behavior as a result of the passion – mimic the political pathology of
the Mexican Revolution during which the novel is set. However, this
atmosphere of pathology is beginning the process of curing other
pathologies; in one sense, Gertrudis breaks free of the sexual repression
of the ranch, and in another sense, as a revolutionary general, functions
as a metaphorical physician who models a cure for a social ill: the
subjugation of Mexican women. In other ways, personal aspects of this
"pathological passion" will later be cured, not in the culinary sense of
treating food to preserve it, but in the medical sense of recovering a
healthy state of balance.

At this point, recovery is distant, and Tita's suffering is likened to the
last food item on the tray, the one no one dares to take lest he or she be
thought a glutton. Starved for warmth and wishing to be chosen, Tita
compares herself to *un chile en nogada olvidado en una charola* [a stuffed
pepper in sauce forgotten on the tray], a rich and spicy delicacy that is
left untried and is headed for the rubbish bin (57). Again Tita sublimates
her passion, throwing her energy into work. She crochets nightly, the
unfinished project reflecting the unconsummated relationship, and her
thoughts fixed in the consideration of heat in all its definitions. Tita translates her pain into creativity in the kitchen as well: "De esta época de
sufrimiento nacieron sus mejores recetas" [From this period of suffering,
her best recipes emerged] (69).

The birth of Roberto as a turning point in Tita's suffering and development direct the reader to the figurative significance of Tita's creativity
in the kitchen. The words "impregnated' (in the description of the rose
petal sauce) and "being born" (referring to Tita's creation of her recipes)
are significant in light of Tita's involvement with Roberto. Soon after,
she delivers Roberto and swaddles him *como taco* [like a taco] (74) to calm
and warm him.[9] Tita is preparing *mole* with three kinds of peppers, pepper
seeds, and onions for the baptism, and she rhythmically pulverizes ingredients in a *metate*. Attracted by the delicious smells from the kitchen,
Pedro enters and is seized by passion when he can't take his eyes off the
sympathetic movement of Tita's unfettered breasts as she moves over the
metate. In her typical way of thinking about life in terms of food, Tita
considers how "el contacto con el fuego altera los elementos [y] en sólo
unos instantes [de mirarlos con passion] Pedro había tranformado los

senos de Tita, de castos a voluptuosos, sin necesidad de tocarlos" [contact with fire alters the elements and in just a few moments of looking at them passionately, Pedro had transformed Tita's breasts from chaste to voluptuous, without needing to touch them] (67). This transformative stimulation may be a precursor of Tita's "miraculous" but physically possible lactation. When Rosaura cannot nurse or nurture Roberto (as her mother could not nurse or nurture Tita), and the wet nurse is accidentally killed in the Revolution, Tita is able to feed him from her own breasts.[10]

Tita and Pedro feel as if they are the parents of Roberto, and Tita takes Rosaura's place at the baptism party when Rosaura is too ill to attend. Mamá Elena notices their happiness, and soon sends Rosaura, Pedro, and Roberto across the border (81–82), ostensibly for better medical care, but science fails. In San Antonio, Roberto dies, as Chencha says, because "todo lo que comía le caía mal" [everything he ate disagreed with him][11] (99). Rosaura, like her mother, lacks Tita's sympathetic nature and cannot access the spiritual support that Tita gets from Nacha. Rosaura cannot cook and has never cared for a baby, so the move is predictably fatal to Roberto.

The news destroys Tita's sanity, and her mental breakdown signals another transition-transformation in her character. When the news arrives, Tita, her mother, and Chencha are making sausage. When her mother refuses to let her grieve, Tita explodes in anger, her mother strikes her, and Tita climbs up to seek refuge in the dovecote, taking with her a young bird that she has been compulsively feeding. The dovecote is the only place Mamá Elena cannot reach her due to her fear of heights. Nearly catatonic and mute after spending the night there, during which her little bird dies from indigestion (a mirroring metaphor for Roberto), Tita refuses to come down, and her mother sends for Dr. John Brown to take Tita to the insane asylum. The sausage they had been preparing soon spoils, a thing that has never before happened on the ranch.[12]

John takes her away, her enormous, multi-colored woven bedspread trailing from his carriage, but he cares for Tita in his own home. Tita has no work to do there and never speaks, but John tells Tita about his work and about his Kikapú grandmother, Luz del amanecer, whose theory about happiness and grief allows Tita to understand her life with Mamá Elena and Pedro. The turning-point is broth – beef, not chicken soup![13] – that is delivered by Chencha, who is now the ranch cook. Chencha's ox-tail soup, hot both in temperature and spice (containing salt, onion, and peppers) conjures up Nacha, bringing about an emotional reconnect that restores Tita's "sanity"(124).

Tita's foresworn return to the ranch is occasioned by injury: the night Chencha returns from John Brown's house, the ranch is attacked,

Chencha is raped by the bandits, and Mamá Elena is paralyzed by a blow when she attempts to defend Chencha (130). Reentering the life where Mamá Elena is a kind of substitute for the child and childcare forbidden to Tita, Tita's care for her is now more labor-intensive than before: Mamá Elena, paralyzed, is truly "as helpless as a baby." Tita prepares broths to help heal her mother, but Mamá Elena repeatedly detects a bitter flavor – the emotion of an unwilling cook. Elena dies as a result of repeatedly dosing herself with syrup of ipecac,[14] in fear of poison, effecting another narrative transition. In an effort to explain her unexpected lack of feeling over her mother's death, Tita turns again to food analogies:

[. . .] Tita no sentía dolor ninguno. Hasta ahora [no] comprendía el significado de la frase de "fresca como una lechuga," así de extraña y lejana se debería sentir una lechuga antes su repentina separación de otra lechuga con la que hubiera crecido. Sería ilógico esperar que sufriera por la separación de esa lechuga con la que nunca había podido hablar ni establecer ningún tipo de comunicación y de la que sólo conocía las hojas exteriores, ignorando que en su interior habían muchas otras escondidas. (137)

[Tita felt no pain. Until that moment she had (not) understood the meaning of the phrase "fresh as a lettuce," just this strange and distant a lettuce would have to feel in its sudden separation from another lettuce with which it had matured. It would be illogical to hope that it might suffer from its separation from that other lettuce with which it had never been able to talk or to have any type of communication and of whom it knew nothing but the outer leaves, unaware that within there were many hidden ones.]

Among her mother's things, Tita discovers that her mother's parents had forbidden her to marry José and that he was shot and killed the night they planned to run away. José is the illegitimate son of a *mulata*,[15] and he becomes the father of Gertrudis after Elena's forced marriage to Juan de la Garza. Juan learns of Gertrudis's parentage when he goes to the tavern to celebrate Tita's birth and suffers a heart attack.[16] When he dies several days later, Tita becomes the family's last daughter and cannot marry. Perhaps in an effort to restore her honor in society and to expiate her guilt over the extramarital affair, Elena remains unmarried, and she sacrifices Tita's innocent life, mirroring a substitute for her own errors.

During the funeral, Pedro and Rosaura, who is about to give birth, arrive at the ranch to discover that John and Tita intend to marry. Esperanza is born, but Rosaura again can't nurse and Tita refuses to nurse her and raises her on *tes* [teas] and *atoles* as Nacha had done with Tita (5, 146) When Rosaura suffers complications with an imbedded placenta,[17] she is unable to have more children though John saves her life with surgery. This pathology and its cure provide another transition–transformation and create a new issue: Rosaura intends to sacrifice Esperanza just as her mother sacrificed Tita.

Following Esperanza's birth, heat imagery abounds, with both Pedro and Tita "boiling," *como agua para chocolate* [like water for chocolate] (151).[18] Pedro is angry and irritable due to Tita's plans to marry John. Tita is upset over Rosaura's plans to imprison Esperanza in caretaking. One day Tita relieves the growing tension with a cool shower (recalling Gertrudis's shower episode). She abruptly realizes that the water is growing warmer: "De pronto empezó a sentir que el agua se entibiaba y se ponía cada vez más caliente hasta empezar a quemarle la piel" [Suddenly she began to feel that the water was getting warm, and it went on getting hotter by the minute until it began to burn her skin] (154). She opens her eyes and discovers Pedro on the other side of the shower planks watching her with eyes that "glow" (*brillar*) in the dusk. The incident figuratively scalds Tita, making her angry, rather than inflaming her with passion (154–55). Before dinner is served, in a tense atmosphere, John asks Pedro for Tita's hand, they discuss details of the wedding, and John presents Tita with a ring. The glittering diamonds remind Tita of the brilliant light in Pedro's eyes earlier in the evening. Late that night, Tita is alone in the kitchen putting away dishes when Pedro, who had concealed himself, throws Tita on Gertrudis's abandoned bed where "la hizo perder su virginidad y conocer el verdadero amor" [he caused her to lose her virginity and to know true love] (159). Their love-making creates a visible show of fireworks, "un resplandor extraño" [a rare brightness] where "[v]olutas fosforescentes se elevaban hacia el cielo como delicadas luces de bengala" [glowing columns rose into the sky like the delicate lights of a flare] (159). Rosaura and Chencha see the fireworks, and Chencha identifies the display as the spirit of Mamá Elena returned from Purgatory. The narrator explains the irony: fear of Mamá Elena now provides "la oportunidad ideal" [the ideal opportunity] for Pedro and Tita's lovemaking (160).

Rosaura, having gained weight and developed digestive problems, asks for Tita's help in recovering Pedro's affection, a recovery or cure that will prove impossible. Rosaura reveals a radical change in her physical representation that recalls Ostriker's critical theory:

> Desde hacía unas semanas tenía graves problemas digestivos, sufría de flato y mal aliento. Rosaura se sintió tan apenada [. . .] que inclusive tuvo que tomar la decisión de que Pedro y ella durmieran en recámaras sepa-

radas. [. . .] No se explicaba por qué desde que regresó al rancho había empezado a engordar tanto. (169–70)

[For several weeks, he had serious digestive problems, suffered from gas and bad breath. Rosaura was so distressed . . . that she also made the decision that she and Pedro would sleep in separate bedrooms. . . . Why she had begun to gain so much weight when she returned to the ranch was unexplained.]

Rosaura's problems, made visible in "un voluminso y gelatinoso cuerpo" [a huge and gelatinous body] temporarily capture Tita's sympathy, but only until Rosaura reaffirms her vow to follow Mamá Elena's example, imprisoning Esperanza in care-taking.

Mamá Elena's spirit appears and confronts Tita for having had relations with Pedro (173) and curses Tita's unborn child. Tita believes that she is pregnant and soon confides in Gertrudis (189–90), who has returned to the ranch as a General in the Revolution and as the wife of Juan, the soldier with whom she ran away (179). Gertrudis reveals that a year before, she gave birth to a *mulato* child and that Juan has not forgiven her for the suspected infidelity; fortunately, Tita can reveal the truth of Gertrudis's parentage and resolve the problem (181).[19] For her part, Gertrudis arranges to discuss Tita's supposed pregnancy within earshot of Pedro (191). These events, which occur in the chapters "Septiembre" [September] and "Octubre" [October], bring to mind Ostriker's mimesis theory in that Gertrudis's experience in the world allows her to put herself in Tita's position and to act decisively for what she sees as Tita's happiness. Tita, for her part, because of her knowledge of their mother, is able to provide information that saves Gertrudis's marriage to Juan.

Whether Tita's pregnancy symptoms point to her true condition or intend to symbolize a false transformation in the form of stress-related amenorrhea, Mamá Elena's ghost validates the pregnancy when she accuses Tita and curses the child.[20] Having had enough of her mother's abuse, Tita rejects her mother with the words, "la odio" [I hate you]: "las palabras mágicas para hacer desaparecer a Mamá Elena para siempre" [the magic words for making Mamá Elena disappear forever] (200). Tita finds that she is no longer pregnant – if she ever was: "Los músculos de centro de su cuerpo se relajaron, dando paso a la impetuosa salida de su menstruación" [The muscles in the center of her body relaxed, giving way to the flood of her menstruation] (200). The purgative confrontation restores Tita's physical – if not her emotional – equilibrium.

The "imponente imagen" [powerful image] of light and heat that is

Mamá Elena's spirit, however, is not quite exhausted and inflicts its final damage on Pedro, and it "se acercó a Pedro girando vertiginosamente, y con furia hizo que el quinqué más cercano a él estallara en mil pedazos. El petróleo esparció las llamas con rapidez sobre la cara y el cuerpo de Pedro" [it drew near Pedro spinning furiously, and it angrily smashed the oil lamp nearest him into a thousand pieces. The lamp oil scattered the flames rapidly across Pedro's face and body], and Pedro, converted into "una antorcha humana" [a human torch], runs along the patio (201). This horrifying scene has the paradoxical effect of restoring Tita's sympathies toward Pedro, and it makes public their relationship when Pedro rejects Rosaura's offer of comfort and clings to Tita (202–203). Tita uses traditional medicine: she treats Pedro's burns with egg whites and raw potatoes.[21] To heal his scars, she seeks the advice of Nacha, who gets the answer from Luz del amanecer: the bark of the *tepezcohuite* tree for which she must send Nicolas to "el mejor brujo de la región" [the best herbalist in the area] (202–203).[22]

The narrative moves to Rosaura's death, many years later (a year before Esperanza's wedding), and again works from paradoxical representations. As if Rosaura were a negative photographic image of Tita, her death is of the most opposite to the delicious food imagery and smells produced by Tita's cooking. Its nature is described as "de lo más extraña" [among the strangest]. Pedro is distracted from his book one evening by the noise of Rosaura's passing gas, described as "estos desagradables ruidos" [those unpleasant sounds] (232). Pedro tells himself "que no era possible que ese prolongado sonido fuera del producto de los problemas digestivos de su mujer" [that is was not possible that that prolonged noise came from the digestive problems of his wife], and he wonders whether the "estruendosos cañonazos la revolución se había reiniciado" [the thunderous shelling of the Revolution had begun again] (233). He remarks (to himself) "un olor [. . .] nauseabundo" [a nauseating odor], which penetrates the rooms "a pesar de haber tomado la precaución de [usar] un trozo de carbon encendido y un poco de azúcar" [in spite of having taken the precaution of using a piece of burning coal and a little sugar] (233). He soon discovers Rosaura "de labios morados, cuerpo desinflado, ojos desencajados, mirada perdida" [with purple lips, her body flat, her eyes askew, her gaze empty], and John Brown pronounces the cause of death "una congestión estomacal aguda" [an acute congestion of the stomach] (233). Rosaura's chronic condition and its symptoms suggest food allergies.[23]

Following Rosaura's death, Esperanza and Alex, John's son, are married on the ranch. This marriage, with Esperanza as *alter ego* for Tita, is a kind of vicarious fulfillment for Tita, and unites the two families in true love. Even more important, the marriage precludes, for all time, any future attempt to sacrifice the innocent in the De la Garza tradition. Esperanza and Alex can look forward to a healthy life because the "illnesses" within the relationships that led to theirs have been "cured."

Esperanza becomes a mirror or a fulfillment of potential for Tita when she describes her response to Alex's gaze on her body. She tells Tita that she feels "como la masa de buñuelo entrando al aceite hirviendo" [like the dough of a *buñuelo* going into the boiling oil] (239), a sentiment and a metaphor that resonates with Tita, who had used it to describe the effect of Pedro's eyes on her at the Christmas party the night he had declared his love: Tita "comprendió perfectamente lo que debe sentir la masa de un buñuelo al entrar en contacto con el aceite hirviendo" [understood completely what the dough of a *buñuelo* must feel when it comes into contact with boiling oil] (15). Tita describes the conversion of her breasts, from "chaste" to "voluptuous" under Pedro's gaze in similar terms. In all these instances, the emphasis is on the change that fire (heat) brings to the "elements" (67). Like Tita, Esperanza is not the boiling liquid of water that is ready for the chocolate, but the low-temperature, "inert" element or ingredient – *chocolate, masa,* or *buñuelo* – that is changed irretrievably and instantly upon contact with heat. This image of joining culinary opposites for an erotic outcome appears in the special dish Tita prepares for Esperanza's wedding, *chiles en nogada,* which blends spicy and savory flavors with sweet ingredients (228).

Two final scenes, both related to Esperanza and Alex's wedding, return to the theme of heat, and this time, the heat of passion provides a searing closure. When Tita and Pedro are finally alone, they begin to make love, but Pedro suffers a heart attack *del éxtasis* [of ecstasy] (246), fulfilling the warning of Luz del amanecer's philosophy of the internal matches (117–18) articulated by John to Tita after Roberto's death:

"Si por una emoción muy fuerte se llegan a encender todos los cerillos que llevamos en nuestro interior de un solo golpe, se produce un resplandor tan fuerte que ilumina más allá de lo que podemos ver normalmente y entonces ante nuestros ojos aparece un túnel esplendoroso que nos muestra el camino que olvidamos al momento de nacer y que nos llama a reencontrar nuestro perdido origin divino. El alma desea reintegrarse al lugar de donde proviene, dejando al cuerpo inerte. . . ." (245–46)

[If because of a very strong emotion one happens to light all the matches that we carry inside at one time, there is a glow so bright that it shines beyond anything than we can normally see and then before our eyes a splendid tunnel appears that shows us the path that we forget at the moment of birth and that calls us to reconnect with our lost divine origin. The soul desires to reunite with the place from which it came, leaving the body lifeless . . .]

Juliet-like, Tita then consumes a bunch of matches and calls upon her memories of Pedro to kindle the fire that her "damp" internal matches and the breath and words of Pedro can no longer inflame.[24] Having achieved her own *extasis*, Tita joins Pedro in the tunnel of origin and returning, and from Tita's passion for Pedro, the ranch catches fire and all is destroyed except the key to the story: Tita's cookbook-journal (246–47).

Esquivel's revisionist mythmaking creates a magical body of narrative over what is a realistic framework of scientific and traditional medicine in *Like Water for Chocolate*. Food transforms, creating a radical change in physical representation through emotional response, and Esquivel shows the alteration working in reverse as Tita's emotions inform her food. Physical and psychological consequences of these catalysts ensue, viewed through Esquivel's scientific and magical representation of the body, illness, injury, treatment, recovery, and death. These events of pathology, leading to cure or resolution, both conceal and reveal Esquivel's work. A part of this process is the characters' mimetic activity: they mirror or mimic other characters, exhibiting or developing identical or similar characteristics or behaviors, as if one character represents or substitutes for the other. Instances of illness, injury, and madness follow a degree of medical and scientific protocol, and these instances work to bring the novel's action to a denouement of equilibrium, to a restoration to health, paradoxically through processes of illness, injury, madness, and heat. These transitions or transformations may be read productively as a narrative that cures, not only for the characters and for the De la Garza family as a social entity, but for Mexican society, and for the narrative that represents it.

Notes

1   Quotations from *Like Water for Chocolate* appear in the Doubleday Anchor paper Spanish edition (*Como agua para chocolate* 1989). Translations into English are the editor's.

    Further background on the home remedies and scientific and medical content of the novel cited below comes from online resources. These appear in the Works Cited under "Medicine, Science, and Home Remedies on the Internet." The notes refer the reader to the online information in the Works Cited by the surname of the first author or the first word(s) of the site's title.

2   In spite of the fictional focus on negative behavior and destructive pathologies, the novel adopts a paradoxical view of these events, mingling grief and joy in some of its most shocking and harrowing scenes.

3   See Ostricker's website (Ostricker, Alicia Suskin). Also of interest are two

of Ostriker's books in critical theory on women's poetry and language (1986).

4 Slicing the onion releases enzymes called allinases; these break down substances like amino acid sulfoxides that are released from the onion cells. Amino acid sulfoxides form sulfenic acids, which rearrange themselves into a volatile gas. When the gas reaches the eyes, it reacts with the water in them, producing a mild form of sulfuric acid, irritating the nerve endings in the eyes and causing them to tear in an effort to neutralize the irritant. See "Why does chopping an onion make you cry?"

5 Salt maintains the electrolyte balance at the cellular level. Human blood contains 0.9% salt, the concentration found in the (USP) sodium chloride compound commonly used to cleanse wounds (Salt Institute). See "Food salt and health."

6 Tears help to relieve depression and stress because tears contain chemical compounds linked to depression and stress. Tears carry these compounds out of the body. See "Healthy Grieving and Mourning."

7 Only the *turrón* [nougat] contains raw eggs (ten egg whites) (34). No eggs go into the *relleno* [filling] or *fondant* [a special confection used as an icing], but the 170 preserved eggs in the cake batter, if not "properly cooked," or if involved in "cross contamination" of substances or surfaces, could have resulted in salmonella food poisoning, whose effects include the symptoms experienced by the guests (nausea and vomiting). Sweets and eggs are among common modes of infection. See "Salmonella enteritidis." Of all the sweets, Nacha samples only the *fondant* (34). See *turrón* in the Glossary.

8 The oils contained in rose petals undergo transformation, especially with heat and salt-related compounds. Rosewater was distilled by the Arabs at least as early as the ninth century (Kitab Kimya' al-'Itr wa al-Tas'idat [Book of Perfume Chemistry and Distillation] qtd. by Hayward). A by-product of rosewater production is said to have great power over the emotions: "It restores hearts that have gone and brings back withered souls." See Hayward.

9 Swaddling creates a slight pressure around the infant's body that seems to provide a sense of security or nervous system "organization." See "Swaddling your baby."

10 Although lactation can be induced without a preceding pregnancy, lactation requires the production of hormones, artificially intense or extended suckling, or both. See Creel.

11 When a child is abruptly weaned and put on cow's milk, diarrhea and vomiting may result from the change, due to an allergic reaction or for digestive reasons. Without adequate treatment, dehydration may ensue. Death may follow quickly if there is no relief. See "Infant Dehydration" and also Krugman.

12 Aggression and emotional disconnect (*e.g.*, dissociative symptoms) can be symptoms of syndromes associated with stress such as acute stress disorder (ASD), which may arise in the first month following a traumatic event.

See "National Center for PTSD." On the science behind the unprecedented spoilage of the ranch sausage, see online *"Curing and Smoking Meats."*

13 Chicken soup, long believed in traditional medicine to be of value in illness, is now known to help with at least respiratory problems, not because of the ingredients, but because of the vapor created by heating, so any kind of broth would have the same effect. See "Coronary Disease/Heart Attack."

14 Ipecac syrup is a plant extract from the *ipecacuanha* shrub found in Brazil. Ipecac is a single-use drug used as a vomitive when one has ingested poison or overdosed on medication. Its misuse can cause severe medical complications (such as heart damage) and result in death. See "Ipecac Abuse."

15 Mamá Elena's parents were undoubtedly scandalized both by José's illegitimacy *and* by his mixed race.

16 Stress may increase magnesium excretion, making the heart more sensitive to electrical abnormalities and vascular spasm, leading to cardiac ischemia. A rise in adrenaline causes the blood to clot more readily. Since stress can constrict the coronary arteries, blood flow to the heart is reduced. See "Coronary."

17 *Placenta accreta* (and its variant conditions) describe a placenta that implants too deeply into the uterine wall to be expelled normally, and hemorrhaging results. As in Rosaura's case, the placenta can be surgically removed to stop the bleeding, and a hysterectomy (removal of the uterus) is necessary. See (David) Miller, esp. "Placenta Accreta."

18 See this expression in the Glossary in this volume.

19 *Mulato* in Mexico is a social distinction. Here, it refers to skin color and hair type since the child has Mamá Elena's blue eyes and presumably her "fine" features (235). See Tomáš J. Fülöpp's online essay, especially its references to Aguirre Beltrán's "caste system." One explanation for this child's appearance is that Gertrudis's unexpressed genes found a match with similarly unexpressed genes carried by Juan.

20 There are many different reasons for lack of menstruation. The issue of "false pregnancy" is also complex. See Hoffman and "'False' Pregnancy," especially the discussion of "blighted ovum."

21 A collection of home remedies advises: "For boils: Take out the inner skin of a raw egg and place on boil. For burns: Scrape the inside of an 'arsh' [Irish] potato until it is a pulp and rub on the burn." See Gorin.

22 MIMOSA TENUIFLORA: Arbusto del sudeste mexicano, también denominado Tepez-cohuite [tepezcohuite]. Posee una importante acción regenerativa del tejido cutáneo y eleva el nivel de hidratación [a shrub from southeast Mexico, also known as "Tepezcohuite." It possesses an important regenerative property of cutaneous tissue and raises the level of moisture]. See "Albert D'Arnal." The bark is sold in ointment form and in powder form today in *herberías*, markets where medicinal herbs are sold.

23 Food allergies, whose symptoms include tiredness, bloating, pain, diarrhea, and constipation, may damage the intestinal tract over time and can lead

to other illnesses such as celiac disease, Irritable Bowel Syndrome (IBS), Crohn's disease, etc. See "Food Allergies" and Marks.

24 Refer to John's explanation of his grandmother's philosophy / metaphor (116–18).

Cultural Identity and the Cosmos: Laura Esquivel's Predictions for a New Millennium

ELIZABETH COONROD MARTÍNEZ

Laura Esquivel's second novel, *The Law of Love* is, like her first, a narrative that concerns itself with Mexican cultural identity.[1] *The Law of Love* anticipates the Mexican future as the earlier novel delved into the pivotal period of Mexico's Revolutionary past. In *Like Water for Chocolate*, Esquivel wrote the history of the Mexican Revolution from a new perspective and invited the reader to consider the female and mixed-race view of contemporary Mexican identity in that historical past. Set eight centuries after the Spanish conquest, *The Law of Love* proposes a potentially dangerous future for Mexico, where, rather than simply touting recognition of the past as is done in the contemporary era, national memory is expressly prohibited. To examine Esquivel's approach to her material in *The Law of Love*, this essay first examines how the novel uses a variety of modes to represent and contest cultural identity and then provides a broad synopsis in order to inform the critical assertions in the third section.

The Law of Love uses a mosaic of Mexican culture, contemporary life, humor, and indigenous philosophy to affirm the endurance of Mexican roots. Esquivel collects strands of indigenous thought and practice, connecting them to the European invasion and to current global issues to depict a future society rife with political maneuverings, where erring actions are paid for with a karma influenced by indigenous beliefs. In the process of their search for identity, Esquivel's characters require spiritual healing that contributes to the wholeness and balance of the entire society, the kind of harmony that is essential to indigenous philosophy.

In these ways, *The Law of Love* continues Esquivel's search for broader understanding of Mexican identity, but with an interesting twist. Rather than emphasize gender as "otherness," *The Law of Love* merges gender in its characters to emphasize the need for spiritual harmony and cosmologic balance. This novel initiates a new genre in fiction, one which unites ancient, indigenous cosmology with modern culture and projects the narrative toward the third millennium. In that space and time, its characters seek identity in harmony – without race or gender as a consideration – that can only be achieved by claiming ownership of their past and present actions.[2]

The narrative weaves philosophic considerations of culture and identity (including Aztec poetry) with the protagonist Azucena's desperate search for her soulmate, Rodrigo. Color drawings provide the reader with graphic images of critical moments in various characters' past lives, and a music CD-ROM of *árias* and traditional Mexican *danzones* suggests the ambient mood in scenes of love and betrayal, in acts of violence, and in mundane occurrences. The reader shares the listening experience with the characters, who listen to a musical selection in order to recover a memory from a past life. Characters must locate a "Walkman," a device forbidden in their society, in order to listen to music that is also forbidden, and the reader becomes involved in Azucena's "astro-analysis" by listening simultaneously with her. Esquivel's strategy is reminiscent of Julio Cortázar's ploy of providing the readers of *Rayuela* (1963; Hopscotch, 1966) with the choices of reading in linear fashion, or of following an out-of-sequence enumeration of chapters which tells the story differently. Esquivel also offers two manners of involvement in her narrative quest for identity, either the multimedia experience or a traditional, linear reading.[3] Esquivel's innovative storytelling through various media is representative of modern life, with its multiple levels of problems and experiences.

Most pertinent to this reading is the fact that *The Law of Love* contests the present by constructing a counter-hegemonic discourse based on non-Western philosophy and the indigenous past.[4] The ancient and the contemporary travel full circle to meet again: in the first chapter, the Spanish conquistador Rodrigo constructs his house on a site that was formerly the pinnacle of the Aztec pyramid of Love (73), and a twenty-third-century character, Isabel, inhabits the same location hundreds of years later. The principal characters travel to a twenty-third-century outdoor market built on the site of a huge, pre-conquest, indigenous market.[5] The novel's first chapter opens with the dismantling of Tenochtitlan around 1519–1520, and the second chapter jumps to the twenty-third century, demonstrating the continuity not only of a people and their culture, but also of their presence in a geographical area.

The characters must seek recognition of their native (autochthonous) roots, in terms of both philosophy and nature. While they are physically in the same space, the only way to recuperate a true Mexican identity according to this novel is to rectify the spiritual or universal disequilibrium of a society out-of-balance since the era of the Spanish conquest. Early on, Azucena's adviser and guardian angel, Anacreonte, states that the gods like disorder and provoke eternal chaos, but that

La naturaleza, al contrario que los Dioses, es bastante ordenada, casi neurótica, podríamos decir, siente la necesidad de entrar en acción para mantener el equilibrio y poner las cosas en donde deben estar (16).

[Nature, contrary to the Gods, is pretty well ordered, almost neurotic, we could say; it feels the need of going into action in order to maintain equilibrium and to put things where they ought to be.]

Esquivel's "Nature" – with guardian angels performing as a forward guard – will attempt to right a state of disequilibrium that is not always visible: "Es muy fácil detectar el desorden en el mundo real y tangible. Lo difícil es encontrar el orden de las cosas que no se ven. Pocos pueden hacerlo" [It's very easy to uncover disorder in the real and tangible world. The hard thing is to find the order of things that are unseen. Few can do it] (15). As an astroanalyst, Azucena is supposed to help people through the process of understanding Nature's order.

In her futuristic setting, Esquivel intertwines autochthonous philosophies in the form of indigenous lore discounted by the contemporary world, making that ancient worldview more accessible to contemporary society.[6] Esquivel projects into the third millennium a recuperation of the value of ancient wisdom by tying it to the continuity of human existence. Only through an examination of past lives can characters understand their inter-connectedness to all existence. Also essential are the novel's validation of stories related by characters from various social levels and the words of songs that help characters find their way through cycles of existence. Esquivel emphasizes the importance of cultural narrative in an interview published shortly before the novel was released (Loewenstein 1994). In the interview, she suggests that the Mexican people's memory is disappearing, especially in Mexico City. Esquivel notes that stories are no longer passed down in Mexican families because both parents work outside the home and "leave the education of their children to the television" (Loewenstein 593). Mexican identity and cultural continunity are lost with the diminished role of cultural narrative.

The Narrative

This loss is represented in Azucena as she seeks her past and her soulmate, Rodrigo. Azucena is an astroanalyst who does psychological analysis by observing, together with her patients, their previous lives, but she is remiss in connecting with her own past lives. Anacreonte, her guardian angel, arrives regularly and communicates this need to Azucena until she banishes him (25). Because Azucena is obsessed with finding her twin soul – her perfect mate – she postpones working on her own past as Anacreonte instructs her to do. Azucena has forgotten that her actions are connected to others' actions throughout the universe. Her single-minded quest is to reunite with Rodrigo, who became lost after their one night together. Rodrigo had planned to return the following day with his possessions, but several strange occurrences prevented the reunion. Azucena hysterically refuses to accept the idea that she cannot somehow retrieve Rodrigo (25–26).

Azucena happens to see a news interview featuring a professional colleague on her *televirtual* (which brings persons and scenes as holograms into one's home) and gets the idea that her colleague, Dr. Díez, may be able to help her locate Rodrigo's aura (27–28). When she visits his office, Dr. Díez tells Azucena that he has created only two machines that can locate an aura: the police have one, and the other is at the Control Universal de Vidas Anteriores [The Universal Ministry of Past Lives] (36), which happens to have an office position available, and Azucena decides to apply in order to obtain access to the machine (37*ff.*). During the required criminal screening of her subconscious, Azucena begins to review her previous lives as she listens to music provided in a headset containing a camera that photographs Azucena's mind (39–40).

Although Azucena passes the test, she still has to obtain an *auragraph* at a government office, where she encounters long lines of people (50). Azucena is now consumed by a new obsession: she wants to hear more of the opera that she listened to during the test; however, the government allows possession of CDs and players (one of which is called a "discman") only to those sufficiently "evolucionados" [evolved], as certified by an astroanalyst (50–51). With her professional status, then, Azucena can obtain a CD player, but she must complete government paperwork, a process that may take a month. Azucena is impatient to get a discman and a CD of the opera because the memory she had begun to recover with the music could take her more quickly to Rodrigo.

As Azucena muses on reconnecting with Rodrigo, a burly man in line behind her tells her about his past lives, including his favorite, as a ballerina dancer (55–57). Azucena tries to ignore him, but she will see him again. When Azucena finally reaches the counter, she explains that she has only a telephone number for Rodrigo (which she has called repeatedly without getting an answer) and that she wants his address. The clerk searches for the information and then informs Azucena that he does not exist (58). As Azucena leaves, she runs into a *coyote* who offers to sell her another body, telling her he has a new shipment of untraceable bodies (bodies without a registered aura) (59–60). Azucena pushes him aside and returns to her apartment, where the superintendent, Cuquita, tells her how to find and purchase CDs and a discman at the Tepito market (77–78). When Azucena returns home from the market with her contraband, she discovers the dead body of a stranger who accidentally entered her apartment through the *aerofónico* (transporter phone booth) when he dialed the wrong number (82).[7] Azucena quickly deduces that someone is trying to kill her, so she decides to find the *coyote* and change bodies (85–86).

The narrative tension accelerates in proportion to Azucena's level of nervous energy as she goes about discovering shards of her past. Having taken on a new body, Azucena returns to her office to find it in disarray and discovers that Dr. Díez, her office neighbor and colleague, has been murdered (94). With her professional life completely "out of order," Azucena begins to realize that she must help others in order to recover her own balance. She returns to her apartment building and explains who she is to Cuquita, who helps get her into her own apartment by changing the code to admit Azucana's new body (92).

The pairing of Cuquita and Azucena represents Mexico's class struggle in the society of the twenty-third century where karma and balance determine social status. Cuquita represents the *no-avanzados* (those who have not progressed), while Azucena and other *evolucionados* are the privileged class because they have ascended by means of several reincarnations, paying for their wrongful actions in earlier lives with subsequent lives. The *evolucionados* have access to greater benefits and services, including higher-status hotels, resorts, and space transport (93). Cuquita criticizes the inaccessible system: "¿Cómo iban a dejar los no evolucionados su baja condición espiritual si nadie les daba la oportunidad de demostrar que estaban evolucionando?" [How were the unevolved people going to leave their low spiritual condition if nobody gave them the opportunity to show how they were evolving?] (93). The bureaucrats have no compassion for Cuquita, who lodges complaints about the frequent beatings her husband gives her, on the rationale that she has *karma* to pay and must endure her suffering. Some citizens, however, have fraudulently ascended the social ladder by installing devices in their brains which make them appear to be *evolucionados*.

Azucena's travails bring her serendipitously to rescue Cuquita from her alcoholic, abusive husband, an act that changes Azucena's luck. One evening after Cuquita's husband beats both her and her grandmother, Cuquita arrives at Azucena's door and appeals for her to take them in (106). They put the grandmother to bed in the livingroom, and Azucena shares her bedroom with Cuquita, who immediately picks up the remote to enjoy Azucena's privileged *televirtual* – Cuquita has only an older model television. Cuquita finds a program coming from Korma, a planet of cave-dwelling, less-evolved humans, where a news crew is reporting on Isabel González, the Mexican candidate for Global President. González is shown handing out food to the planet's inhabitants, including Rodrigo. Cuquita notices that one of Isabel's bodyguards, the burly man who talked to Azucena about being a ballerina in a previous life, is using the former Azucena body. Cuquita wakes Azucena to see the man in Azucena's former body, but instead, Azucena is thrilled to see her beloved Rodrigo (91).

Cuquita and Azucena decide to travel to Korma, but with little money, they must do so on a third-class spaceship owned by their neighbor, *el compadre Julito* (116). The entire group, including Cuquita's abusive husband, boards the spaceship, where *mariachis* practice and all types of people intermingle. To shut out these conditions, Azucena listens to her contraband CD player and recovers a strand of her past that links her to Isabel, whom she sees committing a murder in 1985 (127). Once on Korma, the group locates Rodrigo in a cave, but he does not recognize Azucena, and she soon realizes his memory has been erased. The *coyote* body-changer has traveled with them, and Azucena asks him to switch the bodies of Rodrigo and Cuquita's husband. The group leaves the abusive husband – now in Rodrigo's body – in the cave, and brings Rodrigo – now in the other's body – on board the spaceship (135).

Considerations of Identity and Gender

Body exchanges are common during the twenty-third century of *The Law of Love*, and characters may change gender when ascending from one life to another, blurring traditional concepts of gender more explicitly in *The Law of Love* than in Esquivel's previous and subsequent novels. Esquivel's use of science fiction to make gender a mutable state also serves to broaden her discourse on Mexican identity: Rodrigo in the present century was a woman in the seventeenth century who was raped by her brother-in-law (138–39; 149–50). Prior to that, he/she was a ruthless conquistador who raped an indigenous woman in 1527 (151). Cuquita's sweet, decrepit grandmother was previously an Argentine general who tortured people. In *The Law of Love*, characters can harm one another and destroy cosmic balance, regardless of their gender.

Each character in the narrative world has changed gender and been both good and evil through multiple lives. It is not enough for one gender to acquire the privileges of the other gender (which occurs in Esquivel's first novel) nor does technological progress in the future produce a better world. Deceit and harm continue at the most advanced level of this futuristic society, as in the case of the politician Isabel. She has had a microchip implanted in her brain which makes her appear to have been Mother Teresa in a previous life, but in fact, she is a miserable character, a dreadful mother to her second daughter, Carmela, and a ruthless politician. Isabel's first daughter was born with an inauspicious astral chart that suggests a potential threat to Isabel's political aspirations, and Isabel ordered that the infant be "disintegrated" for a century (69–70). Eventually, Azucena discovers that Isabel is her mother and that she was saved from disintegration by one of Isabel's employees (127–28; 248–49). As the novel ends, Isabel is punished for her many misdeeds and required to serve as Consul to the planet Korma, where she must help restore harmony in the lives of the prisoners there (250). Even Isabel, in spite of being a powerful *evolucionada*, cannot achieve personal happiness or help restore universal spiritual balance until she confronts the deeds of her past lives.

In *The Law of Love*, the true path for making a better future lies not in following one course of politics or another, but rather in finding one's place in the balance of the universe. The principal characters achieve this understanding through their examination of past lives, lived in both genders, and fraught with errors. Revenge and violent actions only cause further disharmony, as this excerpt indicates:

[T]odo lo que ha sucedido forma parte de un mundo equilibrado. Desde la rosa que le regalaron hasta el palo que le dieron en la cabeza. Todo tiene una razón de existir. Entonces, ¿qué tan necesario es contestar el palo? El mundo se ha convertido en una cadena interminable de "él me hizo, entonces yo le hago." Esa cadena se va a romper cuando alguien se detenga, y en lugar de responder con odio lo haga con amor. Ese día comprenderá que se puede amar al enemigo. (133)

[All that has happened is part of universal harmony. From a rose presented to you, to a stick used to hit you over the head, everything has a reason to exist. Why is it so important to answer the blow? The world has become an interminable chain of "he did to me, so I do to him." That chain will break when somebody stops himself, and in place of answering with hate, he answers with love. That day we will understand that you can love your enemy.]

This explantion is the novel's philosophy of universal harmony, the "Law of Love," that Esquivel plays out in a Mexico City that is more imaginative than futuristic. Esquivel asserts that Mexicans must attain a better understanding of their own existence through a quest for individual and universal equilibrium.

Azucena defies the Law early in the novel, rejects community, and is seen as a *self* seeking only personal happiness. Once she is pushed to do so, she becomes involved with those around her and discovers that humans are like the plants in her office.[8] The natural world requires that those who are neglectful of the welfare of others remedy their acts of omission as quickly as possible in order to restore harmony. When Azucena provides Cuquita and her grandmother with shelter, she does so without realizing that her involvement will help restore harmony to her collective existences and to the cosmos. Her less-evolved neighbor Cuquita wisely points this out:

> Usté está buscando obtener la paz y el equilibrio interior recuperando a su pareja original. Está luchando por encontrarse a sí misma en Rodrigo. ¡Está bien! Pero déjeme decirle una cosa, durante su lucha, a quien verdaderamente va a recuperar es a usté misma. Parece que es lo mismo pero no lo es. No es igual recuperar el equilibrio interno como resultado de una armonización interior, que por la unión con otra persona, así sea esa persona nuestra alma gemela. ¿Y cómo va a obtener ese equilibrio? Expandiendo su conciencia. (133–34)

> [You are trying to find peace and internal balance by recovering your first love. You are struggling to find yourself in Rodrigo. Fine! But let me tell you one thing, during your struggle, what you are really going to recover is yourself. It seems like the same thing, but it isn't. It isn't the same to recover your inner balance as a result of finding internal harmony, as (to recover it) by means of union with another person, even though he may be your soulmate. And how are you going to achieve that balance? By expanding your consciousness.]

Cuquita's words reinforce the Law of Love and assure Azucena that what she gains will depend on her willingness to understand a greater truth.

Considerations of Balance

The Law of Love promotes the recuperation of the value of ancient wisdom by tying it to human experience. Just as Tita in *Like Water for Chocolate* discovers spiritual energy in her role as cook, Azucena learns more about the inner guide to her healing by performing astro-analysis on herself (as she listens to music). When Azucena thinks that she has lost her soulmate, as Cuquita explains to her in the quotation above, what she has really lost is her balance in the universe. To regain it, she will have to follow the correct steps according to cosmic law, a process reminiscent of the Jungian perspective. According to Jungian psychologist Clarissa Pinkola Estés, the act of learning the steps required for a cyclical return helps to guide a lost soul, even when errors have been committed in an earlier stage (264). Azucena's quest to find her lost love represents the yearning for a part of one's being which is lost, called a "second skin" or "the soul" by Pinkola Estés. What Esquivel character-izes as "molecules yearning for completion," is, in Jungian thought, the union of the two parts into a cohesive and complete being which could not exist otherwise (265). Azucena thinks she must recover Rodrigo, whom she has identified as her soulmate, but her own essence is what she truly seeks. Azucena's understanding of this idea will strengthen her soul and assure balance in the cosmos.

It is interesting to note that Azucena's name means "lily" and that the word designates a variety of flowers in the lily family. The most familiar example of this family is the large white lily with bright yellow stamens, known in English as the Easter Lily and as a symbol of purity, chastity, and the feminine principle. Its balanced petal shape also suggests the cross, with its associations with the sacrifice and rebirth of Easter.[9] In the spirit of the Easter sacrifice that results in the redemption of others, Azucena assists others and also pursues her own redemption. She finally directs her energy to reconciliation and forgiveness and finds the path to peace and understanding for the future according to the Law of Love.

Individual harmony is not the end, then, but a means to broader harmony. *The Law of Love* demonstrates that a personal connection with greater understanding – the joining of the two separated entities of being – is only possible in harmony with the community, a strong aspect of Amerindian thought. Azucena cannot recuperate her "other half" – Rodrigo – and reach perfection without being involved with her community. After losing her first body, Azucena begins to understand that she must work in cooperation with others. She comes to understand that actions from past centuries are throwing her twenty-third-century society off balance, a state of disequilibrium that will not disappear with the passing of the generation that caused it, but continue until remediating actions rectify it.

Balance in the Capital

Claudia Schaefer discusses futuristic vision in Esquivel's novel, with the city as symbolic condensation of the real and the imagined (109), a "third space" possibility. She sees Esquivel's novelistic D.F. (Mexico City) as a hologram suspended above the concrete city and representing an essential element of Mexico's future. In Schaefer's view, this future does not simply unite the Indian and Conquistador past into a single harmonious race, but supplants Octavio Paz's *Malinche* philosophy.[10] This supplanting vision is launched from "zero," with Rodrigo and Azucena as Adam and Eve (114). Although Schaefer calls the novel "futuristic," she contrasts Esquivel's projection of a new, harmonious life here on earth with Esquivel's earlier view of happiness (in *Like Water for Chocolate*) as possible only in Tita and Pedro's union in the afterlife (Schaefer 116). Calling the Law of Love a mental state, Schaefer points out that the Law responds to the question presented in the first chapter: "¿Cuándo desaparece una ciudad? Cuando no existe más en la memoria de los que la habitaron" [When does a city disappear? When it no longer exists in the memory of those who lived in it] (17).

The residents of Mexico's capital tolerate its deficits and celebrate life there despite its problems. Esquivel provides evidence of that attitude in her characters' enjoyment of eating and other pasttimes and also with sporadic comedic elements which are true to Mexican culture. For example, when Azucena purchases an illegal body (manufactured from human eggs stored in test tubes during the twentieth century, grown into soulless shells or bodies by *coyote* contrabanders) on the black market, she looks over her choices and selects one with the attributes she has always desired: a long-legged blonde (87). As Azucena leaves the clandestine lab and walks down the street in her new body, men greet her with stares and *piropos* [catcalls]. She enters a sandwich shop and hides her legs under the table to put a stop to the attention (88–89). Later, when she is shot and leaves the voluptuous body, Azucena inhabits the body of Cuquita's grandmother who has just died (179–80; 184), which means that she will receive no attention from men. While her community's attitudes toward age, class, and perceived beauty are superfluous to the attainment of cosmic harmony, such humorous accounts add a true Mexican feel to the novel.

In other ways, too, Mexico's popular culture anchors the narrative. Donna M. McMahon has suggested that popular oral tradition – myths and exaggerations coupled with the official story – serves as an intertext in *Like Water for Chocolate* (McMahon 19). *The Law of Love* employs a similar strategy: Mexican popular culture thrives in a twenty-third century of space ships and molecular travel and provides comic relief in familiar Mexican images. While spaceships are public transportation, older ships – like today's older buses – provide third-class transportation. Unemployed mariachis – who frequent Garibaldi Plaza in the twentieth century – now ride this cheap transportation, hoping to be hired for special functions; their music still elicits tears and strong sentiment from twenty-third-century Mexicans. Traditional foods prepared from indigenous products, such as *sopes* (corn-based flatbread with meat and sauces on top), *tamales*, and *atole*, are still popular. Mexican men still make flattering remarks with *piropos*. Invariably, Mexicans must still wait in long lines at public service offices, where bureaucrats remain predictably oblivious to the the crowd's frustrations and needs. Social customs and government requirements continue in Esquivel's twenty-third century as in the twentieth, but the novel's insistence that characters find spiritual harmony by making up for past actions exemplifies a need for the same in the contemporary era.

Considerations of Nature and Indigenous Ethos

Esquivel's characters' romp through the twenty-third century reveals a Mexico that is connected to its indigenous roots in terms of philosophy as well as culture, and where all citizens, regardless of gender, must become aware of the implications of their actions. Mexicans must learn again to salute the four winds and to show respect for their inter-connectedness to the universe. Toward the end of the novel, the key pyramid pinnacle is discovered (in the *Pocito* at the historic Villa de Guadalupe); its renewal restores harmony in the universe, and love and respect govern (250–51). The ancient Tenochtitlan is reproduced in hologram, and Nahua poets sing in unison with Spanish monks. Each understands that the *other* is the same as himself or herself.

Like Carmen Boullosa and other contemporary writers, Esquivel writes in favor of an ecological ethic and proposes Mexico's unique place in a universal ecology, based on its non-Western philosophy. Esquivel's environmental concern extends from Mexico City into the universe. In the novel's final paragraphs, a sort of epilogue for the narrative, the reader learns that Azucena had been one of history's most vicious murderers: in a previous era she blew up three planets with nuclear weapons (261). To make amends, she had to put the Law of Love into operation again and reestablish equilibrium in the universe, a task that she finally accomplishes. Esquivel presents, more than a love story, a place where people have attained greater understanding of each other and of life because they have looked into the past, seen themselves, and sought reconciliation. They know that "La energía en el Universo es una. Está en constante movimiento y transformación [. . . . S]i uno envía ondas de energía negativa, recibirá ondas negativas" [Energy in the universe is one. It is in constant movement and transformation. . . . If one sends out waves of negative energy, he will get back negative waves] (180).

This cyclical philosophy, borrowed from Mexican indigenous cultural tradition, grounds and informs the novel's futuristic present. Just as Equivel recuperates a missing feminine and indigenous perspective on the early twentieth century in her first novel, she urges in *The Law of Love* that Mexico reinstate its ancient indigenous ethos to inform and guide the nation's future. Indigenous heritage in *The Law of Love* stands as a direct and demanding link to the characters' past lives, creating a dialectic between permanence and change in Mexican culture over the centuries, both on an individual and a cosmic level. Characters learn that they must pay for past deeds which have altered or disturbed universal equilibrium. While cosmic payback for past behavior is generally known as *karma*, reincarnation myths are also prevalent in Mesoamerican cultures, which maintain that the individual must seek equilibrium in positive and negative forces.

These principles translate to a respect for the sustaining elements of the universe – an attitude that Esquivel embraces. Esquivel explained her practice of creating an indigenous altar in her office in the Loewenstein interview:

> [Esquivel] Wherever I work I put up an altar in the form of a square that comprises the four elements of nature. I use flowers in one corner to symbolize the earth, in another corner I burn incense to symbolize the air and, in another, I put a vessel of water, and then I burn a candle to symbolize fire.
>
> [Loewenstein] Is the ritual you describe a traditional one?
>
> [Esquivel] Well, I'll tell you. I greatly respect the sacred and ancient traditions and this seems to be one of the very oldest and most sacred traditions that exist. As an example, Rigoberta Menchú says that she does a salutation to the four winds – actually all indigenous people do that kind of salutation because they believe that the four winds form our world. The idea is that the activity you are going to perform on any given day through your work is going to change or alter the cosmos, that is, your activity will alter the equilibrium and so you must ask permission before beginning one's daily routine.
>
> [Loewenstein] So you do this ceremony in the morning?
>
> [Esquivel] Oh yes! In the morning very early one salutes the four elements, and so one maintains an altar with these symbols of respect for the universe. You must show respect, and that's why I have my altar. (598–99)

147

Esquivel honors Mexico's indigenous roots in her private life as in her novels, although in *The Law of Love*, the philosophical basis appears eclectic.

As with her approach to creating a narrative, Esquivel combines aspects of several philosophical systems in *The Law of Love*. She applies the indigenous idea of respect emanating from the individual toward the universe, the process she describes in the Loewenstein interview. In the interview, Esquivel also suggests the Hindu idea of reincarnation and the Zen-Buddhist idea of the primordial absence of a center, ideas also found in Mesoamerican thought. In Eastern religion, no one person has been sacrificed to atone for mankind's sin, but each is responsible for balancing the cosmic books on an individual basis. In Amerindian philosophy, one makes (non-human) sacrifice in order to attain a higher level of meaning or understanding, and upon death, descends to the underworld to travel and later reappear on earth in another form. At every level, the person is responsible for his or her actions. By incorporating these non-eurocentric philosophies, Esquivel – in the mode of other contemporary Latin American writers – deconstructs Latin America's Hispanic identity, separating it from a Spanish- or Western-only construct.

In distinguishing between what is practiced *in* Latin America and what *is* Latin American, Chilean scholar Bernardo Subercaseaux Sommerhoff considers the idea that Latin America has appropriated its policies, movements, and culture, borrowing them as whole cloth from other nations: "[Such a model] rejects the myth of cultural purism and essentialism of any kind because what is Latin American is not something produced or completed, but something that would be constantly developing."[11] Although reincarnation is not a doctrine of the Catholic Church, an institution imported to Mexico with the Conquistadors, Esquivel makes the doctrine essential in a futuristic Mexico where indigenous spirituality and Eastern beliefs come together to locate the soul (and the true essence), bringing past and present culture into harmonious balance.[12]

Mapping Mexico's Future

The Law of Love's Azucena shows the way to an imaginary, but authentic future – if Mexicans will contemplate this future. The novel's use of popular culture and humor suggests that Esquivel seeks the ordinary reader's consideration of this proposition, but most critics did not capture the significance of this strategy. Instead, best-seller women writers' works were derisively categorized as *literatura lite* (associating them with the advertising campaigns for *Pepsi Lite*, or light yogurt, which were in vogue during the 90s) by critics who failed to understand innovative novels such as Esquivel's. Mexican novelist and critic Sara Sefchovich (1987) has noted that most literature since the 1980s tends toward "un retrato crítico de la sociedad, . . . con la mirada sobre un personaje concreto" [a critical portrait of society . . . fixing the gaze on a concrete character] (223).[13] The late twentieth century has seen a new opening among novelists who join the indigenous past with the present in intellectual (rather than romanticized) discourse.

Long before *The Law of Love*, two Mexican women writers, Elena Garro (1916–1998) and Carmen Boullosa (1954–), also suggested a better understanding of the Aztec era by reincarnating Aztec characters into Mexico's contemporary world. In Boullosa's novel *Llanto: Novelas imposibles* (1992. [*Lament: Impossible Stories*]), Moctezuma returns from his sleep in the depths of the earth to twentieth-century Mexico City, where he is confused about the new nature of Tenochtitlan. In Garro's story, "La culpa es de los Tlaxcaltecas" (1962. ["Blame the Tlaxcalans"]), the protagonist, Laura, is both a contemporary character and a reincarnated character from the Aztec past. She last saw her Aztec husband as he left to battle the invading Spaniards, and she is married to a violent, twentieth-century man whose actions connect him to present-day politicians while his appearance connects him to the Spanish conquerors. Her Aztec husband locates her in the twentieth century and eventually persuades her to leave and return with him to their indigenous life. In *The Law of Love*, Esquivel's indigenous characters and pre-Columbian philosophy establish the foundation of her fictional world. This essential core, along with futuristic technology and scenes of Mexican popular culture and language, construct an imaginative novel that requires a culturally and historically informed critical approach.

Esquivel peppers her intellectual discourse with humor – a strategy of Latin American novelists since the Boom – and with elements of global popular culture and contemporary concerns. She prophetically advances a new Bush presidency with an incumbent "Global President," who is called "Pres. Bush." However, he is a person "of color," raised in the Bronx (95). The novel refers to the subversive trafficking of an illegal drug, but in the twenty-third century it is *cacao*, rather than cocaine or heroin, and the chocolate *capos* are arrested (26). By placing *cacao* in her novel, Esquivel reprises an aspect of Aztec civilization: chocolate was the preferred drug of the elite and was used as currency.

In another contemporary political touch, Esquivel's futuristic world is brokering a free-trade agreement, and Isabel, with her eye on the prize, stops at a less-evolutionized planet to address its enactment, knowing that action will help her politically (160). By using names of political leaders and issues of the present era, Esquivel asserts that specific politicians and practices do not produce disharmony, but simply revive old conflicts in another form. Self-interested political practices negatively affect the lives of communities of people and keep the universe from its essential harmony.

In futuristic fiction, the writer – with her readers – seeks a sense of verisimilitude in a created reality. George Orwell's *1984* is an outstanding literary example of a created, plausible reality with detail in a futuristic situation, providing a warning as well as a prediction. *The Law of Love*, likewise, not only provides the reader with amusing entertainment, it shows or "warns" that the present era's pattern of political conflict, materialism, and self-interest predicts a chaotic future. The reader is encouraged to imagine a future where harmony is attainable. In this latter sense, Esquivel creates what one critic calls an "attractive fantasy" in *The Law of Love* (Alkon 8). Although Esquivel merges science fiction trappings with a love story in the novel, it supports a reading apart from science fiction and is much more than soap opera entertainment.

The Law of Love poses the question: *where do we go from here?* Like the European effort to invent the Americas by means of Western discourse during the Colonial era, Esquivel's Mexicans of the twenty-third century undertake a similar task: to invent a present that authentically joins with its past, where cosmic harmony that was honored by the indigenous peoples is finally achieved. The present, leading into the imaginary future, will restore the values of human existence that were active in this hemisphere prior to the arrival of European thought. Esquivel attempts a blueprint for a harmonious future that remains beyond the experience of present societies, a future anchored by a central philosophy that individual wholeness can be achieved only by participation in and on behalf of the community. Esquivel's created space suggests a new process of *decolonization* in which a New America, a new Mexico, or a new Mexico City validates itself with recognition and respect afforded to the foundational values of its native peoples.

Notes

1 Citations from *The Law of Love* come from the Crown Spanish-language edition (New York 1995). English translations are the work of the author and editor.

2 Readings by Ryan Prout (2000) and Claire Louise Taylor (2002) also examine the use of gender in *The Law of Love*. Prout points out that the novel ends with the union of the male and female heterosexual couple, and that the only gay character dies.

3 The use of a combination of communication media to stimulate visual and auditory images is discussed in Concepción Bados-Ciria (1996), Catherine R. Perricone (1999), Ana María Rodríguez-Vivaldi (2003), and Ludmila Kapschutschenko-Schmitt (2004). Martha I. González (1996) calls the mix of media an example of "intertexuality."

4   When I began working on *The Law of Love* in 2000, few critical articles existed on the novel. Now, several studies have been published, some surveying Esquivel's use of indigenous lore and science fiction or futuristic fiction. Prout (2000) and Taylor (2002) both approach the novel from a science-fiction perspective, and Lydia H. Rodríguez, here, focuses on a reading of the novel as science fiction. My reading, however, is that Esquivel's intention is not to create a work of science fiction, but instead, a philosophic novel, transcending contemporary narrative strategies.
    Editor's note: See Coonrod Martínez's *Hispania* review of *The Law of Love* (1998), discussed in the editor's critical introduction in this volume, and additional discussion of the novel's critical reception.

5   A village called Tlatelolco maintained a huge outdoor market that was frequented by people from towns in the Mexican valley. Bernal Díaz del Castillo, who accompanied Cortés, described his amazement at the array of various types of produce, meats, household goods, farm tools, and other items in the market.

6   Rosa Fernández-Levin (1997) focuses on aspects of Aztec myth and narrative in *The Law of Love*, citing Enrique Florescano's point that the introduction of Western discourse to describe the Indian past actually collided with the manner in which indigenous cultures viewed historical events and perceived space and time.

7   The booth works something like *Star Trek*'s "beam" in "Beam me up, Scotty": the body's molecules dissolve, and the user arrives complete at the new destination.

8   In a comic scene, the plants in Azucena's office demonstrate Nature's balance. When Azucena has been absent for several days and has forgotten to plug in the computer that provides water and her own conversation to the plants, they hiss at her when she returns. Their reception surprises her because they are usually "affectionate." Azucena begs their forgiveness, waters and caresses them, and sings to them until they purr with glee (34). Her actions correct an imbalance in nature, foreshadowing a need for the same in her own life. It is relevant in a novel where indigenous philosophy is constantly in play to note in this context that Native American spirituality teaches that each plant has a spirit.

9   See Cirlot's discussion of the lily (189).

10 I refer to Paz's chapter "The Sons of La Malinche" ("Los hijos de la Malinche") in *The Labyrinth of Solitude* (1961. *El laberinto de la soledad* 1950, 2nd ed. 1959). For Paz on La Malinche, see the essays of Jeanne L. Gillespie and Ryan F. Long in this volume.

11 The translation is the author's. Subercaseaux's essay, "Reproducción y apropiación: Dos modelos para enfocar el diálogo intercultural" [Reproduction and Appropriation: Two Models for Bringing Intercultural Dialog into Focus], reads as follows: "El modelo de apropiación cultural se *contrapone a una visión dual* de la cultura de América Latina; por definición el proceso de apropiación niega la existencia de un núcleo cultural endógeno incontaminado, rechaza el mito de purismo cultural y los esen-

cialismos de cualquier tipo, puesto que lo latinoamericano no sería algo hecho o acabado, sino algo que estaría constantemente haciéndose, y que por lo tanto no podría ser comprendido a partir de aproximaciones preconceptuales o precategoriales." (Italics are in the original. 4). See the first note appended to Subercaseaux's paper for additional references. Also see Amaryll Chanady for a reading of Subercaseaux's essay (36). Note: "Sommerhoff" is printed in error as "Sommerhorf" in some versions of his work.

12 As the idea of reincarnation is not acceptable to the Church, Esquivel's use of this concept may have distanced some Catholic readers from the philosophical *modus operandi* of the novel.

13 Also qtd. in Anderson 17.

Laura Esquivel's Quantum Leap in *The Law of Love*

LYDIA H. RODRÍGUEZ

Time and space are two relative and subjective concepts that shape the course of daily life, being themselves governed within the parameters of the twenty-four-hour day and geographical space; alternate propositions would be discarded as false or as imaginary, but science fiction extends the possibilities of time and space. Science fiction, as a genre, allows the extension of time and space where the impossible is possible, where what is absent becomes present, and where reality may be invented, duplicated, and elaborated in imaginative ways. In the fourth and fifth dimensions of science fiction, computers can direct their own computations, and the teleportation of "Beam me up, Scotty" is standard practice. Behind these familiar trappings of "sci-fi," however, is a critical theory of science fiction that seeks to determine how and why it works – or does not work. In order to approach Laura Esquivel's *The Law of Love* as a work of science fiction, I have turned to Robert Scholes's theory of structural fabulation (*Structural Fabulation* 1975) and Jean Baudrillard's *Simulacra and Simulation* (1994) for a productive theoretical approach and will argue for a reading of the novel as grounded in the genre of science fiction.[1]

The Law of Love presents a futuristic universe and a network of imaginative and technical systems. The narrative deconstructs the present to create a twenty-third century where remarkable invention and familiar elements populate a gymnastically-paced text. The characters' yesterdays are accessible as technological simulacra of the past, and the narrative present shifts rapidly in location and perspective to support the pace. The omniscient perspective of the first chapter narrates the conflicts that set the Law of Love (as a cosmic philosophy) in motion, and the rest of the novel, set in the futuristic present, is narrated in the first or third person, the former, from the perspective of Anacreonte, Azucena's guardian angel. Azucena, the impatient and willful protagonist, presents a series of challenges to Anacreonte as she searches for her soul mate, Rodrigo.[2] Dialogues, monologues, and soliloquies structure much of the text.

The Law of Love is known for its multi-media narrative approach: chapter introductions with recorded material, and poetry and six sections of custom-developed narrative images that parallel the text. Selections from Miguel León-Portilla's poetry on the Conquest and the destruction of Aztec culture and Liliana Felipe's contemporary lyrics are printed in some chapters, and Felipe's lyrics are included on the CD-ROM that accompanies the text. At pauses in the narration, the reader is instructed to listen to poetry or music on the accompanying disc. The effect is a multifaceted reading experience in which technology, art, and popular culture enhance the narrative.[3]

Robert Scholes, in *Structural Fabulation*, theorizes that successful (science) fiction must be systematically integrated with reality and present an internally integrated cosmos. Scholes explains that the fiction must present two basic elements, namely, the cognitive and the sublime, and that writing "which accomplishes neither must be bad or no fiction at all" (4). Scholes comments that fiction contains "systematic models which are distinct from reality though they may be related to it in various ways" (5–6). These "ways" include the presence of realistic fictional detail. Fictional reality, of course, cannot be constructed as an identical replica. Fictions work as "model versions of reality, rather than either records of the real or fabrications of the real," and (writers, readers, and critics) "explore the ways in which such models may relate to our existence" (11). Science fiction creates "strange" models of the future in which the reader sees images of present reality.

If the fiction presents too many incredible events, a circumstance with which the criticism of science fiction is concerned, the reader feels distanced from the fiction, so the writer must be conscious of maintaining a balance. Scholes comments that when "[the] fictional world seems deficient in its own natural laws, [it . . .] will fail structurally and cognitively [. . .] though it may retain some sublimative force" (43–44). Writing fiction under this theoretical rubric cannot be about merely emulating reality in its totality, but must also be about adding enough credible material to a created "reality" to allow the reader to place himself in the setting, even when the created reality is quite different from ordinary life.

One of the ways of adding credibility to science fiction is to project history into the future, as Esquivel does in the *Law of Love*. Scholes suggests that "[b]ecause we know that the unexpected happens continually in the history of science itself, fiction has now a license to speculate as freely as it may, in the hope of offering us glimmers of a reality hidden from us by our present set of preconceptions" (18). Scholes affirms that fiction is a "fabulation" offering the reader "a world clearly and radically discontinuous from the one we know, yet [it] returns to confront that known world in some cognitive way" (29). Under this theoretical, *The Law of Love* is "speculative fabulation" or science fiction. Science fiction alters reality through a process of alienation of the known, which it presents as the unknown.

Baudrillard offers a further perspective in his chapter "Simulacra and Science Fiction," where he posits three types of simulacra. A simulacrum (*pl.* simulacra), according to Baudrillard, is *not* merely imitation, duplication, or parody, but "a hyperreal," in which "signs of the real" are substituted for the real ("The Precession of Simulacra" 1–2). Baudrillard's first type is that which is constituted naturally by image, imitation, or falsification, and these aim for "the ideal institution of nature made in God's image" (121). The second is characterized as "productive," created out of energy and force, and its goal is "a Promethean aim" of globalization and expansion by "an indefinite liberation of energy" (121). The third type is a "hyperreality" that aims for total control (121). Baudrillard's second type of simulacrum, involving expansion and globalization, prompts a reading of *The Law of Love* as science fiction. *The Law of Love* presents a narrative world where, as Baudrillard explains, "science fiction adds the multiplication of its own possibilities" (122).

Esquivel's narrative begins in the remote past at the time of the Conquest when the Aztecs and the great Tenochtitlan have just fallen. The second chapter places the reader abruptly into a futuristic world that references the events and characters – Rodrigo and Citlali – of the first chapter. These mortal enemies, Citlali, an Aztec princess, and Rodrigo, one of Cortés's men, are reference points through which the narrative threads run. Additional signs connect the narrative worlds of the distant past and the twenty-third century. These include the Pyramid of Love, a focal point in the opening and close of the novel; an indigenous man playing a conch as a musical instrument; and the place-name Tenochtitlan, the older name of Mexico City. The reader is prompted to reference events, images, and characters that are established in the first chapter through the rest of the novel.

In the *Law of Love*, Scholes's two components of fiction, the cognitive and the sublime, figure in appropriate proportions. The novel connects to the reader's knowledge of historical reality by placing its action in a known existential location formerly known as Tenochtitlan and now familiar as Mexico City. The setting provides an additional basis for resonating with the reader's experience in Esquivel's use of Mexico's colloquial language. *¡Híjole!* [Son of a gun! or My gosh!], a frequent exclamation of surprise, commiseration, or frustration, and the equally frequent conversational *¡Oiga!* [Listen here!] come familiarly to the reader's ear and create an echo of Mexico's daily life.[4] Anacreonte's emotional explanation of Azucena's pride – from which the English translation fails to capture the flavor of the Spanish slang word (shown below in italics) – offers another characteristic example from ordinary speech: "Lo que pasa es que ella está convencida de que triunfó por sus *huevos*, y está en un error" (15, italics added) [So she is convinced that she has triumphed because of her nerve, but that's where she's wrong] (16). The expression *por sus huevos* [*lit.*, "because of her balls"] is another authentic linguistic connection for a reader familiar with Mexico.

Another example of this typically-Mexican language appears in the dialogue between Azucena and a salesman of bodies. The words of interest are italicized:

- *¡Ándale! ¡Anímese!* No va a encontrar mejor precio.
- ¡Qué no! No necesito ningún cuerpo.
- Pues no es por nada, pero yo la veo media maltratada.
- *¡Y eso a usted que le importa!*
- No, *pos yo nomás digo. Ándale*, tenemos algunos [. . .]. (59, italics added)

[– Come on, you won't get a better price anywhere.
- I said no! I don't need a body.
- Well, I don't want to say so, but yours looks a little beat up.
- What's that to you!
- Okay, I'll shut up, but . . . come on, we just got some new ones.
   . . .] (61)

The syntax of the indignant *y eso a usted que le importa* [and what's that to you?] would be familiar to the reader who knows Mexico, and the italics indicate a selection of frequent elements in casual conversation. In this case, the atmosphere is that of a market, and the linguistic markers in syntax and phonology provide a "realistic" model of speech.

Other examples appear in conversations between Azucena and Cuquita, her neighbor. In the following example, Cuquita has just shown Azucena some illegal "virtual reality books," known as VRBs. This example combines the familiar with the strange, making the strange familiar with characters who seem, by their speech, to be twentieth-century transplants to the twenty-third century. The effect is comic:

- ¡No se haga! ¡Nomás le advierto que si le dice a la policía soy capaz de todo! Yo por defender a mi familia . . .
- ¡Ah! No, no se preocupe, no la voy a denunciar . . . Oiga, pero por

favor dígame si donde [. . .] compró [los VRB] también venden compact discs. (77)

[– To the police! Don't even think of it, I'm warning you! Because when it comes to defending my family, I'm capable of anything.
– Oh, don't worry, I won't go to the police. . . . But listen, could you tell me if they also have compact discs where you bought those VRBs? (77)]

The line *soy capaz de todo* is a familiar inchoate threat: I might do something extreme. The hint that this threat of going to extremes is prompted by a family matter is pragmatically accurate: to defend my family (I would do anything). The topic abruptly turns, as it might naturally do, to a practical matter of acquiring a sought-after piece of goods, producing an ironic and realistic connection with the reader.

Other language also serves as a hook to real-world cultural experience. In political culture, Esquivel's narrative converts today's familiar political staple, the PRI (Institutional Revolutionary Party), into the *Partido de Revindicación de los Involucrados"* – The Party for the Retribution of Inequities (93) – still the "known" PRI, but with an "alien" and comic twist. The Plaza Garibaldi and the *mariachi* band that figure in the narrative are other staples of Mexican popular culture with which the reader can identify. When Azucena hears her friend Julito begin "a ensayar *Sabor a mí* con el grupo de mariachis" (91) [to warm up his *mariachi* group with the song "Sabor a mí" (91)], Azucena starts to cry, moved by the lyrics and music. Esquivel uses the repeated presence of the *mariachi* band and the song ("Sabor a mí") made popular by the Mexican trio *Los Panchos* to create a context in which Azucena has a predictable reaction to the romantic lyrics.[5] These cultural connections are elements of Scholes's "cognitive" function of fiction in that they help to create a "systematic model" of a narrative reality that features an element of "distortion" in order to reveal some truth (*Structural Fabulation* 5–8).

In *Structural Fabulation*, Scholes explains that from the two basic functions – and pleasures – of fiction, namely, sublimation and cognition, science fiction emerges as "speculative fabulation" or "extrapolative narrative," in which the writer must determine "the difference between purposeful discontinuity and a magical relaxation of the cosmic structure" (43).[6] Speculative fabulation projects a narrative "universe" that is in some ways "strange," but in other ways, familiar: "Like all speculative fabulations, they [extrapolative narratives] will take their origin in some projected dislocation of our own existence, but their projections will be based on a contemporary apprehension of the biosphere as an ecosystem and the universe as a cosmosystem" (43). The projection and the creation of another universe are based on the present universe, but the created universe separates itself from the familiar: "What is unique in this form of fiction is the way in which it defamiliarizes things" (46). Science fiction asks the reader to take another look at the nature of familiar things that are, because of the narrative, made strange.

Scholes reads Darko Suvin as affirming that "this technique of defamiliarization or estrangement" of the known is "the fundamental principle of science fiction," but Scholes asserts that this has been the basis of all art "since the romantic period" (Scholes 46).[7] The distinction, according to Scholes, is the element that unnerves or perturbs the reader in science fiction by making familiar things strange. For the reader, this is an "estrangement [that] is more conceptual and less verbal. It is the new idea that shocks us into perception, rather than the new language" (46–47). Esquivel's creation of an unfamiliar future-time, future-world in *The Law of Love* creates a strange world built on a familiar one, a circumstance that prods the reader to consider the potential of the present-day environment.

The elements of the known and alien in *The Law of Love* are alternated and juxtaposed. In the first chapter, the Conquistador's cognitive process, available to the omniscient narrator, explains how the strange was imposed on the familiar in the past:

Por eso, el día en que Cortés vio a un indio tocando el caracol frente a los restos de una antigua pirámide, supo que no podía dejar la ciudad en ruinas. Habría sido como dejar un monumento a la grandeza de los aztecas. (2)

[This was why, on the very day Cortés saw an Indian sounding a conch in front of the remains of an ancient Pyramid, he knew he could not leave the city in ruins. It would have been like leaving a monument to the grandeur of the Aztecs.] (2)

Answering his inspired prognostication with action, Cortés decides to erase Aztec civilization and construct a new city. Esquivel's revivification of the historical moment, a mirror of the event that Cortés intended to avoid, is described by Baudrillard as a hallucination with a retrospective truth (23), in which the historical serves as a reflection for the text to come. In the second chapter of *The Law of Love*, the narrative world resembles Mexico of the late twentieth century, and in this new world, the prohibitions of the new technology make the Mexican past of the first chapter in the category of the "strange," "alien," or "unknown." Of course, the Aztec Pyramid of Love has not been completely obliterated by the Spaniards' destruction, and it will reappear.

The reader meets with an example of "alien" technology when Azucena takes "the aerophone booth," the new advance in bus transportation, to go to Tepito to get a compact disc that will help her remember her entire life. Azucena arrives at her destination in seconds, but when "the door of the aerophone" opens, she is "facing a crush of people pushing and elbowing their way into the booth Azucena was vacating" (78). On one hand, the reader faces the strange, futuristic system of transportation, and, on the other hand, the familiar bus system of the Mexican capital with its elbowing (*codazos*) and shoving (*empujones*) as people board and disembark the bus.

Azucena tries to return home after she makes her purchases and again faces the competitive transportation system. She gets to the booth and thinks that she has succeeded:

> Pero su buena fortuna se vio opacada por el empujón que le dio un hombre de prominente bigote que intentó entrar en la cabina antes que ella. [. . .] Con la cara transformada por la rabia, alcanzó al hombre y lo sacó de un jalón. [. . .]
> – Señorita, ¡déjeme utilizar la cabina, por favor!
> – ¡Óigame, no! Me toca a mí. Yo me tardé lo mismo que usted en llegar . . . .
> [. . .] La multitud empezó a chiflar y a tratar de ocupar la cabina que esos dos estaban desaprovechando miserablemente. (80–81)

> [Her feeling of good fortune vanished, however, when she was shoved aside by a man with a large mustache, who forced his way into the booth before her. Infuriated by this latest injustice, her face transformed by rage, Azucena grabbed the man's arm and yanked him back out. . . .
> "Lady! Please let me use the booth!"
> "No, you listen to me! It's my turn. I waited just the same as you to get here." . . .
> People behind them began whistling and shouting, and some of them tried squeezing past the two into the booth.] (80–81)

Even though Esquivel has taken the reader to an unknown world, the known remains apparent: the chaos of present-day Mexico appears, and the reader is assured that the people and the problems of Mexico have not changed so much, not even in the imagination of one of Mexico's leading female writers.

Another entertaining but fantastic sequence of events takes place in Julito's spaceship. In the following scene, Azucena makes an interplanetary trip because she is looking for her soul mate by getting a free ride on Julito's interplanetary spaceship (117), which provides another element of discontinuity. The ship is an unknown and unusual apparatus, but the reader moves closer to the known when the text explains that Julito has to make extra stops on his usual route because he operates two lucrative sideline businesses along the route: "home-delivery grandchildren, and express-mates" (117). The known element here is the projection of a working-class Mexican citizen earning money in a variety of ingenious ways, but Julito's scheme of increasing his income by renting grandsons and spouses will strike the reader as outrageous – and comic.

From the beginning, the narration displays a familiar, known world populated by unknown elements: characters whose reincarnations in various genders and identities are a rapidly changing narrative force; quirky transports; futuristic technology; elements of material culture; a political universe; and so on. These elements are a part of science fiction's duplicating structure, about which Baudrillard has commented: "Science fiction has always played on the double, on doubling or redoubling either [real], artificial, or imaginary" (125). The most obvious doubles in *The Law of Love* begin with Rodrigo and Citlali in their historic setting, where they appear as the nameless Spanish conquistador and the Aztec princess, also with the name of Citlali. Beginning with the second chapter, Rodrigo and Citlali become an inverted image. As the reader stands before an unknown, futuristic world, Rodrigo and Citlali familiarize and anchor the discontinuity at points where the present and past worlds cross, weaving the fabric and mystery of the novel.

The linguistic referents described above create a "sublime" known element for the reader with the Pyramid of Love as the primary element in the process. The Pyramid is Scholes's *sublimation*, the "satisfying shape," the "way of relieving anxiety," and "making life bearable" through the Law of Love and the final scene of reconciliation.[8] The Pyramid's connection to the narrative philosophy becomes increasingly clear over the course of the novel, and the attentive reader eventually understands its importance. It works as the "activating" object, and references to the Pyramid involve the reader in pondering its importance and significance as the reader follows its appearances through the narrative.

In the climax and denouement of the narrative, the Pyramid's power is finally revealed, and the reader sees that its positive energy extends to the characters: "El amor como un huracán borró todo vestigio de rencor, de odio. Nadie pudo acordarse de cuál era la razón por la que se había distanciado de un ser querido" (260) [Like a mighty hurricane, love erased every vestige of rancor, of hatred. No one could remember why they'd ever grown apart from a loved one (264)]. Love, in this telling of the future, conquers all, and Esquivel's novel erases corruption with an explosion of harmony from the Pyramid of Love. *The Law of Love* closes with a positive vision of Mexico's future, a kind of narrative resolution, which Scholes calls *sublimation*, or "turning our concerns into a satisfying shape," as "a way of relieving anxiety, of making life bearable" (*Structural Fabulation* 5). This is what Esquivel's fiction offers the reader.

Structural fabulation is marked in the novel by a complex of futuristic effects, retrospective history, elements of popular culture, the resurrection of doubles, "alienation," and other such self-evident components of successful science fiction. Esquivel's futuristic world seems far removed from the present perspective of the twenty-first century, but its known elements are suggestive and beckoning. In some ways, as Esquivel's "realistic" narrative anchors suggest, the age represented in the *The Law of Love* appears to be lurking just around the corner of a pyramid. We are daily faced with urgent messages that we must make up for past errors in social and economic policies and material consumption with kinder, greener, wiser approaches – the "Law of Love," if you will.

Notes

1   I will focus in particular, in Baudrillard's book, on two chapters, "The Precession of Simulacra" (1–42) and "Simulacra and Science Fiction" (121–27). See Genaro Pérez and Janet Pérez's "Introduction" to the issue of *Monographic Review / Revista monográfica* on the topic *Hispanic Science-Fiction and Fantasy* (1987). In addition to its science fiction elements, *The Law of Love* also employs modes of the detective story, the love story, and the mystery. The close of the novel implies the harmony and happiness of the romance, or, in other terms, a utopia achieved by means of the reconciliation of opposites. None of these is foreign to the genre of science fiction.

2   English quotations from the *Law of Love* come from Crown edition (New York 1996). Spanish quotations come from *La ley del amor* Crown (1995). The pagination in the two Crown versions is proximate, but not always identical. The cover art of the Grijalbo edition suggests the Pyramid of Love spiritually imposed over the Cathedral (Mexico 1995).

3   Note the similarity, in a text supported by narrative images, between *The Law of Love* and *Malinche: A Novel* (2006).

4   For the former, see the exchange in the Spanish edition at 77–78. For *¡Oiga!* see 108–10.

5   See "Eydie Gorme y el Trío Los Panchos" in Works Cited.

6   See Scholes's 4–5 and 43–44, for clarity on these "functions" and "pleasures."

7   Suvin's article, cited by Scholes (*Structural*), appeared in *College English* in December, 1972 (372–82).

8   See Scholes, *Structural Fabulation* (5). The narrative answers to the cognitive and to the sublime, and also to the discontinuity of two worlds. These terms come from Robert Scholes and Jean Baudrillard's theories. Baudrillard's third order extends to hyperreality, in which science fiction

has died. Scholes's theory suggests that Laura Esquivel's novel fits within the parameters of structural fabulation although this essay utilizes only Baudrillard's second order of the simulacrum theory.

The Two Mexicos of
Swift as Desire

ELIZABETH MOORE WILLINGHAM

In her third novel, *Swift as Desire*, Laura Esquivel returns to themes of desire, destiny, and reconciliation – and to a new allegory of Mexico. Lluvia, the novel's protagonist, is engaged in a quest to uncover the truth about her parents' history and estrangement, and by that act, to fill in missing spaces in her understanding of them and of herself. Her search is also about Mexico as a political and cultural entity and about piecing together individual and communal identity. As Lluvia's efforts eventually resolve rancor and bitterness through process of realization for her parents and herself, the narrative implies a parallel potential for Mexico. Esquivel's alternating third- and first-person narratives suggest a shifting perspective that both lives and observes the narrative, in the same way that one lives within a national culture and history, and yet observes it as a witness. The narrative garners an immediate reality in its setting and central problem: Esquivel places the novel in an ordinary, present-day Mexico City apartment, where Lluvia contends with an issue of the moment for her generation, that of caring for a debilitated parent while fulfilling the roles of parent and grandparent.

Lluvia's apartment holds a microcosm of life in the sprawling capital and, indeed, of the vast country around it. Lluvia, a divorced grand-mother-to-be in her early fifties at the opening of the novel, cares for her dying father, Júbilo, whose origins are in the south, and who dreams of the Mayan sea. Lluvia mourns the loss of her father's personality and the shift in roles that his debilitation requires, but as a resourceful daughter of the Capital, she acts with speed and ingenuity to improve his life in the present. Lluvia's older brother, Raúl, supports Júbilo's care financially from his home in the U.S., but he has no other contact with his father or Lluvia, remaining distant geographically and emotionally from the family. Raúl makes no direct appearance in the novel, and his ideas are conveyed through Lluvia's conversations with her mother, Luz María, familiarly known as Lucha. Lucha, uncommunicative by choice and materialistic by nature, comes from the North of Mexico and is as distant as brother Raúl from Júbilo and Lucha's daily lives, yet her history is an essential part of the riddle of the past. Júbilo represents the part of Mexico that remains in touch with its indigenous heritage, that values love and family above material signs of wealth, and that finds itself marginalized, unable to speak, unable to direct or plan its future, living under the shadow of estrangement from the mainstream policy of progress and rapid obsolescence that distances itself from Mexico's past.

The family configuration of *Swift as Desire*, unique to Esquivel's fiction, is significant in that it recreates the basic unit of society, culture, and economy: father, mother, and child. In this family, however, the mother, like other natural–unnatural mothers that Esquivel presents in *Like Water for Chocolate*, *The Law of Love*, and *Malinche: A Novel*, is neither maternal nor emotionally available. Lluvia's beloved father is in a fatal decline. Ironically, despite the patriarchal milieu of Mexico City, the men of Lluvia's family are unable (Júbilo) or unwilling (Raúl) to assume the *jefe de familia* [head of the family] status, and those functions are left to female characters.[1] Lluvia, as the "child," faces a passage in middle-age with the death of her father; she is about to be deposed from what might be called "adored daughter" status. She moves from depending on her father's emotional and financial support, to caring for him, to life without him.

As the novel opens, Júbilo's physical existence is hermetic and solitary, governed by his invalidism, blindness, and inability to speak, and the resulting struggle to understand and surmount physical barriers (that also informed *Like Water for Chocolate* and *The Law of Love*) sets up the immediate problem that Lluvia seeks to address. It is telling that the image of the ill and impaired body of the father, further bounded within the urban apartment, circumscribes the life of the daughter, whose understanding and movements are limited on another level by her lack of knowledge of the past. In spite of these layered prisons, physical and psychological, Lucha's activity and its results extend beyond those boundaries almost limitlessly, like a camera angle that begins in a tight interior space and pans out to take in the city, the state, the nation before the music swells. The overarching problem of understanding the present through the past, of understanding national history and place by understanding one's own, is eventually answered as Lucha works to mediate her father's physical challenges and emotional needs.[2]

In drawing the family groups of *Swift as Desire*, Esquivel has reversed the stereotypical gendered Mexican roles in two successive generations, creating indigenous paternity (Librado) in the first generation and semi-indigenous paternity (Júbilo) in the second.[3] Lluvia's mother, Lucha, and paternal grandmother, Jesusa, represent the Spanish upper-class, the desire for material possessions and the comforts provided by technology and invention. Esquivel writes another reversal of perspective in the discomfort felt by *doña* Itzel Ay at the marriage when "la boda de su hijo con una mujer blanca [la] había dejado con el ceño fruncido de por vida" [her son's marriage to a white woman had left her with her brow furrowed for life] (14), but the healing brought about by a child recalls the effect of Roberto on Tita. *Doña* Jesusa and *doña* Itzel have a history of limited communication with one another, and relations remain strained until Júbilo is old enough to make peace between them.

The good-humored Júbilo, in spite of being only half-Mayan, is intimate with the spiritual and mystical traditions of the Mayan Yucatán, and has a special gift for understanding the *true* message of a speaker or sender of a telegram, as opposed to the spoken or written words. Júbilo's understanding of Mayan language and numerology comes from his grandmother, *doña* Itzel, but his gift for reading thoughts is a component of his own nature. *Doña* Itzel's affectionate response to Júbilo, her last grandchild, is ironic in that none of her other grandchildren by her son Librado and his "white" Spaniard wife, *doña* Jesusa, has had any significant involvement with grandmother Itzel. It is telling that *doña* Itzel's response to Júbilo is also a pragmatic stroke of destiny, in that Júbilo represents her final opportunity to pass on Mayan culture and language. As in *The Law of Love*, before, and in *Malinche*, afterward, Esquivel relies here on Mayan spirituality to theorize the passages between life and death, with which this novel is especially concerned from beginning to end.

Júbilo is born when *doña* Jesusa is laughing uncontrollably at a family gathering, and her water breaks from the force of her laughter. She leaves the table and soon returns with the newborn, her twelfth child. *Doña* Itzel's worried aspect, imprinted by her son's marriage to *doña* Jesusa, is transformed when she sees the newborn Júbilo: "comenzaba a sonreír en cuanto lo veía" [she began to smile as soon as she saw him], and after the birth, *doña* Itzel makes a habit of visiting her son's home, a thing she has never done before (14–15). Júbilo, as the youngest son, bears no heavy burden of parental dreams and expectations, and he is free to find his own way, but his brothers and sisters are accomplished achievers, and he worries about what he might do to be as worthy as they (22–23).

As a child, Júbilo seeks to please the adults around him and to make them happy and peaceful with one another. He discovers his gift for hearing the true messages behind the verbal ones and learns to mediate between warring parties, first with diplomatic kitchen translations between his mother and grandmother (19–20), and later, with the language of the Morse code over the telegraph wires. With this simple and selfless philosophy, the adult Júbilo will practice his trade as a telegraph operator for the good of others. Júbilo is comic, optimistic, passionate, self-sacrificing – and unlucky.

The teenage Júbilo falls in love with Lucha (82), who comes from a privileged family of the North and who appreciates the comfort and advantage of material possessions. Lucha, like Júbilo, the youngest child of a large, well-to-do family, is discontent in her tightly-budgeted marriage to Júbilo because her daily work goes on unassisted by the technology that was available in her parents' home. Wearing the latest fashions in hair and clothing and driving her own car around the Mexican provinces, the newlywed Lucha is modern and stylish – "vestía como artista del cine" [she dressed like a movie actress] (89) – and is dissatisfied with less than the best of everything.

Lucha looks to Europe and the U.S. to seek models for who she is and what she wants life to be. When Júbilo's work as a traveling telegraph operator takes them to the rural communities of Mexico, Lucha misses family and friends, but she also pines for her "Victrola" and the availability of money: "[s]u nueva vida le exigía nueva ropa, nuevo peinado, nuevos zapatos [. . .]" [her new life demanded that she have new clothes, a new hair-do, new shoes] (88–91). Lucha views money as the source of opportunity; the world as "diseñado para los ricos" [designed for the rich]; and the lack of money as provoking "todo tipo de desgracias" [every kind of misfortune] (98). Júbilo's realization of happiness, on the other hand, has little to do with money and possessions and much to do with love and friendship.

Lucha and Júbilo's conflicting natures and the national parallels they suggest are most evident in their approaches to economic problems. Lucha's desire for an immediate solution to her newlywed discontent is "a corto plazo" [short term] – she wants to make some purchases, to go shopping with money in her purse – while Júbilo's idea is for "un alivio definitivo" [long-term relief] – to save as much money as possible to buy them a house (93). Complications arise when they compromise by agreeing that Lucha will purchase "un par de enaguas y un rebozo" [a couple of petticoats and a *rebozo*], and that she will not spend any more of their savings (93). Lucha eventually finds herself a few *centavos* [pennies] short – "el dinero ya se le había esfumado" [the money had just vanished] – when she tries to purchase *velas* [candles] and *aceitunas* [olives] (94).

At this point, the villain of the piece, one *don* Pedro, a self-important, lascivious opportunist raised to power by the Revolution, appears, offers unwelcome financial aid that Lucha cannot manage to refuse, and places an unwelcome kiss on Lucha's hand (95). In spite of that cautionary experience, Lucha retains her determination to have her desires fulfilled by consumption. She finds happiness, for example, when Júbilo's second job can provide them with "un nuevo refrigerador, una lavadora de ropa de rodillos," "su olla express," and "su licuadora" [a new refrigerator, a wringer washer, her pressure cooker, and her blender] (129). Júbilo is happy that Lucha is happy, but Lucha's desire for finery, as well as bare economic necessity, will continue to add to their store of problems.

Though Júbilo and Lucha are inextricably bound to one another by love and desire, *don* Pedro, representing the dark side of Fate, is an incarnation of evil in their lives. His recognition of Lucha's weakness is devilish, indeed, as he lies in wait around the corners of her paths to tempt her and distance her from Júbilo. *Don* Pedro's rapacious and opportunistic nature deftly detects the potential that lies in the opposing forces of Lucha and Júbilo's natures, values, and geographies, and his actions work to cleave an irreparable chasm between them.

Fate comes between Lucha and Júbilo when Júbilo's ability to hear beyond the normal and even mechanical ranges fails on two fatal occasions that occur close together, one impinging upon the other. In the first instance, "manchas solares" [sun spots] prevent Júbilo's communication (as an air-traffic controller) with a plane that crashes, killing many aboard and plunging Júbilo into feelings of guilt and sorrow. Circumstances prevent his being consoled by his wife following this distressing event, and two nights after the plane crash, following an intervening night of lovemaking when Lluvia is conceived, Lucha returns home in the wee hours of the morning to find their second son, Ramiro, dead in his crib.

Júbilo, who can hear "el deslizamiento de los insectos" [the sliding about of insects] (186) and to whom the noises of the city and technology "le llena[n] los oídos de ruidos sibilantes" [fill his ears with whistling noises] (187), in a tragic stroke of irony, has not heard his baby son choking on a blanket. Presumably overcome with horror, grief, and guilt over Ramiro's death, Júbilo reacts to Lucha's late arrival with jealousy and suspicion. For her part, Lucha blames Júbilo for the baby's death, since Júbilo smells of alcohol. Júbilo makes an angry and pained accusation of infidelity that Lucha will not forgive, and they live estranged within the same house until their two remaining children have grown up and moved away. From the day of Lluvia's wedding, they do not see or speak to one another for thirty years, bringing their history to the time of the narrative, with Júbilo dying in Lluvia's apartment.

Like a journalist who gives a voice to those who lack a venue, Lluvia's ingenious efforts to restore her father's power of "speech" result in Júbilo's being able to communicate via an antique telegraph and a computer translation program for Morse code, a pragmatic and serviceable mediation of the old and the new. His old friends from the telegraph office are soon "talking" to him again, sharing his jokes and joy in life. Lluvia discovers that she has her father's propensity for the telegraph, and soon she is able to "talk" to him without using the intermediary of the computer program to translate the telegraph signals.

A visit with Júbilo's Telegraph Office friends and the gift of a 1946 photograph showing Lucha in an advanced state of pregnancy two years before Lluvia was born leads Lluvia on a quest to learn about a series of secrets hidden from her by her parents and her older brother, Raúl. Lluvia suspects that the secret suggested by the photograph lies behind her parents' long estrangement, and she is determined to understand her parents' relationship, her mother's bitterness, and her father's longing by clearing up the mystery. Her opportunity arrives when Lucha comes unexpectedly to Lluvia's apartment to see Júbilo.

Júbilo overcomes the effects of his medication immediately when Lluvia announces, "Papi, despiértate [sic] chiquito [sic] que mi mamá vino a verte . . . ." [wake up, sweetheart, because my mother has come to see you] (187). Lluvia, who has never understood their estrangement, their separate bedrooms, and her father's insistence on remaining in the marriage, suspects, perhaps wishfully, that Júbilo and Lucha's bond is "una fuerza amorosa escondida bajo el alejamiento externo" [a loving force hidden beneath an external separation] (188). Whether one reads this meeting as the re-engagement of estranged, aging lovers *or* as an allegorical encounter of Mexico's opposed worldviews, it is telling that Lucha addresses Júbilo for the first time in thirty years in these words of self-reproach: "Odio odiarte, Júbilo" [I hate hating you, Júbilo] (189). Thus, Esquivel captures thirty – or several hundred – years of emotional distress over a breach in the family.

The subsequent chapter (IX) opens with a narration of the *día fatal* [fatal day] in the couple's relationship and is presented as Lucha's story told to Júbilo (191). For Lucha, Júbilo's accusation that she arrives home late because of a date with *don* Pedro is more than Lucha can bear:

> Don Pedro, esa noche, [. . .] había profanado su propio hogar, había acabado con la imagen que Lucha tenía de Júbilo y la que Júbilo tenía de ella. ¡Cómo era posible que Júbilo dudara su honestidad! [. . . .] En una frase Júbilo había acabado con todo. (200)

> [Don Pedro, that night . . . had profaned their own home, had destroyed the image that Lucha had of Júbilo and the one that he had of her. How was it possible that Júbilo could doubt her faithfulness! . . . With a sentence, Júbilo had destroyed everything.]

Júbilo, fearful about the reason for her unexpected absence, wounds Lucha with his accusation of infidelity, and the truth is so far from his assumption that the breach will not be mended for many years.

Contrary to Júbilo's accusation of her unfaithfulness, Lucha has passed the hours away from home caring for Lolita, an unmarried friend and co-worker, who is raped by *don* Pedro when Lucha rebuffs him (198). Júbilo learns in the morning newspapers that *don* Pedro (Ramírez) has been shot and killed the previous night by a "mujer misteriosa" [mysterious woman] who is only described as "muy bien vestida" [very well dressed] (203). Júbilo cannot forget "que una mujer bien vestida había asesinado a don Pedro en un arrebato de celos y la misma noche" [that a well-dressed woman had killed *don* Pedro in a jealous rage the same night) (204) that Ramiro had died in his crib. Lucha, for her part, cannot forget Júbilo's unjust accusation against her character, and she blames Júbilo for not awakening to save Ramiro because Júbilo, she believes, was in a drunken sleep (204).

Neither, of course, is completely correct, but the misunderstanding is deep. Júbilo reacts to Ramiro's death and his estrangement from Lucha by drinking for months until he must be hospitalized (207). Lucha, who becomes pregnant the night before Ramiro dies, is seven months pregnant when Júbilo is released from treatment and arrives home. Significantly, a storm breaks as they embrace, and Júbilo connects Lucha's embrace and the falling rain. The effects merge in his consciousness, and he feels renewed, "cómo le volvía el alma al cuerpo" [how his soul was returning to his body]; moreover, he senses that the rain offers him a rebirth: "la lluvia representaba la resurrección de esas gotas de agua" [the shower represented the rebirth of those drops of water] (209). Lucha's embrace is his own "resurrección," an event that is both spiritual and sexual, as are other such embraces in Esquivel's fiction. Lucha and Júbilo's third child is born late that afternoon, a seven-months baby whom Júbilo names *Lluvia*, "como un regalo del cielo" [like a gift from heaven] (210).

After Lucha's tale has been told, filling the empty and mistaken spaces in Júbilo's memory, Júbilo responds in a rapid-fire sending of Morse code that Lucha cannot interpret, and she calls for Lluvia to translate (211). Like Júbilo before her, Lluvia "translates" a message that will bring peace between two people she loves, just as Júbilo had "translated" the messages between his mother and grandmother. That is to say, what Lluvia translates is not precisely what Júbilo has encoded, "pero le encantaba ver que su hija así lo había interpretado" [but it was enchanting to him that his daughter had interpreted it in that way] (211). For Lluvia, this translation gives voice to her own desires and silence:

Finalmente, ella se había atrevido a dar voz a sus deseos. [. . .] Y estaba convencida de que no había inventado nada, que sólo había repetido las palabras que mucho antes había escuchado, cuando aún [. . .] esperaba en el vientre de su madre el mejor momento para nacer. (212)

[Finally, she dared to give voice to her desires. . . . And she was convinced that she had invented nothing, that she had only repeated the words that she heard long ago when she was still waiting in the womb of her mother for the right time to be born.]

Lluvia not only has her father's gifts for translation and quick-thinking diplomacy, she possesses the deepest desire of a child to justify her existence in the context of her parents' love for one another. Read politically, the Mexican state can no more be content with "Father" and "Mother" living estranged, rancorous, and uncommunicative, than children with contentious parents can live happily. For the sons of Cortés and Malinalli to be happy, the reconciliation must transpire, even if someone with a vested interest has to provide a creative, last-ditch translation born of a desire for deep-rooted harmony.

Lluvia's moment as the older generation arrives in the final pages of the novel and is spoken in terms of memoir, in first-person narration, more earnestly and intimately than in the foregoing narrative that was "about" Lluvia. In these pages, a revelatory and comforting dream and a box of Proustian mementos push Lluvia toward a resolution that may never be complete, but that will continue to prod and inspire her. The narrator's activity and determination are also a hallmark of Lluvia's approach to life, and the narrative exchange between the present and memory continue to structure the narration in this first-person section following Júbilo's death.

Lluvia and the nurses prepare her father's body at home, according to his instructions: "lo vestimos con su traje de lino blanco, con el que bailaba danzón con mi mamá y llamamos a la funeraria" [we dressed him in his white linen suit, the one he wore when he danced the *danzón* with my mother, and we called the funeral home] (216). In a timely way, the narrator moves to make appropriate disposition of Júbilo's clothing and personal possessions (217–18), and her plan to pass on her father's non-material legacy has already begun to take shape: "[H]e vuelto de tomar clases de astronomía [. . . y] estoy aprendiendo Maya" [I have begun again to take astronomy classes . . . (and) I am learning Maya] (220). Moreover, she will teach her grandson what she learns so that the indigenous legacy will endure for another generation.

In *Swift as Desire*, Esquivel again attaches individual history, culture, and destiny to the macrocosm that is Mexico, and the basic unit of society, economy, and culture, realized here in Júbilo, Lucha, and Lluvia, speaks meaningfully of Mexican experience and worldview. The fictional world of the novel is shaped and driven by principles of attraction and communication: life and death exercise complementary forces, attracting life into the world and calling life toward death at the appropriate time[4];

characters are not only attracted to one another by love, but also by the workings of Fate; the passion of lovers is eternal, and their shared feelings for one another travel instantaneously, setting up communication and attraction between them. In this fictional world, happiness may be impossible, and the innocent carry forward the burden of the past until it can be mediated. Lluvia's voice speaks of transcendent themes and the quest for lasting reconciliation.

That Esquivel taps into the individual and the personal is an aspect of women's writing that has caused some readers discomfort and others to hear a resonant voice.[5] As she has done in her other novels in the historical past and in the imagined future, Esquivel asks the reader to consider Mexico's historical dialogue and the enduring truths in a present-day context. Here, she fashions a marginal, hermetic space located in a small, urban apartment in today's densely populated Mexico City into an expansive, mediated space characterized by activity and creativity, within which her characters realize a reconciliation that had once seemed impossible.

Notes

1   On the subject of Latin American women writers narrating patriarchy, writing in its shadow, or creating themselves there, see essays of Eunice Doman Myers and Joan Torres-Pou, both in Susana Cavallo's collection of essays (1998). The latter essay is of interest to the question of the critical reputation of Latin American women writers generally, especially 251–53.

2   Of interest to this fundamental Latin American quest for national identity through fiction is Sara Rosenberg's interrogative essay on representing the nation in Argentine fiction (2009). The search for individual identity at the moment of death or within a troubled family in which certain matters are obscure or hidden has caught the popular, as well as the literary imagination. Isabel Allende's extended autobiographical reflection in *Paula* seeks an understanding of identity and purpose, individual and collective. Carlos Fuentes narrates an introspective fictional version of the search for identity of the dying title character in *The Death of Artemio Cruz*. Fiction as distinct in setting as Amy Tan's *The Bonesetter's Daughter* and Rebecca Wells's *Divine Secrets of the Ya-Ya Sisterhood* and Fannie Flagg's *Fried Green Tomatoes at the Whistlestop Cafe* have this search at their core. Stephen King's *Dolores Claiborne* also falls into this genre. Female protagonists – and some of the male protagonists, too – of dramatic television series such as *Bones*, *Closed Case*, *Crossing Jordan*, and *Law and Order: Special Victims Unit* augment the drama and add an extra layer to a conflicted character by incorporating side-bar searches for reconciliation and knowledge related to disruptions involving parents and unresolved mysteries in their family histories.

3   Recall that Esquivel also makes this reversal in *Like Water for Chocolate*

when Tita discovers (in "July") that Mamá Elena, a daughter of the border gentry, fell in love with José Treviño, an illegitimate *mulato*, born of a liaison between a Mexican father of the same name and "una guapa negra" [a handsome black woman] (Doubleday Spanish 130).

4   In *Celebrations of Death: The Anthropology of Mortuary Ritual*, Peter Metcalf and Richard Huntington describe a ritualized drama practiced among the Bara people of Madagascar where death is a "birth," and ancestors receive the dead as if the body were being "born" into the opening of the tomb (esp. 128–30). Note *Swift as Desire*'s narrative connection with the Bara view of death (130, final paragraph).

5   In his essay in this collection, Alberto Julián Pérez references this propensity of feminist fiction as Unamuno's "intrahistory."

Malinche: Fleshing out the Foundational Fictions of the Conquest of Mexico

JEANNE L. GILLESPIE

Laura Esquivel's *Malinche: A Novel* (hereafter, *Malinche*) is a subtle *mestizaje* narrative that layers indigenous and European conventions and systems to present a flesh-and-blood representation of the title character. Though the novel's title suggests a negative set of references in Mexican history, philosophy, popular culture, and language, Esquivel's treatment sets up a context for revising the popular conception of the historical person upon whom the novel is based. In Mexican popular culture, "Malinche" (or "La Malinche") signifies the indigenous woman who acted as translator for Hernán Cortés (1485–1547). The name "Malinche" is linked to the pan-Hispanic curse *hijo de puta* [son of a whore], a malediction that condemns the mother of its object as sexually aggressive and smears him with the iniquity of his mother. The emphatic phrase ¡*hijo de puta*! is used frequently by male speakers as a curse that expresses contempt of another male. This aspersion is recast in Mexico as *hijo de la chingada* [son of the raped or violated woman]. Instead of a "whore" – a woman dedicated to illicit sexual pursuits – the term *chingada* is a close equivalent to English "fucked." While the sexual activity of the mother is implicit in both curses, in the Mexican version, *hijo de la chingada*, she is the recipient of unwelcome sexual contact and does not instigate or profit from it. In both cases, the mother is the conduit of blame and dishonor that falls on her children.

The expression was elaborated philosophically and brought into Mexico's public dialogue in Octavio Paz's essay "The Sons of La Malinche" ("Los hijos de la Malinche"), in which the indigenous woman represented by "La Malinche" *is* "la chingada."[1] For male Mexican writers such as Paz and Carlos Fuentes, the debate is whether the Mexican – in particular the Mexican male, who is the ostensible audience and object of their discourse – can overcome being viewed and viewing himself as a product of miscegenation and violation. Fuentes narrates the shame of the mother and the son in his novel *The Death of Artemio Cruz*, and Paz explains that the term *la chingada* is the essence of *mexicanidad*.[2] For Paz, the expression attains the status of an ironic battle cry of Mexican *mestizo* pride in the refrain, "*Viva! Los hijos de la chingada*" [long live the sons of the "accursed" woman], and is also a cosmic scar that confirms Mexican inferiority as the product of a violent coupling between a Spanish father and an indigenous mother.

In all of its interpretations, however, the embodiment of *la chingada* for Paz's Mexican audience is La Malinche, or, in Esquivel's view, Malinalli, the Nahuatl-speaking girl who was sold as a slave by her mother to the Maya-speaking leader of Tabscoob (Tabasco), and whose resultant linguistic skills made her Cortés's personal translator[3] and, eventually, the mother of his son, the first *mestizo* – if not in fact, at least symbolically so. In contemporary Mexican slang, the term *malinchista* signifies a person who "sells out," especially to a *yanqui* or other foreign aesthetic. This meaning asserts, as Paz comes close to doing, that the Conquest of Mexico was due to Malinalli's bad character and was not Cortés's doing, nor that of the four hundred European soldiers with their three hundred African slaves, nor that of the 60,000 Tlaxcalans and other neighbors of the Aztecs who fought against them with Cortés, nor the "fault" of the Aztecs themselves for their violent regime.[4] Whether she was forced to take part or was a willing participant, Malinalli is singled out for culpability as "La Malinche." Thus Malinalli, also known as "Doña Marina," "Malintzin," and "La Malinche," has become the most ubiquitous, complex, and controversial figure in Mexican history, popular culture, and literature. In the following discussion of the historical and fictional woman, I will refer to the historical figure as "Doña Marina," to the cultural figure as "La Malinche," and to Esquivel's character as Malinalli.

Doña Marina in History and Culture

Doña Marina's image was frequent and powerful in Colonial Mexican art, for which it was an immediate and useful link between the hegemony of the Spanish and the indigenous Mexican communities and the Catholic Church, yet its force and significance at that period remain relatively unexplored. In post-Conquest examples, the colonial Catholic Church used Doña Marina's image to represent its intention to convert native populations to Christianity. As an indication of this appropriation, a Bible clasp found in western Florida shows a woman in Nahua dress speaking and gesturing. The figure closely reproduces the image of Doña

Marina in the *Lienzo de Tlaxcala* [*The Tlaxcala Panel*], a mid-sixteenth-century, native-produced text.[5] Doña Marina's first appearance in the *Lienzo,* in the illustration "Uliuocan" [Reception], shows Doña Marina standing in front of Cortés, who is seated on a horse, and both gesture with one hand uplifted and a finger pointing, a typical posture for speakers in medieval manuscript illustration and a common representation from Mesoamerican pictorial texts as well.[6] In this and other images from the document, Doña Marina is presented as a central and integral participant in the process of conquest and conversion.

The *Lienzo*'s honorific presentation of Malinche is particularly interesting since the document's authors, the Tlaxcalans, were Cortés's closest allies against the Mexica. The Tlaxcalans portray Doña Marina as a Marian figure throughout the *Lienzo* and in their oral narratives of the Conquest. Interestingly, this Marian figure is directly related to Conquest warfare for the Tlaxcalans since they fight alongside Cortés's soldiers, who carry a wooden image of "María Conquistadora" [Mary, the Conqueror] into the battle. Not only do the Tlaxcalans adopt Mary, they also show Santiago [St. James] as a Christian figure who comes to assure military victory against the Mexica. In the *Lienzo* narrative, Tlaxcalan victories are "blessed" by the Amerindian divinities invoked by the Tlaxcalans as well as by the Christian saints, asserting that the Tlaxcalans, now converted to Christianity, receive the support of European divine intervention. In the *Lienzo de Tlaxcala*, these assertions become the basis for evangelization throughout the new colonies.[7]

Sandra Messinger Cypess establishes that Doña Marina's nineteenth-century image as the object of Spanish desire was "fertile territory" for conquest and conversion. She is also viewed in this period as having offered herself to Cortés as a facilitator of the Conquest and as a woman, and he is viewed as possessing her politically and sexually. An indication of this negative perception of Doña Marina appears in the "first" Mexican novel *Jicoténcatl* (or *Xicoténcatl*), an anonymous work attributed to Félix Varela and published in Philadelphia in 1826. The novel casts Doña Marina – more correctly "La Malinche" – as the evil temptress who betrays "la patria" [the fatherland] (*Xicoténcatl* 10). Although Cortés takes advantage of Doña Marina's intellectual talents and her body – quite likely by physical or emotional coercion or both – Doña Marina bears the blame in this version of events. The motif of her complicit and willing relationship with Cortés retains its currency throughout the nineteenth century.

The idea of a Mexican nation state gained popularity in the middle years of the nineteenth century following Benito Juárez's mid-century rebellion against the Emperor of Mexico, Maximilian of Hapsburg. Mexican literature of the period reflected strongly nationalistic sentiments, celebrating the role of the indigenous proletariat in Juárez's successful revolt and the emergence of a new socio-political organization that celebrated the native heritage of the Mexican nation. In *Foundational Fictions* (1991) Doris Sommer comments on the process of creating romantic literary figures to exemplify the emerging Latin American nation states and explains the synergy inherent in the coupling: "Romantic novels go hand in hand with patriotic history in Latin America. The books fueled a desire for domestic happiness that runs over into dreams of national prosperity; and nation-building projects invested private passions with a public purpose" (7). While the romance novel – a genre directed at the female reader – created a domestic utopia for the new order, the literary constructions created by these novels contrasted sharply with the chaos and disorganization that would characterize post-Revolutionary Mexico.

In the early years of the next century, the Mexican Revolution (1910–1920) established a powerful image of the *mestizo* nation that cast out the European colonial powers in the previous century, and by the time of post-Revolutionary Mexico, Doña Marina is viewed as the victim of the Conquest, forced against her will to participate, yet condemned as *la chingada*. In *La Malinche in Mexican Literature*, Sandra Messinger Cypess locates post-Revolutionary texts in which *La Malinche* is recast as *la puta* [the whore], and this Mexican revolutionary rhetoric, harkening back to the Colonial period for its recontextualization, persevered through the twentieth century, aided by the kind of discourse exemplified by Octavio Paz in the 1950s. Paz's *la chingada* considers "La Malinche" as a weak, female victim of the Conquest, and Diego Rivera's twentieth-century murals reflect the same view. Rivera's fellow muralist José Clemente Orozco's rendering of Cortés and La Malinche/Doña Marina does nothing to romanticize the interpreter, and she appears subjugated by Cortés.[8]

Representations of La Malinche in today's popular culture reflect the durability of these assumptions. Her image appears in folk dances throughout Mexico, including *matachines* dances in which she is the central character, and in dance reenactments of the fifteenth-century Spanish Reconquest, which is associated by indigenous people with the Spaniard's Conquest of Mexico.[9] La Malinche appears as menacing in the huge parade puppets called *mojigantes*, and she is sometimes conflated with *X'tabay*, who seduces Maya men at the base of the giant *ceiba* tree, and also to *La Llorona*, who wails in the night, seduces wayward travelers, and steals children from their families. As *La Llorona*, she is the terrible mother whose children are cursed because of her whorish behavior.[10]

In the last quarter of the twentieth century, however, Chicana writers and artists transformed the image of La Malinche into their model of *mexicanidad* and rejected gender-biased representations of her, like that of Paz, as efforts to undermine women's status on "natural" moral grounds and to cast women as no more than sexual objects and predators.[11] Norma Alarcón explains the perceived historical manipulation of this historical figure by the Mexican and – by extension – Mexican-American patriarchal system:

> In our patriarchal mythological pantheon, there exists even now a woman who was once real. Her historicity, her experience, her true flesh and blood were discarded. [. . .] Malintzin's excruciating life in bondage was of no account, and continues to be of no account. Her almost half a century of mythic existence, until recent times mostly in the oral traditions, had turned her into a handy reference point not only for controlling, interpreting or visualizing women, but also to wage a domestic battle of stifling proportions. (182)

Because Doña Marina "sold out" to Cortés, Mexican women have suffered as her heirs, but Alarcón contends that by reclaiming her "La Malinche" image, some Mexican and Mexican-American women have been able to assert their own power in the societal structure.

Recent scholarship on Doña Marina has tended to support an honorific view as well and has examined her as a woman whose life was engaged in surviving a difficult destiny. Frances Karttunen examines Doña Marina as a symbol co-opted by both the native allies of the European Conquest and the Catholic Church to communicate their intentions in the post-Conquest political organization of New Spain.[12] Coming logically out of this period of reexamination, Esquivel uses the mode of fiction to propose a "flesh and blood" version of Doña Marina's experience and to prod her readers toward a reconsideration of the armaments in the "domestic battle" Alarcón cites.

"Domestic Tranquility" vs. "Domestic Battle"

While Laura Esquivel's so-called "romance novel" *Like Water for Chocolate* catapulted Esquivel into the international literary limelight, the twists that Esquivel weaves through her novels, in fact, offer complex portraits of anti-nation states where domestic happiness is continually thwarted, and where women and men attempt to deal with the realities – and sometimes with "magical realities" – that life brings them. *Like Water for Chocolate*, in fact, mostly takes place in the Revolutionary period, yet it asserts that the most oppressive factors in that period in Mexico were internal, family matters as opposed to external political forces. *Like Water for Chocolate* is clearly antithetical to the romance novel's requirement of achieving a standardized happy ending for the heroine – Sommer's "domestic tranquility." Tita never attains "domestic tranquility," despite her efforts to achieve it. Tita is successful in freeing her niece, Esperanza, from the cycle, so a certain amount of cosmic tranquility can be inferred in the *extra*-novel or *post*-novel, even if domestic tranquility is fleeting in the novel proper; ironically, Tita's sister Gertrudis is freed *from* "domestic tranquility" by becoming a general in the Revolutionary army.[13]

In *Malinche*, Esquivel moves closer in some ways to Sommer's construction of a narrative that seeks to establish a link to a historic past and then to create a space of "domestic tranquility" within it. However, with Esquivel, genres are never what they seem, and in *Malinche*, she explores a mediation between the literary traditions and cultures of Anahuac and Europe. In a sense, *Malinche* is a "romance novel": there is a "love story," the protagonist is fascinated by the "wrong man," and she is loved from a distance by the "right man"; however, as she did with Tita, Esquivel has awakened another passionate and resilient female protagonist who won't be pigeon-holed, and neither will the novel.

Esquivel's Malinalli

Esquivel makes no pretense of historical recreation, though she has done her research in documents and histories that mention the Nahua translator and includes a modest bibliography following the conclusion of the novel.[14] Despite the preparation, Esquivel aims toward nothing more than a deeply felt and historically informed fictionalized account of Malinalli's life in the context of events that transpired around her. Esquivel indicates that she intends to focus primarily on her protagonist's rationales and motivation, rather than on historical events, and so she does (185).

For Esquivel, Malinalli is a sympathetic and complex figure – and who would not find her so at some level? In Esquivel's narrative, she is sold into slavery, abandoned at the age of five by her mother after suffering the death of her guardian and grandmother, whom she calls *Citli* [Grandmother].[15] Malinalli is thus forcibly severed from her family and culture and, according to this version, becomes a slave to a Maya ruler.[16] Having matured in slavery, she is then given to the Europeans by the Maya and, probably in late adolescence, she is made the concubine of Cortés. Malinalli becomes the mother of two *mestizo* children, at least one of them, Cortés's. Viewed as a facilitator in the destruction of the Aztec Empire, she is again given away, this time to become the wife of a *conquistador*. Esquivel has reasonably suggested that if Malinalli's role in the Conquest merits a new perusal, then perhaps the foundational idea of Mexican culture and nationhood – that of *los hijos de la chingada* – should be re-examined, too.[17]

In Esquivel's narrative, Malinalli's response to sexual victimization is to "purify" her perpetrator by bringing Cortés into the *temascal* – a steam bath and ritual purification that is still practiced in some Mesoamerican communities to cleanse physical and psychological stains. In the *temascal* scene, Esquivel explores Malinalli's passion for telling stories and her dedication to her cultural heritage, as well as her fascination with Cortés's power. Malinalli remains a slave to Cortés until he marries her to his aide Jaramillo, in spite of the fact that her intellect and linguistic talents have earned for her the honorific name *la Lengua* [the Tongue], indicating her importance to Cortés. Malinalli becomes Cortés's voice – his tongue – to the indigenous people. She is so essential to the negotiations that the indigenous forces call Cortés "Malinche," meaning "Malinalli's Master," denoting *him* with her Nahua name.[18]

Esquivel thus reexamines the violation and servitude that made the girl Malinalli into the demon *La Malinche* – *la chingada* as identified by Paz – but Esquivel rejects Malinalli's subjugation in these contexts as the overarching message of the protagonist's life. While Esquivel presents Malinalli's violation, it is only one defining moment of her eventful life, and only one of the telling interactions between her and Cortés. What is remarkably different about Esquivel's casting of these events is that neither the Europeans nor the Mexica play the role of the "good guys." Esquivel's novel represents narratives of "domestic battles" on several levels, as well as the destruction of a civilization and the painful birth of a new culture, that of *los hijos de la chingada*. Esquivel's fiction, indeed, reverses models of the traditional romance novel and familiar constructs of Mexican national identity.

A "Flesh and Blood" Malinalli[19]

Esquivel recounts Malinalli's life and historical events from birth to death from Malinalli's perspective. The reader witnesses Malinalli's dramatic birth, for which her grandmother serves as midwife. In Nahua society, the midwife acted as mediator between life and death and was charged with rites of purification, of cleansing the stains caused by ordinary experience or by coming too close to the Divine. At one point, Esquivel's treatment of Malinalli's complicated birth focuses on the midwife's charge to dismember the fetus with an obsidian knife in the event that the infant's umbilical cord, wrapped around the neck, prevents the child from being born. At the moment the grandmother-midwife has decided she must perform that gruesome task on her own grandchild in order to spare her daughter-in-law, Malinalli emerges from the birth canal with the cord between her lips (2). The image of the newborn with the cord held in her mouth is reminiscent of the Mexican flag's eagle perched on a cactus and holding a serpent in its mouth, an image that resonates in Nahua culture, and one to which I will return later. This scene has the important task of prefiguring the guiding force in Malinalli's life, the midwife-grandmother who saves her at birth. Her grandmother will rescue her again several years later and will mold Malinalli's character, teach her useful skills, and provide her with a spiritual anchor.

When Malinalli's father dies before her third birthday (24), her mother takes a new husband and determines to erase the past – including Malinalli – from her life by selling the girl. The grandmother rebuffs this first attempt by Malinalli's mother to sell the child to a neighboring ruler, and the grandmother further insists that Malinalli must remain with her as long as the grandmother is alive. The grandmother explains her role in the care of Malinalli: "Yo estoy aquí para regalarle el camino, para suavizar su existencia, para mostrarle que el sueño en el que vivimos puede ser dulce, lleno de cantos y flores" [I am here to show her the way, to ease her existence, to show her that the dream in which we live can be sweet, full of flowers and songs] (26). The grandmother wins the argument, and Malinalli, content and protected for the time being, remains with her.

From her grandmother, Malinalli learns the ways of her people, about the nature of the gods, and her relationship with the cosmos. It is important that the grandmother's discourse reflects pre-Hispanic narrative codes, some of which are concerned with memory and the painting of codices. In several scenes, the grandmother teaches Malinalli to "dibujar codices mentales para que ejercitara el lenguaje y la memoria" [to draw mental codices in order to train her language skills and her memory] (27). The grandmother then has Malinalli narrate the codices to her because the grandmother is blind.

Toward the end of her life, Malinalli is able to compose her own codex because of her skill in interpreting memory. The grandmother explains to the child how memory works in creating a codex:

"La memoria," le dijo [la abuela a Malinalli], "es ver desde dentro. Es dar forma y color a las palabras. Sin imagines no hay memoria." Luego le pedía a la niña que dibujara en un papel un códice, o sea, una secuencia de imagines que narraran algún acontecimiento. [. . .] La abuela se divertía mucho descubriendo la imaginación y la inteligencia que su nieta tenía para interpretar las imágenes de un lienzo. (27)

["Memory," her grandmother told her, "is seeing from within. It is giving form and color to words. Without images, there is no memory." Later she would ask the child to draw a codex on paper, that is, a sequence of images that narrate an event. (. . .) The grandmother delighted in the discovery that her granddaughter had the imagination and intelligence to interpret the images from a manuscript.]

In relating this process, Esquivel sets Malinalli's adult skill with language and memory within the context of her early upbringing – through age five – under her grandmother's Anahuac tutelage.

Malinalli's skills, both those for survival and those for enhancing her existence, are her grandmother's cultural legacy. Malinalli helps her grandmother to plant and harvest corn and to make tortillas, and these are activities that she will continue to associate with her grandmother throughout her life. Indeed, Esquivel represents Malinalli's grandmother with the symbol of corn, the organizing principle of Mesoamerican society, and when her grandmother dies and she is sold into slavery, Malinalli carries her grandmother's seed corn and other gifts from her grandmother into her new life in the household of a neighboring ruler. Following her grandmother's death, Malinalli uses the memories of her grandmother to guide her choices and determine her values.

Upon the arrival of the Europeans, Malinalli faces another radical change. When the Maya offer Malinalli as a gift to the Spanish soldiers, the Spaniards soon discover her linguistic talents, and she eventually becomes "la Lengua" and is responsible for the communication between Nahuatl, Maya, and Spanish speakers. Perhaps one of the most striking insights into Esquivel's Malinalli is the translator's meditation on her role as "La Lengua:

Ser "la Lengua" era una enorme responsabilidad. No quería errar, no quería equivocarse y no veía cómo no hacerlo, pues era muy difícil traducir de una lengua a otra conceptos complicados. Ella sentía que cada vez que pronunciaba una palabra uno viajaba en la memoria cientos de generaciones atrás. Cuando uno nombraba a Ometéotl, el creador de la dualidad Ometecihtli y Omecíhuatl, el principio masculino y femenino, uno se instalaba en el momento mismo de la Creación. Ése era el poder de la palabra hablada. (60)

[Being "the Tongue" was an enormous responsibility. She didn't want to make a mistake, she didn't want to misunderstand, and she couldn't see how not to do it, because it was very difficult to translate complex ideas from one language to another. She felt that every time she pronounced a word she was traveling back hundreds of generations in memory. When one spoke the name of Ometéotl, the creator of the dual natures Ometecihtli y Omecíhuatl, the masculine and feminine principles, one was putting oneself into the very moment of Creation. That was the power of the spoken word.]

Here Malinalli struggles to incorporate European ideas and constructions into her narrative strategies, and, as the translator, she feels the weight of meaning and linguistic history on her shoulders.

In her struggle with translation, however, Malinalli also assumes that just as her Mesoamerican narrative structures embody spiritual concepts, the essence of European religious beliefs must also be contained in narrative forms. Under this assumption, she muses over Cortés's revelation that the European god has no spouse and attempts to convey to him the impossibility of such an idea. Incredulous, Malinalli explains to Cortés that God must have a wife:

"Porque sin vientre, sin oscuridad, no puede surgir la luz, la vida. Es en lo más profundo que la madre tierra produce las piedras preciosas, y es en la oscuridad del vientre que toman forma humana los hombres y los dioses. Sin vientre no hay dios." (60)

[Because without a womb, without darkness, the light – life – cannot come forth. It is only in the deepest places that Mother Earth produces precious stones, and it is in the darkness of the womb that men and gods take human form. Without a womb, there cannot be god.]

While Cortés is fascinated by her mention of "piedras preciosas" [precious stones], Malinalli continues to think in non-material terms and muses that "[s]er 'la Lengua' implica un gran compromiso espiritual" [to be "the Tongue" involves a serious spiritual commitment] (62).

Malinalli's view of spiritual matters and man's relationship to the gods urges her participation in the events of the Conquest, including the massacre at Cholula, which I will treat below. While she is dedicated to the memory of her grandmother and her pre-Conquest teachings, Malinalli expresses disdain for the blood sacrifice practiced by the current Mexica Empire and the region's other ruling entities. As she processes her new information about the Europeans, considering the prospect of her freedom at their hands and her death should the Mexica Empire triumph, Malinalli struggles to reconcile her construction of the pre-Hispanic divinity Quetzalcóatl with Spanish religious beliefs. The theme of the return of Quetzalcóatl permeates Colonial narratives of the Conquest, and Esquivel weaves this motif into her narrative structure and into Malinalli's professions of faith, both Nahua and Christian. Some pre-

Hispanic texts claim that Quetzalcóatl formally prohibited human sacrifice at the ancient city of Tula and that the community subsequently broke the god's interdict, angering the god and inviting retribution, and this is the construction of Quetzalcóatl to which Malinalli subscribes.[20]

This is also the construction of Quetzalcóatl used by the missionary priests in order to link Quetzalcóatl to Jesus Christ. In the scene of Malinalli's conversion to Christiantity, the baptism of Cortés's female slaves offers Malinalli the first sign that European religious beliefs might be akin to those of Mesoamerica. Malinalli expects a transformational ceremony like those of her culture, and she arrives appropriately adorned in an embroidered *huipil* that she has threaded with religious significance, but the European rite and her European name, "Marina," leave her unmoved:

> Vestía como una devota fiel pero nadie parecía notarlo. [. . .] Al único que parecía deslumbrarle su atavío era un caballo que tomaba agua en el río y que nunca le quitó la vista durante [. . .] la ceremonía del bautizo. (42)

> [She was dressed like a true-believer but no one seemed to notice. . . . The only one who appeared to take note of her attire was a horse that was drinking in the river and that never took his eyes off her during . . . the baptism ceremony.]

Later, when the priest explains that the meaning of her name is "la que provenía del mar" [that which comes from the sea], Malinalli wishes for something more profound: "Ella esperaba que el nombre que le estaban adjudicando los enviados de Quetzalcóatl tuviera un significado mayor. [. . .] Su nombre tenía que significar algo importante" [She was hoping that the name given her by the emissaries of Quetzalcóatl might have greater meaning. (. . .) Her name should mean something important] (42).

Malinalli's spiritual crisis culminates when a woman from Cholula tells her that the locals are planning to ambush the Spaniards. Malinalli will either betray the city of Cholula by telling the Europeans about the plan, or else betray her new position as "la Lengua" to Cortés by failing to reveal the Cholulans' plan. As she washes clothes in the river, Malinalli meditates on the decision she must make, favoring neither the Mexica and their leader Moctezuma, nor the Spaniards and Cortés. When Malinalli enters the river to bathe, Cortés, arriving at the same moment with the same intention, discovers her and enters the water with her (74). While the two naked young bathers discuss the nature of the Mesoamerican divinity Tlaloc, the Rain God, Cortés becomes sufficiently aroused that he decides to possess Malinalli and her god at the same time ("quiso poseer a Malinalli y a su dios al mismo tiempo") and just has time to ask her what her god is like before throwing himself on top of her ("lanzarse sobre ella") (75).

Esquivel's construction of cosmic passion, lust, water, and spiritual searching culminates in a violent thunderstorm at the moment of Cortés's violation of Malinalli. In Malinalli's experience of the moment, her senses are overwhelmed by silence and water:

Mientras, llovió tan fuerte que esa passión y ese orgasmo quedaron sepultados en agua, lo mismo que las lágrimas de Malinalli, quien por un momento había dejado de ser 'la Lengua' para convertirse en una simple mujer, callada, sin voz [. . .]. (76)

[All the while, it rained so hard that that passion and that orgasm became entombed in water, the same as the tears of Malinalli, who, for a moment, had ceased to be "the Tongue" to become just a woman, silent, without a voice . . .].

In an Esquivelian touch, Malinalli's future husband and Cortés's faithful officer, Jaramillo, witnesses these events and finds her unforgettable (77).

Following this turbulent union, Malinalli leads Cortés to the *temascal* for healing and purification, the scene to which I referred above. In the *temascal*, Malinalli takes the lead, instructing Cortés (and non-Mexican readers) in the practices of the *temascal*:

Si entras al temascal, si te desnudas de todos tus atavíos, de todos tus metales, de todos tus miedos y te sientas sobre la Madre Tierra, junto al fuego, junto al agua, podrás renovarte, renacer, elevarte, navegar por el viento como lo hizo Quetzalcóatl, dejar a un lado tu piel, tu vestimenta humana y convertirte en dios y solo un dios como ése puede vencer a los mexicas. (84)

[If you enter the *temascal*, if you strip yourself of all your gear, of all your metal, of all your fears, and you sit on Mother Earth, next to the fire, next to the water, you will be able to renew yourself, to be reborn, to lift yourself up, to sail on the wind like Quetzalcóatl, to leave your skin aside, your human trappings, and to become a god, and only as a god can you defeat the Mexica.]

In the *temascal*, Malinalli answers Cortés's questions about Quetzalcóatl, explaining his rule and fall at Tula, as well as the divinity's incarnation as the Morning Star. After Malinalli's lesson in Mesoamerican spirituality and the purification of their bodies in the *temascal* ceremony, Cortés and

Malinalli exit the "womb" of the *temascal* and return to the business at hand: Cholula.

In Esquivel's construction of events, culminating in the scene at the river, Malinalli asserts that the Mexica, in their obsession with human sacrifice, have strayed from the teachings of Quetzalcóatl (*i.e.*, to eliminate human sacrifice at Tula); however, Malinalli's dedication to Quetzalcóatl is threatened by the massacre of Cholula, which remains an important site in the veneration of the god. In fact, Cortés's informants (probably the Tlaxcalans) alert the Spaniards and preempt Malinalli's conflict, and the Europeans plot a massacre to assure that the Cholulteca will not hinder their passage to Tenochtitlan. In Esquivel's narrative, when Cholula falls, Malinalli questions her faith and her role in the event, and she wonders at the fact that Quetzalcóatl did not help the indigenous forces defeat the invaders (103).

At this crisis, Malinalli discovers that in addition to memory, "forgetting" is also an important aspect of her narrative:

Ahora deseaba olvidar.

No quería que las imágenes de la destrucción de Tula formara un códice en su mente. Quería olvidar también el día en el temascal, en el que confió que Quetzalcóatl había humedecido en Cortés el recuerdo de dios. Ya no quería hablar, ya no quería salvar su libertad. No a ese precio. No através de la muerte de tantos inocentes, de tantos niños, de tantas mujeres. Antes que ello prefería que de su vientre salieran serpientes que se enrollaran por todo su cuerpo, que le ahogaran el cuello, que la dejaran sin respiración, que la volvieran nada, palabra en la humedad de la lengua, símbolo, glífo, piedra. (103)

[Now she wished to forget.

She did not want the images of Tula's destruction to form a codex (a series of images) in her memory. She wanted to forget also the day in the *temescal* when she had trusted that that Quetzalcóatl had moistened the memory of god for Cortés. She did not want to talk, to get her freedom. Not at this price. Not by means of the murder of so many innocent people, so many children, so many women. Before that, she would rather have serpents come from her womb and wind around her whole body, choking her around the neck, leaving her without breath, making her nothing, a word in the wetness of the tongue, a symbol, a glyph, a stone.]

Perhaps it is at this moment that Malinalli is the most chingada.

Regardless of the involvement of the Tlaxcalans, an image from the

Lienzo de Tlaxcala presents "Malintzin" speaking in the midst of full blown battle, as interpreter of and witness to the Massacre of Cholula. This is one of the most frequently reproduced images of her participation in the Conquest, and it is interpreted as depicting her betrayal of the native forces. In the historical accounts, nevertheless, the Tlaxcalans were seen as the traitors. In Esquivel's narrative, from this point onward, Malinalli begins to redefine herself and to distance herself from Cortés, despite her continued fascination with the *conquistador*.

Beyond *la chingada*

As the events of the Conquest unfold, Malinalli's codex makes clear her connections with Tonantzin, the female divinity called the "mother of the people," who will be linked with the Virgin of Guadalupe in the Colony, and who was connected in pre-Columbian times with the *Cihuateteo*, women who died in childbirth and who are linked with the *Tzitzimime*.[21] Malinalli is also disturbed by the fanaticism with which Cortés pursues his expedition to conquer the Hibueras. During the campaign, when Malinalli asks that Cortés follow her to a secluded place in order that she may "tell him something," he expects her to impart a military secret. When finally he demands, "¿[Q]ué es lo que quieres?" [What do you want?] (152), she delivers an unprecedented scolding:

Lo que quiero no puedo tocarlo. Está lejos de mí. Lo que quiero es sentir la piel de nuestro hijo. [. . .] Tú me prometiste libertad y no me la has dado. Para ti, yo no tengo alma ni corazón, soy un objecto parlante que usas sin sentimiento alguno para tus conquistas. [. . .] Lo que quiero es que despiertes y que aceptes la oportunidad que te ofrezco de ser felices, de ser una familia, de ser un sólo ser. [. . .] Olvídate de esta idea absurda de ir a conquistar las Hibueras, por favor, Hernán, destierra de tu mente esa locura. (152–53)

[What I want, I cannot touch. It is far from me. What I want is to feel our son's skin. . . . You promised me liberty, and you have not given it to me. To you, I have no soul, no heart, I am a talking object that you use without any feeling to achieve your conquests. . . . What I want is for you to wake up and to accept the opportunity I am offering you to be happy, to be a family, to be one being. . . . Forget this absurd idea to conquer the Hibueras; please, Hernán, drive this crazy idea from your mind.]

Malinalli has made her choice. She does not wish to participate in war ever again. She wants to be a wife and a mother, to be free. She offers Cortés a home and family – "domestic tranquility" – and he rejects the idea and her advice categorically, telling her to "get it together" ("Vuelve a la razón, Marina" 153).

At this moment, in the midst of these historical events, the "foundational fictions" of Sommer's domestic tranquility are possible, at least in Malinalli's thinking. Cortés refuses Malinalli, but he later gives her the opportunity for a peaceful life and a family by marrying her to Jaramillo (155–56). Even as the act of "giving" Malinalli to another serves to separate her from Cortés and his service, the marriage to Jaramillo works to liberate Malinalli from her destiny as "la Lengua." The night of the wedding, she lies awake, her thoughts on her role in Cortés's success:

> Pensó en los momentos en que la boca de Cortés y su boca fueron una sola boca y el pensamiento de Cortés y su lengua una sola idea, un universo nuevo. La lengua los había unido y la lengua los separaba. La lengua era la culpable de todo. Malinalli había destruido el imperio de Moctezuma con su lengua. Gracias a sus palabras, Cortés se había hecho de aliados que aseguraron su conquista. Decidió entonces, castigar el instrumento que había creado ese universo. (157)

> [She thought about the times when her mouth and Cortés's mouth were one mouth, when Cortés's thoughts and her tongue were one idea, a new universe. Her tongue had united them and her tongue was separating them. Her tongue was capable of anything. Malinalli had destroyed Moctezuma's empire with her tongue. Thanks to her words, Cortés had made alliances to assure his conquest. She decided, then, to punish the instrument that had created that universe.]

In a punishment that reflects auto-sacrificial rites performed throughout Mesoamerica, Malinalli uses a maguey spine to pierce her tongue so that she could never again be the instrument of conquest. She ceases to be "La Lengua" and refuses to be dominated by Cortés or to participate in the Conquest. Cortés's campaign to the Hibueras, like the potential relationship between Cortés and Malinalli, ends in failure (160). She moves beyond *la chingada*.

Malinalli now begins to experience life as a free woman, a wife, and a mother. On the voyage home from the Hibueras, she gives birth to her daughter and names her "María," which pleases Jaramillo (158–59). From the ship, Malinalli tosses the baby's umbilical cord to the sea, making a connection between the salty liquid of birth and the liquid forces of nature found in the ocean. As she nurses the baby, Malinalli realizes that

187

she has become the divine liquid that she sought in her spiritual quest: "Entonces Malinalli se volvió líquida, leche en sus pechos, lágrimas en sus ojos, sudor en su cuerpo, saliva en su boca, agua de agradecimiento" [Then Malinalli became liquid: milk in her breasts, tears in her eyes, sweat on her body, saliva in her mouth, the water of gratitude] (160). She reconnects with her spiritual essence, with the liquid of Nahua religious practices: blood from her pierced tongue, water, milk, sweat, and saliva. Here, she begins to extract herself from the "grave spiritual compromise" that she suffered when she became "la Lengua."

She recovers Martín, her son by Cortés (160–65), and with Martín, Jaramillo, and María, she settles in Coyoacan (169 *ff.*). Jaramillo plays a doting husband and father and makes woodcarvings of the Spanish Virgin of Guadalupe, remembered from his childhood in Extremadura. Malinalli prepares meals and experiments with ingredients, and he and Malinalli design a patio garden that recalls his visit to the *Alahambra* and Malinalli's memories of Tula, the ancient Mexican city of Quetzalcóatl (170–71). In Malinalli's garden, Spain's Arabic heritage converges with Mexico's indigenous forms and values, and Jaramillo's carved images of the Virgin of Guadalupe contribute a polyvalent sign to their domestic life. While the Mexican Virgin appeared to "Juan Diego," a Nahua man in Tepeyaca, and offered him the "roses of Castile" as proof of her appearance to him,[22] the Virgin of Guadalupe known to Jaramillo as a boy in Spain was (and is) a black Virgin, carved from black wood, adding further ethnic and cultural layers to the Virgin's image. In Malinalli's beautiful garden where waters flow to the four cardinal directions and create a polyvalent cross at their intersection, Malinalli finds the domestic tranquility that is realized by Sommer's star-crossed lovers in new nations. The difference here is that Malinalli finds bliss beyond – and in spite of – her association with the dashing Cortés, not because of it.

Like those of many female protagonists in Latin America's romantic novels, Malinalli's meditations on historical events explore the personal concerns of a woman, in contrast to the kinds of concerns that would trouble a historian. In many instances, reading *Malinche* is like turning the pages of Malinalli's diary. While this is a much more personal narrative than those usually seen in the Nahua oral and pictorial tradition, Esquivel makes Malinalli a potential *tlacuilo* (codex painter), but one who is exceptional in that she records her own story in the pictographic style of pre-Hispanic Mexico. Malinalli's personal codex appears integrated into the book jacket, printed on the reverse side and depicting events of Malinalli's life in images modeled on pre-Hispanic and Colonial art. The images are likewise a narration of the novel, so the "codex" reflects an experiment with Mesoamerican literary forms, as well as an experimental technique added to the novel.

As she did with music and sets of illustrations in *The Law of Love* (1995), Esquivel reaches beyond the traditional form of the novel with the reversible, double-coded book jacket. The inside jacket, "Malinalli's codex," places the indigenous form of expression as equivalent to the invader's text. In her introduction, Esquivel explains:

> Algunos historiadores han considerado que la imagen [era la técnica] más importante para la conciliación cultural de la conquista española en tierras americanas y que es la imagen de la Virgen de Guadalupe [que] ha sido concebida y plasmada como una de las formas más sofisticadas de[l] códice. [. . .]
> Por esta razón decidí era indispensable que un códice acompañara esta novela. (viii)

> [Some historians have considered that the image was the most important (technique) in the cultural conciliation of the Spanish Conquest on American soil and that it is the image of the Virgin of Guadalupe (which) has been conceived and promulgated as one of the most sophisticated forms within the codex. . . .
> For this reason, I decided that it was indispensable to have a codex accompany the novel.]

In addition to the balance and inclusiveness Esquivel seeks with the commission of the codex, she is at pains to privilege certain Nahuatl forms of address and oral narration within the pages of her narrative, among them the *huehuetlatolli* [the speech of elders], *oraciones* [prayers], and *xochicuicatl* [the flower song]. Esquivel, in particular, explores specific *huehuetlatolli* techniques using rich, dense metaphoric images to instruct and inform a Nahua audience.

The *huehuetlatolli* is particularly important in the discourse styles of Malinalli's father and grandmother. Elders would use the *huehuetlatolli* in offering advice to children and young people, so it is appropriate that the grandmother uses this narrative form since it reinforces her role as an "elder" passing on her cultural connections to Malinalli. The words of the grandmother (quoted above) as she explains to Malinalli's mother why she must be allowed to rear the child for as long as she lives, reflect the *huehuetlatolli*, and the final image of her speech, that of a "sweet" life full of "songs and flowers," suggests the *xochicuicatl* [flower song] that was important in the narration of military events and histories (26). The *xochicuicatl* is also important in the context of Malinalli's formative influences since many of these songs are also connected to visual representations of historical events; to the celebration of beauty that appears in songs, poetry, and dance; and to the painting of mnemonic texts that would be called "códices" by the Spaniards.

189

Malinalli's father's first utterances to his newborn daughter include the Mesoamerican *oraciones* [prayers] that are customarily offered to welcome a new life. These words could have been taken directly from Nahua sources:

> Aquí estás mi hijita, la esperada por mí, la soñada, mi collar de piedras finas, mi plumaje de quetzal, mi hechura humana, la nacida de mí. Tú eres mi sangre, mi color, en ti está mi imagen. Mi muchachita, mira con calma: he aquí a tu madre, a tu señora, de su vientre, de su seno, te desprendiste, brotaste. Como si fueras una yerbita, así brotaste. Como si hubieras estado dormida y hubieras despertado. Ahora vives, has nacido, te ha enviado a la tierra el Señor Nuestro, el dueño del cerca y del junto, en hacedor de la gente, el inventor de los hombres. (6)

> [Here you are my little daughter, my awaited one, dreamed one, my necklace of fine stones, my quetzal plumage, my human creation, the one born of me. You are my blood, my color, my image is within you. My little girl, look calmly: here I have your mother, your lady, from her womb, from her breast you loosened yourself, you came forth. As if you had been a little plant, thus you sprouted. Now you live, you have been born, you have been sent to earth by Our Lord, the Ruler of the Near and the Close, the Maker of People, the Inventor of Men.]

The final epithets refer to the god Quetzalcóatl and relate the safe birth of the child and her destiny to the god's intention. The first phrase is very close to the one Malinalli will adopt to tell Martín, her son by Cortés, who he is in relation to her (162).

Also interesting in this scene is that Esquivel has the father break from tradition and include his own "predictions" for the child's life: "Hija mía, vienes del agua y el agua habla" [My daughter, you come from the water and the water speaks] (6). He references here Malinalli's intimate kinship with water, to which she is drawn throughout her life. Her father also foreshadows her role in history: "Y tu lengua será palabra de luz y tu palabra, pincel de flores, palabra de colores que con tu voz pintará nuevos codices" [And your tongue will be the word of light and your word, your paintbrush of flowers, of colors; you will paint new codices with your voice] (7). As her father predicts, Malinalli's voice and words will contribute to new codices, and she will later avail herself of the models used by her father and grandmother to form her own speeches.

In the final discourse given to Malinalli in the novel, the former translator communicates with the female Mesoamerican divinity often called Tonantzin [Our Revered Mother], who will emerge years afterward as the Virgin of Guadalupe, the image of an indigenous Mary who serves as the patron saint of Mexico. In their "conversation," Tonantzin advises Malinalli that the nature of the divine as constructed by the Amerindians will change, but that "the ancient gods, the unchanging, those of the near and close, those who have no beginning or end, will not change except in form" (178). Malinalli's *huehuetlatolli* begins:

> A ti, silencio de la mañana, perfume del pensamiento, corazón del deseo, intención luminosa de la creación, a ti, que levantas las caricias en flores, y que eres la luz de la esperanza, el secreto de los labios, el diseño de lo visible, a ti te encargo lo que amo, te encargo a mis hijos, que nacieron del amor que no tiene carne, que nacieron del amor que no tiene principio, que nacieron de lo noble, lo bello, de lo sagrado, a ti que eres una con ellos, te los entrego para que estés en su mente, para que dirijas sus pisadas, para que habites en sus palabras, para que no pierdan el deseo de vivir. [. . .] Ellos, que son la mezcla de todas las sangres – la ibérica, la africana, la romana, la goda, la sangre indígena y la sangre del medio oriente [. . .] Preséntate ante ellos con tu collar de jade, con tus plumas de quetzal, con tu manto de estrellas, para que puedan reconocerte, para que sientan tu presencia. [. . .] Fortalece el espíritu de la nueva raza que con nuevos ojos se mira en el espejo de la luna, para que sepa que su presencia en la tierra es una promesa cumplida del universo. Una promesa de plenitud, de vida, de redención y de amor. (179–80)

> [To you, silence of the morning, perfume of thought, heart of desire, luminous intention of creation, to you, who lifts up caresses with flowers, and who is the light of hope, the secret of lips, the design of the visible, to you I entrust what I love, I entrust my children, who were born from a love that has no flesh, who were born from a love that has no beginning, who were born from what is noble, beautiful, and sacred; to you who are one with them, I entrust them to you so that you are in their thoughts, so that you direct their steps, so that you exist in their words, so that they do not lose the will to live. . . . They, who are a mix of all bloodlines – Iberian, African, Roman, Visigoth, indigenous blood, and Middle Eastern blood. . . . Present yourself to them in your jade necklace, with your quetzal feathers, with your robe of stars, so that they can recognize you, so that they can feel your presence. . . . Strengthen the spirit of the new race so that it sees itself in the mirror of the moon, so that it knows that your presence on the Earth is a promise fulfilled in the universe. A promise of prosperity, of life, of redemption, and of love.]

Malinalli's petition to the goddess is thoroughly *huehuetlatolli*, but within the form, she places indigenous cultural heritage with Iberia's multicultural heritage: European, African, Visigoth, Roman, Christian, Jewish, and Muslim.

As Malinalli becomes "La Lengua" and then ceases to be "La Lengua" though Esquivel's narrative, the reader is made aware of the processes through which Malinalli learns, from her grandmother and others, how to craft a story and how to represent a narrative properly in Mesoamerican cultures: it is to be told out loud and painted on *amatl* [bark paper]. In keeping with this principle, Esquivel enlarges the printed narrative with the "Malinche codex" contained inside the book jacket, where the narrative appears in Mesoamerican pictorial form. As Esquivel crafted her standard narrative, she guided her *tlacuilo* [illustrator, book painter], Jordi Castells, in setting down the signifying images into a pictorial text. Wrapped around the book and concealed within the jacket, these images invite the reader who "discovers" them to explore an ancient form of art and narrative.

By pointing outside itself at this "painted book," the narrative voice attempts to involve the reader in a different kind of reading – "reading" Mesoamerican style. The attentive reader learns to interpret the pictographic signs through reading the book, and also to anticipate events of the written narrative by examining the signs in the codex. Like traditional Nahua texts, Esquivel's narrative is auto-referential, pointing at its own narrative strategies and techniques: the arts of codex writing, of image painting, of reconstructing events, of narrating, and of remembering.

In the final image of the codex, as in Malinalli's final *huehuetlatolli*, Esquivel combines signifiers from multiple cultures. Malinalli smokes a European-style pipe with her beloved Jaramillo in an Arabic-inspired courtyard with water running from four directions – a powerful Mesoamerican image. Her children play in the garden that Jaramillo has built to remind them of his Spanish home. Jaramillo carves images of the Spanish Virgin of Guadalupe – who is connected to the coming Mexican Virgin through Tonantzin to whom Malinalli directs her prayer for the well-being of her children at the sacred mountain of Tepeyac – where Juan Diego will encounter the Mexican Virgin in 1531. In the same way that Esquivel incorporates and subjects historical figures to her artistic vision, she shapes literary conventions and cultural artifacts from many cultures in order to reinterpret them as "Mexican." Her narrative thus becomes a *mestizaje* of indigenous and European constructions, images, codes, and participants.

Esquivel's Malinalli embodies Mexico as a *mestizo* nation; she is the mother who conceived and bore the children who founded the nation, and she prays, inexplicably associating Jaramillo's Spanish Virgin with Tonantzin (180), to a *mestizo* heaven for the nation's protection and prosperity. From the moment that Malinalli emerges from her mother's womb with the umbilical cord grasped in her mouth, to her pilgrimage to Tepeyac to commune with Tonantzin; from Jaramillo's carving of his Virgin of Guadalupe suspended above their marriage bed, to the death in which Malinalli's soul is united with the Mexica cosmos and Quetzalcóatl, the most powerful images of Mexico converge in the Nahua translator.

As the mother of the first *mestizo*, "La Malinche" has long stood as the mother of the *mestizaje* created by the fusion of European and Amerindian cultures, but that maternity has been problematic. As the historical woman of Chicana discourse of the last century, "La Malinche" was invested with autonomy, rationale, and power. Esquivel, taking that signal further, portrays a "flesh and blood" woman who is an equal of – even superior to – both Cortés and Moctezuma; moreover, Esquivel's narrative honors her Malinalli as a voice that nurtures the inevitable union of two cultures, neither perfect nor utopic, but each with elements that enrich and inform life at every level.

Whether Malinalli can or should be called *puta* or *chingada* is not an issue in Esquivel's narrative. In its final chapters, Malinalli moves beyond the blame and the horrific events of the Conquest to live the life she desires. "Domestic tranquility" (Sommer's term) is achieved in the awareness that despite imperfect ancestors and horrific memories of suffering, a family might yet be able to enjoy a fruitful life together. While Adriana López's review of the novel postulates that Doña Marina "overcame her condition as a slave to take part in a crusade that would liberate her from the Aztec rule," it is more accurate to say that in Esquivel's construction of the "hero" (or "anti-hero"), Malinalli consciously withdraws from political history, scarred and exhausted, to enjoy her family and find herself again. In this world, no romantic hero conquers all. Malinalli is, in the end, a mother who yearns for the best future for her beloved children. Esquivel creates a woman as flawed, as thoroughly motivated, and as rational as those powerful male actors in the drama of the Conquest, distancing her from the cultural icon and historical stigma of *la chingada*.

Notes

1 Paz (1914–1998) included "The Sons of La Malinche" as the fourth chapter in *The Labyrinth of Solitude* (1961. *El laberinto de la soledad* 1950, 2nd ed. 1959). See the recent Penguin Spanish edition (1997).
2 Literally, "Mexican-ness," *i.e.*, what it means to be "Mexican," or the essential nature of being "Mexican." On Carlos Fuentes, see Poniatowska's essay (in English), n. 11.
3 The adjective *Nahua* refers to the culture practiced by speakers of the

Nahuatl language. The Mexica-Tenochca (commonly referred to as "Aztecs") were one group of Nahuatl speakers, but the Tlaxcalans and other Mesoamerican groups also spoke Nahuatl. Cortés's translation corps included Maya-speaking Spanish priest Gerónimo de Aguilar, who had lived as a captive with the Maya in the Yucatán for seven to eight years by the time Cortés landed there and took him on board ship ("rescued him"). Malinalli also spoke Maya as well as her native Nahuatl dialect. She translated from Nahuatl to Maya, and Aguilar, from Maya to Spanish. After a short time, her Spanish was adequate to perform the task without Aguilar. Bernal Díaz de Castillo (1496–1584) describes this process in his chronicle of the period; see n. 14, below.

4　The *Lienzo de Tlaxcala*, referred to below (n. 5) in a separate context, affirms the participation of the indigenous allies of Cortés who helped defeat the Aztec empire. Also see n. 14, below.

5　The *Lienzo* contains a series of panels depicting the Conquest of Mexico and post-Conquest exploration. Tulane University's Latin American Library mentions "three so-called lost 'originals,'" rather than a single "original"; see The Latin American Library at Tulane in the Works Cited

　　The Glasgow University Library Special Collections Department sponsors online images of the manuscript with accompanying tutorials to honor the Royal Academy of Arts (London) exhibition *Aztecs* (16 November– 11 April 2003). The narrative provides the information that scribes "used natural dyes on prepared animal skin, on paper made from the bark of the fig tree, or from cotton" to create "pictograms" (Aztecs – Painted Books), models for the "codex" Esquivel commissioned for *Malinche*. See *Historia de Tlaxcala* and *Aztecs – Painted Books* in the Works Cited.

　　A facsimile of the *Lienzo de Tlaxcala*, edited and published by Alfredo Chavero in 1892 for the Mexico Antiquities Commission in celebration of the 400th anniversary of Columbus's first voyage, shows careful consideration of the role of Malinalli given in the Tlaxcalan version of the Conquest. See also n. 4, above, and n. 15, below.

6　The *Lienzo de Tlaxcala* contains various images of Malinalli. For further discussion of her role in the Tlaxcalan narratives, see Gillespie (2004) chapter five.

7　See Gillespie (2004) chapter two.

8　See Orozco's *Cortés and Malinche* (1926); the detail of the mural showing Cortés and Malinche is reproduced in Susan Schroeder, Stephanie Wood, and Robert Stephen Haskett's edited collection (298) from the original in the stairwell at the Antiguo Colegio de San Ildefonso, Mexico City.

9　Max Harris describes the conflation of the "Conquests" and their representation in the *matachines* dances.

10　*La Llorona* dates to the sixteenth century in the manuscript of the *Florentine Codex* (Biblioteca Medicea Laurenziana, the Laurentian Library, Florence, Italy), which shows her as a wailing woman (9). For the *Florentine Codex*, see Sahagún, Bernardino de (d. 1590) in "Works Cited" in this volume.

11　See Mary Louise Pratt's article on Chicana views of Malinche. See also

Cypess, especially 12–13.

12 See Frances Karttunen's article, especially 291. See also, Gillespie, especially chapter five.

13 Quotations in this essay from *Like Water for Chocolate* / *Como agua para chocolate* come from the Spanish edition by Doubleday, 1993. The reader will recall that Esperanza is dead during the narration and that her daughter is narrating. Gertrudis is addressed as *"mi generala"* [*lit.* "my general"] by her aide, Treviño (180). In the novel, see especially "Capítulo 10: Octubre: Torrejas de natas" [Chapter 10, October: Cream Fritters (the Christensens' translation of the chapter title)].

14 The historical record on Esquivel's subject is scanty. Ironically, Malinalli's voice, while powerful in the events of the Conquest, is seldom recorded. Cortés's *Letters from Mexico* (1986. *Cartas de Relación*), which are generally considered historical documents rather than literature, mentions the interpreter only once, and Bernal Díaz de Castillo (1496–1584), who accompanied Cortés to Mexico, speaks briefly of her life in his *The History of the Conquest of New Spain* (2008. *Historia verdadera de la conquista de Nueva España*), which is also principally of historical interest. Both works have seen several editions in English and many in Spanish. Doña Marina is also mentioned in letters to the court of Spain from her descendants and from men who were formerly a part of Cortés's army. Joanne Danaher Chaison discusses the contents of the "Shäfer Index" (516 *ff.*) and of Mariano Cuevas's *Cartas y otros documentos de Hernán Cortés* [Letters and Other Documents of Hernán Cortés] in regard to statements and documents related to Doña Marina. See Chaison's references to these sources and her lengthy footnote on older works on Diaz de Castillo's Doña Marina as "Malinche" (522–23 n. 31). Doña Marina's personal history and her activity during the Conquest are documented mainly through Amerindian sources. *Lienzo de Tlaxcala* shows her image twenty-four times in its first forty-eight scenes (see n. 5, above).

15 *Citli* is Nahuatl for "grandmother." See Paul Radin's article for Mesoamerican kinship terms.

16 For a fascinating discussion that offers some insight into Malinalli's indenture to the Maya ruler, see McCafferty and McCafferty.

17 See Gabriel San Roman's blog for "Laura Esquivel Visits Santa Ana [California]."

18 See Ryan F. Long's essay in this volume on the linguistic explanations for the name "Malinche" as applied to Cortés and to Malinalli. Karttunen addresses the matter (292–93), as does Chaison, from a slightly different perspective (514–15, 514 n. 2).

19 Quotations come from the Spanish edition of the novel. Translations are those of the author and editor.

20 Despite post-Conquest claims suggesting that Quetzalcóatl eliminated human sacrifice in the Mexican highlands, archaeological evidence indicates that sites dedicated to the worship of Quetzalcóatl – including Cholula – did, in fact, practice human sacrifice. See Anamaria Ashwell

(*Elementos*) and Suárez Cruz and Martínez Arriaga (*Monografía*). Tula, also known as Tullán, was the Toltec capital.

21 Esquivel mentions the Cihuateteo in describing Malinalli's patio design (182). See studies of the Virgin of Guadalupe by Richard Nebel (*et al*) and Edmundo O'Gorman for the Virgin's origins in Spain and the development of the legend in Mexico. See Woodrow Borah's summary of the Mexican and Spanish legends, especially 328–330, and his account of the documentary evidence. *Cihuateteo* and *Tzitzimime* appear in the Glossary of this volume.

22 As Louise M. Burkhart notes, there is scant archaeological evidence of pre-Conquest worship at this shrine, a site apparently dedicated to an indigenous female divinity; however, the worship of a chthonic [*Gk*. of or from the earth] Mother / Grandmother divinity was prevalent in Nahua culture.

Esquivel's Malinalli: Refusing the Last Word on *La Malinche*

Ryan F. Long

Laura Esquivel's *Malinche: A Novel* christens its title character "Malinalli," thus negotiating the vexed problem of naming a character with too many names and no certain name and, interestingly, choosing the famous pejorative as the title that names her novel.[1] In these and other ways, the text acknowledges the nature of the author's task as open-ended and ripe for further interpretation, as it simultaneously acknowledges the title character's lack of control over her destiny, identity, and legacy within the fiction. The novel not only affirms the nature of "Malinche" as myth, but it also reflects upon the diverse and unpredictable revisions that her mythical identity has undergone continuously since the period of the Conquest. The text seeks a middle ground between Malinalli's autonomy and Malinche's predetermination, combining historical accounts with plausible conjecture based on Nahua culture and Esquivel's authorial invention.

Those who approach the matter of naming Malinche from a documentary perspective are more tentative in their assertions than Esquivel, whose task accords her creative license. Sandra Messinger Cypess (1991) outlines the mystery surrounding Malinche's probable name, but cautions that "we should not think we know with certainty her original name" (33). According to scholars such as Ricardo Herren (1993), the name *Malinche* is a plausible cross-linguistic adaptation of either the Nahuatl name *Malintzin* or the Spanish *Marina*. "Marina" is documented as the baptismal name given to the girl who was to become the concubine of Hernán Cortés (1485–1547). "Marina" was baptized in Tabasco on March 20, 1519, five days after Cortés and his men received a group of about twenty female slaves, "Marina" among them, from local Mayan leaders (25–26).

197

If the original name of the woman who would become Cortés's translator was indeed *Malinalli*, and she was recognized as being of noble birth, then *Malinche* is possible as a Spanish-language corruption of the Nahuatl *Malintzin*, which combines *Malinalli* with the honorific Nahuatl suffix *-tzin*. On the other hand, the Spanish name Marina, with its medial /r/ (a lateral alveolar tap in the Conquest period as today), would have presented an obstacle for Nahuatl speakers to perceive and reproduce since Nahuatl contains no such sound. Nahuatl speakers would probably have produced [l] (an alveolar lateral, with velarization following /a/) in the effort to pronounce /r/, and thus would have produced [malina] and possibly have added the suffix *-tzin* as a sign of respect for her position as adviser to Cortés.[2]

As Jeanne L. Gillespie points out in the preceding essay, two of the most influential views of Cortés's translator are found in Bernal Díaz del Castillo's sixteenth-century chronicle, *The History of the Conquest of New Spain*, and in Octavio Paz's mid-twentieth-century philosophical musings on the Mexican psyche in "The Sons of La Malinche.[3] Díaz de Castillo refers to her honorifically as "Doña Marina," but Paz casts her as "La Malinche," the consummate traitor, the female responsible for Mexico's collective psychological trauma, whose sexual sin is unpardonable. Recent critics continue to take those characterizations as starting points in considering the cultural and literary significance of the translator. Cypess points out that Díaz de Castillo "compares her to models from the Bible and the Spanish literary tradition that were well known to his readers" in order to imply that the Conquest was an evangelical and noble enterprise (28). Countering Paz, Chicana feminist writers, like Cherríe L. Moraga (1981), reinterpret the translator in positive terms and call attention to the misogyny at the heart of blaming her for the fall of the Aztec Empire.[4] Díaz de Castillo presents Doña Marina's nobility as factual, and contemporary scholars such as Herren, Cypess, and Camilla Townsend (2006) accept it as probable. Esquivel presents as uncontested Malinalli's noble origins, as well as her birth year, though the birth year is an educated guess. Scholars, however, consider Esquivel's choice of the birth year plausible.[5] Esquivel's use of 1504 as her protagonist's birth year allows her to present Malinalli's birth as coincident with Cortés's documented arrival in the "New World," a neat fit of fictional destiny.

Esquivel constructs Malinalli as innately associated with destiny, embodying and responding to historical events and cosmic tendencies beyond her control: "Todas estas nociones del tiempo son las que acompañaban a cada ser humano desde el momento en que nacía. Malinalli había nacido en la casa doce. [. . .] El significado del doce es el de la resurrección" [All these ideas of time are those that go with every person from the moment of birth. Malinalli was born in the twelfth house. . . . The meaning of "twelve" is resurrection] (41).[6] With the idea of resurrection in play, Esquivel attempts to resurrect "La Malinche" as Malinalli, beginning at the beginning. The novel opens with a detailed recreation of the heroine's birth in Mexico, presented as simultaneous with Cortés's landing on the island of Hispaniola in 1504 (7–10).

Malinalli–Malinche's Open-Ended Tale

The newborn is named "Malinalli" in accord with the Nahua tradition of naming children for the day they were born.[7] Malinalli receives her name and its significance from *Citli* [grandmother],[8] Malinalli's father's mother, who acts as midwife to her daughter-in-law at the dangerous birth. In the ceremonial "baptism" several days later, *Citli* suggests a deeper meaning of Malinalli's name when she declares to the infant that "A partir de hoy serás llamada Malinalli, ese nombre será tu sino, el que por nacimiento te corresponde" [From this day you will be called Malinalli; this name will be your destiny, which is your birthright] (6). The infant's father then enlarges the meaning by alluding to a destiny that is tied inextricably to her words and tongue and to her "giving voice": "Tu palabra será el fuego que transforma todas las cosas [. . . .] Y tu lengua será palabra de luz y tu palabra, pincel de flores, palabra de colores que con tu voz pintará nuevos codices" [Your word will be the fire that transforms all things. . . . Your tongue will be a word of light and your word, a brush of flowers, a word of colors that with your voice will paint new codices] (6–7). Esquivel suggests that Malinalli will realize her destiny and define her place in history through spoken and written language, and later enlarges on the meaning of *malinalli*, connecting the name cross-culturally with images of indigenous and Spanish spirituality.

Esquivel offers sophisticated imagery and associations that suggest productive, layered ways of interpreting Malinalli–Malinche, and, ironically, point to Esquivel's limitations as Malinalli–Malinche's "interpreter."[9] In one of these layered passages, the child Malinalli has discovered that her grandmother is blind and is surprised when her grandmother "sees" the world around her in a uniquely intuitive way that implies a parallel procedure for "reading" the absences in the historical record. Standing outside their dwelling in the rain, *Citli* tells Malinalli to look at the sky because *Citli* "sees" eagles flying overhead. When Malinalli asks how *Citli* can "see" the eagles despite being blind, *Citli* responds, "[C]uando llueve, el agua me habla, el agua me indica la forma que tienen los animales cuando los acaricia" [When it rains, the water talks to me, the water tells me the forms of the animals as it touches them] (54). *Citli*'s perception consists in her being able to distinguish the rain-defined contours around an absence of rain, an image that serves as a particularly apt metaphor for interpreting La Malinche as Malinalli, for giving form to a historical absence by means of the space created by that absence.

Esquivel suggests that in order to know who "La Malinche" was, we think about her in terms of the empty spaces at the heart of her signification, and Esquivel models that approach in her text. Malinalli is shown struggling to comprehend a series of losses: the deaths of her father, her grandmother, her people, and the "old gods"; her mother's abandoning her; her rape by Cortés; the destruction and massacres of the Conquest; her separation from her son; her reunion with the mother who abandoned her; and her final separation from Cortés. Malinalli's coming-of-age / coming-to-eternity journey is an individual, internalized experience, partly an evolution and partly a quest.

The mutability in these and other passages suggests that Esquivel intends a specific kind of layered reading: the first directs the reader to become involved in the fiction of Malinalli, and the other is a reflective reading – or a post-reading reflection – intended to add color to Malinche, the figure of symbol and legend, and is also open to multiple interpretations. Such passages in the novel suggest a self-reflective position for the text and urge the reader to consider not only the experience of Malinalli as it develops in Esquivel's efforts to translate "her" translator, but that of Malinche, who has been "translated" many times by many fictions.

Esquivel communicates an authorial consciousness of herself as one of the "translators" of Malinche when Malinalli goes to have her future read by a *tlachique* [fortune teller] in grains of corn. That Malinalli's fortune is revealed in corn is meaningful because corn is associated in the novel with Malinalli's grandmother, *Citli* – the novel's index of emotional integrity, unconditional love, and indigenous wisdom – and Malinalli considers corn to be "la manifestación de la bondad" [the manifestation of goodness] (18). As a commentary on the trajectory of the "historical" and unknowable Malinche and her changing symbolic significance, the *tlachique*'s reading of the corn suggests that the anxiety Malinalli experiences upon becoming Cortés's translator is to be resolved in a way that will affirm Malinalli's value and power. The *tlachique* interprets the corn to her:

> "Malinalli, el maíz te dice que tu tiempo no podrá medirse, que no sabrás en su extensión cuál será su límite, que no tendrás edad, pues en cada etapa que vivas descubrirás un nuevo significado y lo nombrarás y esa palabra será el camino para deshacer el tiempo. [. . .] Ésta es la voz del maíz." (19)

["Malinalli, the corn tells you that your time is measureless, that you will not understand in your lifetime what your limits may be, that you will have no age, but that at each stage while you live, you will uncover a new meaning, and it will name you and that word will be your way of canceling time. . . . This is the voice of the corn."]

Malinalli is thus led to lie awake pondering the idea that *she* is part of some organic, dynamic destiny. Esquivel acknowledges, too, that her work in interpreting Malinalli's past has a destiny beyond the "meaning" that Esquivel gives her.

Malinalli's destiny – including that "timeless" destiny of becoming Malinche – looks toward an unlimited future in which meaning and interpretation will be constantly evolving. Most interesting is the notion of "undoing time" (*deshacer el tiempo*), which points away from a stable, fixed definition toward a productive ambivalence that belies any rigid, teleological conception of how meaning is produced. Malinalli–Malinche, viewed with esquivelian optimism, will be less the result of an accumulation of layers of meaning, and more a sign that demands a freely moving process of reinterpretation. Significantly, in proposing that Malinalli's trajectory will be without end, Esquivel acknowledges that in the case of *Malinche: A Novel*, the novel will not have the last word.

Another example of this layered reading is Esquivel's emphasis on Malinalli's abhorrence of the practice of human sacrifice, which Malinalli views as Moctezuma's great error in kingship, an idea that is grounded in historical data. Malinalli thinks of the practice as "La enorme culpa que Moctezuma cargaba sobre sus espaldas" [The great guilt that burdens Moctezuma] (65). Malinalli's rejection of human sacrifice motivates her to aid Cortés and the Spaniards as "los [. . .] enviados del Señor Quetzalcóatl" [the ones sent by the Lord Quetzalcóatl] (65) – an assumption that prepares Moctezuma to accept his defeat – but Malinalli's stronger impulse is her desire for freedom. She wants to live as a free person: "Tenía muchos deseos de vivir en libertad, de dejar de pasar de mano en mano, de llevar una vida errante" [She was anxious to live in freedom, to stop passing from master to master, living a wandering life] (66). Malinalli's desire for liberty is animated, then, by the idea that the Spaniards who offer her freedom are aligned with the powerful Nahua deity she follows. The further implication is that one may credit that motivation to La Malinche, a traditionally demonized figure from whom Malinalli gains a purifying distance in Esquivel's vision.

The idea of escaping a life of slavery motivates her agreement when Cortés asks Malinalli to serve as his translator in exchange for freedom, but the reality she finds in her role as La Lengua is a fiercer form of servitude:

Cortés, entonces, le pidió a Malinalli que lo ayudara a traducir y a cambio le daría su libertad. A partir de ahí los acontecimientos se habían ido sucediendo con una velocidad extraordinaria y ahora Malinalli se encontraba presa de una vorágine que no le permitía escapatoria. (70)

[Cortés, then, asked Malinalli to help him translate and in return, he would give her freedom. From there, events had transpired with astonishing speed, and now Malinalli found herself a prisoner in a maelstrom that would not allow her a means of escape.]

The irony in this passage plays on the reversals in Malinalli's quest for "liberty" and suggests a similar conundrum in the trajectory of Malinche. As Malinalli earns her freedom through the Conquest, she finds its very events pulling her into a place where her liberty is increasingly difficult to negotiate. Malinalli's "freedom" alongside Cortés is thus limited in the novel, and, in much the same way, Malinche's symbolic meaning has been held captive, to differing degrees, in a *vorágine* of interpretations, Esquivel's included.[10]

Malinalli's witness of the massacre at Cholula is a particular moment of crisis in her life with Cortés. The destruction of the city, the silence of the dead, the abyss of lost knowledge and wasted human life take over Malinalli's senses and memory, leaving her empty at the core: "Los miles de cadáveres desmembrados, sin vida [. . .] tomaron presa el alma de Malinalli. [¶] Su espíritu ya no le pertenecía, había sido capturado durante la batalla por esos cuerpos inertes, indefensos, insalvables. [. . . Ella] estaba muerta y cargaba sobre sus espaldas cientos de muertos" [The thousands of dismembered, lifeless bodies . . . took Malinalli's soul prisoner. ¶ Her spirit was no longer hers, but had been captured during the battle by those motionless corpses, undefended, indefensible. . . . (She) was dead and carried hundreds of the dead on her back] (93). This moment of spiritual darkness is the catalyst for a period of introspection and doubt and of radical separation from her identity and culture.[11] The remainder of Esquivel's novel concerns itself predominantly with the ways in which Malinalli struggles to put her life back together in the face of almost overwhelming trauma.

Domestic Fiction

Another position from which Esquivel translates Malinche into Malinalli requires that Esquivel impose her view of feminism on the tale. By imagining Malinalli's coming of age experiences, her encounters with the Spanish and Cortés, and the cultural and political negotiations of her life,

Esquivel closes the narrative on what one might shallowly distill as a tale of true love and domesticity. Certainly Esquivel's feminism balances precariously between embracing patriarchy and resisting it. While some of Esquivel's characters offer determined resistance to patriarchal values – represented most vehemently by women characters like Mamá Elena (*Like Water for Chocolate*) and Lucha (*Swift as Desire*) – Esquivel leans toward the "embrace" in an interview with Verónica Ortiz in February 2004:

> A que desde los griegos estamos acostumbrados a catalogar como lo femenino a aquello que tiene que ver con los mundos íntimos, que tiene que ver con la vida, con la muerte, con otro tipo de orden que es más cósmico. Lo masculino es aquello que tiene que ver con un orden social, con el mundo público. (182)

> [From the time of the Greeks, we have been accustomed to identifying as "feminine" that which has to do with intimate things, with life, with death, with other kind of order that is more or less cosmic. The masculine is that which has to do with social order, with the public world.]

Esquivel here compartmentalizes activity by gender, and in *Malinche: A Novel*, the characters of Malinalli and Cortés fit the dichotomy she proposes – though the characters of Jaramillo and even Malinalli's father offer some grounds for nuance.

What is more to the point here and elsewhere in Esquivel's fiction are the signifiers of successful domestic life as not only the core of social and political equilibrium, but also as individual self-realization. Elena Poniatowska has pointed to Esquivel's intimate relationship with domesticity, noting that Esquivel's first novel single-handedly established a standard for literary symbolism centered on women's domestic life: "Laura Esquivel sacralizó la cocina y le dio sentido a los pucheros. Su *Como agua para chocolate* es a la literatura lo que [es] *El festín de Babette* para la cinematografía. Laura le otorga un rango especial a ser la reina del hogar" [Laura Esquivel made the kitchen sacred and gave meaning to stew-pots. Her *Like Water for Chocolate* is to literature what *Babette's Feast* is to film. Laura conferred a special honor upon being the queen of the hearth] (qtd. in Ortiz 12).[12] Malinalli accepts that "honor," too, and her domestic union with Juan Jaramillo is presented as Malinalli's source of "la paz, el cielo en la tierra" [peace, heaven on earth] (173). By the novel's end, Malinalli has settled into relative happiness and peace, and she dies content with her role as the co-founder of *mestizaje*. While Esquivel's female characters often represent failed domesticity – Gertrudis and Rosaura in *Like Water for Chocolate*, Lucha in *Swift as Desire*, Malinalli's mother in *Malinche: A Novel* – the character of Malinalli wavers along the failed domestic path of her mother, but in the end, she achieves her domestic dream.[13]

Malinalli's marriage to Jaramillo provides her an escape from slavery and from Cortés's ambition and violence, as well as the context for reconciling the indigenous and Spanish belief systems and worldviews that evolved into the syncretism that marks Mexican national identity.[14] The positive aspects of the union between Malinalli and Jaramillo are represented in the patio of their home and in Jaramillo's carving of the Spanish Virgin of Guadalupe that they place above their bed (172). The Spanish Virgin presides beneficently over their marriage and descendants, and she will soon be transfigured into a Mexican Virgin at a site sacred to the warlike, maternal Nahua deity named Tonantzin. The new Virgin will be the spiritual *mediatrix* to all of Mexico.[15]

The connection between Malinalli and Juan Diego's vision of the Mexican Virgin is grounded in the narrative by Malinalli's destiny. Having been born in the twelfth house, Malinalli is connected to the Nahua concept of resurrection, which is represented by a glyph showing a skull in profile, crowned with an adornment of the sacred grass *malinalli*:

> Curiosamente, fue con malinalli, la fibra de la que estaba hecha la manta que Juan Diego portaba el día en que en el año de 1531 se le apareció la Virgen de Guadalupe sostenida por la luna, el día doce del doceavo mes y a los doce años de la llegada de Hernán Cortés a México. (41)

> [Curiously, it was with *malinalli*, the fiber with which was woven the tilma that Juan Diego was wearing that day in the year 1531 when the Virgin of Guadalupe appeared to him, held aloft by the moon, on the twelfth day of the twelfth month, twelve years after Hernán Cortés's arrival in Mexico.]

Thus, by means of destiny and the interpretation of signs, Esquivel's novel transforms Paz's misogynistic view of "La Malinche" as traitor into the affirmative construction of Malinalli, a symbol of reconciliation and unity, of honorific *mestizaje*. She becomes the mortal equivalent to the spiritual convergence of culture and spirituality represented by the Mexican Virgin of Guadalupe.

The pilgrimage that Malinalli makes shortly before her death illustrates this point (177–82). She visits Tepeyac, the site of a shrine to the Aztec deity Tonantzin, where, not coincidentally, Juan Diego would witness the first appearance of the Virgin of Guadalupe in 1531. At Tepeyac, Malinalli communes with the goddess, and Jaramillo's recollections of the

Spanish Virgin of Guadalupe come unbidden into her mind: "Sin saber por qué, recordó a la Virgen de Guadalupe, esa virgen morena cuya imagen Jaramillo y ella tenían colgada sobre la cabecera de su cama" [Without knowing why, she remembered the Virgin of Guadalupe (the Spanish one), that dark-skinned Virgin whose image she and Jaramillo had hung above the head of their bed] (180). The reader, having the vantage point of hindsight, understands that Malinalli's mystical experience at the Tepeyac shrine presages the convergence of the two female figures into the future patron saint of Mexico.

Assured at Tepeyac by Tonantzin that the old gods ("los dioses antiguos") would change only in form and endure in essence (178), Malinalli regains the peace that she lost when she witnessed the Spaniards' brutality against the Mexica, of which she was reminded in her last encounter with Cortés (178–79). At Tepeyac, the prospect of future peace is the dominant image:

> Ese día Malinalli, sentada en el cerro del Tepeyac, después de enterrar su pasado, se encontró a sí misma, supo que era dios, supo que era eterna y que iba a morir. [. . .] Malinalli sintió la fuerza del viento en su rostro, en su cabello, en todo su cuerpo y el corazón del cielo se abrió para ella. (181)

> [That day, seated on the hill of Tepeyac, after having buried her past, she found herself, she realized that she was god, that she was eternal, and that she was going to die. . . . Malinalli felt the wind's strength on her face, in her hair, all over her body, and the heart of the sky opened itself to her.]

Telescoping the centuries of conflict and tension implicit in Mexico's religious past, Esquivel's narrative proposes Tonantzin/Guadalupe as the stable origin of a new tradition, one that allows Malinalli to be reconciled to the past and to welcome the promise of a syncretic future for her children and the coming of death for herself.

Malinalli's thoughts in this scene, affirming resolution, peace, and mediation, stand in meaningful contrast to the associations she makes with Cortés. Cortés's disruptive presence, his ambition for material wealth, his connection with "la guerra, el destierro, y el odio" [war, destruction, and hate] (173) are the forces that send Malinalli on her pilgrimage to reestablish her spiritual heritage at Tepeyac. Cortés finds no comparable moment of enlightenment, atonement, or reconcilation, which is damning indeed in Esquivel's cosmos. Cortés, "convencido que la fortuna favorece a los valientes" [convinced that Fortune favors the brave] (33), disappears from the fiction into history, and Malinalli dies, having constructed with Jaramillo the symbolic domestic negotiation of space and cultural artifacts that is their home together.

Negotiating Space

If the novel's effort is to contain Malinche's story, its task is rendered ultimately futile by the text itself. But if its value is to add a fresh and thoughtful narrative layer onto the continuing efforts to interpret this ineffable character, the task has been accomplished. Neither is absolute, and this is appropriate in a text whose mode can be no more than suggestive and whose valuable contribution to this story is to remind readers how difficult but necessary it is to continue reading and rereading the raindrops that surround the period of the Conquest, whether the contours seem irretrievable or already defined.

The middle ground between determination and contingency, between fate and free will, is of course complemented by the middle position of embracing *mestizaje* as the solution to the destruction of the Conquest and the coming of the Spaniards. The place Malinalli occupies in the closing pages of the novel is one that is as much left to her as created by her. This space both defines Malinalli within Esquivel's fictional world and recalls the mediated space of small gains and great sacrifices that other characters in other Esquivel novels claim as the prizes available to them in Mexico's patriarchy. If *Malinche: A Novel* may be considered as a romance novel – as I suggested was possible earlier – the genre is yet another middle ground that Esquivel herself negotiates and redefines.

Notes

1   The full name of the novel is retained in this chapter to avoid confusion with the name *Malinche* (written in italics as a non-English word) in the discussion of naming.
2   See Cypess 33, 180–81 n. 24; Herren 34–36 for evidence of the accuracy of Esquivel's translation of the Nahuatl name into Spanish.
3   For Bernal Díaz del Castillo (1496–1584), see Gillespie in this volume, n. 14. For Paz, also see note 4, below.
4   Gillespie's essay treats the changing intellectual and popular culture perspectives on La Malinche, including the influence of Paz. See also Van Delden.
5   Cypess remarks that it is "generally accepted that she [La Malinche] was born either in 1502 or 1505" (33) whereas Herren observes that "[P]odemos suponer que había nacido entre 1502 y 1504" [We can suppose that she was born between 1502 and 1504] (40).
6   All translations to English in this essay belong to the author and editor.
7   Esquivel writes that the birth occurs "en el tercer carácter, de la sexta casa"

[in the third character of the sixth (twelfth?) house]. The text poses this internal conflict – or error – between the "sixth" house (3) and the "twelfth" house in an extended exposition (41).

8   See Paul Radin for kinship terms.

9   In contrast to more poetic passages, stands the clumsy description of Malinalli and Cortés's first coupling, which juxtaposes clinical terms within a richly embroidered pathetic fallacy (74–75).

10 This is an allusion to *The Vortex* (1935. *La vorágine* 1924), the famous novel of the Columbian jungle by José Eustasio Rivera (1888–1928).

11 When Malinalli hears of the temple massacre at Tenochtitlan, perpetrated by Pedro de Alvarado (130), her previous experience in Cholula allows her to "live" the unseen massacre in horrifying detail.

12 *Babette's Feast*, written by Isak Dinesen (Karen Blixen 1885–1962), was first published in the United States in the *Ladies Home Journal* (June 1950) and collected in *Anecdotes of Destiny* (New York: Random House, 1958). *Babette's Feast* gained little popular currency prior to the 1988 film version, so Poniatowska refers to the film as primary.

13. See Doris Sommer's standard work on "national romances" (1991), and also Gillespie's treatment of this aspect of the novel in this volume.

14 See Butler Murray in this volume, his n. 4 on "syncretism" as an approach to understanding Mesoamerican religious practices.

15 Pope John Paul II visited Tepeyac and recognized the Virgin of Guadalupe as the "patron saint" of all "America" in March 1999. Juan Diego was not canonized until 2002. See Virgilio P. Elizondo.

Esquivel's Fiction in the Context of Latin American Women's Writing

ALBERTO JULIÁN PÉREZ[1]

Esquivel's novels, beginning with *Like Water for Chocolate* in 1989 and continuing through *Malinche: A Novel* in 2006, stand as important contributions to the new fiction published over the past twenty-odd years by Latin American women writers.[2] Today's Latin American women writers, some of whom enjoy a global audience, follow in the footsteps of a notable group of earlier women writers in the region, particularly Mexican women writers working around mid-century. Mentioning only three of them will serve to carry the point: Rosario Castellanos (1925–1974), who made memorable contributions to the *indigenista* novel in *Nine Guardians* (1992. *Balún Canán* 1957) and *The Book of Lamentations* (1998. *Oficio de tinieblas* 1962); Elena Poniatowska (1932–), the creator of the new genre of testimonial literature such as *Here's to You, Jesusa* (2001. *Hasta no verte Jesús mío* 1969) and *Massacre in Mexico* (1975. *La noche de Tlatelolco* 1971); and Elena Garro (1916–1998), dramatist and novelist, best known for *Recollections of Things to Come* (1969. *Los recuerdos del porvenir* 1963).[3] Subsequent writers owe a great deal to these and other women writers working in the two decades after 1950.

Since the early 1980s, the number of novels published by Latin American women has created its own "boom." The late-1980s were especially fruitful for criticism on that body of literature. Such publishing events as the release of Chilean Isabel Allende's first best seller, *The House of the Spirits* (1985. *La casa de los espíritus* 1982) and the publication of *Like Water for Chocolate* at the end of the decade, followed by the release of films based on the two novels within a two-year period (1992–1994) brought international prominence to Latin American women writers.[4] The 1990s saw increased activity among women writers throughout Latin America, as I will detail below.

To the influence of figures like Garro, Castellanos, Poniatowska, and others whom I will mention below, one must add the pervasive extra-literary influence of Frida Kahlo (1907–1954), whose work has increased in relevance year after year because of her singular and penetrating portrayal of the Mexican woman as a suffering, wounded, feminine voice. Kahlo's art is a counterpoint to the celebratory, epic tone of the great post-Revolutionary muralist of Mexico, Diego Rivera (1886–1957), in the same way that women writers have created a counterpoint to male-authored historical-period novels dating from the nineteenth century forward.[5] Esquivel's work over the past twenty years and the work of younger Mexican women writers like Eve Gil (1968–), Vicky Nizri (1954–), Susana Pagano (1968–), Guadalupe Nettel (1973–), and their counterparts throughout Latin America arguably owe a great deal to those earlier writers and artists.

Critical work in the field has had much to do to keep pace with the fiction it considers. In 1989, the year that Jean Franco's *Plotting Women* and *Like Water for Chocolate* were coincidentally published, Sharon Keefe Ugalde, in a review-article concerning several books on women in Latin American literature, refers to the "energetic state of women's literature in Latin America" (222). Other studies related to women's writing in Latin America continued to emerge through the 1990s, like Joanna O'Connell's study of Castellanos's essays and fiction, and reference works intended to consolidate information on Latin American women writers, filmmakers, artists, and politicians.[6] In a review of works in literary criticism in the field published in the 1990s, Judy Maloof refers to the last two decades of the twentieth century as the period of "the mushrooming corpus of women's writing" (243) and notes the concomitant activity in criticism and teaching on Latin American women's writing.[7]

Recent events have again aimed a spotlight on fiction written by Latin American women as an important and developing literary event. The 2007 awarding of the biennial International Rómulo Gallegos Novel Prize [Premio Internacional de Novela Rómulo Gallegos] to Poniatowska for an immense novel on the Mexican railroad workers' union activity in 1958–1959 sent another positive message to Latin America's women writers. *El tren pasa primero* (2005. [*The Train Passes First*]) is in the "testimonial-biographical" tradition of which Poniatowska is the acknowledged master. This award makes the second Gallegos prize to a woman writer in Spanish America, and it is notable that the first, in 1997, also went to a Mexican, Ángeles Mastretta (1949–) for *Lovesick* (1997. *Mal de amores* 1996). In 2008, an academic congress, The Boom Femenino in Mexico, held at University College Cork, Ireland, sought to explore the "phenomenon of the literary boom *femenino* in Mexico," a phenomenon whose beginnings organizers Nuala Finnegan and Jane E. Lavery date approximately at 1980 and define as "the dramatic increase in [women's] publishing in Mexico." This recent recognition of Mexican women writers in prominent international venues suggests that the "boom" in Latin American women's writing continues to evolve in a strong way in the third decade of its development and to be especially vital in Mexico – as two international awards over a ten-year period and Esquivel's "best-seller" affirm.

With that in mind, it is useful to consider the writing of Mexican women authors apart from the whole in order to make an important distinction within the context of the historical-period novel. The writing of Mexican women novelists shows an interest in history and a willingness to experiment with modes and approaches. These writers focus on the chronicle of "everyday life," and their narrative is "history" viewed from the perspective of an individual, a circumscribed group, or a family. This approach, consciously or not, enacts Miguel de Unamuno's theory of *intrahistory*, which seeks an understanding of history through the individual or community (family, village), through the private over the public, political versions of history.[8] Mexican women writers narrate a "deep history" in which their characters are both victims whose lives are influenced by national or political history, and participants who must contend with related events. For Mexican women writers like Poniatowska, Esquivel, and Castellanos, and the artist Kahlo, the individual is the deeper truth, and issues of gender, self-realization, and individual and communal struggle and survival take precedence over History with the capital letter.[9]

Along with this women writers' view of history, which I particularly set in Mexico, a second critical element that has much to do with Latin American women's fiction is their positive attitude toward popular genres often considered low-brow and sub-literary – the serialized romance novel and the melodrama. In their novels, we find those genres combined with the critically valued approaches of the high literary novel, such as the genealogical-historical approach, or the portrait of contemporary life among the urban middle class. Recently, readers have shown an increased interest in intimate narratives that explore an individual's interior emotional life in the context of narrative surroundings and routines, in contrast to fiction that imagines broad approaches to large social problems. Poniatowska's work communicates this value, for example, through her investigative approach and testimonial style. In this shift of genre and taste – or priority – Latin America's woman writer has assumed a central role, aided in part by feminist movements and the feminist cultural agenda, especially in the last two decades of the twentieth century.[10]

Before exploring these ideas further, it will be helpful to consider the effect that cultural movements have on the history of literature. I am referring to "cultural movements" that appear when a group of writers organizes its efforts around a program of action or a project in order to alter the literary landscape of their time and replace it with their own proposal, as happened with the *Modernistas* and the *Vanguardistas* [Modernist and Vanguard groups] that became cultural protagonists in Latin America at the beginning of the past century.[11] These literary groups, born between emergent literary generations, derived their esthetic proposals in part from ideas emerging in European metropolitan centers that they transformed according to their cultural necessities. Their works achieved originality and played a singular role in the history of our literature – consider for example the poetry and poetics of Rubén Darío (1867–1916), Pablo Neruda (1904–1973), and César Vallejo (1832– 1938). At the end of the heterogeneous, postmodern, skeptical, and consumer-based twentieth century though, great literary "accords" were difficult to achieve. The fact is that our new century, lacking Modernism and Vanguardism's aesthetic motivations, is unlikely to see an early change in that atmosphere.

One of the few cultural movements that has achieved progressive growth, legitimacy, and rapid global representation from the second half of the twentieth century through the beginning of the twenty-first century is feminism. Feminism, unlike Modernism and Vanguardism, is not mainly an aesthetic movement because it sets its claims in the realms of ethics, justice, and freedom. In most of its manifestations, it seeks to establish equal opportunity, access, rights, and compensation for women. It is noteworthy that feminist art and literature – that which is inspired by the increasing currency of feminist perspectives and values – has points in common with the revolutionary literature of Social Realism produced at the beginning of the 1930s, a literature that arose from the cultural politics of the Russian Communist Party, with an artistic interest subordinated to the ethical. The ethics-driven nature of Social Realism did not, however, impede the creation of a literature of great artistic merit in Latin America, yielding notable works such as the late poetry of Vallejo, the *Canto general* (1950) of Neruda, the poetry of Ernesto Cardenal (1925–), and that of Roque Dalton (1935–1975).[12]

In a little over three decades at the close of the twentieth century, U.S. and European feminism initiated a wide-ranging reassessment of culture intended to demonstrate the historical and social situation of women, giving special attention to the revaluation and legitimization of works in the arts produced by women in the past and in the present, as Sandra Gilbert and Susan Gubar amply illustrate. Using Virginia Woolf's *A Room of One's Own* (1929) as a point of departure, feminist criticism has continued to extend its horizons.[13] Catharine Stimpson (1989) points out that Woolf's book posed early on some of the questions around which feminist criticism later developed, specifically Woolf's interest in women as a subject of inquiry and in the problems of heterosexuality and the dominant patriarchal structure (130). Within the context of sexual behavior and feminist revisionism, studies about women's "desire" compose "a category of their own," to borrow an expression from Woolf, and these studies have been heralded as replacing Freudian psychoanalytic theory. These feminist interests in desire and the body are relevant to criticism of Esquivel's fiction, as well as to other Mexican women's writing, a point addressed below in the context of *Like Water for Chocolate*.

The broader objective of this revisionist critical movement, supported by the work of leading contemporary critics such as Julia Kristeva (Bulgaria 1941–), Luce Irigaray (Belgium 1932–), and Hélène Cixous (France 1937–), is to elucidate the notion of a feminine writing (*écriture*) that narrates the woman's body of desire as an entity set apart from the traditional patriarchal culture, eliminating its traditional binary oppositions.[14] Historical or sociological feminist criticism, for its part, has questioned such things as ideas of authorship, genre, canon, or nationality, to determine the ideological weight in the formation of those concepts (Gilbert and Gubar 147). This historical and sociological feminist critical model, linked to the Marxist explanation of the processes of social alienation and reification in the modern industrial capitalist society, has had a major impact in Latin America, given the strong Marxist tradition among its intellectuals through the twentieth century.[15] In addition to this beneficial linking of Feminism with Marxism, the activist and political character of the feminist movement was able to create effective channels of communication to disseminate and debate its ideas. In Latin America, these means of communication with one another and the public have included media and public events, specialized journals, and academic volumes dedicated to studies of women's issues.[16] In the literary arena, one notes the proliferation of feminist publication, including periodicals and volumes of research and editorial support for women's writing.[17]

In considering all of Latin America in the context of women's publishing, it seems to me that Mexico's women writers, in particular, have secured a solid position in the nation's letters with an excellent *corpus* of women's fiction over an extended period. The nature of this achievement has been validated by national and international awards, and as Mexican critic and creative writer Margo Glantz (1930–) has suggested, one need only cite a few names to support the point: Castellanos, Poniatowska, Garro, Esquivel, Mastretta, and Carmen Boullosa (1954–). To those, one might add Nellie Campobello (1900–1986), Luisa J. Hernández (1928–), Inés Arredondo (1928–1989), Julieta Campos

(1932–2007), María Luisa Puga (1944–), María Luisa Mendoza (1938–), Bárbara Jacobs (1947–), and Glantz herself.[18] These women writers represent a broad chronological awakening of Latin American women's writing that gained significant momentum in the final decades of the twentieth century and that has been fundamental to a re-examination of the female point of view within the imaginative structure of fiction written by women. The writing of these women has also evolved into a publishing phenomenon, and in this regard, the novels of Allende and Esquivel are especially visible in that they have sold millions of copies internationally, have been translated from Spanish into English, French, German, and other languages, and have been made into films.

Such events as *Like Water for Chocolate*'s becoming the most successful film in the history of Mexican cinema and Allende's *Daughter of Fortune* (1999. *Hija de la Fortuna*) being featured in its English translation as Oprah's Book Club choice in 2000 have given Latin American women writers broad cultural currency outside Latin America.[19] This level of commercial success and favorable public exposure for such diverse fiction as Esquivel and Allende's novels indicates that Latin American women writers have enjoyed a positive creative environment in which their work has been considered on a par with men's writing – at least in some venues – and that they have been able to express "feminist" ideas without adhering to specific and militant ideas of any single feminist group. This is especially clear in the work of Esquivel, whose ideas do not conform to any standard feminist position.[20]

Esquivel's Fiction

Esquivel's confidence in her mode and material is self-evident in the bold and playful subtitle of *Like Water for Chocolate: A Novel in Monthly Installments with Recipes, Romances and Home Remedies*, in which the author explicitly confronts us with our suppositions (and prejudices) about what a novel is or should be. The author declares that her work is a "novel," associating it with a major literary genre, but she reduces it to the old-fashioned serial presentation of a "novel in monthly installments," making it a work of popular consumption. Such writing is commonly relegated to the broad category "light" – "lite" – literature or sub-literature, which includes popular romance and melodrama and other kinds of work that critics of serious literature do not deign to consider.[21]

Esquivel's novel, to confuse the question of category further, explicitly juxtaposes narrative and – what are generally considered to be – non-narrative elements (*i.e.*, recipes and home remedies), but all of them become a part of the organic narrative structure. Recipes and home remedies appear with frequency in home magazines directed at women, but rarely in novels, so these modes in fiction were off-putting to some critics. The romantic relationships that one finds in *Like Water for Chocolate*, *The Law of Love*, and *Swift as Desire* may be viewed as unlikely, exaggerated, or melodramatic, like those of formulaic romantic fiction – the *novela rosa* of Latin American popular fiction – but Esquivel's handling of these relationships caught the critical imaginations of scholars and casual readers alike.

Esquivel acknowledges in her interview with Argentine journalist Jorge Halperín that incorporating recipes into a work of fiction had already been utilized by Spanish author Manuel Vázquez Montalbán (1939–2003) "in another form" (6–7), but Esquivel, unlike Vázquez Montalbán, features recipes as more than a mere appended resource. Rather, she places them at the center of the narrative and points to them in the title, and creates a culinary experience that whets the readers' curiosity and relates food preparation and consumption to the episodes of love and romance within the novel. These are "tales of romance" by a woman who cooks, written for women who cook, and the tales all begin, in one way or another, in the kitchen.

The kitchen also provides the raw ingredients for the novel's second unexpected element, home remedies, as formulas for poultices and health-giving foods with instructions for administering them to the sick and wounded. Esquivel's use of home remedies also underscores her intention to narrate women's knowledge of healing and their power to heal and to portray women as characters who heal, and whose knowledge and activity are intimately connected with the body and with health, life, and death. Esquivel's use of recipes and home remedies makes her a writer of "the body" (a category referred to in the previous discussion of feminist revision), which has apparently inspired some critical name-calling, directed at Esquivel and at other women writers like Allende. One of these terms is *fodongas* [unkempt, sloppy, unattractive], and Halperín explains that such terms are equivalent in Argentina to calling these women writers *escritoras grasas* [low-class or hack writers] (6).[22]

In Esquivel's subtitle of the novel, she implies an exploration into the particular space of the feminine world as it is represented by the home, which we understand as the place where women make love, give birth, nourish, heal, and die. In the home, the circle of life is completed. Within it, the woman who cooks is the executive high priestess of an ancestral ritual: that of offering the food of life. In her interview with Halperín, Esquivel describes the nature of food preparation and consumption from a feminist point of view, and with respect to her own experience:

I almost didn't leave the house, especially the kitchen [. . . .] When I married and had children, I began to realize that the kitchen isn't the place of punishment; it's the most sacred space there is [. . .] by means of the ritual of the meal, a communion is constructed with all people. I even believe that they reverse gender roles with men: now he has to be passive and the woman is active. She penetrates him by means of her cooking. (6)

Cooking in Esquivel's novel has an allegorical, archetypical significance, without making *Like Water for Chocolate* an ideological or conceptual novel. To Halperín, Esquivel says that she views the cook "as an alchemist or as a priestess" (7). When the journalist asks her what relationship exists between the kitchen and literature, Esquivel responds without hesitation: "sensuality." She adds that the idea of the book came to her while she was cooking, and that the inspiration arrived associated with the smells of the kitchen, not only those of her own kitchen, but also those recalled from her mother's and grandmother's kitchens (7).

For this reason, I characterize *Like Water for Chocolate* as a novel where the narrative emerged "organically," grounded in individual experience and family history. In concert with Unamuno's *intrahistoria* theory, Esquivel's two historical-period novels (*Like Water for Chocolate* and *Malinche*) focus on individual experience, are isolated and intensely personal in point of view, and leave the sweeping and epic narratives of history to other writers. Esquivel eschews another connection to mainstream regional narrative when she confesses to Halperín that she does not feel an affinity with so-called "magical realism," because what she narrates, she says, seems real: "Everything that seems exaggerated really has to do with reality. I do not see it as something magical. I believe that I did not invent anything because I speak from my own experiences" (7). While this affirmation should be considered within the context of the Latin American novel, where it is impossible to break with realism without alluding, consciously or unconsciously, to magical realism, Esquivel is not the first Mexican woman writer to make such a protest. Elena Garro likewise rejected "magic realism" and also asserted that she wrote "realism" based on experience, but that she did so with "irony and humor" (Prado 35).

In spite of the kinds of innovations introduced by independent and liberated feminine voices in Latin America's contemporary narrative, these innovations alone cannot have given women writers the space they have won within contemporary literature's preeminent genre, which is not characterized with an adjective of gender, as "women's," but merely the *novel* itself. Esquivel's ambiguous approach to the novel allows her to write in ways that successfully address her primary reading public, which is presumably female, since all her principal characters are women who contend with "women's things" of one kind or another, yet Esquivel also writes in ways that establish her work within the broad tradition of the novel. Addressing this question, critic Beatriz González Stephan considers Esquivel a "revolutionary writer" because Esquivel "attacks all of the codes of censorship and binary principles" (211). For González Stephan, *Like Water for Chocolate* uses parody and the grotesque to desacralize the world of high-brow literature, and *Like Water for Chocolate* is an attack on "authoritative discourses" that seeks to transgress "the established order" (211). One might read *The Law of Love* or *Malinche: A Novel* from a similar perspective, yet while González Stephan's assessment proposes interesting questions, her position may be overstated in the case of *Like Water for Chocolate*.

Mastretta's *Tear this Heart Out* (1997. *Arráncame la vida* 1985), published in Mexico only a few years before *Like Water for Chocolate*, can be considered a transgressive demythification of *machista* culture in the post-Revolutionary period in Mexico. Indeed, demythification is what Mastretta's novel is essentially about. On the other hand, the attitude toward power and gender in *Like Water for Chocolate* is ambiguous, as Esquivel confirms in the Halperín interview cited above. She confronts the genre by devising variations and avoiding its most common tendencies. If we consider Esquivel's fiction in relation to Mexico's novelistic tradition, especially with respect to the writers of the Revolution, who are considered the founding fathers of Mexico's contemporary novel, we find that Esquivel connects her work with theirs by setting the central part of its chronology during the Revolution. Although events take place during that period, and the action of the Revolution intervenes in the plot of the novel in important ways, Esquivel presents the events in a contained space that is isolated, for the most part, from the Revolution. One notes a desire of affiliation rather than non-conformity on the part of the author. The major characters who are connected with the Revolution, like Gertrudis and Treviño, are admirable, energetic, and effective.

In considering the question of *machista* culture, one would have to say that certainly Esquivel confronts gender, but in a way that envisions unique circumstances and avoids the most common tendencies of narrating gender. The author blames the existing order on Mamá Elena, the feudal mother-father, a matriarchal figure who runs the ranch in a patriarchal way. Mamá Elena best parallels the figure of the rural despot popularized in the novels of the land, like *Doña Bárbara* (1929) by Rómulo Gallegos (1884–1929). In Esquivel's *Swift as Desire*, the sexual predator and local "boss" don Pedro fills this role, and in *Malinche: A Novel*, Mexico's first Spanish empire-building "despot," Hernán Cortés, is insecure, self-aggrandizing, and dangerous. In *Like Water for Chocolate*,

Esquivel links two sub-genres of the Latin American novel: that of the Revolution in its chronological setting and that of the land in its geographical setting, and the *malvada de la historia* [the story's villain] is a ranch-owning widow and "single mother." *Like Water for Chocolate*, then, is an amalgam; it is the product of authorial "plotting" – to borrow a key term from Franco – that is associative, additive, and heterogeneous.

To pursue the point of contested gender, consider the sometimes ambiguous gender of Esquivel's characters, in whom masculine and feminine tendencies combine to one extent or another. As Patrick Duffey, Jeffrey Oxford, Ryan F. Long, and Elizabeth Coonrod Martínez have pointed out in their essays in this volume, gender is an area of authorship (and criticism) that is especially malleable and suggestive in Esquivel's fiction. In the world of fiction, characters are often asexual, pre–Oedipal, or trans-gendered so that elements of maleness and femaleness can be rearranged and displaced independently of gender. It is easy to associate Esquivel with other novelists who have utilized stereotypically feminine characters and those of melodrama, but her approach to gender is really more akin to that of Argentine writer Manuel Puig (1932–1990), with his strange and successful alternation of the masculine-feminine and the blurring of gender distinctions – a mode reminiscent of Esquivel's gender-shifting in *The Law of Love*.

The authoritative, patriarchal, masculine model in *Like Water for Chocolate* is displaced from male characters and located in one woman, Mamá Elena. The relationship between mother and daughters, in particular between Mamá Elena and Tita, reveals the central conflict of the work. The despotic mother condemns her youngest daughter to the kitchen and makes Tita her servant until the day of Mamá Elena's death. Tita is circumscribed from participating in love and marriage, but she takes the locus of her exclusion and achieves important degrees of self-realization and liberty – but almost always within certain boundaries. She escapes the house at one point, as Gertrudis had done before her, but Tita's exile, however liberating it is, is also the product of Mamá Elena's ordering her life and the life of the ranch. In many scenes, Tita's imposed "disability" within the ranch transforms itself into a fairly effective weapon as she gains skill and understanding of her domestic domains. When she returns from exile on the other side of the border, she is more fit to contend with her mother, and following an empowering conversation with Gertrudis, banishes her mother's "spirit" forever.

Among the women on the ranch (sisters Gertrudis, Rosaura, and Tita; and Mamá Elena, Nacha, and Chencha), Esquivel creates a system of alliances and oppositions. Rosaura, as Mamá Elena's most favored daughter, identifies with her mother, and when her mother is dead, Rosaura tries to assume her authority. Tita, however, aligns herself with

Gertrudis, the illegitimate child of Mamá Elena, and has the spiritual and physical support of Nacha and Chencha. Gertrudis mocks all dangers – fire, sensuality, and self-realization – and her passion allows her – or impels her – to pass from the private realm of history (that of the house and the brothel) to the national stage of history as an officer in the Revolution.

In the narrative's paradigm of alliances and oppositions, envy, mistrust, violence, victimization, egoism, negation of others, and general destruction operate to circumscribe Tita's activity. As essays in this volume have demonstrated, Tita's longing and love for Pedro stand in opposition to Mamá Elena's power and her capacity for violence. When Pedro accepts Mamá Elena's exchanging Rosaura for Tita, he participates in the novel's displacement of sexual desire and sacrifice and does so in order to be close to Tita. This triadic displacement, in which both Tita and Pedro participate, mirrors the role of a parent toward her children when the mother sacrifices in order to comply with the wishes of the child. Self-sacrifice for a loved one is traditionally a feminine strategy, yet both genders employ it in *Like Water for Chocolate*. The author disgenders the psychology of the sacrifice: Pedro takes the crumbs rather than the cookies, and Tita gets the leftovers from her sister's wedding cake, so to speak.

In other ways, too, *Like Water for Chocolate* presents gender ambiguously. Like most of the men in this novel, Pedro is usually passive. Tita's father dies at the beginning of the work, upon hearing that his wife's second daughter is the child of a lover. This child, Gertrudis, dominates her revolutionary lover and her troop of soldiers. John Brown, the passive and long-suffering doctor, altruistically accepts Tita's changing desires, and like a good mother, is willing to accept whatever she can offer him. The centers of power and authority belong to women, and women are the heroes in *Like Water for Chocolate*. The same is true of Esquivel's recent historical-period novel, *Malinche*, in spite of the presence of Cortés and Moctezuma. In an important sense, female characters are omnipotent and central, and male characters remain subordinate in both novels.

In addition to following Boom and post-Boom tendencies to exploit gender categories, Esquivel's novels consistently mine the central element of the traditional *indigenista* novel, an important feature in the fiction of Esquivel's compatriot Castellanos, in whose work the white or *mestizo* woman learns from the indigenous woman in a transcultural exchange.[23] In *Like Water for Chocolate*, Esquivel presents three indigenous women, two of whom live at the De la Garza ranch: Nacha, the cook, and Chencha, the servant. *Swift as Desire* and *Malinche: A Novel* feature similar characters as emotionally anchoring for the novels' heroines. In *Malinche*, however, both the young female protagonist (Malinalli) and the maternal figure (Citli, Malinalli's grandmother) are indigenous. For Tita, Nacha becomes the adoptive mother, the mother of Tita's affection, who supplies the love that Mamá Elena is not capable of giving Tita. With Nacha and other indigenous women characters, Esquivel shows a nurturing face of maternity to oppose the perverse, distant, and abusive natural mothers.

In *Like Water for Chocolate*, the character of Dr. John Brown represents "positive femininity" in that Dr. Brown learns indigenous healing arts from his Kikapú grandmother and combines his medical education with her teachings. The kitchen and Tita's cookbook are other means of transculturation. In the kitchen, Tita is born into Nacha's hands, and Nacha rears and educates Tita there. The cookbook is one means by which that world and its myths and secrets are transmitted from generation to generation. The cookbook's centrality to the narrative is made clear when it is the only material object to survive the conflagration that consumes the ranch as the product of Tita and Pedro's final, ceremonial tryst.

The most interesting and innovative aspect of Esquivel's fiction is the feminine point of view on a world that turns exclusively around the interests and motivations of the female protagonist with whom the female reader – at least – can sympathize. Many aspects of Esquivel's novels move the reader: the experience of negation as a consequence of another's selfishness or envy; the narration of a life threatened in its innocent years; and, in *Like Water for Chocolate* and *The Law of Love*, a sort of stylized vision of stock sentimentality and evil that unfolds with irony. Esquivel's talent as a narrator is her ability to utilize varied modes and approaches and to change them without destroying the narrative equilibrium, permitting an easy communication with her audience. Hers is an eclectic, fortuitous art that alerts the senses. With Esquivel there is a deliberate – or intuitive – sensual plotting that communicates by means of the sensory marks and tracks of the perceived world, rather than through an ideological synthesis; there are flavors, smells, tactile experiences, the sounds of the life. It is a world armed and plotted through the experience of Laura Esquivel as author.

Esquivel's representations – allegorized, mythologized, realized – of the world of women's desires speaks to the female reader, who, in contrast to the experience of reading a male author's imagined woman, encounters a narrative voice with the ring of authenticity. As a contrastive example of reader response, I, as a male reader, feel a bit uncomfortable about how the pain and pleasure and the good and the evil are dealt out in *Like Water for Chocolate*. I mean by this that the mother is not good and selfless, but tyrannical and masculine, and the sensual, seductive and dangerous woman is an admired, liberated, revolutionary commander. Perhaps what surprises the male reader in the portrait of society that

Esquivel creates is that the forces that one expects to be high-minded and fine are essentially punitive, cruel, and destructive in nature, and it is the women characters who plan, achieve, and accomplish tasks.

Happily for us, Esquivel has written a story that is not excessively psychological, but rather has much of the fable to it, and in the end, love and the good triumph over all when Tita and Pedro are practically transformed into angels, and Esperanza and Alex achieve what Tita and Pedro were not able to enjoy, while the evil have already suffered their punishment. In *Like Water for Chocolate* and in the opening scenes of *Malinche*, evil arises from the action of a selfish mother, and its consequences weigh on the victimized daughter. Once the physical and psychic obstacles disappear, goodness and love triumph, reconciliation is possible, future generations begin on an improved footing, and the narrative world regains its balance in the close of the novel.

Some of these assumptions concerning the female reader's connection to Esquivel's fiction and to Esquivel's way of plotting are validated in Esquivel's statements about her experience and her writing. Rather than an impersonal narrator, genderless or masculinized, Esquivel has preferred in the two novels most resonant of her life experience, *Like Water for Chocolate* and *Swift as Desire*, to narrate in the female voice, and in *The Law of Love*, the alternating narrative voices remain feminine – even if a guardian angel is supposed to be male. Speaking with Halperín about *Like Water for Chocolate*, Esquivel recalls that she spent her childhood "in the kitchen, beside my mother and grandmother, hearing the stories of thousands of women" (6). Those stories populated Esquivel's imagination and became a part of her worldview and experience. Like her mother and grandmother, Esquivel tells stories about women.

The world that the feminine imagination presents is not necessarily the one that the masculine imagination envisioned. This expectation is not frustrated only because Esquivel and other Mexican women writers prefer *intrahistory* and mixing the "low-brow" and popular genres with the mainstream ones. It is frustrated because the world that Esquivel paints is sometimes a wounding, injurious world, one where envy, jealousy, hate, and vengeance flourish, and in this, perhaps we see the psychology of the melodrama appealing for its place in higher literature. In Esquivel's work – another departure from masculine expectations – the heroine obliterates or reconciles destructive elements and mediates a space of reconciliation and self-realization.

Until a short time ago, literature that expressed a feminine sensibility was generally branded – perhaps condemned – as sentimental or extravagant, written for "popular" consumption rather than as "serious" literature. But that "lesser genre" is growing, and it possesses political and historical content, though it is not necessarily partisan or ideological in the political sense. Its politics are liberating and mediating in that they "plot" a space where characters live and achieve peace and coherence, if not for themselves, as in the case of Tita and Malinalli (*Malinche*), then for those who follow them. This "new women's novel" revives a human space, psychologically realistic and sympathetic, to stand as the woman's world, representing her necessities and desires. It comes closest to being a search for human and civil liberty, long promised and long delayed in Latin America.

Notes

1   Patrick Duffey and Harrison L. Parks translated Professor Pérez's original Spanish essay, prior to its rewriting and editing in English. A grant from Austin College (Sherman, Texas) supported the translation. The original Spanish essay (1995) appears in *La nueva mujer en la escritura de autoras hispánicas: ensayos críticos*, edited by Juana Alcira Arancibia and Yolanda Rosas. Juana Alcira Arancibia is director of the Instituto Literario y Cultural Hispánico, which published the collection. While the present study is distinct in its aims and coverage and considerably expanded from the original treatment, we would like to thank the editors of the volume in which the essay appeared for their kind permission to make use of Pérez's earlier essay. Translations of the quotations cited are those of the translators (Duffey and Parks), the author, and the editor.

2   Quotations from *Like Water for Chocolate* come from the Doubleday Spanish edition, 1993.

3   The *indigenista* novel is a Latin American novel whose material is focused on the native peoples of a region. Glantz's essay (in Kohut) is referenced here several times and is useful in this context (esp. 122).

4   Allende (1942–) has at least seventeen books that have been translated into English. Among these are the autobiographical memoir *Paula* (1995. *Paula* [Spanish] 1994) and the short-story collection *The Stories of Eva Luna* (1991. *Cuentos de Eva Luna* 1991). The rest are works of fiction.

5   See Jean Franco's discussion of Kahlo's images in *Plotting Women* (106–12).

6   Diane E. Marting's *Spanish American Women Writers* (1990); Aurora Tovar Ramírez's *Mil quinientas mujeres* (1996); Schuma Schumaher and Érico Vital Brazil's *Diccionario Mulheres* (2000); and Cynthia Margarita Tompkins and David William Foster's *Notable Twentieth-Century Latin American Women* (2001), for example, have updated the numerous publications of the 1980s that treated Latin American women writers, such as Sandra Messinger Cypess's *Women Authors of Modern Hispanic South America* (1989). Some of the newer references are extended to include Latin American women whose field of endeavor is not principally creative writing. María Claudia André and Eva Paulina Bueno have edited a new compilation of critical biography essays on Latin American writers (2008).

7   Maloof provides an excellent bibliography of works in Latin American

feminist criticism in the books she formally reviews in this article and in her note No. 3 (244).

8   In *En torno al casticismo* (1902. [*Return to the Love of Castilian Unity*]), Unamuno asserts that true history is found in rural places in the lives of rural people, that "truth was found in the single souls of men," as Peter G. Earle writes in his study of the complexities of Unamuno's views of history (319). *En torno al casticismo* is available in reprints of the Espasa-Calpe (1902) edition and in Unamuno's *Obras Completas* [*Complete Works*]. See Peggy W. Watson's study of Unamuno's fiction in the context of "Intra-historia" (1993). See also Sandra Benítez's *Bitter Grounds*, a work that constructs Salvadoran history though the voices of women in two "very different" families. Barbara Belejack, reviewing the book, explains that Benitez and her informants are engaged, like Esquivel, Allende, and others, in "wrest[ing] the novel and national history [away] from the male writers who dominated the so-called Boom" (24). Critics such as Gastón Lillo and Monique Sarfati-Arnaud (1994), Claudine Potvin (1995), and John H. Sinnigen (1995) discuss the treatment of Mexican history and the Revolution in the film and novel of *Like Water for Chocolate* within the context of postmodernity. Potvin, for example, asserts that that the "voice" in the novel and film speaks from a place outside historical discourse; that the novel outcome lacks social, historical, or cultural awareness; that the women in the novel lack agency, having their actions and desires dictated by the hegemonic culture; and that history's social and political referents are absent (64). See the critical introduction to this volume on the views of Lillo and Sarfati-Arnaud, Potvin, Sinnigen, and others who consider the question of history in *Like Water for Chocolate*.

9   See the "Introduction" to the 2003 *Monographic Review* (Pérez and Pérez) and its collection of treatments of the "nueva novela histórica" [new historic novel] in Latin American and Peninsular literature. The essay of Elizabeth Coonrod Martínez in that volume is of particular interest to the issue of how women are involved in Mexican history, suggesting how women perceive their roles in history and how women writers represent historical female figures.

10   Márgara Russotto develops this idea (23–42). See also Naomi Lindstrom's essay on two novels of Argentine writer Roberto Arlt (1900–1942) for its insightful perspectives on myth, feminism, and discourse in Arlt's deconstructive process of giving his female protagonist an authentic voice.

11   Earlier literary movements such as Spanish American *modernismo*, led by Rubén Darío, and the *vangardista* movements that emerged in the Spanish-speaking world in the first half of the twentieth century, promulgated cultural models and permitted a rapid diffusion of the movement's goals and ideals and the consolidation of a reading public. They attracted interest and editorial support (coming from newspapers, literary magazines, and publishing houses), which created a modest "market" around this literature and produced generally enduring and constructive consequences for the Spanish-speaking world. Juxtaposed with these examples of collective

success, there are always segments of the cultural world that cannot fit within the new paradigm. One example of literary marginalization created by the "movement attitude" is the belated recognition given José María Arguedas, as compared with the critical attention and immediate diffusion accorded the writers of the Boom. Another such injustice is the lack of serious critical attention placed on the work of Mexican writer Nellie Campobello.

12 Neruda's fifteen *Cantos* were translated by Jack Schmitt (1991). See Lindstrom (*The Social Conscience*) on the debates within feminist circles on theory and terminology; she points out that the Latin American system of education is geared toward a Marxist perspective (125–27). I must also reiterate the importance of *Plotting Women* by Jean Franco, a British critic of Latin America, widely read there, who combines Marxist methodology with feminist criticism.

13 Virginia Woolf (1882–1941) advised, "A woman must have money and a room of her own if she is to write fiction" (2005–4). See Poniatowska's essay in English in this volume (n. 5).

14 See Gilbert and Gubar (151). See also Gubar's "What Ails Feminist Criticism" (883 and n. 10).

15 See the testimonies, interviews, essays, and reviews collected in a special issue of *Revista Iberoamericana* dedicated to the study of Spanish American women writers and edited by Rose Minc (1985). Carmelo Virgilio and Naomi Lindstrom's 1985 collection of essays on women characters in Latin American literature is especially useful. Becky Thompson (2002) provides a helpful and insightful historical view of the movement in the U.S. and suggests a reassessment from the perspective of multi-racial feminism and its debates. From a global rather than Latin American perspective, Susan Gubar (1998) and Danielle Bouchard (2004) address some of the challenges that Feminism faces in the academic setting, from basic terminology to theoretical debates, and also in bridging from its academic disciplines to social concerns and in claiming and revitalizing its political roots, no small part of which is its relevance to minority women's issues.

16 Mágara Russotto's 1990 book (especially 112–72) and Sheila Radford-Hill's 1986 essay point to the diffusion of Feminist ideas and goals from the point of view of the mid-to-late 1980s and provide discussion and details of feminist movements up to that time.

17. See Russotto's treatment of this issue in the 1970s and 1980s (113–72).

18 See Glantz's discussion at 121–29.

19 The film version of *Como agua para chocolate* for which Esquivel wrote the screenplay is discussed in this volume in the editor's introduction and in Duffey's essay on the film. See also Halperín's 1993 interview with Esquivel (6). Reviews for *Daughter of Fortune* are featured at the Oprah Book Club site, <http://www.oprah.com/obc/pastbooks/isabel_allende/obc_pb_20000217_rev.jhtml>.

20 González Stephan describes the critical environment as related to Latin American women writers in the closing decades of the twentieth century.

21 González Stephan describes how Esquivel's "cultural discourses," displaced by the literary establishment, constitute a literary text (210).

22 Esquivel complains: "They do this [impose pejorative labels] to those of us who write about the body in our works" (Halperín 6).

23 Glantz points out that Castellanos achieves "transculturation" with this juxtaposition of women from two different Mexican cultural backgrounds (126).

Glossary of Spanish and Nahuatl Words and Phrases

Usage for words and phrases in the Glossary, unless otherwise indicated, applies to Mexican Spanish. As usual, the definite or indefinite article should be disregarded for alphabetizing purposes. Pronunciation helps are intended to guide an English speaker toward a mediated pronunciation and do not reflect the International Phonetic Alphabet or Spanish vowel pronunciation.

la abnegada a Mexican archetype; a suffering woman, a wife and / or a mother, who denies her own comfort and well-being for the sake of the family, spouse, or children. She draws her happiness in life from seeing them better provided for than she.

adobo a marinade for meats, fish, seafood, or *chiles*.

Anahuac in Nahuatl, "the land between the waters"; the geographical location of the Aztec capital, now the Valley of Mexico (Valle de México).

El Ariel the Academia Mexicana de Artes y Ciencias Cinematográficas [Mexican Academy of Motion Picture Arts and Sciences] established the Ariel awards in 1946 to recognize excellence in Mexican film. The Ariel is paralleled in the U.S. by the Academy of Motion Picture Arts and Sciences' "Oscar." See *Ariel* in the Works Cited.

atole a hot drink made of corn.

buñuelo a yeast dough that is flavored with anise and deep fried. After frying, the *buñuelo* may be dipped into or sprinkled with powdered sugar, brown sugar, *pilloncillo* (a cone of unprocessed cane sugar), or cinnamon or some combination. It is customarily made for Christmas celebrations. Many cultures have a similar food, sometimes mixed with or made of fruit or vegetables.

cabaretera a seductive female character working in a dancehall, saloon, nightclub, or a restaurant with entertainment; she is assumed to be a woman of easy virtue, and is often a prostitute. As Duffey writes in his essay in this volume, she is "a sexual siren" who uses "sex to express anger and exact vengeance."

225

cacao (Nahuatl) See **chocolate**. For this and other Nahuatl words or derivations, see Fermín Herrera's *Concise Dictionary* for further information.

chabela the wedding cake that Tita prepares in chapter two, "February," in *Like Water for Chocolate*.

charro the Mexican cowboy and horseman. He is familiar in his impeccable and elaborate costume at parades, festivals, and *charreadas*, the *charro* "rodeo" (*lit.* "round-up"). Francis Edward Abernethy evokes the *charro*'s traditional costume as the horseman's "beautiful charro regalia and the splendid trappings for his horse" (1). Abernethy calls the *charro* "the best of men on horseback" and writes that the image of the *charro* recalls the Mexican desire for independence and the "heroic and dramatic in Mexican history and tradition" (2). See Abernethy's "Preface" in *Charreada* and Olga Nájera-Ramírez's article on the *charro*.

chatarra – literatura chatarra trashy or low-brow literature, a term given to women's literary forms such as romance, and also, now or in the past, to science fiction, detective fiction, horror, suspense, and the like. *lit.* discards, junk, or cast-offs; "scrap" or "salvage" materials, like iron, collected and sold for reuse or recycling. The English "junk food" is *comida chatarra*, the culinary equivalent to **literatura chatarra**.

chicana a descriptor that characterizes a woman of Mexican heritage born in the United States. *Latina*, as a descriptor, refers to a woman of Hispanic heritage born in the U.S. and encompasses the descriptor *Chicana*.

chido Mexican slang for "cool," "awesome." For *Chido Guan*, see the essays of Ledford-Miller (Biography), Poniatowska, and Duffey in this volume.

chiles en nogada a dish prepared with *chiles poblanos* (*poblano* peppers), which are cleaned and prepared and then filled with a *picadillo* (stuffing) that might consist of nuts (walnuts, almonds), fresh and dried fruits (raisins, apples, peaches), vegetables (onion), and pork, and served in a cream sauce. This is the final dish that Tita prepares before her death, in "December" of *Like Water for Chocolate*.

chinampas a small rectangle of land established by containing and layering material in an otherwise wet area to allow for planting of crops; *chinampas* were the "floating gardens" described by Europeans seeing them for the first time. See Phil Crossley's work on *chinamapas* in Xochimilco.

chocolate a drink made from *cacao* beans crushed on the *metate* and added to water that has been brought to a boil. The drink may include spices and herbs. It has long been reputed to enhance male sexual performance, and Moctezuma is said to have used it for that purpose. See *como agua para chocolate*.

chorizo norteño the subject of "May" in *Like Water for Chocolate*, a traditional pork sausage, requiring great care in its preparation, and using the intestines of the hog as its "skin"; therefore, a "link" sausage.

Cihuateteo (*pronun*. se-wha-te te' oh) the goddess-spirits of women, "women gods" (141), who as "women warriors" had died in childbirth. They guarded the sun from noon to sunset and waited to take children who chanced to be outdoors or passers-by who came to crossroads at ill-starred times. See H. B. Nicholson 422; Sylvia Marcos 168; and Willard Gingerich 233. For a cautionary legend from Xochimilco in which Cihuateteo is a serpent that takes the milk from nursing mothers, putting its tail in the child's mouth to keep it from crying, see Vania Salles and José Manuel Valenzuela (149). Cihuateteo is a probable error for – or a conflation with – Cihuacoatl (se-wha-ko-ah'-til). Cihuacoatl, as the suffix -*coatl* indicates, has a "serpent" form, and was a handy referent, along with Tonantzin, for colonial period Christian evangelists who wished to make an Eve–Serpent–Mother–Mary association in the Nahua system of deities. See *Tzitzimime*.

comedia ranchera a form of Mexican film, dating to 1936 that, according to Olga Nájera-Ramírez "romanticized life on the hacienda [the estate or ranch] and the relationship between landowners and workers" (7). Nájera-Ramírez notes that in *comedia ranchera*, the *charro* represented the "'true Mexican'" (7). The term has been translated in various senses, each with its own truth. Dianna C. Niebylski (2004) calls the genre "ranch melodrama" (263). Andrea Noble (2005) calls the genre (without using the Spanish phrase) "rural comedy" (96). "Rural" or "country" modifying "musical comedy-drama" is possibly more fully indicative of what comprises the genre. Care is indicated in translations like Niebylski's since *rancho* and "ranch" can refer to several distinct entities, and "comedia" covers a range of theater and film types, not all of which are "melodrama." Nájera-Ramírez calls *comedia ranchera* "cowboy comedy" because it features the *charro*, the Mexican cowboy, singing and strumming a guitar, perhaps on horseback. See Gloria Ribe's brief documentary of the genre (*Comedia ranchera)* and the television series *Los que hicieron nuestro cine* [*Those who Created Our (Mexican) Film*] directed by Alejandro Pelayo Rangel (1996), in the "Film" and "Television Programming" sections, respectively, of the Works Cited. The

227

comedia ranchera is featured in volume 5 of a recorded set, originally 63 episodes of 30 minutes each (IMDb).

como agua para chocolate "like water for chocolate," literally, from culinary practice, "at the boil." Figuratively, in the context of the novel, at the end of one's rope, about to explode emotionally, or at the point of taking some action. See Tita's description of herself in the Doubleday Spanish edition (1993 141) and in the Doubleday English translation (1992 151). To prepare Mexican *chocolate* (a hot drink), water is brought to a boil, the chocolate dropped in, and the mixture taken off the fire and beaten. The mixture is then returned to the fire to come to a rolling boil, perhaps several more times, and removed from the fire and beaten again each time. See the articles of Francisco Villegas (1955 28) and Jack Emory Davis (1961 74) on their interpretations of the expression in real-life and literary examples, respectively.

coyote in real life, a person who makes his or her living by transporting illegal immigrants from Mexico and Central America across the U.S.–Mexican border. In *The Law of Love*, the *coyote* character deals in untraceable bodies (bodies having no registered "aura"), which he sells to those who do not want to be recognized.

danzón a traditional musical style and its dance originating in Cuba and attributed to African influence; the danzón has long been popular around the Caribbean and on the adjoining coast of Mexico. The *danzón* is represented in the music CD of *La ley del amor* according to Concepción Bados-Ciria (1996). The *danzón* is the centerpiece of a 1991 Mexican film *Danzón* (1991).

fondant a confection used as an icing.

guacamole (from Nahuatl, *ahuacatl* [testicle] + *mulli* [sauce, gravy, soup]) a salad of mashed or whipped avocados seasoned with minced vegetables (tomato, peppers, onions), and spices (cilantro, garlic, salt, lemon or lime).

guan or *guán* the English-language number one with Spanish phonology and spelling imposed.

huipil (Spanish, güipil) (*pronun.* we' pil) a native over-blouse, loomed in the form of a rectangle with arm openings and varying degrees of embroidered decoration. Examples of the *huipil* may be long or short. Josué Mario Villavicencio Rojas describes the *huipil* as "Camisa de algodón, sin mangas, con bordados" [a sleeveless, embroidered cotton shirt] (48).

huacal / salir del huacal according to Rosa María Roffiel, "es salir de los límites que la sociedad patriarcal te ha marcado" [exceed the boundaries that the patriarchy has set for you] (Costantino 1992

29). *Juacal* literally signifies a wooden box constructed with thin strips of wood spaced at intervals that is used to hold and transport fruits and vegetables; *salir(se) del juacal* is to move beyond strictures or control, to free oneself from established social restrictions or authority. Costantino notes that the word comes from Nahuatl, *huacalli*, "cage" (41 n. 8).

literatura chatarra See *chatarra*.

lienzo a woven cloth, like cotton or linen.

machista an adjective used to describe a cultural phenomenon (language, dance, art, politics, dress, treatment of women, *etc.*) or a complex of cultural phenomena that assert male superiority.

(*bollitos de*) *mandinga* the term used by Elena Poniatowska in her essay here to name a dish in Jorge Amado's *Dona Flor and Her Two Husbands*. In Amado's Portuguese text, *bolinhos de bacalhau* signify Brazil's deep fried "codfish balls," and the phrase is translated from Portuguese to Spanish as *bollitos de bacalao*, and as "codfish balls" in English. Poniatowska writes "bollitos de mandinga." The *cocina afromestiza* (African-*mestizo* cooking) in Mexico's Veracruz region of the town of Mandinga and Lake Mandinga may be the source of the alternative name. The Mandinga Restaurant there is one of many known for its seafood. See Nancy Zaslavsky's *A Cook's Tour of Mexico* (1995 186).

malinchismo the betrayal of one's own people for gain, based on the perception that (La) Malinche (Doña Marina, Malinalli) was a traitor to her people.

malinchista a traitor, a sell-out. See *malinchismo*, above.

mestizaje the individual and communal cultural experience of being *mestizo*; *mestizaje*, in addition to its reference to "mixed" blood, ethnicity, or race, implies life experience, and elements of economic and social life and popular culture, such as language, food, music, art, and poetry. See *mestizo*.

mestizo a person of mixed indigenous and European blood.

metate a stone upon which grains, seeds, and other foods are crushed and ground into powder or milled into flour by hand using a *mano del metate*, an elongated grinding stone held in the hands and repeatedly drawn over the grains or seeds to pulverize them. The *metate* may be basically flat, may have a bowl-like center, may have raised sides to make the center a trough, or may be in the shape of a long, low "v." Some of the variations in shape result from use. The *metate* may have three or four legs or a short platform supporting it, or it may rest flat on the floor.

mole m. (Nahuatl *mulli*) a thick gravy or sauce made from ingredients that give the sauce a distinctive color and flavor and that often assign it to a region of Mexico. *Mole* is served on enchiladas, meats, and other dishes.

mortadela or **mortadella** (Brazil, U.S.) a sausage roll of ground meat with spices, cheese, and other ingredients, sliced or cubed and eaten on bread or toast; a bologna.

Nahua – Nahuatl "Nahua" refers to the culture, cultural artifacts, and people whom Cortés found when he landed in what is today Mexico. Nahuatl refers to their language.

novela rosa literally, "the pink novel," meaning a "woman's" or "romance" novel, one in which a love interest and the complications and tensions surrounding star-crossed lovers are the primary focus, and in which the lovers eventually overcome the obstacles facing them for a happy ending.

pambazo a large rounded bun or bread; an overflowing sandwich that may include crumbled chorizo and avocado in a big bun soaked in chocolate *mole*.

pan de muerto literally, the "bread of the dead," All Soul's Bread, available from October 21 through November 1–2, depending on the area, and consumed in large quantities in Mexico during the Day of the Dead observances. The bun may resemble the English "hot cross bun," with a dough cross laid on top before the baking, but is more likely to be a large bun ornamented with dough "bones" that may or may not resemble a skull, and further decorated with sugar or colored sprinkles. Many imaginative variations are possible.

pelado *n.* literally, a bald man, used contemporarily in the sense of a "guy"; during the Revolution, a Federal soldier (draftee, conscript), whose head is shaved for hygienic reasons, also a pejorative term.

piropos flirtatious remarks, whistles, or catcalls, intended to compliment women and to attract the attention of women in public places.

Porfiriato the period of Mexican history during which Porfirio Díaz was dictator of Mexico. The Porfiriata, as it is also called, ended with the coming of the Mexican Revolution in 1910. See also **The Revolution, The Mexican Revolution**.

ranchera (*adj.*) having to do with the country or cowboys, not as *vaqueros* (literally, cowboys or cowhands, or wranglers), but as *charros*. See **charros** and **comedia ranchera**.

rancho a farm where crops and animals are raised, a ranch where herding animals are the economic focus. *Rancho* is also used (in an ironic sense) for an urban apartment or living space, or a (small) farmhouse or cabin in the countryside. The expression *hacer rancho* means to "make a space" or "step aside."

rebozo a traditional, rectangular one-piece woven article of apparel that is worn around the shoulders (like a shawl) by women in Mexico. It may be used to support infants and small children and be used to carry burdens such as firewood.

refranes *plu.* traditional, popular pithy sayings, terse and rhyming, such as "*Mujer que sabe latín ni tiene marido ni buen fin*" [A woman who knows Latin won't get a husband or come to a good end]. The epigraph for *Like Water for Chocolate* is "*A la mesa y a la cama, una sola vez se llama*" [You come to the table or to bed the first time you are called].

relleno any stuffing or filling used in food preparation.

The Revolution, The Mexican Revolution usually bounded within the dates 1910–1920, this war has been described as a "hurricane" and as a "wind that swept Mexico." In Anita Brenner's little book *The Wind that Swept Mexico*, published in 1943, the dates are given in the title as 1910–1942, and one sees that some observers view the Revolution beyond the armed conflict (the so-called "destructive" years) that made Pancho Villa and Emiliano Zapata's names and images known in Mexico and the Southwestern U.S. Stephen E. Lewis calls the period of 1910–1917 the "destructive" stage and 1917–1940 the "constructive" stage. Michael J. Gonzáles's text on the Revolution (2002) sets the upper limit at 1940. Brenner's work includes 184 photographs of historical and cultural interest, some of which are reprinted in Gonzáles's work.

rosca de Reyes a cake or bread formed in the shape of a crown or wreath to commemorate Epiphany (Twelfth Night, January 6). It may be filled with a cream filling. A token for good luck in the form of a coin, the figure of an infant, or other image is placed into the cake, and the person who gets it, is to give a party on Candelaria day, February 2, when the faithful take images of the infant Jesus to receive a blessing from the local priest.

salsa de molcajete the *molcajete* is a small lava-stone bowl, conical in shape, that is used to grind small amounts of vegetables such as peppers, cilantro, onion, tomato, and seasonings such as garlic, salt, and dried peppers to create fresh sauces – *salsas* – with traditional texture and flavor.

tamales (s. *tamal*) literally, "carefully wrapped" in Nahuatl, *tamales* are the ritual food of choice for special celebrations in Mexico and Guatemala. The preparation of *tamales* is labor intensive. Basically, *tamales* consist of some mixture of food that is steamed in corn-husks or banana leaves. More specifically, the term refers to a carefully wrapped bit of specially ground corn dough (*masa para tamales*) mixed with other ingredients. A filling of meat, such as

231

pork, chicken, or fish, may be seasoned and cooked and laid down vertically along the center of a rectangle of *masa* (a mixture of ground corn, fat, and liquid having the consistency of a thick bread dough) that has been spread on a corn husk (softened in water) or on a banana leaf. The wrapping is folded up at one end and "rolled" to enclose the filling with the *masa*, leaving the upper end open. Several finished tamales may be grouped together and tied (like a faggot of grain or sticks), and the bundle is placed, standing, on a rack in a large cooking utensil containing water. When all the bundles are arranged, the water will be brought to a boil and the tamales cooked and then cooled until they are "set." The filling, methods of preparation, and style of *tamales* in Mexico and Guatemala may vary by region. In the U.S. Southwest, the singular is often anglicized as "tamale," rather than *tamal*. See Christie's chapter on "kitchenspace" in this volume for *tamal* preparation, as well as her book on Mexico's kitchen culture (2008).

temascal (*pronun.* tay mahs kahl') a Mesoamerican enclosed, sacred space (structure) in which to perform ritual mind-body-spirit purification; also, the ritual cleansing of mind, body, or spirit that goes on within the space. The *temascal* is the site of a scene of reconciliation in *Malinche: A Novel.*

tilmatli – tilma (*pronoun.* til mat' tli) a mantle or cloak worn over the shoulders or at the back by tying or fastening, or used for carrying burdens. The *tilmatli* of Juan Diego bears the image of the Virgin of Guadalupe and is on view in the Basilica of the Virgin in Mexico City.

Tonantzin (*pronun.* toe nahn' tzeen) *Tonan* usually given as "mother" or "our mother," with the honorific suffix (*-tzin*) appended. Tonantzin is the Nahua maternal goddess whose sacred site at Tepeyac was appropriated by the Spanish Christians when Juan Diego, an indigenous convert, saw there a vision of a dark-skinned Virgin, comparable in the Spanish experience to the "dark" Virgin of Guadalupe of Extremadura, Spain. She brought with her "roses of Castille," suggesting, again, her Spanish provenance. See Wayne Elzey's synthesis of the debate over the nature of the goddess. For further bibliography, see Woodrow Borah's review of a group of books on the subject (1996).

tortilla a flat bread, most traditionally made of corn ground on the *metate*, mixed with water, patted into a round shape, and cooked on a hot, flat stone or iron. It is eaten in the course of being used as a utensil to hold or scoop other food. The traditional preparation process is highly labor intensive and members of the family might have consumed three to five tortillas each at a meal. *Tortilla* is the Spanish word applied to the Mesoamerican article, *tlazcali* or *tlaxcalli*. See Christie's essay in this volume for information on contemporary tortilla culture. *Malinche: A Novel* uses the tortilla as an important symbol of Malinalli's connection to her grandmother and indigenous heritage.

trufas *f.* truffles are a highly regarded fungal delicacy (hypogenous fungi) or a confection (candy) so named for its resemblance to the fungal variety. **trufar** = to fill poultry or other foods with truffles (the fungal type).

turrón nougat. A light confection that may be made of nuts (usually almonds), egg whites (for light texture and color), fruits, flavoring, and honey or sugar; *turrón* is used as a filling in candies or spread between wafers. In *Like Water for Chocolate*, the *turrón* is prepared as a cake filling.

Tzitzimitl (*pronun.* tzi tzi mee' tul) *plu.* **Tzitzimime** (*pronun.* tzi tzi mee' may) one or a group of Nahua star-demons, formerly warriors whose souls were made into stars, and who come to earth at night at certain spaces in the calendar to trouble mortals (Klein). Michael Graulich aptly styles them "demons of darkness" (357). Their activity was linked reciprocally to that of the *Cihuateteo.* Early in Colonial rule, the *Tzitzimime* were formally conflated with the Christian devil, acting on earth to ensnare the unwary (Burkhart, Sousa). See *Cihuateteo.*

villista a soldier or officer aligned with Villa's army.

Abbreviations Used in the Volume

BFI The British Film Institute.

BUAP Benemérita Universidad Autónoma de Puebla [The Distinguished Independent University of Puebla] located in the colonial city of Puebla de los Ángeles in the state of Puebla, MX.

Chasqui *Chasqui: Revista de literatura latinoamericana*, a journal of literary and cultural criticism issued in two numbers per year, formerly three.

col. column, as that of a newspaper or magazine printed with multiple columns on the page.

D.F. El Distrito Federal, The "Federal District." This designation for Mexico City is comparable with that of Washington, DC, as the "Federal District" of the U.S.

Dir. – dir. Director(s), used in a bibliographic citation related to film or television. Capitalization depends on whether the abbreviation precedes or follows the director's name.

DR *The Drama Review*, a quarterly journal published by the MIT Press Journals.

Ed. – ed "Edited by" or "editor(s)," respectively, in a bibliographic citation. Capitalization and the reading depends on whether the abbreviation precedes or follows the editor's / editors' name(s).

Exec. Prod. executive producer, used in a bibliographic citation related to film or television.

f. feminine in gender; grammatically, a noun unless otherwise specified.

FCE Fondo de Cultura Económica, a Mexican publishing house, or *editorial*.

ff. signals the reader to continue reading from the page number given in a citation to a logical stopping point, such as the end of a section or chapter.

FSG Farrar Straus Giroux, a New York publishing firm.

Gk. Greek, as a word derived from the Greek language.

Hispania *Hispania: the Journal of the American Association of the Teachers of Spanish and Portuguese.*

HR *The Hispanic Review*, a quarterly journal based in the Department of Romance Languages at the University of Pennsylvania.

IMDb Internet Movie Database. <http://www.imdb.com>.

LARR *Latin American Research Review: The Journal of the Latin American Studies Association*, now based at McGill University and published of the University of Pittsburgh Press.

LASA the Latin American Studies Association, an international professional organization.

lit. literally, as opposed to a figurative or popular significance.

LSU Louisiana State University.

m. masculine in gender; grammatically, a noun unless otherwise specified.

México Mexico City. Bibliographic citations providing "México" as the place of publication refer to the city, México, MX, D.F.

MLA the Modern Language Association, whose *MLA Handbook for Writers* (7th ed. 2009) is the basis for documentation format in literary and language studies. See *MLA*, below.

MLA (italics) a part of the title of a publication sponsored by the MLA or a regional organization of the MLA, such as SCMLA, the South Central MLA. See *PMLA*, below.

MLN *Modern Language Notes*, a journal published five times per year by the Johns Hopkins UP.

MLR *The Modern Language Review*, a quarterly journal published by the Modern Humanities Research Association.

MNC Andrea Noble's *Mexican National Cinema*. (National Cinemas Series. London and New York: Taylor & Francis Routledge, 2005). The page number from *MNC* is given following the data in question (director, title, year of release) without "p."; for example, (MNC 31). *MNC* provides translations of Spanish film titles, along with film cast lists and plot synopses.

Mortiz The *editorial* [publishing house] of Joaquín Mortiz, founded in 1962 (Anderson 1996 3).

MR *Monographic Review/Revista Monográfica*, an annual journal on a topic in Hispanic literature edited by Janet Pérez and Genaro Pérez (Texas Tech University, Lubbock).

MX. Mexico, the nation, as distinguished from Mexico City; used in bibliographical references to Mexican states, shown in Spanish (with the accent) in Spanish-language contexts. See **México**.

n. (italics) a noun, given to disambiguate a word that might be read as an adjective or other form.

n. (plain font) indicates a footnote or an endnote attached to the page(s) of the work cited. A citation reading "36 n. 4," refers to note four on page thirty-six of the work cited.

n.d. "no date" of publication or, in the case of a website, posting or last revision; found in bibliographic entries.

NYT *The New York Times*, a newspaper published in New York, the largest U.S. daily. The *NYT Book Review* is a weekly folio supplement to the newspaper.

P Press, given as a part of publication information as in "UP of Florida," meaning the University Press of Florida. "Press" is spelled out where "P" might cause confusion. See **U** and **UP**, below.

p. "page," used sparingly, as necessary to clarify the purpose of a number.

pl. plural.

PMLA *Publications of the Modern Language Association*, the quarterly journal of the MLA.

Prod. "Producer," as a part of a citation related to film or television.

PW *Publishers Weekly*, a weekly news magazine serving the publishing industry.

qtd. quoted (in); wording quoted from a secondary source rather than from the original.

rpt. reprinted (in); an essay or article reprinted in a second collection, journal, *etc.*

SR *The Southwest Review*, a quarterly literary journal published at Southern Methodist University (Dallas, Texas).

U and **UP** "University" and "University Press," respectively, given as a part of publication information, as in "U of Minnesota P" or "U P of Florida."

UNAM La Universidad Nacional Autónoma de México [The National University of Mexico].

Vol. Volume, used in a citation to indicate which of the volumes of a multi-volume work is being cited.

vols. volumes, the number of volumes in a single work.

WRB *The Women's Review of Books* is currently a bi-monthly publication of the Wellesley Centers for Women and Old City Publishing (Philadelphia).

The Contributors

Debra D. Andrist is Professor of Spanish and founding Chair of the Department of Foreign Languages at Sam Houston State University in Huntsville, Texas. She formerly held the Cullen Chair of Spanish and Chair of Modern & Classical Languages at the University of St. Thomas in Houston. Dr. Andrist's publications include language-acquisition textbooks, a translation of a book of short stories, and a book on literary theory, as well as articles, translations, reviews, and interviews that have appeared in the *South Central Review, Letras femeninas, Revista de Filología y Lingüística de la Universidad de Costa Rica*, and *Bulletin of the Cervantes Society of America,* among others. She has pioneered several specialized language programs, including three for medical professionals. She is past president of the South Central Modern Language Association and is editor of the *Southwest Conference of Latin American Studies Boletín*. She is Senior Vocal of the Asociación de Literatura Femenina Latinoamericana.

The Reverend Dr. Stephen Butler Murray is College Chaplain and Assistant Professor of Religion at Endicott College in Beverly, Massachusetts, and Senior Pastor of the First Baptist Church of Boston. In higher education, he previously served as the chaplain and on the faculty of Skidmore College and Suffolk University, and as an administrator at the Dwight Hall Center for Public Service and Social Justice at Yale University. He also has taught at Union Theological Seminary in New York City and Auburn Theological Seminary. He is Managing Editor of *The Journal of Inter-Religious Dialogue*, and his research and teaching focus on the history of Christian theology, religious ethics, interfaith relations, and the interplay of race, class, and gender in religion. He is a past President of the North American Paul Tillich Society and serves as the Board of Trustees of the Massachusetts Bible Society.

María Elisa Christie is Program Director for Women in International Development at Virginia Tech's Office of International Research, Education, and Development. Christie's professional involvement in various aspects of international development concerning women and agricultural workers has allowed her to explore the intersections of gender, culture, and environment with particular attention to the spaces of everyday life. Her articles have appeared in the *Geographic Review; Gender, Place and Culture; Journal of Latin American Geography*; and *Revista de Literatura Mexicana Contemporánea*. She served as guest editor for a special issue of *Geographical Review: People, Place and Gardens*. Her book *Kitchenspace: Women, Fiestas, and Everyday Life in Mexico* (2008) is published by the University of Texas Press.

Elizabeth Coonrod Martínez is Professor of Latin American Literature and Chair of the Department of Chicano and Latino Studies at Sonoma State University in northern California. She is the author of *Josefina Niggli, Mexican American Writer: A Critical Biography* (U of New Mexico P 2007), *"Lilus Kikus" and Other Stories by Elena Poniatowska* (U of New Mexico P 2005), and *Before the Boom: Latin American Revolutionary Novels of the 1920s* (University Press of America 2001). She is currently working on a six-book series on Latin American culture titled *Aperturas: La cultura lati-noamericana en su formación, con antología literaria* (Boston: Focus Publishing: vol. I, México, in press; vol. 2, El Latino/Hispano en los Estados Unidos, in press; vol. 3, América Central; vol. 4, El Caribe; Vol. 5, La región andina y amazónica; vol. 6, El cono sur y Brasil).

Patrick Duffey is Dean of Humanities and Professor of Spanish at Austin College, Sherman, Texas. Duffey's primary area of research has been the impact of film on Hispanic cultures. In recent years, he has published numerous articles and delivered invited lectures on the impact of U.S. silent film in Latin America and Spain during the 1920s and 1930s. He is author of *De la pantalla al texto: La influencia del cine en la narrativa mexicana del siglo XX* (1997).

Jeanne L. Gillespie is Associate Professor of Spanish and Associate Dean for Research and Interdisciplinary Studies in the College of Arts and Letters at the University of Southern Mississippi. She is the author of *Saints and Warriors: Tlaxcalan Perspectives on the Conquest of Tenochtitlan* (2004) and co-editor of *Women's Voices and the Politics of the Spanish Empire: From Convent Cell to Imperial Court* (2008) with Jennifer Eich and Lucia Guzzi Harrison. Recent articles include "Talking out of Church: Women Arguing Theology in Sor Juana's *loa* to the *Divino Narciso*" (*Unruly Catholic Women and their Writings*. New York: Palgrave Macmillan, 2007) and "Amerindian Women's Voices in Aztec Society and the Spanish Colony" (*Cuaderno internacional de estudios hispánicos y lingüística*. Spring 2005). Her current project, *Performing Spanish Louisiana: Isleño Décimas and the Narratives of St. Bernard Parish*, is a collection of Isleño texts, images, and folklore.

The Contributors

Linda Ledford-Miller is Professor of Spanish and Portuguese and Chair of the Department of Foreign Languages and Literatures at the University of Scranton in Scranton, Pennsylvania, where she teaches Spanish, Portuguese, and American Minority Literature. She has held Fulbright grants to Brazil, Guatemala, and Mozambique. Her research interests include travel writing on Guatemala and Mexico and women writers.

Ryan F. Long is Assistant Professor of Spanish at the University of Oklahoma. His research focuses on culture and politics in Mexico, especially the late twentieth century. He has published articles on a range of topics, including the conflict in Chiapas, Mexican cinema, and a number of writers, such as Ignacio Manuel Altamirano, Álvaro Mutis, and Luis González de Alba. His book, *Fictions of Totality: The Mexican Novel, 1968, and the National-Popular State*, was published in 2008 by Purdue University Press.

Jeffrey Oxford is Professor of Spanish and Chair of the Department of Spanish and Portuguese at the University of Wisconsin at Milwaukee. Oxford is co-author of *Eduardo Mendoza: A New Look* (2002); author of *Vicente Blasco Ibáñez: Color Symbolism in Selected Novels* (1997); and editor of Blasco Ibáñez's *La barraca* (Juan de la Cuesta 2003) and Juan Valera's *Pepita Jiménez* (2005). He is the author of over two dozen scholarly articles, including several articles on feminist theory. One of his recent articles is "'Well-behaved women seldom make history,' ni la cuentan: El papel de la mujer en *Muertes de perro*" (*Hispania* 89.4 [2006]: 759–65). Oxford is co-editor of volumes on Virginia Woolf and Eduardo Mendoza, and co-edited *The Languages of Addiction* (1999). His current research project studies aspects of social justice in the life and works of Vicente Blasco Ibáñez, and he serves as Managing Editor of *Monographic Review/Revista Monográfica*.

Alberto Julián Pérez, Argentine literary critic, is Professor of Spanish and Director of Latin American and Iberian Studies at Texas Tech University. Pérez has specialized in the work of Domingo Faustino Sarmiento and is President of the Instituto Sarmiento de Texas. His publications include *La poética de Rubén Darío: Crisis post-romántica y modelos literarios modernistas* (1992); *Modernismo, Vanguardias, Posmodernidad: Ensayos de literatura hispanoamericana* (1995); *Los Dilemas Políticos de La Cultura Letrada: Argentina Siglo XIX* (2003); *Imaginación Literaria y Pensamiento Propio: Ensayos de la Literatura Hispanoamericana* (2006); and numerous articles in *Revista literaria* and other journals of literary criticism.

The Contributors

Elena Poniatowska Amor is an internationally known journalist, novelist, essayist, lecturer, and political activist. She is a founder of the Mexican newspaper *La Jornada* and the feminist magazine *Fem*. Poniatowska's *Massacre in Mexico* (*La noche de Tlatelolco* 1971) and *Here's to you, Jesus* (*Hasta no verte, Jesus mío* 1969) gave her an international reputation as a journalist and author. She was the first woman to receive Mexico's National Journalism Award in 1979. Her recent work includes *El tren pasa primero* (Alfaguara 2005. [*The Train Passes First*]) and *Tlapalería*, a short-story collection (2003). Her most recent book, *Amanecer en el Zócalo: Los 50 días que confrontaron a México* (Planeta 2007 [*Dawn in the Zócalo: Fifty days that Challenged Mexico*]), chronicles the fifty days she spent in the streets of downtown Mexico City with thousands of other citizens who protested the electoral fraud that stole the presidency from leftist candidate Andrés Manuel López Obrador in 2006. Poniatowska holds the highest rank of The French Legion of Honor (2004), and she was honored with The Maria Moors Cabot Prize for outstanding reporting on Latin America and the Caribbean (1972), the Premio Mazatlán de Literatura [Mazatlán Prize for Literature] twice, in 1971 and 1993, the Premio Alfaguara de Novela [Alfaguara Novel Prize 2001], and the Rómulo Gallegos Prize (2007). The International Women's Media Foundation recognized Poniatowska with its Lifetime Achievement Award in 2006. She holds honorary doctorates from Columbia University, Manhattanville University, the New School of Social Research, and Florida Atlantic University, among others.

Lydia H. Rodríguez, a native of Mexico, is Associate Professor in the Department of Spanish and Classical Languages at Indiana University of Pennsylvania. Her research interests include Latin American women writers and Chicana literature. She is author of *El mestizaje del canon: Helena María Viramontes* (Pliegos 2005) and *Helena María Viramontes en sus propias palabras* (Nuevo Espacio 2006), and is co-editor for *Mosaico literario sobre autoras latinoamericana y caribeñas* (Universidad Católica Andrés Bello 2008). Rodríguez has been an invited lecturer in Colombia and Venezuela, and in 2005 was recognized by Mayor Adrián Rivera Pérez of Cuernavaca, Mexico, for promoting Spanish language and culture abroad.

Elizabeth Moore Willingham is Associate Professor in the Department of Modern Foreign Languages at Baylor University (Waco, Texas). She has published on topics in Latin American women's fiction, Laura Esquivel's fiction, Medical Humanities, Historical Language, and medieval Miracle and Arthurian literature. She has served as president and executive director of the Southwest Council of Latin American

Studies. She is series editor for The *Lancelot* of Yale 229 (Brepols) and volume editor for *Essays on the Lancelot of Yale 229* (2007) and editions of *La mort le Roi Artu* (2007) and *La Queste del Saint Graal* (2010). The *Agrauains* edition, supported by the National Endowment for the Humanities, is expected in 2012.

Works Cited

Works Cited comprises:
Primary and Secondary Literary and Critical Sources
Films Cited
Film Reviews and Box Office Reports
Television Programming
Resources in Medical Humanities

Primary and Secondary Literary and Critical Sources

Abernethy, Francis Edward. "Preface." *Charreada: Mexican Rodeo in Texas.* Photographer, Al Rendón. Series Ed. Francis Edward Abernethy. Publications of the Texas Folklore Society 59. Denton, TX: U of North Texas P, 2002. 1–5.

Aguiar, Sarah Appleton. *The Bitch is Back: Wicked Women in Literature.* Carbondale, IL: Southern Illinois UP, 2001.

Aínsa, Fernando. "Invención literaria y 'reconstrucción' histórica en la nueva narrativa latinoamericana." Kohut 111–21.

——. "La reescritura de la historia en la nueva narrativa latinoamericana." *Cuadernos americanos* 4.28 (1991): 13–31.

Alarcón, Norma. "Chicana Feminist Literature: A Re-Vision Through Malintzín/Malinche: Putting the Flesh Back on the Object." Moraga and Anzaldúa 182–90.

——. "*Tradutora Traditora*: A Paradigmatic Figure of Chicana Feminism." *Cultural Critique: The Construction of Gender and Modes of Social Division* 13 (1989): 57–87.

Alarcón, Norma, Ana Castillo, and Cherríe Moraga, ed. *Third Woman: The Sexuality of Latinas* 4. Berkeley: Third Woman P, 1989.

Aldaraca, Bridget. "'El ángel del hogar:' The Cult of Domesticity in Nineteenth-Century Spain." *Theory and Practice of Feminist Literary Criticism.* Eds. Gabriela Mora and Karen S. Van Hooft. Ypsilanti, MI: Bilingual P, 1982. 62–87.

Aldrich, Robert and Garry Wotherspoon. *Who's Who in Contemporary Gay and Lesbian History, from WWII to Present Day.* New York: Routledge, 2001.

Alkon, Paul K. *Origins of Futuristic Fiction.* Athens, GA: U of Georgia P, 1987.

Allende, Isabel. *La casa de los espíritus.* Barcelona: Plaza & Janés, 1982.

Works Cited

——. *Cuentos de Eva Luna*. Barcelona: Plaza & Janés, 1990.

——. *Daughter of Fortune: A Novel*. Trans. Margaret Sayers Peden. New York: HarperCollins, 1999.

——. *Hija de la Fortuna*. Barcelona: Plaza & Janés, 1999.

——. *The House of the Spirits*. Trans. Magda Bogin. New York: Knopf, 1985.

——. *Inés del alma mía*. Barcelona: Plaza & Janés, 2006.

——. *Inés of My Soul*. Trans. Margaret Sayers Peden. New York: HarperCollins, 2006.

——. *Paula*. Barcelona: Plaza & Janés, 1994.

——. *Paula*. Trans. Margaret Sayers Peden. New York: HarperCollins, 1995.

——. *The Stories of Eva Luna*. Trans. Margaret Sayers Peden. New York: Atheneum, 1991.

Amado, Jorge. *Dona Flor e seus dois maridos: história moral e de amor*. São Paulo: Martins, 1971.

——. *Doña Flor y sus dos maridos: Edificante historia de amor*. Trans. [Portuguese to Spanish] Lorenzo Varela. Buenos Aires: Losada, 1961. Madrid: Alianza, 1981.

——. *Doña Flor y sus dos maridos: Historia moral y de amor*. Trans. Amalia Sato. New York: Vintage Español, 2008.

——. *Dona Flor and Her Two Husbands: A Moral and Amorous Tale*. Trans. Harriet de Onís. New York: Knopf, 1969.

Amerlinck, Fernando. "1904: Nada pasa; todo queda." (February 6, 2007) *Asuntos Capitales*. 11 November 2009 <http://www.asuntoscapitales. com/default.asp?id=3&ids=2&idss=16&ida=1904>.

Anderson, Danny J. "Creating Cultural Prestige: Editorial Joaquín Mortiz." *LARR* 31.2 (1996): 3–41.

——. "Difficult Relations, Compromising Positions: Telling Involvement in Recent Mexican Narrative." *Chasqui* 24.1 (1995): 16–29.

André, María Claudia, and Eva Paulina Bueno, eds. *Latin American Women Writers: An Encyclopedia*. New York: Routledge, 2008.

Andreu, Alicia G. *Galdós y la literatura popular*. Madrid: Sociedad General Española de Librería, 1982.

[Anonymous/Staff.] "[Review of] *Malinche*." *PW* 253.9 (February 27, 2006): 31.

[Anonymous/Staff.] "[Review of] *Swift as Desire*." *PW* 248.29 (July 16, 2001): 165.

Ariel: Historia del Ariel. (August 21, 2009 [updated daily]). Academia Mexicana de Artes y Ciencias Cinematográficas A.C. 11 November 2009 <http://www.academiamexicanadecine.org.mx/historiaAriel.asp>.

Arredondo, Inés. *Obras Completas*. México: Siglo XXI, 1988. 2nd ed. 1991.

——. *Río subterráneo*. México: Mortiz, 1979.

——. *Underground River*. Trans. Cynthia Steele. Lincoln, NE: U of Nebraska P, 1996.

Ashwell, Anamaría. "Cholula: ¿Qué hay en un nombre?" *Elementos: Ciencia y cultura* 9.48 (2002–2003): 39–47.

Aztecs – Painted Books. (November 16, 2002–April 11, 2003). The Royal

Works Cited

Academy of Arts: 11 November 2009 <http://www.aztecs.org.uk/en/books.html>.

Bados-Ciria, Concepción. "*La ley del amor* de Laura Esquivel: ¿Por qué la opera, el danzón y el comic?" *Revista de Literatura Mexicana Contemporánea* 1.3 (1996): 38–42.

Baker, Phyllis L. "'It Is the Only Way I Can Survive': Gender Paradox among Recent Mexicana Immigrants." *Sociological Perspectives* 47.4 (2004): 393–408.

Barrientos, Tanya. "[Review of] *Malinche*: Invented Story of a Real Woman, Cortés's Translator and Mistress." *Philadelphia Enquirer* (August 16, 2006): E02.

Baudrillard, Jean. *Simulacra and Simulation*. Trans. Sheila Faria Glaser. Ann Arbor, MI; U of Michigan P, 1994.

Beckman, Pierina E. "*La ley del amor*: más allá de las barreras literarias." *Fem* 23.192 (1999): 44–46.

Belejack, Barbara. "In the Midst of Terror: [Review of] *Bitter Grounds* by Sandra Benítez." *WRB* 15.9 (June 1998): 24.

Benítez, Sandra. *Bitter Grounds*. New York: Hyperion, 1997.

Blanco, José Joaquín. *Se llamaba Vasconcelos: Una evocación crítica*. Vida y pensamiento de México. México: FCE, 1977.

Blasco Ibáñez, Vicente. *Obras completas*. Vol. 2. Madrid: Aguilar, 1987.

Borah, Woodrow. "[Review article] Queen of Mexico and Empress of the Americas: 'La Guadalupana' of Tepeyac." *Mexican Studies / Estudios Mexicanos* 12.2 (1996): 326–39.

Bordo, Susan. "The Cartesian Masculinization of Thought." *Signs* 11 (1986): 239–56.

Boschetto, Sandra María. "The Demythification of Matriarchy and Image of Women in *Chronicle of a Death Foretold*." *Critical Perspectives on Gabriel García Márquez*. Ed. Bradley Shaw and Nora Vera-Godwin. Lincoln: Society of Spanish and Spanish-American Studies, 1986. 125–37.

Bouchard, Danielle. "Women's Studies' Guilt Complex: Interdisciplinarity, Globalism, and the University." *Journal of the Midwest MLA: The University* 37.1 (2004): 32–39.

Boullosa, Carmen. *Llanto: Novelas imposibles*. México: Era, 1992.

Bower, Anne L., ed. *Recipes for Reading: Community Cookbooks, Stories, Histories*. Amherst, MA: U of Massachusetts P, 1997.

Bracho, Diana. "El cine mexicano: ¿y en el papel de la mujer . . . Quien?." *Mexican Studies / Estudios Mexicanos* 1.2 (1985): 413–23.

Bratton, Jacky, Jim Cook, and Christine Gledhill, eds. *Melodrama: Stage Picture Screen*. London: BFI, 1994.

Brenner, Anita, and George R. Leighton, Ed. of Photography. *The Wind that Swept Mexico: The History of the Mexican Revolution 1910–1942*. New York: Harper, 1943. Austin, TX: U of Texas P, 1971.

Brunner, José Joaquín. "Latin American Identity – Dramatized." Trans. Shara Moseley. *Latin America Writes Back: Postmodernity in the Periphery*. Ed. Emil Volek. New York: Routledge, 2002.

Bunzel, Ruth. *Chichicastenago: A Guatemalan Village*. American Ethnological Society 22. Seattle, WA: U of Washington P, 1952.

Burkhart, Louise M. *Before Guadalupe: The Virgin Mary in Early Colonial Nahuatl Literature*. Albany, NY: Institute for Mesoamerican Studies, U at Albany, State U of New York, 2001.

Burton, Kate. "Frida Kahlo 9 June–9 October: Tate Modern." *Tate Modern: Past Exhibitions: Frida Kahlo*. 13 November 2009 <http://www.tate.org. uk/modern/exhibitions/kahlo/roomguide.shtm>.

Butler, Judith. *Bodies that Matter: On the Discursive Limits of "Sex."* London: Routledge, 1993.

——. *Gender Trouble: Feminism and the Subversion of Identity*. London: Routledge, 1990.

Burton-Carvajal, Julianne. "Mexican Melodramas of Patriarchy." *Framing Latin American Cinema: Contemporary Critical Perspectives*. Ed. Ann Marie Stock. Minneapolis, MN: U of Minnesota P, 1997. 186–234.

Byars, Jackie. *All That Hollywood Allows: Re-reading Gender in 1950s Melodrama*. Chapel Hill, NC: U of North Carolina P, 1991.

Cammarata, Joan. "*Como agua para chocolate*: Gastronomía erótica, magicorrealismo culinario." *Explicación de Textos Literarios* 25.1 (1996–1997): 87–103.

Campos, Julieta. *Obras reunidas*. Ed. Fabienne Bradu. México: FCE, 2005.

——. *She Has Reddish Hair and Her Name is Sabina: A Novel by Julieta Campos*. Trans. Leland H. Chambers. Athens, GA.: U of Georgia P, 1993.

——. *Reunión de familia*. México: FCE, 1997.

——. *Tiene los cabellos rojizos y se llama Sabina*. México: Mortiz, 1974.

Cantú Corro, José. *La mujer a través de los siglos*. México: Botas, 1938.

Carlsen, Robert S., and Martin Prechtel. "The Flowering of the Dead: An Interpretation of Highland Maya Culture." *Man* 26 (1991): 23–42.

Carpentier, Alejo. "On the Marvelous Real in America (1949)." Zamora and Faris 75–88.

Carrasco, David. *City of Sacrifice: The Aztec Empire and the Role of Violence in Civilization*. Boston, MA: Beacon, 2000.

——. "Jaguar Christians in the contact zone: Concealed narratives in the histories of religions in the Americas." Olupona 128–38.

——. *Religions of Mesoamerica: Cosmovision and Ceremonial Centers*. San Francisco, CA: HarperSanFrancisco, 1990.

Carreño, Manuel Antonio. *Manual de urbanidad y buenas maneras: El manual de Carreño*. Caracas: Libros de El Nacional, 2001.

Castellanos, Rosario. "Woman and Her Image." Trans. Ahern, Maureen. *A Rosario Castellanos Reader: An Anthology of Her Poetry, Short Fiction, Essays, and Drama*. Ed. Maureen Ahern. Austin, TX: U of Texas P, 1988. 236–44.

——. *Balún Canán*. Lecturas mexicanas. México: FCE, 1957, 2004.

——. *The Book of Lamentations* [*Oficio de tinieblas*]. Trans. Esther Allen. New York: Penguin, 1998.

——. *Mujer que sabe latín*. México: Secretaría de Educación Pública, 1973.

——. *Nine Guardians* [*Balún Canán*]. Trans. Irene Nicholson. Columbia, LA: Readers International, 1992.

——. *Oficio de tinieblas*. México: Mortiz, 1962.

Castillo, Debra A. "Anna's Extreme Makeover: Revisiting Tolstoy in *Karenina Express*." Lambright and Guerrero 93–109.

——. *Easy Women: Sex and Gender in Modern Mexican Fiction*. Minneapolis, MN: U of Minnesota P, 1998.

——. "Reading Loose Women Reading." *The Places of History: Regionalism Revisited in Latin America*. Ed. Doris Sommer. Durham, NC: Duke UP, 1999. 165–79.

Cavallo, Susana, Luis A. Jiménez, and Oralia Preble-Niemi, eds. *Estudios en honor de Janet Pérez: El sujeto femenino en escritoras hispánicas*. Potomac, MD: Scripta Humanistica, 1998.

Chaison, Joanne Danaher. "Mysterious Malinche: A Case of Mistaken Identity." *American Academy of Franciscan History* 32.4 (1976): 514–23.

Chanady, Amaryll. "Latin American Imagined Communities and the Postmodern Challenge." *Latin American Identity and Constructions of Difference*. Ed. Amaryll Chanady. Minneapolis, MN: U of Minnesota P, 1994. ix–xlvi.

Chanan, Michael. *The Cuban Image: Cinema and Cultural Politics in Cuba*. Bloomington, IN: Indiana UP, 1985.

Christie, María Elisa. "Kitchenspace, Fiestas, and Cultural Reproduction in Mexican House-lot Gardens: Rural Spaces in Increasingly Urban Contexts." *The Geographical Review* 94.3 (2004): 368–90.

——. "Kitchenspace: Gendered territory in central Mexico [*sic*]." *Gender, Place & Culture: A Journal of Feminist Geography* 13.6 (2006): 653–61.

——. *Kitchenspace: Women, Fiestas, and Everyday life in Mexico*. Austin, TX: U of Texas P, 2008.

——. "Naturaleza y sociedad desde la perspectiva de la cocina tradicional mexicana: género, adaptación y resistencia." *Journal of Latin American Geography* 1.1 (2002): 21–54.

Cirlot, Juan Eduardo. *A Dictionary of Symbols*. New York: Dorset, 1991.

Claudel, Paul. *Break of Noon*. Trans. Wallace Fowlie. Chicago: Regnery, 1960.

——. *Partage de midi*: premiére version. *Théatre* I. Ed. Jacques Madaule and Jacques Petit. Bibliothèque de la Pléiade. Paris: Gallimard, 1967. 981–1062.

Cohn, Deborah N. "A Tale of Two Translation Programs: Politics, the Market, and Rockefeller Funding for Latin American Literature in the United States during the 1960s and 1970s." *LARR* 41.2 (2006): 139–64.

Colina, Enrique and Daniel Díaz Torres. "Ideología del melodrama en el viejo cine latinoamericano." *Cine cubano* 73/74/75 (1971): 14–26.

Cooke, Rachel. "[Review] Pleasure Zone: *Swift as Desire*. Laura Esquivel." *New Statesman* 130.4552 (August 27, 2001): 39.

Coonrod Martínez, Elizabeth. "The Subversive Role of Women in the Making of History: Pre-Revolution Mexico and Teresa Urrea." *MR* 19 (2003): 224–35.

——. "[Review of] *La ley del amor* by Laura Esquivel." *Hispania* 81.4 (1998): 891–93.

Cortázar, Julio. *Hopscotch*. Trans. Gregory Rabassa. New York: Pantheon, 1966. London: Collins, Harvill, 1967.

———. *Rayuela*. Buenos Aires: Sudamericana, 1963.

Cortés, Hernán. *Cartas de relación*. 10th ed. México: Porrúa, 1978.

———. *Letters from Mexico* [*Cartas de relación*]. Trans. and Ed. Anthony R. Pagden. New Haven, CT: Yale UP, 1986.

Costantino, Roselyn. *Resistant Creativity: Interpretative Strategies and Gender Representation in Contemporary Women's Writing in Mexico*. Dissertation, Arizona State U (Tempe, AZ), 1992.

Contreras, Joseph and Scott Johnson. "Mexico's New Wave: Using Brutal Realism and Bold Subject Matter, A Fresh Generation of Directors and Actors is Testing The Country's Freedom of Expression." *Newsweek* (November 24, 2003). 11 November 2009 <http://www.newsweek.com/id/60648>.

Counihan, Carole M. and Penny Van Esterik, eds. *Food and Culture: A Reader*. New York: Routledge, 1997.

Crossley, Phil. "The Chinampas of Mexico." 11 November 2009 <http://www.chinampas.info/>.

———. "Xochimilco: Don't Float by the Gardens." (August 1995) Chinampas/Planeta.com. 11 November 2009 <http://www.planeta.com/planeta/95/0895chinampa.html>.

Cruz-Lugo, Victor. "The Poet and the Visionary: A Conversation with World-Renowned Writer Laura Esquivel." *Hispanic Magazine* 19.4 (April 2006): 28–30.

Csordas, Thomas J., ed. *Embodiment and Experience: The Existential Ground of Culture and Self*. Cambridge Studies in Medical Anthropology. Cambridge, UK: Cambridge UP, 1994.

Curtin, Deane W. and Lisa M. Heldke, ed. *Cooking, Eating, Thinking: Transformative Philosophies of Food*. Bloomington, IN: Indiana UP, 1992.

Cypess, Sandra Messinger. *La Malinche in Mexican Literature: from History to Myth*. Austin, TX: U of Texas P, 1991.

Cypess, Sandra Messinger, David R. Kohut, and Rachelle Moore. *Women Authors of Modern Hispanic South America: A Biography of Literary Criticism and Interpretation*. Metuchen, NJ: Scarecrow, 1989.

Davies, Lisa. "Monstrous Mothers and the Cult of the Virgin in Rosario Castellanos' *Oficio de tinieblas*." *New Readings* 6 (December 5, 2000). Cardiff University, Wales, UK. 11 November 2008 <http://www.cardiff.ac.uk/euros/subsites/newreadings/volume6/davisl.html>.

Davis, Jack Emory. "Picturesque 'Americanismos' in the Works of Fernández de Lizardi." *Hispania* 44.1 (1961): 74–81.

De Valdés, María Elena. *The Shattered Mirror: Representations of Women in Mexican Literature*. Austin, TX: U of Texas P, 1998.

———. "Verbal and Visual Representations of Women: *Como agua para chocolate / Like Water for Chocolate*." *World Literature Today* 69 (1995): 78–82.

Díaz del Castillo, Bernal. *The Discovery and Conquest of Mexico, 1517–1521. Edited from the only exact copy of the original ms (and published in Mexico) by*

Genaro García. Trans. and ed. A. P. Maudslay. New York: Grove, 1956.

——. *Historia verdadera de la conquista de la Nueva-España*. Madrid: Impr[esa] del Reyno, 1632.

——. *The History of the Conquest of New Spain by Bernal Díaz del Castillo*. Ed. Davíd Carrasco. Albuquerque, NM: U of New Mexico P, 2008.

Dinesen, Isak [Karen Blixen]. *Anecdotes of Destiny*. New York: Random House, 1958.

Dobrian, Susan Lucas. "Romancing the Cook: Parodic Consumption of Popular Romance Myths in *Como agua para chocolate*." *LARR* 24.48 (1996): 56–66.

Dueñas, Guadalupe. *Tiene la noche un árbol*. México: FCE, 1958.

——. *Imaginaciones*. México: Jus, 1977.

——. *Antes el silencio*. México: FCE, 1991.

Duffey, J. Patrick. *De la pantalla al texto: La influencia del cine en la narrativa mexicana del siglo veinte*. Trans. Ignacio Quirarte. México: UNAM, 1996.

Earle, Peter G. "Unamuno and the Theme of History." *HR* 32.4 (1964): 319–39.

Eco, Umberto. *Postscript to the Name of the Rose*. New York: HBJ, 1984.

Elias, Thomas. "The Miracle Worker: How Alfonso Arau's *Water for Chocolate* Dream Came True." *Chicago Tribune* March 6, 1994. Section 13: 19.

Elizondo, Virgilio P. "Our Lady of Guadalupe: A Guide for the New Millennium." (December 1999) *St. Anthony Messenger*. 11 November 2009 <http://www.americancatholic.org/Messenger/Dec1999/feature2.asp#F2>.

Elmore, Peter. *La fábrica de la memoria: La crisis de representación en la novela histórica latinoamericana*. México: FCE, 1997.

Elsaesser, Thomas. "Tales of Sound and Fury: Observation on the Family Melodrama." *Monogram* 4 (1972): 2–15. [Rpt. in] *Home Is Where the Heart Is: Studies in Melodrama and the Woman's Film*. Ed. Christine Gledhill. London: BFI, 1987: 43–69.

Elu de Leñero, María del Carmen. *¿hacia dónde va la mujer mexicana? (resultados de una encuesta nacional): proyecciones a partir de los datos de una encuesta nacional* [sic]. México: Instituto Mexicano de Estudios Sociales, 1969.

Elzey, Wayne. "A Hill on a Land Surrounded by Water [sic]: An Aztec Story of Origin and Destiny." *History of Religions* 31.2 (1991): 105–49.

Escaja, Tina. "Reinscribiendo a Penélope: Mujer e identidad mejicana en *Como agua para chocolate*." *Revista Iberoamericana* 66.192 (2000): 571–86.

Esquivel, Laura. *Between Two Fires: Intimate Writings on Life, Love, Food & Flavor*. Trans. Stephen Lytle. New York: Crown, 2000.

——. *Como agua para chocolate: Novela de entregas mensuales con recetas, amores y remedios caseros*. New York: Doubleday, [April] 1993.

——. *Como agua para chocolate: Novela de entregas mensuales con recetas, amores y remedios caseros*. New York: Anchor-Doubleday, 1989.

——. *Como agua para chocolate: Novela de entregas mensuales con recetas, amores y remedios caseros*. México: Planeta, 1989.

——. *Como agua para chocolate: Novela de entregas mensuales con recetas, amores y remedios caseros*. [Paper] New York: Anchor-Doubleday, [June] 1994.

——. *Como agua para chocolate*. Perf. Yareli Arizmendi. [audio cassette] Madrid: Alfaguara Audio, 1994. [CD] New York: Random House Audio, 2006, 2007.

——. *La Estrellita marinera: una fábula de nuestro tiempo*. México: Planeta, 1999.

——. "Foreword." *An Appetite for Passion*. Ed. Lisa Fine, Ivana Lowell, and John Willoughby. New York: Miramax, 1995.

——. "Foreword." *The Secrets of Jesuit Breadmaking: Recipes and Traditions from Jesuit Bakers Around the World*. Rick Curry. New York: Morrow, 1995.

——. *Íntimas suculencias: tratado filosófico de cocina*. Madrid: Ollero & Ramos, 1998.

——. *The Law of Love*. Trans. Margaret Sayers Peden. New York: Crown-Random, 1996.

——. *The Law of Love: A Novel with Music*. Perf. Yareli Arizmendi. New York: Random House Audio, 1996.

——. *La ley del amor*. Barcelona: Plaza & Janés, 1995.

——. *La ley del amor*. México: Grijalbo, 1995.

——. *La ley del amor*. New York: Anchor, 2001.

——. *La ley del amor*. New York: Crown-Random, 1995.

——. *El libro de las emociones: son de la razón sin corazón*. Barcelona: Plaza & Janés, 2002.

——. *Like Water for Chocolate: A Novel in Monthly Installments with Recipes, Romances and Home Remedies*. Trans. Carol Christensen and Thomas Christensen. New York: Doubleday, 1992.

——. *Like Water for Chocolate*. Perf. Kate Reading. [audio cassette]. New York: Doubleday/Anchor, (1992?), 1993. New York: Random House/Listening Library, 2006. Random House Audio, 2007.

——. *Malinche: A Novel*. Trans. Ernesto Mestre-Reed. New York: Atria, 2006.

——. *Malinche: A Novel*. New York: Washington Square, 2007. [Atria's English translation, paperback. Only "*Malinche*," as the title, appears on the cover.]

——. *Malinche: novela*. New York: Atria, 2006.

——. *Malinche: novela*. Perf. Lucía Méndez. Fonolibro, 2006.

——. "Prólogo." *La cocina del chile*. Patricia Van Rhijn. México: Planeta, 2003.

——. *Swift as Desire*. Trans. Stephen A. Lytle. New York: Crown-Random, 2001.

——. *Swift as Desire*. Perf. Elizabeth Peña. New York: Random House Audiobooks, 2001.

——. *Tan veloz como el deseo*. Barcelona: Plaza & Janés, 2001.

——. *Tan veloz como el deseo*. New York: Anchor-Doubleday, 2001.

Estrada, Oswaldo. "(Des)Encuentros (arque)típicos con la nueva ficción histórica en *Malinche* de Laura Esquivel." *Cien años de lealtad En* [sic] *honor a Luis Leal / One Hundred Years of Loyalty In* [sic] *Honor of Luis Leal*. 2 vols. Ed. Sara Poot-Herrera, *et al*. Santa Barbara, CA: U of California, Santa Barbara, UC-Mexicanistas; Instituto Tecnológico de Monterrey; UNAM; Universidad del Claustro de Sor Juana, 2007. Vol. I 617–37.

Works Cited

"Eydie Gorme y el Trio Los Panchos – 'Sabor a mí' – 1964." Momentosdetango. 11 November 2009 <http://www.youtube.com/watch?v=JwEhvccG3Ac>.

Feracho, Lesley. *Linking the Americas: Race, Hybrid Discourses, and the Reformulation of Feminine Identity*. SUNY Series in Latin American and Iberian Thought and Culture. Albany, NY: State UP, 2005.

Fernandes, Carla. "Poètes du monde aztèque, Tenochtitlan, Mexico et le premier roman multimedia." *Caravelle: Cahiers du Monde Hispanique et Luso Brésilien* 76–77 (2001): 667–75.

Fernández-Levin, R[osa]. "Bridging the Gap: Mythical and Historical Discourse in *La ley del amor*." *Journal of Latin American Lore* 20.2 (1997): 333–46.

Finnegan, Nuala, and Jane E. Lavery. *The Boom Femenino in Mexico: Reading Contemporary Women's Writing*. (2007) University of Southhampton, Ireland. [An academic congress] 11 November 2009 <http://www.lang.soton.ac.uk/boomfemenino/project.html>.

Flagg, Fannie. *Fried Green Tomatoes at the Whistlestop Cafe*. New York: ImPress, 1999.

Flores, Ángel. "Magic Realism in Spanish American Fiction (1955)." Zamora and Faris 109–17.

——. "Magical Realism in Spanish American Fiction." *Hispania* 33.2 (1955): 187–92.

Florescano, Enrique. *National Narratives in Mexico: A History*. Norman, OK: U of Oklahoma P, 2006.

Fox-Anderson, Catherine. "*Mysterium coniunctionis*: La boda alquímica de Tita y Pedro en *Como agua para chocolate: una novela de entregas mensuales con recetas, amores y remedios caseros*." *Explicación de textos literarios* 29.2 (2000–2001): 92–103.

Franco, Jean. "A Touch of Evil: Jesusa Rodríguez's Subversive Church." *DR* 36.2 (1992): 48–61.

——. "La Malinche y el Primer Mundo." Glantz 153–67.

——. *Plotting Women: Gender and Representation in Mexico*. New York: Columbia UP, 1989.

Freud, Sigmund. "Some Psychical Consequences of the Anatomical Distinction Between the Sexes" (1925). *The Standard Edition of the Complete Psychological Works*. Vol. 19. London: Hogarth, 1953. 248–58.

Fuentes, Carlos. *Los años con Laura Díaz*. Madrid: Alfaguara, 1991.

——. *The Death of Artemio Cruz*. Trans. Alfred MacAdam. New York: FSG, 1964.

——. *The Eagle's Throne*. Trans. Kristina Cordero. New York: Random, 2006.

——. *El gringo viejo*. México: FCE, 1985.

——. *La muerte de Artemio Cruz*. México: FCE, 1962.

——. *The Old Gringo*. Trans. Margaret Sayers Peden and Carlos Fuentes. New York: Perennial, 1986.

——. *La región más transparente*. México: FCE, 1963.

——. *La silla del águila*. México: Alfaguara, 2003.

——. *Where the Air is Clear*. Trans. Sam Hileman. New York: Obolensky, 1960.

——. *The Years with Laura Diaz*. Trans. Alfred MacAdam. New York. FSG, 2000.

Gallegos, Rómulo. *Doña Bárbara*. Barcelona: Araluce, 1929.

——. *Doña Barbara*. Trans. Robert Malloy. New York: Cape and Smith, 1931.

Gant-Britton, Lisbeth. "Mexican Women and Chicanas Enter Futuristic Fiction." *Future Females, the Next Generation: New Voice and Velocities in Feminist Science Fiction Criticism*. Ed. Marleen S. Barr. Lanham, MD: Rowman & Littlefield, 2000. 261–76.

García, Gustavo. "Melodrama: The Passion Machine." *Mexican Cinema*. Ed. Paolo Antonio Paranaguá. Trans. Ana M. López. London: BFI, 1995. 153–62.

García Canclini, Néstor. *La globalización imaginada*. Buenos Aires: Paidós, 1999.

García Lorca, Federico. *The Rural Trilogy: "Blood Wedding," "Yerma," and "The House of Bernarda Alba."* Trans. Michael Dewell and Carmen Zapata. New York: Bantam, 1987.

——. *Teatro Mayor: "Bodas de Sangre." "Yerma." "La casa de Bernarda Alba."* Nicolás Dorr. Habana: Instituto Cubano del Libro, 1972.

García Márquez, Gabriel. *Cien años de soledad*. Buenos Aires: Sudamericana, 1967.

——. *Del amor y otros demonios*. New York: Penguin, 1994.

——. *Of Love and Other Demons*. New York: Knopf, 1995.

——. *One Hundred Years of Solitude*. Trans. Gregory Rabassa. Franklin Center, PA: Franklin Library, 1970.

Garro, Elena. "La culpa es de los Tlaxcaltecas." *La semana de colores: (Cuentos)*. Ficción 58. Xalapa, MX: Universidad Veracruzana, 1964. 9–33.

——. *Recollections of Things to Come*. Trans. Ruth L. C. Simms. Austin, TX: U of Texas P, 1969, 1986.

——. *Recuerdos del porvenir*. México: Mortiz, 1963.

Gilbert, Sandra, and Susan Gubar. "The Mirror and the Vamp: Reflections on Feminist Criticism." *The Future of Literary Theory*. Ed. Ralph Cohen. New York: Routledge, 1989. 144–66.

Gill, Mary, Deana Smalley, and Maria Paz Haro. *Cinema for Spanish Conversation* 2nd ed. Newburyport, MA: Focus (Pullins), 2006.

Gillespie, Jeanne. *Saints and Warriors: Tlaxcalan Perspectives on the Conquest of Tenochtitlan*. University Press of the South, 2004.

Gingerich, Willard. "Three Nahuatl Hymns." *Mexican Studies / Estudios Mexicanos* 4.2 (1988): 191–244.

Glantz, Margo. "Las hijas de la Malinche." Kohut 121–29.

——, ed. *La Malinche: Sus padres y sus hijos*. México: Facultad de Filosofía y Letras, UNAM, 1994.

Gledhill, Christine, ed. *Home Is Where the Heart Is: Studies in Melodrama and the Woman's Film*. London: BFI, 1987.

Glenn, Kathleen M. "Postmodern Parody and Culinary-Narrative Art in Laura Esquivel's *Como agua para chocolate*." *Chasqui* 23.2 (1994): 39–47.

Gonzalez, Martha I. "El efecto de la intertextualidad en la invención del mundo narrativo en *La ley del amor* de Laura Esquivel." *Revista de Literatura Mexicana Contemporánea* 1.3 (1996): 43–47.

Gonzáles, Michael J. *The Mexican Revolution 1910–1940*. Albuquerque, NM: U of New Mexico P, 2002.

González Olvera, Pedro. "El laborioso poeta de 'Inventario.'" *Áncora* (Costa Rica, Sunday, August 16, 2009). nacion.com/áncora. 11 November 2009 <http://www.nacion.com/ancora/2009/agosto/16/ancora2051223. html>.

González Stephan, Beatriz. "Para comerte mejor: cultura calibanesca y formas literarias alternativas." *Nuevo Texto Crítico* 9/10 (1992): 201–15.

Granillo Vázquez, Lilia del Carmen. "Cien años y más de literatura espiritual femenina, entre *Staurófila* y *La ley del amor*." *Letras femeninas* 27.2 (2001): 102–21.

Graulich, Michel. "Aztec Human Sacrifice as Expiation." *History of Religions* 39.4 (2000): 352–71.

Gubar, Susan. "What Ails Feminist Criticism?." *Critical Inquiry* 24.4 (1998): 878–902.

Guenther, Irene. "Magic Realism, New Objectivity, and the Arts during the Weimar Republic." Zamora and Faris 33–73.

Guerrero, Elisabeth. "Stirring up the Dust: The Healing History of a *Curandera* in *La insólita historia de la Santa de Cabora*." *Rocky Mountain Review* 56.2 (2002): 45–59.

Guerrero, Elisabeth, and Anne Lambright. "Introduction." Lambright and Guerrero 11–32.

Halevi-Wise, Yael. "Simbología en *Como agua para chocolate*: las aves y el fuego." *Revista hispánica moderna* 52.2 (1999): 513–22.

——. "Storytelling in Laura Equivel's *Como agua para chocolate*." *The Other Mirror: Women Narrative in Mexico 1980–1995*. Ed. Kristine Ibsen. Westport, CT: Greenwood, 1997. 123–31.

Halperín, Jorge. "Cómo se cocina un éxito." *Clarín Cultura y Nación* July 22, 1993. 67.

Hamnett, Brian R. "Benito Juárez, Early Liberalism, and the Regional Politics of Oaxaca, 1828–1853." *Bulletin of Latin American Research* 10.1 (1991): 3–21.

Harding, Sandra. *Whose Science? Whose Knowledge? Thinking from Women's Lives*. Ithaca, NY: Cornell UP, 1991.

Hart, John Mason. *Revolutionary Mexico: The Coming and Process of the Mexican Revolution*. 10th Anniversary Edition. Berkeley and Los Angeles: U of California P, 1997.

Hart, Stephen M. *A Companion to Latin American Film*. Woodbridge, Suffolk, UK: Tamesis, 2004.

Hart, Stephen M., and Win-chin Ouyang, ed. *A Companion to Magical Realism*. Woodbridge, Suffolk, UK: Tamesis, 2005.

Harris, Max. "The Return of Moctezuma: Oaxaca's 'Danza de la Pluma' and New Mexico's 'Danza de los Matachines.'" *DR* 41.1 (1997): 106–34.

Heidegger, Martin. *Poetry, Language, Thought*. Trans. Albert Hofstadter. New York: Harper, 1971.

Heller, Tamar. "Asking for More: [Review of] *Through the Kitchen Window: Women Explore the Intimate Meanings of Food and Cooking* by Arlene Voski Avakian." *WRB* 15.1 (1997): 7–8.

Heller, Tamar, and Patricia Moran, ed. *Scenes of the Apple: Food and the Female Body in Nineteenth- and Twentieth-Century Women's Writing*. Albany: SUNY P, 2003.

Herren, Ricardo. *Doña Marina, la Malinche*. México: Planeta Mexicana, 1993.

Herrera, Fermín. *Nahuatl-English English-Nahuatl (Aztec) Concise Dictionary*. New York: Hippocrene, 2004.

Historia de Tlaxcala: Mexico: 1585. [shelf mark] Sp. Coll. MS Hunter 242 (U.3.15). (January 2003) Glasgow University Library Special Collections Department. 11 November 2009 <http://special.lib.gla.ac.uk/ exhibns/ month/jan2003.html>.

Houston, Robert. "[Review of] *The Law of Love*." *NYT Book Review* (November 17, 1996): 11.

Hutcheon, Linda. *A Poetics of Postmodernism: History, Theory, Fiction*. London: Routledge, 1988.

Ibáñez Moreno, Ana. "Análisis del mito de la madre terrible mediante un estudio comparado de *La casa de Bernarda Alba* y *Como agua para chocolate*." *Especulo: Revista de estudios literarios* 32 (2006): [no pagination, 8 pages]. 11 November 2009 <www.ucm.es/info/especulo/numero32/mitomad. html>.

Ibargüengoitia, Jorge. *Dead Girls*. Trans. Asa Zatz. London: Chatto & Windus, 1983.

——. *The Lightning of August*. Trans. Irene del Corral. New York: Avon, 1986.

——. *Las muertas*. México: Mortiz, 1977.

——. *Los relámpagos de agosto*. 2nd ed. México: Mortiz, 1965.

——. *Las ruinas que ves*. México: Novaro, 1975.

Ibarra, Jesús. *Los Bracho: Tres generaciones de cine mexicano*. México: UNAM, 2006.

Ibsen, Kristine. "On Recipes, Reading and Revolution: Postboom Parody in *Como agua para chocolate*." *HR* 63.2 (1995): 133–46.

The Internet Movie Database (IMDb). [Opening page] 11 November 2009 <http://www.imdb.com>. [IMDb].

Irizarry, Estelle. "Aventura y apertura en la nueva novela española; *Queda la noche* de Soledad Puértolas." Ed. Delia V. Galvan, Anita K. Stoll, and Philippa B. Yin. *Studies in Honor of Donald W. Bleznick*. Newark, DE: Juan de La Cuesta, 1995. 59–73.

Jaggi, Maya. "Guardian Profile: Carlos Fuentes." *The Guardian* May 5, 2001. guardian.co.uk. 11 November 2009 <http://books.guardian.co.uk/ departments/generalfiction/story/0,,486073,00.html>.

Jaffe, Janice A. "Latin American Women Writers' Novel Recipes and Laura Esquivel's *Like Water for Chocolate*." Tamar and Moran 199–213.

Jameson, Fredric. "On Magic Realism in Film." *Critical Inquiry* 12.2 (1986): 301–25.

Works Cited

Johnson, Heather. "20th-Century American Bestsellers: Esquivel, Laura: *Like Water for Chocolate*." (1999) Graduate School of Library and Information Science, University of Illinois at Urbana-Champaign. 11 November 2009 <http://www3.isrl.uiuc.edu/~unsworth/courses/bestsellers/search.cgi?title=Like+Water+for+Chocolate>.

Johnson, Kathleen. "*Como agua para chocolate*: Tita, una nueva imagen de la mujer latinoamericana." *South Carolina Modern Language Review* 1.1 (2002): 29–43.

Kaminsky, Amy. *Reading the Body Politic, Feminist Criticism and Latin American Women Writers*. Minneapolis, MN: U of Minnesota P, 1993.

Kaplan, E. Ann. *Motherhood and Representation: The Mother in Popular Culture and Melodrama*. London: Routledge, 1992.

Kapschutschenko-Schmitt, Ludmila. "El texto multimedia de Laura Esquivel." *Actas del XIV Congreso de la Asociación Internacional de Hispanistas IV*. Ed. Isaías Lerner, Robert Nival, and Alejandro Alonso. Newark, DE: Juan de la Cuesta, 2004. 303–308.

Karlin, Susan. "Sweet Shortcut for Hot 'Chocolate.'" *Variety* 352.3 (August 30, 1993): 1, 34.

Karttunen, Frances. "Rethinking Malinche." Schroeder, Wood, and Haskett 291–311.

Kellerman, Carol. "[Audiobook Review] *Swift as Desire*. Laura Esquivel. Trans. by Stephen Al Lytle. 2001. Read by Elizabeth Peña." *KLIATT* 36.1 (January 2002): 47–48.

King, John. *Magical Reels: A History of Cinema in Latin America*. London: Verso, 1990.

King, Stephen. *Dolores Claiborne*. New York: Viking, 1993.

Klein, Cecelia F. "The Devil and the Skirt: An iconographic inquiry into the pre-Hispanic nature of the tzitzimime [*sic*]." *Ancient Mesoamerica* 11 (2000): 1–26.

Kohut, Karl, ed. *Literatura mexicana hoy del 68 al ocaso de la revolución*. Madrid: Iberoamericana. Frankfurt: Vervuert, 1991.

Labanyi, J. M. "[Review of] *Nueva narrativa hispanoamericana* by Donald L. Shaw." *MLR* 78.1 (1983): 214–16.

Laforet, Carmen. *Nada*. Barcelona: Destino, 1945.

——. *Nada: A Novel*. Trans. Edith Grossman. New York: Random House-Modern Library, 2008.

Lara, Agustín. "Mujer." Perf. Placido Domingo. *Por amor*. CD. WEA-Atlantic, 1998.

Lawless, Cecilia. "Cooking, Community, and Culture: A Reading of *Like Water for Chocolate*." Bower 216–35.

——. "Experimental Cooking in *Como agua para chocolate*." *MR* 8 (1992): 261–72.

Leal, Luis. "Female Archetypes in Mexican Literature." Miller 227–42.

——. "Magic Realism in Spanish American Literature (1967)." Zamora and Faris 119–24.

Levins Morales, Aurora. *Medicine Stories: History, Culture and the Politics of Integrity*. Cambridge, MA: South End, 1998.

Lewis, Stephen E. "Teaching the Mexican Revolution: The Essential Survey Text." *Latin American Perspectives: The Struggle Continues: Consciousness, Social Movement, and Class Action* 31.6 (2004): 110–11.

Lida, Clara Eugenia, and ["in collaboration with"] José Antonio Matesanz. *La Casa de España en México*. Centro de Estudios Históricos. Jornadas 113. México: El Colegio de México, 1988.

Lillo, Gastón, and Monique Sarfati-Arnaud. "*Como agua para chocolate*: determinaciones de la lectura en el contexto posmoderno." *Revista canadiense de estudios hispánicos* 18.3 (1994): 479–90.

Lindauer, Maragaret A. *Devouring Frida: The Art History and Popular Celebrity of Frida Kahlo*. Middleton, CT: Wesleyan UP, 1999.

Lindstrom, Naomi. "Arlt's Exposition of the Myth of Woman." *Woman as Myth and Metaphor in Latin American Literature*. Ed. Carmelo Virgillo and Naomi Lindstrom. Columbia: U of Missouri P, 1985. 151–66.

——. "Feminist Criticism of Hispanic and Lusophone Literatures: Bibliographic Notes and Considerations." *Cultural and Historical Grounding for Hispanic and Luso-Brazilian Feminist Literary Criticism*. Ed. Hernán Vidal. Minneapolis, MN: Institute for the Study of Ideologies and Literature, 1989. 19–51.

——. *The Social Conscience of Latin American Writing*. Austin, TX: U of Texas P, 1998.

Loewenstein, Claudia. "Revolución interior al exterior: An Interview with Laura Esquivel." *SR* 79.4 (1994): 592–607.

Lombardo de Caso, María. *La culebra tapó el río*. Xalapa: Universidad Veracruzana 1962.

——. *Muñecas de niebla*. México: Nuevo Mundo, 1955.

——. *Obras completas*. Ed. Luis Mario Schneider. Puebla, Puebla: Secretaría de Cultura, Gobierno del Estado de Puebla, 1999.

——. *Una luz en la otra orilla*. Letras Mexicanas 47. México: FCE, 1959.

López, Adriana. "Laura Esquivel – Reconquering Malinche." (February 15, 2006) *Criticas: An English Speaker's Guide to the Latest Spanish-Language Titles*. 11 November 2009 <http://www.criticasmagazine.com/article/CA6305733.html>.

López, Ana M. "Tears and Desire: Women and Melodrama in the 'Old' Mexican Cinema." *Mediating Two Worlds: Cinematic Encounters in the Americas*. Ed. John King, Ana M. López, and Manuel Alvarado. London: BFI, 1993: 147–63.

López Austin, Alfredo. "Guidelines for the study of Mesoamerican religious traditions." *Olupona* 118–27.

López-Rodríguez, Miriam. "Cooking Mexicanness: Shaping National Identity in Alfonso Arau's *Como agua para chocolate*." *Reel Food: Essays on Film and Food*. Ed. Anne L. Bower. New York: Routledge, 2004. 61–73.

Macias, Anna. "Women and the Mexican Revolution, 1910–1920." *The Americas* 37.1 (1980): 53–82.

Works Cited

Malinche: novela [Audiobook promotion]. (March 2, 2007) Fonolibro. 11 November 2009 <http://www.youtube.com/watch?v=7h-6cHlu5fk/>.

Maloof, Judy. "Recovering and Discovering Another Perspective: Recent Books on Latin American Women Writers." *LARR* 35.1 (2000): 243–55.

Marcos, Sylvia. "Indigenous Eroticism and Colonial Morality in Mexico: The Confession Manuals of New Spain." Trans. Jacqueline Mosio. *Numen: International Review for the History of Religions* 39.2 (1992): 157–74.

Marquet, Antonio. "La receta de Laura Esquivel: ¿Cómo escribir un best-seller?." *Plural* 237 (1991): 58–67.

Martínez, Victoria. "*Como agua para chocolate*: A Recipe for Neoliberalism." *Chasqui* 33.1 (2004): 28–41.

Marting, Diane E., ed. *Spanish American Women Writers: A Bio-bibliographical Source Book.* Westport, CT: Greenwood, 1990.

Mastretta, Ángeles. *Arráncame la vida.* México: Océano, 1986.

——. *Lovesick* [*Mal de amores*]. Trans. Margaret Sayers Peden. New York: Riverhead, 1997.

——. *Mal de amores.* México: Alfaguara, 1996.

——. *Tear this Heart Out* [*Arráncame la vida*]. Trans. Margaret Sayers Peden. New York: Riverhead, 1997.

McAnany, Patricia A. *Living with the Ancestors: Kinship and Kingship in Ancient Maya Society.* Austin, TX: U of Texas P, 1995.

McCafferty, Geoffrey G., and Sharisse D. McCafferty. "The Malinche Code: the Symbology of Female Discourse in Postclassic Mexico." (February 2005) Seeing the Past, Stanford Archaeology Center Conference, Stanford University. 11 November 2009 <http://traumwerk.stanford.edu:3455/SeeingThePast/315>.

McMahon, Donna M. "From the Kitchen to Eternity: The Feminine Voice in Laura Esquivel's *Like Water for Chocolate.*" *Cine-Lit II: Essays on Hispanic Film and Fiction.* Ed. George Cabello-Castellet, *et al.* Portland, OR: Portland State U, 1995. 19–28.

Meacham, Cherie. "*Como agua para* chocolate: Cinderella and the Revolution." *Hispanic Journal* 19.1 (1998): 117–28.

The Mendoza Codex. Oxford University Bodleian Library MS. Arch. Selden. A. 1. Mexico: Mid-sixteenth century.

Menton, Seymour. *Historia verdadera del realismo mágico.* México: FCE, 1998.

——. "In Search of a Nation: The Twentieth-Century Spanish American Novel." *Hispania* 38.4 (1955): 432–42.

——. "Jorge Luis Borges, Magic Realist." *HR* 50.4 (1982): 411–26.

——. *Latin America's New Historical Novel.* Austin, TX: U of Texas P, 1993.

——. *Magic Realism Rediscovered, 1918–1981.* Philadelphia: Art Alliance, 1983.

Merchant, Carolyn. *The Death of Nature: Women, Ecology, and the Scientific Revolution.* New York: Harper, 1980.

——. "The Realm of Social Relations: Production, Reproduction, and Gender in Environmental Transformations." Ed. B. L. Turner. *The Earth as Transformed by Human Action: Global and Regional Changes in the Biosphere over the Past 300 Years.* Cambridge, UK: Cambridge UP, 1990. 673–84.

Metcalf, Peter, and Richard Huntington. *Celebrations of Death: The Anthropology of Mortuary Ritual.* 2nd ed. Cambridge, UK: Cambridge UP, 1991.

Miller, Beth, ed. *Women in Hispanic Literature: Icons and Fallen Idols.* Berkeley and Los Angeles, CA: U of California P, 1983.

Minc, Rose, ed. *Revista Iberoamericana: Número Especial dedicado a las Escritoras de la América Hispánica* 51.132–133 (Julio–Diciembre 1985): 443–980.

Modern Language Association of America. *MLA Handbook for Writers of Research Papers.* 7th ed. New York: MLA, 2009.

Modleski, Tania. "Time and Desire in the Woman's Film." *Cinema Journal* 23.3 (Spring, 1984): 19–30.

Monsiváis, Carlos. "Landscape, I've Got the Drop on You." *Studies in Latin American Popular Culture* 4 (1985): 236.

———. "Sexismo en al literatura mexicana." *Imagen y realidad de la mujer: Ensayos compilados por Elena Urrutia.* Ed. Elena Urrutia. México: Secretaría de Educación Pública, 1975. 102–25.

Moraga, Cherríe, and Gloria Anzaldúa, eds. *This Bridge Called My Back: Writings by Radical Women of Color.* 2nd ed. New York: Kitchen Table: Women of Color P, 1981, 1983.

Moreno Villa, José. *Cornucopia de México.* México: Casa de España, 1940.

———. *Cornucopia de México y Nueva cornucopia mexicana.* Colección Popular 296. México: FCE, 1985, 1992.

Moseley, William W. "An Introduction to the Chilean Historical Novel." *Hispania* 43.3 (1960): 338–42.

Mujica, Barbara. "[Review of] *La ley del amor.*" *Americas* (English) 48.6 (November–December 1996): 61.

Mulvey, Laura. "Melodrama Inside and Outside the Home." *Visual and Other Pleasures.* Bloomington, IN: Indiana UP, 1989: 63–77.

Muñiz-Huberman, Angelina. *Enclosed Garden.* Trans. Lois Parkinson Zamora. Pittsburgh, PA: Latin American Literary Review P, 1988.

———. *Huerto cerrado, huerto sellado.* México: Oasis, 1985.

Myers, Eunice Doman. "El cuento erótico de Marina Mayoral: transgrediendo la Ley del Padre." Cavallo, Jiménez, and Preble-Niemi 39–52.

Nájera-Ramírez, Olga. "Engendering Nationalism: Identity, Discourse, and the Mexican Charro [*sic*]." *Anthropological Quarterly* 67.1 (1994): 1–14.

Nebel, Richard, Carlos Warnholtz Bustillos, and Irma Ochoa de Nebel. *Santa María Tonantzin, Virgen de Guadalupe: Continuidad y transformatión religiosa en México.* México: FCE, 1995.

Neruda, Pablo. *Canto general.* México: Talleres Gráficos de la Nación, 1950.

———. *Canto general.* Trans. Jack Schmitt. Berkeley: U of California P, 1991.

Nicholson, H. B . "Religion in Pre-Hispanic Mexico." *Handbook of Middle American Indians.* Vol. 10. *Archeology of Northern Mesoamerica, Part 1.* Ed. Gordon Ekholm and Ignacio Bernal. Austin, TX: U of Texas P, 1971: 395–445.

Niebylski, Dianna C. *Humoring Resistance: Laughter and the Excessive Body in Latin American Women's Fiction.* Albany, NY: State U of New York [SUNY] P, 2004.

——. "Heartburn, Humor, and Hyperbole in *Like Water for Chocolate.*" *Performing Gender and Comedy: Theories, Texts and Contexts.* Ed. Shannon Eileen Hengen. Amsterdam, The Netherlands: Gordon & Breach, 1998. 179–97.

——. "Passion or Heartburn? The Uses of Humor in Esquivel's and Arau's [*sic*] *Like water for Chocolate.*" *A Companion to Literature and Film.* Ed. Robert Stam and Alessandra Raengo. Malden, MA: Blackwell, 2004. 252–70.

Noble, Andrea. *Mexican National Cinema.* National Cinemas. London: Routledge, New York: Taylor & Francis, 2005. [MNC]

O'Connell, Joanna. *Prospero's Daughter: The Prose of Rosario Castellanos.* Austin, TX: The U of Texas P, 1995.

O'Gorman, Edmundo. *Destierro de sombras: Luz en el origen de la imagen y culto de Nuestra Señora de Guadalupe del Tepeyac.* México: UNAM, 1986.

O'Gorman, Rochelle. "[Audiobook Review] *Swift as Desire.* Laura Esquivel." *Book* [no volume] (March–April 2002): 78.

O'Keefe, Alice. "Myths of Conquest." *New Statesman* 136.4839 (April 9, 2007): 52.

Olupona, Jacob K., ed. *Beyond Primitivism: Indigenous religious traditions and modernity* [*sic*]. New York: Taylor & Francis, 2004. [The 1996 conference from which the book title is taken placed "Primitivism" in quotations.]

O'Neill, Molly. "At Dinner with Laura Esquivel; Sensing the Spirit In All Things, Seen and Unseen." *NYT* March 31, 1993. C1, C8 [jump page head: "A Spirit in all Things, Seen and Unseen."].

Oprah's Books: Oprah's Book Club. "*Daughter of Fortune* by Isabel Allende." (February 17, 2000) Oprah.com. 11 November 2009 <http://www.oprah.com/article/oprahsbookclub/pastselections/obc_pb_20000217_about>.

Oropesa, Salvador A. "*Como agua para chocolate* de Laura Esquivel como lectura del *Manual de urbanidad y buenas costumbres* de Manuel Antonio Carreño." *MR* 8 (1992): 252–60.

Ortiz, Verónica. "Laura Esquivel." *Mujeres de Palabra.* México: Mortiz, 2005. 161–86.

Orwell, George. *1984.* New York: New American Library, 1949.

Ostricker, Alicia Suskin. *Alicia Suskin Ostriker: Poet Critic Madrashist* [*sic*]. (2008) Rutgers University, New Brunswick/Piscataway. 11 November 2009 <http://www.rci.rutgers.edu/~ostriker/home.htm>.

——. *Stealing the Language: The Emergence of Women's Poetry in America.* Boston, MA: Beacon, 1986.

——. *Writing Like a Woman.* U of Michigan Poets on Poetry Series. Ann Arbor, MI: U of Michigan P, 1983.

Pacheco, José Emilio. "Inventario: Rosario Castellanos o la literatura como ejercicio de la libertad." *Excelsior: Diorama* 58.4 (August 11, 1974): 16.

Páez de Ruiz, María de Jesús. "Apuntes sobre el español en México a través de la novela *Como agua para chocolate* de Laura Esquivel." Session 66 Spanish Linguistics. *South Central Review: Convention Program Issue* 7.3 (1990): 69.

Patmore, Coventry. *The Angel in the House.* Cassell & Company (1891). David Price, Project Guttenberg. Victorianweb.org. 11 November 2009

Works Cited

<http://www.victorianweb.org/authors/patmore/angel/index.html>.

Paz, Octavio. *El laberinto de la soledad y otras obras.* New York: Penguin, 1997.

———. *El laberinto de la soledad.* México: Cuadernos Americanos, 1950. 2nd ed. México: FCE, 1959.

———. *The Labyrinth of Solitude: Life and Thought in Mexico.* Trans. Lysander Kemp. New York: Grove, 1961.

Peña, Magdalena Maiz, and Luis H. Peña. "Sabores y sinsabores: diseño de la subjetividad femenina en *Como agua para chocolate* de L[aura] Esquivel." Asociación de Literatura Femenina Hispánica [and] *Letras Femeninas*: Texto Narrativo y Dialéctica. *Rocky Mountain Review of Language and Literature: Convention Issue* 45.3 (1991): 168.

Pérez, Alberto Julián. "*Como agua para chocolate*: La nueva novela de mujeres en Latinoamérica." *La nueva mujer en la escritura de autoras hispánicas: ensayos críticos.* Ed. Juana Alcira Arancibia and Yolanda Rosas. Westminster, CA.: Instituto Literario y Cultural Hispánico. Montevideo, Uruguay: Editorial Graffiti, 1995. 41–57.

Pérez, Genaro and Janet Pérez. "Introduction." *MR: Hispanic Science-Fiction / Fantasy and The Thriller* 3.1–2 (1987): 11–18.

———. "Introduction." *MR: The "Nueva Novela Histórica" in Hispanic Literature* 19 (2003): 9–27.

Pérez, Genaro, Janet Pérez, and Tim McVay. "Introduction." *MR: Canon Formation and Exclusion: Hispanic Women Writers* 13 (1997): 9–23.

Perricone, Catherine R. "Allende and Valenzuela: Dissecting the Patriarchy." *South Atlantic Review: Spanish American Fiction in the 1990s* 67.4 (2002): 80–105.

———. "Laura Esquivel's *La ley del amor*: The Eclectic Novel." *La Chispa '99: Selected Proceedings.* Ed. Gilbert Paolini and Claire J. Paolini. The Twentieth Louisiana Conference on Hispanic Languages and Literatures. New Orleans, LA: Tulane U, 1999. 293–300.

Peyre, Henri. "Paul Claudel (1868–1955)." *Yale French Studies* 14 (1954): 94–97.

Phillips, Rachel. "Marina/Malinche: Masks and Shadows." Miller 97–114.

Piedras Negras, Coahuila. "Mejor calidad de vida para todos." (2006–2009) Presidencia Municipal de Piedras Negras, Coahuila, México. 11 November 2009 <http://www.piedrasnegras.gob.mx>.

———. *Historia de Piedras, Negras.* "Fundación de Piedras Negras." (2006–2009) Presidencia Municipal de Piedras Negras, Coahuila, México. 11 November 2009 <http://www.piedrasnegras.gob.mx/historia/historia.html>.

Pilcher, Jeffrey. "Recipes for Patria: Cuisine, Gender, and Nation in Nineteenth Century Mexico." Bower 200–15.

Pinkola Estés, Clarissa. *Women Who Run With the Wolves: Myths and Stories of the Wild Woman Archetype.* New York: Ballantine, 1992.

Pizzichini, Lillian. "[Review of] *The Law of Love.*" *Times Literary Supplement* 4881 (October 18, 1996): 23.

Podalsky, Laura. "Disjointed Frames: Melodrama, Nationalism, and Representation in 1940s Mexico." *Studies in Latin American Popular Culture* 12 (1993): 57–73.

Works Cited

Poniatowska [Amor], Elena. *Hasta no verte, Jesús mío.* México: Era, 1969.
——. *Here's to you, Jesusa.* Trans. Deanna Heikkinen. New York: FSG, 2001.
——. *Massacre in Mexico. [Noche de Tlatelolco]* Trans. Helen R. Lane. New York: Viking, 1975.
——. *La noche de Tlatelolco: Testimonios de historia oral.* México: Era, 1971.
——. "Prólogo." *Mujeres de palabra.* Ortiz. 9–21.
——. *Las Soldaderas.* México: Era and El Instituto Nacional de Antropología e Historia, 1999.
——. *Las Soldaderas: Women of the Mexican Revolution.* El Paso, TX: Cinco Puntos P, 2006.
——. *El tren pasa primero.* México: Alfaguara, 2005.
Potvin, Claudine. *"Como agua para chocolate:* ¿parodia o cliché?." *Revista canadiense de estudios hispánicos* 20.1 (1995): 55–67.
Prado, Gloria. "Lazos de familia." *Elena Garro: Lectura múltiple de una personalidad compleja.* Eds. Lucía Melgar and Gabriela Mora. Pubela, MX: BUAP and Fomento, 2002. 23–36.
Pratt, Mary Louise. *Imperial Eyes: Travel Writing and Transculturation.* New York: Routledge, 1992.
——. "'Yo Soy La Malinche': Chicana Writers and the Poetics of Ethnonationalism." *Callaloo: On "Post-Colonial Discourse": A Special Issue* 16.4 (1993): 859–73.
Prescott, William Hickling. *The Conquest of Mexico.* 2 vols. New York: Henry Holt, 1922.
Price, Helene. "Unsavoury Representations in Laura Esquivel's *Like Water for Chocolate.*" Hart and Ouyang 181–90.
Prout, Ryan. "Cosmic Weddings and a Funeral: Sexuality, Techno-Science, and the National Romance in Laura Esquivel's *La ley del amor.*" *Tesserae: Journal of Iberian and Latin American Studies* 6.1 (2000): 43–54.
Puértolas, Soledad. *Queda la noche.* Barcelona: Planeta, 1989. 2nd ed. Barcelona: Anagrama, 2002.
Radford-Hill, Sheila. "Considering Feminism as a Model for Social Change." *Feminist Studies / Critical Studies.* Ed. Teresa de Lauretis. Bloomington, IN: Indiana UP, 1986. 157–72.
Radin, Paul. "Maya, Nahuatl, and Tarascan Kinship Terms." *American Anthropologist: New Series* 27.1 (1925): 100–102.
Ramírez Berg, Charles. "Cracks in the *Macho* Monolith: *Machismo,* Man, and Mexico in Recent Mexican Cinema." *New Orleans Review* 16.1 (Spring, 1989): 67–74.
Ramos Escandón, Carmen. "Receta y femineidad en *Como agua para chocolate.*" *Fem* 15.102 (1991): 45–48.
Richards, Judith. "Letters." *WRB* 10.7 (April 1993): 4.
Richardson, Miles. "Being-in-the-market versus Being-in-the-plaza: Material Culture and the Construction of Social Reality in Spanish America." *American Ethnologist: Economic and Ecological Processes in Society and Culture* 9.2 (1982): 421–36.
——, ed. *Place: Experience and Symbol.* Geoscience and Man 24. Baton Rouge,

LA: Geoscience Publications, Department of Geography and Anthropology, Louisiana State U, 1984.

Riding, Alan. *Distant Neighbors: A Portrait of the Mexicans.* New York: Knopf, 1984. New York: Vintage, 1989.

———. *Vecinos distantes: Un retrato de los mexicanos.* Trans. Pilar Mascaró. México: Mortiz, 1987.

Riquer Fernández, Florinda. "La identidad femenina en la frontera entre la conciencia y la inter-acción social." *La voluntad de ser: mujeres en los noventa.* Ed. María Luisa Tarrés. México: Programa Interdisciplinario de Estudios de la Mujer, El Colegio de México, 1992. 51–64.

Rivera, José Eustasio, *La vorágine.* 9th ed. New York: Andes, 1929.

———. *The vortex: La vorágine.* [Translated from the 9th ed.] Trans. Earle K. James. New York: Putnam, 1935.

Rocheleau, Dianne, Barbara Thomas-Slayter, and Esther Wangari, eds. *Feminist Political Ecology: Global Issues and Local Experiences, International Studies of Women and Place.* London. New York: Routledge, 1996.

Rodríguez-Vivaldi, Ana María. "Shaking the Soul, the Mind, and the Reader: Laura Esquivel and the Multimedia Novel." *Pacific Coast Philology* 38 (2003): 25–32.

Roffiel, Rosa María. *Amara.* México: Planeta, 1989.

Roh, Franz. "Magic Realism: Post-Expressionism (1925)." Zamora and Faris 15–31.

Rose, Gillian. "Geography as a Science of Observation: the Landscape, the Gaze and Masculinity." *Human Geography: An Essential Anthology.* Ed. John Agnew, David N. Livingstone, and Alisdair Rogers. Malden, MA: Blackwell, 1996. 341–50.

Rosenberg, Sara. "La frágil frontera de los géneros de la ficción." *Cuadernos hispánicos* 707 (May 2009): 23–27.

Russotto, Márgara. *Tópicos de retórica femenina: Memoria y pasión del género.* Caracas: Monte Ávila, 1990.

Ruta, Suzanne. "In Grandmother's Kitchen: [Review of] *Like Water for Chocolate: A Novel in Monthly Installments with Recipes, Romances and Home Remedies* by Laura Esquivel; [Trans.] Carol Christensen and Thomas Christensen." *WRB* 10.5 (February 1993): 7.

Sabia, Saïd. "La novela multimedia: un nuevo reto para la crítica literaria." (2005) *Espéculo: Revista de estudios literarios.* Universidad Complutense de Madrid. 11 November 2009 <http://www.ucm.es/info/especulo/ numero29/ssabia.html>.

Sahagún, Bernardino de. *Florentine Codex: A General History of Things of New Spain* [*Historia general de las cosas de Nueva España: English and Nahuatl*]. Ed. Arthur J. O. Anderson and Charles Dibble. Monographs of the School of American Research 14.1–13. Santa Fe, NM: School of American Research. Salt Lake City: U of Utah P, 1950–1982.

Salas, Elizabeth. *Soldaderas in the Mexican Military: Myth and History.* Austin, TX: U of Texas P, 1990.

Salkjelsvik, Kari S. "El desvio como norma: La retórica de la receta en *Como*

Works Cited

agua para chocolate." *Revista Iberoamericana* 65.186 (1999): 171–82.

Salles, Vania, and José Manuel Valenzuela. "Ámbitos de relaciones sociales de naturaleza íntima e identidades culturales (Notas sobre Xochimilco)." *Revista mexicana de sociología* 54.3 (1992): 139–73.

Saltz, Joanne. "Laura Esquivel's *Como agua para chocolate*: The Questioning of Literary and Social Limits." *Chasqui* 24.1 (1995): 30–37.

Sánchez, Marta E. "La Malinche at the Intersection: Race and Gender in *Down These Mean Streets.*" *PMLA* 113.1 (1998): 117–28.

Sánchez-Flavian, Patricia. "*Como agua para chocolate* as a Novel of Self-Discovery Formulated Through Parody." (July 11, 2004) *Ciberletras* CUNY. 1 January 2010. <http://www.lehman.cuny.edu/ ciber-letras/v11/sanchezflavian. html>.

San Roman, Gabriel. "Laura Esquivel Visits Santa Ana." (May 16, 2006) Gabriel's Blog. Uprisingradio.com. 11 November 2009 <http://uprisin-gradio.org/home/?p=436>.

Santiago, Sylvia. "[Review] *Swift as Desire* by Laura Esquivel." *Herizons* (Summer 2002): 35.

Santos-Phillips, Eva L. "Discourses of Power in the Film Versions of *The House of Bernarda Alba* and *Like Water for Chocolate.*" *Hispanic Journal* 18.1 (1997): 9–22.

Sarabia, Rosa. *Poetas de la palabra hablada: Un estudio de la poesía hispanoameri-cana contemporánea.* London; Rochester, NY: Tamesis, 1997.

Schaefer, Claudia. "¿Panteón o paraíso? Visiones milenarias de la ciudad de México en *La ley del amor* de Laura Esquivel." *Texto Crítico* 5.10 (2002): 107–18.

Scholes, Robert. *Structural Fabulation: An Essay on the Fiction of the Future.* Notre Dame, IN: U of Notre Dame P, 1975.

Schroeder, Susan, Stephanie Wood, and Robert Stephen Haskett, eds. *Indian Women of Early Mexico.* Norman, OK: U of Oklahoma P, 1997.

Schumaher, Schuma, and Érico Vital Brazil, eds. *Diccionario Mulheres do Brasil: de 1500 até a Atualidade.* Rio de Janeiro: Zahar, 2000.

Seamon, David, and Robert Mugerauer, ed. *Dwelling, Place and Environment: Towards a Phenomenology of Person and World.* Dordrecht, The Netherlands, and Boston, MA: Nijhoff, 1985.

Sedgwick, Eve Kosofsky. *The Coherence of Gothic Conventions.* London: Routledge, 1986.

Sefchovich, Sara. *México: País de ideas, país de novelas: Una sociología de la liter-atura mexicana.* México: Grijalbo, 1987.

Segovia, Miguel A. "Only Cauldrons Know the Secrets of their Soups: Queer Romance and *Like Water for Chocolate.*" *Velvet barrios: Popular Culture & Chicana/o Sexualities.* Ed. Alicia Gaspar de Alba. New York: Palgrave McMillan, 2003. 163–78.

Selby, Henry, *et al.* "The women of Mexico and the neoliberal revolution [*sic*]." *Women, the Household, and the Work Place under Neoliberalism.* Southern Labor Studies Conference. Austin, TX. October 27, 1995; *Anuario de Estudios Urbanos* 3 (1996): 75–91.

Semo, Alejandro, and Juan José Giovannini. "El arte de la novela como una forma culinaria." *Excelsior* (8 April 1990): 5.

Shaw, Deborah [A.]. "Laura Esquivel." *Encyclopedia of Latin American Literature.* Verity Smith, ed. New York: Taylor & Francis, 1997. 117–18.

——. "Seducing the Public: Images of Mexico in *Like Water for Chocolate* and *Amores Perros* [*sic*]. *Contemporary Cinema of Latin America: 10 Key Films.* Deborah [A.] Shaw [author]. London: Continuum, 2003. 36–70.

Shaw, Donald L. "Introduction." *South Atlantic Review: Spanish American Fiction in the 1990s* 67.4 (2002): 6–9.

——. *Nueva narrativa hispanoamericana.* Madrid: Cátedra, 1981.

Simoons, Frederick. *Eat Not This Flesh: Food Avoidances from Prehistory to the Present.* 2nd ed. Madison, WI: U of Wisconsin P, 1994.

Sinnigen, John H. "*Como agua para chocolate*: Feminine Space, Postmodern Cultural Politics, National Allegory." *CIEFL Bulletin* 7.1–2 (1995–1996): 111–31.

Sklodowska, Elzbieta. *La parodia en la nueva novela hispanoamericana.* Philadelphia: Benjamins, 1991.

Solé, Carlos A., ed., and María Isabel Abreu, associate. ed. *Latin American Writers.* New York: Scribner's, 1989.

Soliño, María Elena. *Women and Children First: Spanish Women Writers and the Fairy Tale Tradition.* Potomac, MD: Scripta Humanistica, 2002.

Sommer, Doris. *Foundational Fictions: The National Romances of Latin America.* Berkeley: U of California P, 1991.

Sousa, Lisa. "The Devil and Deviance in Native Criminal Narratives from Early Mexico." *The Americas: The Devil in Latin America* 59.2 (2002): 161–79.

Spindler, William. "Magic Realism: A Typology." *Forum for Modern Language Studies* 39.1 (1993): 75–85.

Stevenson, Mark. "Mexican government's proposal to cut arts funding prompts fears of an American cultural invasion" (November 13, 2003). Associated Press Archive. [<http://www.ap.org/>].

Stimpson, Catharine. "Our Project: The Building of Feminist Criticism." *The Future of Literary Theory.* Ed. Ralph Cohen. New York: Routledge, 1989. 129–43.

Suárez Cruz, Sergio, and Silvia Martínez Arriaga. *Monografía de Cholula, Puebla.* Puebla, México: Ayuntamiento Municipal Constitucional de San Pedro Cholula, Puebla, 1993.

Subercaseaux Sommerhoff, Bernardo. "Reproducción y apropiación: Dos modelos para enfocar el dialogo intercultural." [n.d.]. 11 November 2009 <http://www.dialogosfelafacs.net/dialogos_epoca/pdf/23-11BernardoSubercaseaux.pdf>.

Suvin, Darko. "On the Poetics of the Science Fiction Genre." *College English* 34.3 (1972): 372–82.

Tan, Amy. *The Bonesetter's Daughter.* New York: Putnam's, 2001.

Taylor, Claire Louise. "Body-Swapping and Genre-Crossing: Laura Esquivel's *La ley del amor.*" *MLR* 97.2 (2002): 324–35.

Works Cited

Tenenbaum, Barbara A. "Why Tita Didn't Marry the Doctor, [*sic*] or Mexican History in *Like Water for Chocolate*." *Based on a True Story: Latin America at the Movies*. Ed. Donald F. Stevens. Wilmington, DE: Scholarly Resources, 1997. 157–72.

Thompson, Becky. "Multiracial Feminism: Recasting the Chronology of Second Wave Feminism." *Feminist Studies: Second Wave Feminism in the United States* 28.2 (2002): 337–60.

Tompkins, Cynthia Margarita, and David William Foster, eds. *Notable Twentieth-Century Latin American Women: A Biographical Dictionary*. Wesport, CT: Greeenwood, 2001.

Torres-Pou, Joan. "Positivismo y feminismo en la producción narrativa de Mercedes Cabello de Carbonera." Cavallo, Jiménez, and Preble-Niemi 245–56.

Tovar Ramírez, Aurora, ed. *Mil quinientas mujeres en nuestra conciencia colectiva: Catálogo biográfico de mujeres de México*. México: Documentación y Estudios de Mujeres, 1996.

Townsend, Camilla. *Malintzín's Choices: An Indian Woman in the Conquest of Mexico*. Albuquerque, NM: U of New Mexico P, 2006.

Tulane: The Latin American Library at Tulane University: Collections: Manuscripts. "Rare Copies of Unknown, Lost or Damaged Pictorial Manuscripts at the Latin American Library." [n.d.] Tulane University, New Orleans, LA. 11 November 2009 <http://www.tulane.edu/~latinlib/ collections/manuscripts/rare_copies.htm>.

Tulchin, Joseph S., ed. *Encyclopedia of Latin American History and Culture*. New York: Scribner's, 2007.

Ugalde, Sharon Keefe. "Process, Identity, and Learning to Read: Female Writing and Feminist Criticism in Latin America Today." *LARR* 24.1 (1989): 222–32.

Unamuno y Jugo, Miguel de. *En torno al casticismo*. Colección austral 403. Madrid: Espasa-Calpe, 1902, 1943, 1968.

——. *En torno al casticismo*. *Obras Completas*. Vol. I. Madrid: Escélicer, 1966. 783–869.

Vance, Birgitta. "The Great Clash: Feminist Criticism Meets Up With Spanish Reality." *Journal of Spanish Studies: Twentieth Century* 2 (1973): 109–14.

Van Delden, Maarten. "Past and Present in Víctor Hugo Rascón Banda's *La Malinche* and Marisol Martín del Campo's *Amor y conquista*." *South Central Review* 21.3 (2004): 8–23.

Varela, Félix. *Xicoténcatl*. Austin, TX: U of Texas P, 1999 [Philadelphia,1826].

Villavicencio Rojas, Josué Mario. *Mojigangas y pachecos: Leyenda, tradición y magia en la mixteca oaxaqueña*. Puebla, Puebla, MX: BUAP, 1998.

Villegas, Francisco. "El Argot Costarricense." *Hispania* 38.1 (1955): 27–30.

Viramontes, Helena María. "'Nopalitos': The Making of Fiction: (Testimonio)." *Breaking Boundaries: Latina Writing and Critical Readings*. Ed. Asunción Horno-Delgado, *et al.* Amherst, MA: The U of Massachusetts P, 1989. 33–38.

Virgilio, Carmelo, and Naomi Lindstrom, ed. *Woman as Myth and Metaphor in Latin American Literature*. Columbia, MO: U of Missouri P, 1985.

Watson, Peggy Whitten. *Intra-historia in Miguel de Unamuno's Novels: A Continual Presence*. Potomac, MD: Scripta Humanistica, 1993.

Wells, Rebecca. *Divine Secrets of the Ya-Ya Sisterhood*. New York: HarperCollins, 1996.

Whittingham, Georgina J., and Lourdes Silva. "El erotismo ¿fruto prohibido para la mujer? en *Como agua para chocolate* de Laura Esquivel y *Del amor y otros demonios* de Gabriel García Márquez." *Texto Crítico* 4.7 (1998): 57–67.

Willingham, Elizabeth M. "Apocalypse, Where is Thy Sting?: Apocalyptic Context in Laura Esquivel's *Como agua para chocolate.*" *MR: Hispanic Millennial / Apocalyptic Literature* 14 (1998): 122–34.

———. "Leer es placer y más: Elements of the *Märchen*, the Local Legend, and the Folk Tale Shape Reader Response to *Como agua para chocolate*." Hijas del Quinto Sol. St. Mary's University. San Antonio, Texas. July, 1998.

———. "[Review of] *Tan veloz como el deseo* by Laura Esquivel." *Hispania* 85.4 (2002): 864–65.

Woolf, Virginia. *A Room of One's Own*. London: Hogarth, 1929.

———. *A Room of One's Own*. Intro. Susan Gubar. New York: Harcourt-Harvest, 2005.

———. "Professions for Women." *The Death of the Moth and Other Essays*. New York: Harcourt Brace-Harvest, 1942 (1970). 235–42.

Wu, Harmony H. "Consuming Tacos and Enchiladas: Gender and the Nation in *Como agua para chocolate*." *Visible Nations: Latin American Cinema and Video*. Ed. Chon A. Noriega. Minneapolis, MN: U of Minnesota P, 2000. 174–92.

———. "Eating the Nation: Selling *Like Water for Chocolate* in the USA." (April 17–19, 1997) LASA Congress Guadalajara, México. U of Pittsburgh. 11 November 2009 <http://lasa.international.pitt.edu/LASA97/wu.pdf>.

Young-Eisendrath, Polly. *Gender & Desire*. College Station, Texas: Texas A&M UP, 1997.

Yourcenar, Marguerite. *Le jardin des chimères*. Paris: Perrin, 1921.

———. *Quoi? L'Éternité*. Paris: Gallimard, 1988.

Zamora, Lois Parkinson, and Wendy B. Faris, eds. *Magic Realism: Theory, History, Community*. Durham, NC: Duke UP, 1995.

Zamudio-Taylor, Victor, and Inma Guiu. "Criss-Crossing Texts: Reading Images in *Like Water for Chocolate*." *The Mexican Cinema Project*. Ed. Chon A. Noriega and Steven Ricci. Los Angeles, CA: UCLA Film and Television Archive, Research and Study Center, 1994. 45–51.

Zaslavsky, Nancy. *A Cook's Tour of Mexico: Authentic Recipes from the Country's Best Open-air Markets, City Fondas, and Home Kitchens*. New York: St. Martin's, 1995.

Zubiaurre, Maite. "Culinary Eros in Contemporary Hispanic Female Fiction: From Kitchen Tales to Table Narratives." *College Literature* 33.3 (2006): 29–51.

Works Cited

Films Cited

All That Heaven Allows. Dir. Douglas Sirk. 1955.
Amores perros. Dir. Alejandro González Iñárritu. 2000.
Babette's Feast. Dir. Gabriel Axel. 1988.
El compadre Mendoza. Dir. Fernando de Fuentes. 1933 [MNC p. 31]. [IMBD1934].
El Chido Guan: Tacos de oro. Dir. Alfonso Arau. Screenwriter, Laura Esquivel. 1985.
La comedia ranchera. Dir. Gloria Ribe. Screenwriter, Francisco Sánchez. 1996. [Documentary 27 minutes]
Como agua para chocolate [*Like Water for Chocolate*]. Dir. Alfonso Arau. Screenwriter, Laura Esquivel. 1992. U.S. 1993 [IMBD].
Crouching Tiger Hidden Dragon. Dir. Ang Lee. 2000.
Cuando los hijos se van. Dir. Juan Bustillo Oro. 1941.
Danzón. Dir. and Screenwriter, María Novaro. 1991.
Doña Bárbara. Dir. Fernando de Fuentes. 1943.
Dona Flor e seus dois maridos. Dir. Bruno Barreto. 1976.
Frida, naturaleza viva. Dir. Paul Leduc. 1984.
The House of the Spirits. Dir. Bille August. Germany 1993. U.S. 1994 [IMBD].
Pan's Labyrinth. Dir. Guillermo del Toro. 2006.
Señora Tentación. Dir. José Díaz Morales. 1948.
Soledad. Dir. Miguel Zacarías.1947.

Film Reviews and Box Office Reports

Ansen, David. "*Like Water for Chocolate*." *Newsweek* 121.11 (March 15, 1993): 74.
Corliss, Richard. "Kitchen Magician: *Like Water for Chocolate*." *Time* 141.14 (April 5, 1993): 61. 11 November 2009 <http://www.time.com/time/printout/0,8816,978142,00.html#>.
Like Water for Chocolate (1993). Box Office Mojo. 11 November 2009 <http://www.boxofficemojo.com/movies/?id=likewaterforchocolate.htm>.
Crouching Tiger Hidden Dragon (2000). Box Office Mojo. 11 November 2009 <http://www.boxofficemojo.com/movies/?id=crouchingtigerhidden-dragon.htm>.
Geist, Kenneth L. "*Like Water for Chocolate*." *Films in Review* 44.5–6 (May-June, 1993): 191.
Karlin, Susan. "Sweet Shortcut for Hot '*Chocolate*.'" *Variety* 352.3 (August 30, 1993): 1.
Kauffmann, Stanley. "Books & The Arts: Stanley Kauffmann on Films: Midwinter Roundup: *Like Water for Chocolate*." *The New Republic* 208.9 (March 1, 1993): 24, 26.
Kraniauskas, John. "*Like Water for Chocolate*." *Sight & Sound* 3.10 (October 1993): 42–43.
Lane, Anthony. "*Like Water for Chocolate* (director: Alfonso Arau; 1993)." (March 8, 1993) *The New Yorker*. 11 November 2009.

<http://www.newyorker.com/arts/reviews/film/like_water_for_choco-late_arau>.

Maslin, Janet. "Emotions So Strong You Can Taste Them: *Like Water for Chocolate*." *NYT* February 17, 1993. B4(N), C13(L). 3 August 2009 <http://movies.nytimes.com/movie/review?res=9F0CE7DA1438F934A 25751C0A965958260>. [11 November 2009, site requires membership for access.]

NYT. Like Water for Chocolate. NYTimes.com. "Movies." [DVD Critic's Pick] 11 November 2009 <http://movies.nytimes.com/movie/29363/Like-Water-for-Chocolate/dvd>.

Pan's Labyrinth (2006). Box Office Mojo. 11 November 2009 <http://www.boxofficemojo.com/movies/?id=panslabyrinth.htm>.

Romney, Jonathan. "Eating Her Gut Out: *Like Water for Chocolate*." *New Statesman & Society* 6.272 (October 1, 1993): 33–34.

Tanitch, Robert. "Like Water for Chocolate." *The Times Literary Supplement* [London] 4724 (October 15, 1993): 17.

Television Programming

Bones. Dir. Greg Yaitanes. Writer and Creator Hart Hanson. Exec. Prod. Hart Hanson, Barry Josephson. Far Field, Josephson Entertainment, and 20th Century Fox Television, 2005–2009.

Closed Case. Dir. Roxann Dawson, *et al*. Writer Meredith Stiehm, *et al*. Exec. Prod. Jerry Bruckheimer, Jonathan Littman, *et al*. JBTV, 2003–2009.

Crossing Jordan. Dir. Alan Arkush, *et al*. Writer, Tim Kring, *et al*. Creator and Exec. Prod. Tim Kring. Exec. Prod. Dennis Hammer, Alan Arkush *et al*. Tailwind and NBC Entertainment, 24 September 2001–16 May 2007.

Cuna de lobos. Dir. and Prod. Carlos Téllez. Dir. Antonio Acevedo. Writer, Carlos Olmos. Televisa. 1986.

Law and Order: Special Victims Unit. Dir. David Platt, *et al*. Creator and Writer, Dick Wolf. Wolf Films and NBC Universal, 1999–2009.

Los que hacen nuestro cine. Dir. Alejandro Pelayo Rangel. UNAM. 1994.

Resources in Medical Humanities

Albert D'Arnal. "Diccionario: Mimosa Tenuiflora." [n.d.] *Albert D'Arnal International*. 11 November 2009 <http://www.albertdarnal.com/paginas/esp/diccionario/diccionario_3.asp> .

Becker, Kyra, MD; Elaine Skalabrin, MD; Danial Hallam, MD; and Edward Gill, MD. "Ischemic Stroke During Sexual Intercourse: A Report of 4 Cases in Persons With Patent Foramen Ovale." *Archives of Neurology* 61.7 (July 2004): 1114–1116. 11 November 2009 <http://archneur.ama-assn.org/cgi/content/full/61/7/1114>.

"Coronary Disease/Heart Attack." (May 30, 2009) Diagnose-Me.com. 11 November 2009 <http://www.diagnose-me.com/cond/C70120.html>.

Creel, Scott R., Steven L. Monfort, David E. Wildt, and Peter M. Waser. "Spontaneous lactation is an adaptive result of pseudopregnancy." *Letters to Nature* 660–662. (June 20, 1991). Nature Publishing Group. 11 November

2009 <http://www. nature.com/cgi-taf/DynaPage.taf? file=/nature/ journal/v351/n6328/abs/351660a0.html>.

Curing and Smoking Meats for Home Food Preservation. (2002). The National Center for Home Food Preservation: Guide and Literature Review Series: Smoking and Curing. "Curing and Smoking Meats for Home Food Preservation. Literature Review and Critical Preservation Points." Brian A. Nummer and Elizabeth L. Andress. February 2010 <http://www.uga.edu/nchfp/publications/nchfp/ lit_rev/cure_smoke_ rev.html>.

"'False' Pregnancy." (2003–2009) MedHelp.org. 11 November 2009 <http://www.medhelp.org/forums/maternal/archive/1389.html>.

"Food Allergies." [n.d.] PhysiciansPlus Medical Group. 11 November 2009 <http://www.docwong.com/health/foodaler.htm>.

"Food salt and health." (2009) Salt Institute. 11 November 2009 <http://www.saltinstitute.org/Issues-in-focus/Food-salt-health>.

Fülöpp, Tomáš J. "Latin America and the Concept of Social Race." (June 30, 1997) Vacilando. 11 November 2009 <http://vacilando.net/ node/264470>.

Gorin, Sandra K. "Tip #170: Old Time Remedies." (August 6, 1997) Roots Web. 11 November 2009 <http://archiver.rootsweb.ancestry. com/th/read/KYRESEARCH/1998-08/0902404184>.

Hayward, Michael R. "The Roses of Taif." (November/December 1997; 2004–2008) Saudi Aramco World. 11 November 2009 <http://www.saudi-aramcoworld.com/issue/199706/the.roses.of.taif.htm>.

"Healthy Grieving and Mourning to Release Broken Bonds." (2000–2009) CharmingHealth.com. 11 November 2009 <http://www.charminghealth. com/self-help/healthygrieving.htm>.

Hoffman, David L. "Amenorrhea." (n.d.) Organic Spa Magazine. 11 November 2009 <http://www.healthy.net/scr/Article.asp?Id=1180>.

"Infant Dehydration: Dehydration in Infants can be Life-Threatening." (2000. Rev. 2004) University of Iowa Health Science Relations. University of Iowa Children's Hospitals, University of Iowa Health Care. 11 November 2009 <http://www.uihealthcare.com/topics/medicaldepartments/pedi-atrics/infantdehydration/index.html>.

"Ipecac Abuse." (2009) Rader Programs. 11 November 2009 <http://www.raderprograms.com/special-issues/ipecac>.

Jackson, Graham. Sex, the Heart and Erectile Dysfunction. London: Taylor & Francis, 2004.

Krugman, Scott D., and Howard Dubowitz. "Failure to Thrive." (September 2003) American Family Physician. 11 November 2009 <http://www. aafp.org/afp/20030901/879.html>.

Marks, Jay. "Information on Intestinal Gas (Belching, Bloating, Flatulence)." (1996–2009) Ed. Leslie J. Schoenfield. MedicineNet.com. 11 November 2009 <http://www.medicinenet.com/intestinal_ gas_belching_bloating_ flatulence/article.htm>.

Miller, David A., M.D. "Obstetric Hemorrhage" (February 2, 2004) Obfocus.

11 November 2009 <http://www.obfocus.com/high-risk/bleeding/hemorrhagepa.htm>.

National Center for PTSD: Post Traumatic Stress Disorder. (August 3, 2009) United States Department of Veterans Affairs. 11 November 2009 <http://www.ncptsd.va.gov/ncmain/researchers/>.

Prabhakaran, Shyam, MD, and John W. Krakauer, MD. "Multiple Reversible Episodes of Subcortical Ischemia Following Postcoital Middle Cerebral Artery Dissection." *Archives of Neurology* 63.6 (June 2006): 891–893. 11 November 2009 <http://archneur.ama-assn.org/cgi/content/full/63/6/891>.

"Salmonella enteritidis." Centers for Disease Control and Prevention. 11 November 2009 <http://www.cdc.gov/ncidod/dbmd/ diseaseinfo/salment_g.htm>.

Spadaccini, Jim. "The Sweet Lure of Chocolate." [n.d.]. *Exploratorium Magazine* [page]8. 11 November 2009 <http://www.exploratorium.edu/exploring/exploring_chocolate/choc_8.html>.

"Swaddling your baby." Baby Center Medical Advisory Board. (December 2006. 1997–2009) Babycenter.com. 11 November 2009 <http://www.babycenter.com/0_swaddling-your-baby_125.bc>.

"Why does chopping an onion make you cry?." Everyday Mysteries: Fun Science Facts from the Library of Congress (February 12, 2009). Library of Congress. 11 November 2009 <http://www.loc.gov/rr/scitech/mysteries/onion.html>.

Index

The index lists the names of authors, scholars, critics, indigenous peoples, historical and fictional figures, films, television programming, and geographic places referred to in the essays and ancillaries of this volume. We also index elements of genre, approaches to criticism, and topics of interest in Latin American and Mexican literature and culture and Esquivel criticism under key words and phrases that we expect to be useful. Works of fiction, theater, and poetry should be sought under the names of the their authors; films and television programs, by title. Glossary headwords are not indexed, but the names of persons, places, and topics that appear within Glossary entries are indexed with the appropriate Glossary headword in parenthesis following the page number, *e.g.*, Abernethy, Francis Edward, 226 (*charro*).

With two exceptions (Sahagún, Bernardino de, and Unamuno, Miguel de) Hispanic surnames are indexed in full; therefore, see "De la Garza, Ethel" and "García Lorca, Federico." Religious figures are indexed under their full religious names: Sor Juana Inés de la Cruz, for example. The index does not contain internal references to the volume's contributors, but only references to their external work. (See Notes on Contributors for further information on the essayists.) Specific medical and health topics and medical writers' names are not indexed separately; for those references, see "Medical Humanities" in the Index and the corresponding Works Cited section.

Index

271

Index

Index

Index

Index

Index

Index

Index

Index

Index

Index

281